Seeking Sustainability in an Age of Complexity

Seeking Sustainability in an Age of Complexity explains why sustainability is hard and why 'collapse' can occur. In the last 20 years the theory of complexity has been developed – complex systems science (CSS) speaks to natural systems and particularly to ecological, social and economic systems and their interaction. Due to the growing concern over the huge changes occurring in the global environment, such as climate change, deforestation, habitat fragmentation and loss of biodiversity, Graham Harris sets out what has been learned in an attempt to understand the implications of these changes, and suggests ways to move forward. This book discusses a number of emerging tools for the management of 'unruly' complexity, that facilitate stronger regional dialogues about knowledge and values, that will be of interest to ecologists, sociologists, economists, natural resource managers and scientists in state and local governments, as well as to those involved in water and landscape management.

GRAHAM HARRIS is Director of ESE Systems Pty Ltd. in Tasmania, Adjunct Professor at the Centre for Environment at the University of Tasmania and an Honorary Research Professor at the Centre for Sustainable Water Management at Lancaster University, UK.

Seeking Sustainability in an Age of Complexity

GRAHAM HARRIS

Centre for Environment, University of Tasmania, Hobart, Tasmania, Australia
Centre for Sustainable Water Management, Lancaster Environment Centre,
Lancaster University, UK

CAMBRIDGE
UNIVERSITY PRESS

10683079

CAMBRIDGE UNIVERSITY PRESS
Cambridge, New York, Melbourne, Madrid, Cape Town, Singapore, São Paulo

Cambridge University Press
The Edinburgh Building, Cambridge CB2 8RU, UK

Published in the United States of America by Cambridge University Press, New York

www.cambridge.org
Information on this title: www.cambridge.org/9780521873499

© G. Harris 2007

First published 2007

Printed in the United Kingdom at the University Press, Cambridge

A catalogue record for this publication is available from the British Library

ISBN 978-0-521-87349-9 hardback

ISBN 978-0-521-69532-9 paperback

To Chris, my wife and best mate, for her forbearance, support and love

Epigraph

I can think of no better way to put it.

> This book does not run a straight course from beginning to end. It hunts; and in the hunting, it sometimes worries the same raccoon in different trees, or different raccoons in the same tree, or even what turns out to be no raccoon in any tree. It finds itself balking more than once at the same barrier and taking off on other trails. It drinks often from the same streams, and stumbles over some cruel country. And it counts not the kill but what is learned of the territory explored.
>
> From the Foreword to *Ways of Worldmaking* by Nelson Goodman. Published by Hackett Publishing, Indianapolis and Cambridge, 1978

In his review of John Horgan's book *The End of Science*[1] in 1996 John Casti argued strongly that we have by no means run out of 'big questions' that remain to be answered. He concluded his review thus:

> All that is needed is a 'big question' requiring new concepts and new methods. For example, many systems constituting the warp and weft of everyday life – say a stock market or a traffic network – involve a collection of agents (traders or drivers) interacting on the basis of limited, local information. Moreover, these agents are intelligent and adaptive: their behaviour and interactions are determined by rules, just like those governing the behaviour of planets or molecules. But unlike these lifeless objects, adaptive agents are ready to change their rules in accordance with new information that comes their way, continually adjusting to their environment to prolong their own survival. So far, there is nothing remotely close to a formalism, or set of scientific rules, for even stating, let alone understanding, questions surrounding the weird and wondrous ways of such processes.[2]

NOTES

1. John Horgan. *The End of Science: Facing the Limits of Knowledge in the Twilight of the Scientific Age.* (New York: Helix (Addison-Wesley), 1996).
2. J. L. Casti. Lighter than air. *Nature*, **382** (1996), 769.

Contents

Acknowledgements

This book is the product of years of osmosis, so I wish to acknowledge and thank all those – too numerous to mention individually – who have shared ideas and provided wise counsel to me over many, many years. I thank all of you with whom I have worked and collaborated over the decades; you have all been very generous. Science is about ideas and people and the two are inextricably intertwined. It has been a privilege to know you and work with you. Of course the usual caveats apply: the responsibility for what I have now done with it all is mine alone.

Maxime Fern and Michael Johnstone provided much-needed assistance in dark times and were the stimulus I needed to keep going. This would probably never have been written without your timely intervention. Maxime also introduced me to the writings of Gregory Bateson, a key influence. Bob Beeton contributed much to my knowledge of multiple capitals and rural community engagement and introduced many new ideas. Andrew Olivier introduced me to the work of Elliott Jaques. Nancy Bray and Andrew Olivier provided insights and criticisms of early drafts and improved my thinking in many ways through long discussions about key concepts. Louise Heathwaite provided critical insights into the science and also knowledge of the UK scene. Paul Harris provided critical comment on the later chapters. Richard Sanders sharpened my thinking on biophysical limits and the role of markets. I thank you all for your assistance.

This book was begun while I was at CSIRO and continued through a Retirement Fellowship, which gave me access to library and computing facilities. I am grateful for that support. The book was completed at the University of Tasmania. I particularly thank Andrew Glenn, Pro-Vice Chancellor (Research) at the University, and other colleagues there for providing a supportive environment and the creative space for me to complete the task. I also thank Wayne Meyer of CSIRO Land and Water, Adelaide, for permission to use the cover image, which so elegantry expresses the intent of this book.

Finally Alan Crowden, my editor, kept on nagging me and believing in me for nigh on ten years. Thank you, Alan; I just hope that the result was worth the wait!

1   Preamble: the world we are in

From the first members of the human species wandering the African savannahs down to the present day we have witnessed ice ages, extreme events of various kinds and a plethora of cultural, political, historical and other changes. We live in a changing world and it was ever thus. But things are different now. At the beginning of the third millennium we have a nexus of social, economic, technological and environmental trends the like of which has not been seen before.[1] Population growth has brought us to the point where we are the dominant species on this planet, and there is growing evidence of our power to modify the global climate. Human activity is affecting the global biosphere in ever more complex ways as a result of technological development, resource use and industrialisation.[2] We are approaching global constraints on our activities, particularly through our modification of global cycles of energy, water and nutrients.[3] We have unprecedented global connectivity through advanced transportation and telecommunications systems. Our social organisation and our economic activity have grown to the point where we have reached and exploited just about every corner of the globe; so we are now the dominant planetary engineers.[4] In the past thirty years there has therefore been a sea change in our relationship with the planet on which we live. We now have a much more complex and recursive relationship with ourselves and with nature.[5] This is why I am going to argue in this book that there is something different this time, something that is a challenge we have not faced before. I am going to argue that there is something qualitatively and quantitatively different this time around in terms of the nature of the constraints, the speed of change, and the magnitude and complexity of the tasks we face if we are to achieve sustainability.

The process of growth and development has not been linear or constant. There are both long-term trends in the human condition – population growth, cultural development, global exploration, resource use – and cyclical patterns of political and economic activity and technological development. Human societies have grown and collapsed many times in human history. The causes of growth and collapse are many and varied, arising from a mix of intrinsic and extrinsic factors.[6] Certainly some of the past collapses have been associated with regional environmental degradation, such as deforestation and soil erosion; in other cases social and economic factors have dominated. The one long-term trend that is focusing minds at the present time is population growth, resource use and the possibility of global change. For the first time in human history we have the potential to make irreparable changes to the entire global fabric, including atmospheric chemistry, global nutrient cycles, climate, water distributions, land use and biodiversity. The constraints are now global as well as regional. These are the long-term drivers on our present thinking about the human condition, which may lead to the predicted 'singularity': when technology and environmental change reach a new convergence point.[7]

Technology development, innovation and resource use has also led to a number of quasi-cyclical changes in economic activity during the past two centuries in particular. Each cycle has been characterised by upswings and downswings in economic activity and intensity of energy and resource use.[8] Although their existence is debated, some claim to have identified approximately fifty-year cycles of economic activity over the past two centuries (known after their first proponent as Kondratiev cycles). Technology development has characterised each cyclical period of economic growth and resource use in the modern era: steam engines, canals, iron production from coke and spinning machines in the (so-called) first Kondratiev cycle beginning around 1789; coal, railways, steamships and the telegraph in the second cycle beginning around 1846; oil, automobiles, electricity, wireless and telephones in the third cycle beginning around 1897; jet aircraft, television, nuclear power and computers in the fourth cycle beginning around 1950. At the turn of the new millennium, it is said, we are about to enter a new cycle – the fifth Kondratiev cycle – which is likely to be dominated by such technologies as wireless communications, multi-media, nanotechnology, genetic engineering, superconductors and what has been called 'friction-free' capitalism.[9] We are progressively 'dematerialising' the global economy.

Whatever the precise timing and nature of these cyclical patterns in economic and sociocultural activity, when taken together with the longer term drivers of human population growth, resource use and ever greater global mobility and connectivity, we are brought to a particularly significant turning point in the present 'fifth' cycle. Table 1.1 summarises some of the current global driving forces.

A more sustainable future for all inhabitants of the global biosphere requires some reconciliation and consilience between these various time varying drivers and responses. The key products of technological advances in the late modern era – loss of biodiversity, resource depletion, impacts on global elemental cycles (including climate change), rising energy prices, global flows of financial capital and global markets for products and services (including culture, sport and the arts) – are affecting all our lives. Convergence between many of these driving forces means that we live in a time of rapidly increasing complexity and of changing relationships, both between ourselves as individuals and as global communities and between ourselves and the natural world.[10]

Before we go any further there is an important point that must be made. Despite the evident problems at the turning of the millennium, and although there is need for concern over the speed and magnitude of change and for some urgency, we should not lose sight of the successes of the modern era. Life really was 'nasty, brutish and short' for all before the advent of Western humanist

Table 1.1 *Major global trends and key issues at the beginning of the twenty-first century*

Population growth
De-ruralisation and urbanisation
Poverty, inequality, terrorism
AIDS, avian influenza
Water supply, sanitation

Changes to global biogeochemical cycles[11]
Climate change, greenhouse effect
Environmental degradation, loss of ecosystem structure
Habitat destruction, land use change
Loss of biodiversity

ICT revolution
Computers, digital communications, World Wide Web, Internet
Mobile telephony
Multi-media convergence

Biotechnology, biosensors
Nanotechnology
Advanced materials

Globalisation of finance
Commoditisation
Growth of China and India
Growth of externalities
Increasing cost of some resources (oil)

Complex systems
Postmodernism (or Radical Modernism)
Feminism

ideals. Even those who believe that it has all gone wrong and that we now live in the wreck of Western culture accept that progress has been made.[12] Now this, of course, is very much a Western view. There are far too many people in this world for whom the evident successes of the modern era do not apply, and the very fact that we have a set of United Nations Millennium Development Goals[13] is an indication that there is still much to be done. There are still too many for whom clean water, sanitation and sewers, health care and reliable supplies of varied foodstuffs are but a dream. Poverty and inequality remain and must be addressed, and progress in the West has been bought at a price. Sustainability and development are therefore closely interconnected and, because of the close link between global sustainability, development, health and freedom, following Amartya Sen I would definitely add public health and freedom to the list of achievements and issues to be worried over.[14]

A global network society is emerging, shrinking time and space through information and communications technologies (ICT), mobile telephony and the World Wide Web.[15] The ICT revolution is daily bringing us added information about the ever-increasing human impact on the planetary biosphere, the dramatic reductions in biodiversity and the threat of global climate change. In his book *The Condition of Postmodernity* David Harvey argued that the West experienced a sea change in its experience of time and space after about 1972, into a condition of postmodernity.[16] (Looking back on it we can now see that the 1970s were a time of change in many aspects of the human experience. As well as the many social changes during that decade – including changing attitudes to Nature and the environment – Tim Flannery has shown that the global climate went through a 'magic gate' in 1976 as global warming suddenly became more evident.[17] Certainly, as I shall show later, the climate over parts of Australia changed suddenly in that year.) Without including the climate changes, Mark Taylor[18] insists that this present period of change is as far reaching as that at the end of the eighteenth century: the industrial revolution. The ICT revolution brings us information and builds knowledge with unprecedented speed and scope, and widens the reach of our intellect. Web search engines and television news bring us access to global databases and snapshots of global events; time and space are telescoped and fragmented.[19] Some have argued that an 'extended mind' is emerging.[20] Certainly there is now a need to pay heed to the social construction of mind and the possibilities for creative collaboration that the new technologies bring.

As knowledge is being made more accessible there is a trend throughout the Western world towards subsidiarity: the pushing down of decision making to local and regional communities and the shrinking of central governments.[21] In his book *The Third Way* Anthony Giddens[22] discussed the challenges and ethical issues of governing in this new and fragmented world and identified the trend towards 'double democratisation' – of managing both globalisation and subsidiarity simultaneously – as a major issue to be dealt with. Subsidiarity empowers local and regional decision making; as I shall argue, this is both a good and a bad thing, but in the end sustainability will depend on the decisions that individuals take in the context of signals received and incentives provided by markets, government policies and global interactions. In 1988 Joseph Tainter wrote about the historical and archaeological evidence for relationships between growing complexity and the collapse of past attempts at constructing sustainable human societies. The present experiment has global implications. One of the major themes of this book will be the importance of regional, local and individual actions and the ways in which, when played out in the context of global and national information sources, signals and incentives of various kinds, they determine larger-scale outcomes. In ecological, social and economic systems and their interactions, the microscopic really does determine the macroscopic outcome. Globalisation and subsidiarity place huge demands on individuals and communities for increased capacity and improved decision making under conditions of complexity and uncertainty.[23] The 'extended mind' is both a boon and a challenge. This increased complexity of information flows and relationships from the individual to the global is a feature of the modern world which adds to the level of personal challenge. So the present ICT revolution has also led to conceptual and philosophical advances in the area of complexity and complex systems that in many ways bring greater realism to our world view. In this respect the idea of the 'extended mind' has real merit.

Relationships, collaboration, trust and social capital[24] are the keys to success in this more complex technological, social, environmental and economic context in which we all live. The social science literature has much to offer us in this regard. This book could in many ways be seen to be an extended commentary on Anthony Giddens' *The Consequences of Modernity* in the context of the management of natural resources and the environment at the turn of the new millennium.[25] Perhaps nowhere else has the effect of these changes struck so hard. The influences of new scientific knowledge revealing complex interactions and fundamental limitations on human actions, and the setting of that knowledge in new economic, technological, institutional and social contexts, have totally changed the way we view, value and manage our biosphere and natural resources. Science is being dragged into the world of Realpolitik, an uncomfortable position in which it finds itself ill suited to exist. This is a world of uncertainty and risk, quite different from the controlled world of disciplinary science.[26] Nevertheless this is inevitable and things are changing. The position I take here is one of attempting to understand and explain complexity and systems behaviour; one in which I lean towards John Ralston Saul's view on the importance of the apprehension of context and of shared responsibility.[27] Anyone who studies systems in all their complexity can do no other.

Ideas are changing rapidly, long-standing theories and practices are being overturned and new concepts are being developed. The rising concern over sustainability merely adds to the complexity of our daily decision making, so we can add environmental factors to the social and economic challenges of the 'third way'. Above all we must now accept and cope with greatly increased complexity at all levels in our lives: individually, at the level of the community, nationally and even internationally. Do we as individuals and institutions have the capacity to adapt and grow under these circumstances? For that to happen there must be a strong dialogue between institutions and individuals in a changing world. This isn't rocket science – it is much harder. If it was easy we would have figured it out by now.

The importance of context

So to understand how we got here requires an appreciation of social, economic and intellectual history because the present situation has deep historical and contingent roots. The landscape in which we live in the West (and in other parts of the world) very much reflects a period of faith in progress and expansionism: the Modern Era. Safety, security, wealth and improved public health were the drivers of behaviour and values. Acts of enclosure changed medieval landscapes to 'modern' ones and brought with them the beginnings of pollution and urban blight. 'Where there's muck there's brass' was a common saying in Northern England during the heyday of its industrial period of mills and densely populated cities. What the industrial revolution created was a modern (Western) semiotics of place, a set of signs and symbols that were used to define and describe our sense of place in the landscape. These semiotics were different depending on class, social standing and place of birth, but taken together there was a defined set of values and sensibilities that described the modern world. The modern era similarly produced a set of urban semiotics. Modern cities are now almost the same everywhere in terms of architectural design and scale, and the expansion of modern techniques of water storage and supply, power generation and distribution, manufacturing and transport, have led to an urban modernist sameness all across the globe.

Each new technological advance and each new cycle of development brought periods of change; the early cycles of the industrial revolution were no exception. It was also a period of great social and economic change.[28] There are parallels with the present time. Not only was the relation between science, nature and society then changing rapidly (as it is now), but basic concepts and understanding were undergoing major revisions also. The cultural and philosophical context – what we (think) we know, how we know it and what we do with the knowledge we have – has changed over time in quite fundamental ways. Whereas the limitation during the industrial revolution was social capital (natural resources were thought to be unlimited) there is now a dawning recognition of both a need for a dramatic increase in social capital and capacity to deal with complexity as well as an urgent need to live within a limited stock of natural capital and resources.

There are huge sunk costs which limit our present options and determine our course of action.[29] Even if we determined to change our ways and become sustainable overnight (even assuming we knew how to do this) it would take generations to achieve the result. We are hedged about by many words that begin with the letter C: culture, community, capitals, constraints, complexity, connectivity and context. Cultural persistence is an important aspect of the *longue durée*, which determines many aspects of human life.[30] So, first: culture, community values and semiotics do not change rapidly. Ideas, concepts and values are slow to change; we are much more dependent on the past than many realise.[31] Second, there are many forms of capital that must be considered in addition to the more familiar financial capital. To be sustainable we must balance the growth of financial capital with various other forms of infrastructure development (physical capital) and the critical forms of human, social and knowledge capital. All this is set in the context of the use, conservation and restoration of environmental or natural capital. Third, there are biophysical limitations and **constraints**. Changes in global and regional stocks and flows of key elements and materials are now evident, and response times may be long. Drastic cuts in global carbon dioxide emissions do not lead to immediate reductions in the concentration of carbon dioxide in the atmosphere because of the long residence times involved. Water supply is limited by climate and rainfall; building new dams does increase the total water supply for human use, but only by the amount harvested from catchments and diverted from their component ecosystems. The huge investments required and the lifetimes of our built infrastructure (from home appliances such as toilets and washing machines, to major power, water and transport infrastructure) mean that we cannot re-engineer our built environments overnight. Fourth, the interactions between the biosphere and the human-dominated world (sometimes called the anthroposphere) are highly complex and variable in space and time and form a set of complex interacting and adaptive systems. Complex adaptive systems are those in which the nature of the networks of interactions (the connectivity) between components changes with time and is influenced by the context so that novel properties emerge, which are not predictable from the behaviour of individual components. Some of our 'limits to growth' arise from these recursive interactions.

The concepts of place and human dominion

A series of concepts and values that were centred on progress, domination and exploitation of the natural world and a requirement for certainty and security were appropriate when the world seemed limitless. In a time when nature seemed boundless and threatening the plan was to have dominion over the natural world, to subdue it and exploit it for human benefit. We made particular efforts to provide safety and security for the human race in the face of risk and variability. We were highly successful in this aim.

Since the earliest times *Homo sapiens* has been a curious animal; curious firstly in the sense of our constant search for knowledge about the world and for explanation and security[32] and secondly in the sense of quirky or peculiar. Our success as a species is a direct result of the success of the first strategy, but we have never succeeded in freeing ourselves from our evolutionary history. The evolutionary context is crucial. As bipedal primates of a particular longevity and stature we see the world in particular ways and have a predilection for some types of explanation over others. What we know, how we know it and what we do with the knowledge gained is always set in a biological, cultural and historical context, which changes slowly with time.[33] We always were very good at particular time and space scales, particularly those that suited a two-metre-high primate that lives for decades, but very bad at perceiving others, particularly the very small and the very fast and the very large and slow. We have numerous curious (peculiarly human) perceptions of cause and effect, some of which we shall have cause to (re-)consider as this book unfolds.

Now that we have come to dominate the planet it is high time to understand what is going on at those inconveniently large and small scales and to lift the level of the debate around critical issues such as the need for security and the impact of our actions around the globe. Throughout the world there is land clearing, habitat fragmentation, loss of biodiversity, degradation of water quality and increasing dryland salinity.[34] Make no mistake, there is urgent need for action on all fronts: more than 40% of the original planetary biomes have now been destroyed and the figure will reach more than 60% by 2050.[35] Over half of the world's major river systems are seriously affected by fragmentation and flow regulation resulting from the construction of dams.[36]

It would be disingenuous of me to deny that there is debate about the so-called 'litany' of environmental degradation. There are many who deny that the world is going to hell in a hand basket, and many who insist that statements such as those I have made above about climate change and biodiversity loss are merely the usual 'litany' and just more 'green' scaremongering.[37] There is a debate about whether 'business as usual' is not just as good a strategy as wholesale sackcloth and ashes. There should be such a debate. Part of the basis of the debate comes from political, religious and social attitudes to the natural environment: we do not all share the same values or land ethics, and no-one is free from bias. Part of the debate also comes from some fundamental issues around the nature of the evidence and varying interpretations and appreciations of uncertainty, risk and even outright indeterminism. Nothing is as simple as it might seem and the world is indeed very complex. We hold vigorous debates and take firm positions in opposition while standing on quicksand. This endangers all involved. There is, however, in my view, a growing sense of realism abroad.

The human population is now about 6 billion; even so there is no question that the lot of the average global inhabitant has improved dramatically in the past hundred years, even the past fifty. Wealth and longevity are increasing, major diseases have been defeated and the average calorific intake per capita is increasing. This is, however, being bought at a cost to the natural environment and limitations are now beginning to be seen in the depletion of natural capital.[38] This is the direct result of the 'Davy Crockett syndrome': once the world was large enough that it was always possible to find another forest to cut down, or another fish population to exploit in even deeper water. If we could not live off the interest from the local natural capital we could always live off the capital itself and then move somewhere else and repeat the trick. Now we have explored and altered the far corners of the Earth and over-fished the ocean depths,[39] dominion must give way to negotiation and constraint. Debates rage about how much has been lost, the nature of the evidence for loss and ways of knowing. The stories we tell ourselves are changing. Science, which once meant power and wealth for the few and human domination of the biosphere by many, has become a matter of contention. The nuclear bomb, Chernobyl, radioactivity, genetically modified organisms (GMOs), bovine spongiform encephalopathy (BSE) and 'foot and mouth' disease have all called into question the relationships between knowing things, and using and distributing the information.

There is a growing consensus that the next fifty years or so are going to be critical. If we can manage the transition we have a chance to set a new course to a more ethical and sustainable future. E.O. Wilson has written of a potential 'bottleneck' in the next fifty years[40] and raises the important issue of how much progress we can make in areas such as climate change and biodiversity conservation before we irreversibly damage the fabric of the planet. Certainly there is growing evidence that we are reaching the physical limits of the globe in terms of population growth, our use of available land for agriculture[41] and impacts on global elemental cycles.[42] We face the problems of maintaining food production through intensive production practices.[43]

The importance of ethics and systems thinking

I am not going to address the global 'litany' at length here. The arguments have been well made by others, especially and most elegantly by E.O. Wilson. What I wish to address here is the question: 'Can we grasp the complexity of it all and, if so, what do we do about it?' Given the fundamental nature of the problem – the destruction of the biosphere and its ecosystem services together with the huge changes going on in human societies and cultures driven by globalisation and technological change – the precautionary principle would suggest that even if the epistemology is flawed, the data are partial and the evidence is shaky, we should pay attention to the little we know and do whatever is possible to mitigate the situation even if we fundamentally disagree about the means and the ends. The only ethical course of action is, as John Ralston Saul writes,[44] based on 'a sense of the other and of inclusive responsibility'. We know enough to act. Ethics is about uncertainty, doubt, system thinking and balancing difficult choices. It is about confronting the evidence.

Over the past two or three decades, as there has been an increasing appreciation of the importance of good environmental management, and as western societies have become more open and the ICT revolution has made information much more widely available there has been a growing debate between the worlds of science, industry, government and the community around environ-mental ethics and environmental issues and their management. During this period new knowledge has been gained, ideas have changed (sometimes quite fundamentally) and there have been huge changes in government and social institutions and policies. We are all on a recursive journey together: we are lit-erally 'making it up as we go along'. This is not easy and there are no optimal solutions. This is an adaptive process requiring feedback from all parts of the system. Yes, there will be surprises. This is why it is so important that when we act we constantly reflect on what we know and what we are doing about it and where it is all going.

As we reach the physical limits of the global biosphere the values we place on things are changing and must change further. A new environmental ethic is required, one that is less instrumental and more embracing. Traditionally there has tended to be a schism between those who take an anthropocentric view (that the world is there for us to use) and those who take the non-anthropocentric view (those who value nature in its own right). Orthodox anthropocentrism dictates that non-human value is instrumental to human needs and interests. In contrast, non-anthropocentrics take an objectivist view and value nature intrinsically; some may consider the source of value in non-human nature to be independent of human consciousness.[45] What is required is a more complex and systems view of ethics which finds a middle ground between the instrumen-talist and objectivist views. Norton,[46] for example, proposes an alternative and more complex theory of value – a universal Earth ethic – which values processes and dynamics as well as entities and takes an adaptive management view of changing system properties. For sustainable development to occur, choices about values will remain within the human sphere but we should no longer regard human preferences as the only criterion of moral significance. 'Humans and the planet have entwined destinies'[47] and this will be increasingly true in many and complex ways as we move forward. There are calls for an Earth ethic beyond the land ethic of Aldo Leopold.[48] The science of ecology is being drawn into the web.[49] Ecologists are becoming more socially and culturally aware and engaged[50] and the 'very doing' of ecology is becoming more ethical.[51] Some scientists are beginning to see themselves more as agents in relationships with society and less as observers.

One important consequence of this is that conservation biology is becom-ing less of a movement that is concerned with the setting aside of the world's 'last great places' and more one that is concerned about the 'rest of nature': the place in which we all live.[52] What we have attempted to do in the past is the geographical separation of the instrumentalist and the objectivist views – setting areas of natural capital aside from our focus on physical and financial capital growth on the rest of the planet – but this policy, the conservation of bio-diversity through the establishment of special reserves, simply is not working.

For example, reserves in West Africa are being plundered for bush meat when other sources of protein are lacking.[53] We have suddenly realised that protection of the fabric of the biosphere, conservation of biodiversity and restoration of ecosystem function are all going to require us to value the 'ordinary' and find ways of living more sustainably with nature.[54] This is going to require nothing less than a fundamental rethink of many conservation policies and a focus not just on physical and economic capital as separate from natural capital but more on the intertwining of the various forms of capital that make up sustainable development. We must find ways of balancing, protecting and valuing all six forms of capital; natural, physical, financial, human, social and knowledge.[55] This is a major challenge to conservationists and is a way to end the usual conflict between proponents of 'business as usual' and environmentalists.[56] It does, however, raise all kinds of issues about managing the complexity of these interactions and the development of the necessary capacity in human societies. We are moving from a belief in certainty into complexity, uncertainty and doubt.

So these chapters are about ecology, the way it is done and the way it is used. They are also about landscapes and waterscapes, what we know about them, how they work and how they can be managed. Inevitably they are also about society, culture, place, values and other ways of knowing. I will assert that the world is much more complex and precarious than we have hitherto assumed and that this realisation, together with the increasingly complex relationships within and between society and the environment, will have major implications for the way we conserve, manage and restore landscapes, catchments and aquatic ecosystems.

The importance of water

I have chosen to focus on water because water is *the* issue for the twenty-first century. Water is essential for life and for quality of life (not just for human species). The global stock of water is finite. Rising population means pressure on water resources, so water is a model for all issues: culture, values, knowledge, management, complexity, policy, governance and society. Water is also an excellent model for understanding and managing what are called common pool resources – such as the atmosphere, water, fisheries, forestry – resources that are held in common and suffer from particular kinds of natural resource management problems which arise from issues around ownership, regulation and institutional difficulties as well as deep cultural, philosophical and ethical considerations.

Water is fundamental to almost all common pool resource management issues around the world. It is also inextricably tied up with numerous social and economic issues. The problem with water supplies for people in both the West and developing countries is not just the quantity of supply. (The ready availability of potable water is something we all take for granted in developed countries but it is a major issue in many parts of the world.) The water supply must be fit for purpose and that means, in most cases, breaking the link between faecal and oral contamination. To provide water supplies for human consumption, for agriculture and for industry most of the world's accessible rivers are now dammed (and as many as 250 new dams are being built each year, even now[57]). Many rivers are dammed more than once on their way from the mountains to the sea. Agriculture is usually the biggest water user and irrigation areas continue to expand across the globe. As a result river flows are regulated and diverted, salinity is increasing and inland lakes and seas, like the Aral Sea, are drying up. What freshwaters remain are being degraded, aquatic biodiversity is declining more rapidly than that on land,[58] wetlands and swamps are being drained, overfishing is rife and nutrient pollution from cities, industry and agricultural runoff is widespread.

So water embodies all the complexity and conflict which lies at the nexus between rational use and conservation, extraction for consumptive and productive use versus protection of natural flow regimes and water quality, recycling and reuse, protection of biodiversity and ecosystem function, sustainability and the concern for the 'triple bottom line': balancing environmental, social and economic sustainability. Science has a key role to play but so do social and cultural values, politics and economic interests. By flowing through, under and across the landscape water connects together and integrates much of what we do, both on the land and in the water. The connection between human society, land use change, ecosystem function and water quantity and quality is a complex and intimate one, which makes water a model subject for this study.

Water is not just the freshwater we see in streams, rivers and lakes. There are a series of complex interactions between evaporation (largely from the oceans), rainfall, infiltration, groundwater and surface runoff. The water in rivers, soils and lakes is only about 0.014% of the total global water[59] so that the water we use (the so-called 'blue' water) is only a small fraction of the total global water flux which maintains the biosphere, its ecosystems and functions (the 'green' water).[60] We are totally dependent on the proper functioning of the biosphere and its ecosystem services and hence on the 'green' water fluxes. Ecosystem services are all those (apparently) free services that the biosphere provides for us; services such as the provision of food, fuel, fibre, pollination, pest control, fertile soils, clean water, balancing the atmospheric gas composition and so on.[61] Without the 'green' water fluxes there would be no natural capital, no ecosystem services and no conservation of biodiversity. By focusing on the security of supply of 'blue' water at the expense of the biosphere we have, as I shall show, knocked the much larger 'green' water flows out of balance and this is causing widespread landscape-scale damage. We have focused on turning natural capital ('green') into financial capital ('blue') through the construction of physical infrastructure; 'blue' water is often bought and sold through market mechanisms. Wealth and human wellbeing are clearly growing year by year but the global environment is suffering a loss of water and biodiversity.

Externalities

There is clear evidence of human domination of the biosphere, especially in the changes to the global cycles of the major elements, carbon, nitrogen, sulphur and phosphorus. Carbon is building up in the air through energy generation and industrial activity and causing global warming. The present concentration of carbon dioxide in the atmosphere is at unprecedented levels, at least as far back as the present records go, which is about 650 000 years. We are in uncharted waters and the past is no guide to the future. In a world of unprecedented technological, environmental and social change and rapidly increasing connectivity and complexity we are in for surprises. Now, it is true (and this is where we can have an argument about the evidence for the 'litany') that there have been some spectacular local and regional successes: forests have regrown, species have recovered and been conserved, pollution levels in our major cities have decreased, human health and water quality have been improved. There are some spectacular examples of conservation and innovation in action which we should celebrate, but the evidence coming in daily from our new range of sensors in space, from cameras on the ground and under water, and from remote monitors coupled to computer models and huge data banks (our new and extended mind) is that human activity is changing the face of the planet at an ever-quickening pace. So, somehow, we must find ways to link the local successes with the less encouraging global picture – to link the micro- and the macro- more effectively across scales.

In economic terms we are beginning to face an exponential increase in 'externalities': impacts on, and costs associated with, all those goods and services that are outside the traditional sphere of economic activity.[62] The stocks and flows of non-market goods and services are being modified, often in ignorance and by mistake. In particular we face a growing loss of ecosystem services as landscapes and waterscapes are degraded and biodiversity declines.[63] By focusing on security, wealth generation and profit and not including the 'externalities' in our cost–benefit calculations we have managed to improve the lot of most, if not all, people on this planet, but the biosphere is paying the price for a narrow view of growth. We are not balancing the various forms of capital. Some take the 'business as usual' and highly instrumental view that democratic reform, market forces and economic globalisation will solve all our problems. Furthermore, adherents to this view would probably discount most of the environmental 'litany'.[64] In short, physical and financial capital growth outweighs other considerations and if we are doing some environmental damage in the process, well, there will be time to fix that up later. At the other extreme we have many environmental groups and non-governmental organisations (NGOs) who oppose globalisation and all that it stands for, and who tend to take an objectivist view and value natural capital above all else. Interestingly, most of the managerial and economic literature about globalisation and its discontents[65] focuses more on the social and economic capital impacts and less on the environmental capital aspects of the problem. This is also true of much of the development literature,[66] although in recent times this has been changing.[67] Similarly, 'green' groups tend to focus more on the changing patterns of (charismatic) biodiversity rather than on the more complex changes to ecosystem function and process. Others take a less instrumental and more patient and broadly ethical middle-ground view, favouring a more 'social democratic' stance in which human, social, financial and physical capitals are balanced through regional differentiation and selective market engagement. This is consistent with a complex systems view of the problem of development and sustainability.[68]

A more broadly sustainable framework is now required as we seek a more ethical and system-based view of the global economy and society. This involves walking into a very complex and contested middle ground. 'Here be monsters.' Traditional economic management has led to a demonstrable degradation of many renewable and non-renewable resources. The global supplies of both oil and water are finite. Both are, or once were, controlled by the activities of the biosphere. In the end every economy is a wholly owned subsidiary of the environment and will remain so as long as we are carbon- and water-based life forms with primate origins. There is an urgent requirement for a 'great transition' to a more sustainable future – and soon. Maybe the next fifty years – the years of the next economic and resource use cycle and the years of technological, social and environmental convergence – really are going to be critical. About the only viable solution is going to be an economy of nature in which we take a more inclusive and ethical view. Of necessity it will include more of the complex and adaptive interactions between the 'systems of systems' that make up the world in which we live. This is a major challenge of comprehension, capacity and managing complexity. This also requires a very new and different form of leadership: one in which context, community, constraints and complexity are the watchwords of a more nuanced style.

So, until now, we have done an excellent job of dominion, and of providing ever-increasing levels of safety and security for our species. We have used up a lot of our stocks of natural and other capital. We still have a very long way to go to address all the issues of poverty, deprivation and inequality on this planet. We do have much to do, but life is better for more people in many areas. We now need to lift the level of the debate and comprehend the changing nature and scale of the challenges we face. There have been massive changes in the past thirty years as the postmodern revolution has hit home. And revolution it truly is.

NOTES

1. Some argue that we are heading for a very special time in human history – a 'singularity' – when all kinds of social, technological and environmental trends all come together in ways which will forever change human civilisation. Around 2050 computing power might well exceed the power of the human brain. We are also seeing exponential increases in complexity, connectivity in the World Wide Web, genetic sequence data and the speed of uptake of new inventions such as mobile phones and the internet. See R. Kurzweil. Human 2.0. *New Scientist*, 24 September 2005, pp. 32–7; also R. Kurzweil. *The Singularity is Near: When Humans Transcend Biology*. (New York: Viking, 2005).

2. See the results from the Millennium Ecosystem Assessment, released 30 March 2005: www.millenniumassessment.org.

3. V. Smil. *Cycles of Life: Civilization and the Biosphere*. (New York: Scientific American Library, 1997).

4. B. H. Wilkinson. Humans as geologic agents: a deep-time perspective. *Geology*, **33** (2005), 161–4.

5. The complexity of the human condition is well explained by John Urry. *Global Complexity*. (Cambridge: Polity Press, 2003).

6. J. A. Tainter. *The Collapse of Complex Societies*. (Cambridge University Press, 1988); Jared Diamond. *Collapse*. (London: Allen Lane, Penguin Press, 2004).

7. R. Kurzweil. *The Singularity is Near: when Humans Transcend Biology*. (New York: Viking, 2005).

8. There are various interpretations of the precise timing of these cycles. For a summary of the evidence for the role of innovation in long-term business cycles and a discussion of Kondratiev cycles see M. Hirooka. Nonlinear dynamism of innovation and business cycles. *Journal of Evolutionary Economics*, **13** (2003), 549–76; also H. A. Linstone. Corporate planning, forecasting and the long wave. *Futures*, **34** (2002), 317–36.

9. B. J. L. Berry. Long waves and geography in the 21st century. *Futures*, **29** (1997), 301–10.

10. Joseph Tainter was the first to bring together the arguments surrounding the links between complexity and culture, and the increased possibility of collapse as the complexity of societies increased. Rycroft and Kash have discussed the challenge of manufacturing and delivering the increasing complexity of products and services. See R. W. Rycroft and D. E. Kash. *The Complexity Challenge: Technological Innovation for the 21st Century*. (London: Pinter, 1999).

11. The combined effects of biology, geology and chemistry on the cycling of elements through the biosphere are together known as biogeochemistry.

12. J. Carroll. *The Wreck of Western Culture: Humanism Revisited*. (Melbourne: Scribe Publications, 2004).

13. See www.un.org/millenniumgoals/.

14. A. Sen. *Development as Freedom*. (Oxford University Press, 1999).

15. Urry, *Global Complexity*. (See Note 5.)

16. D. Harvey. *The Condition of Postmodernity*. (Oxford: Blackwell, 1989).

17. See T. Flannery. *The Weather Makers*. (Melbourne: Text Publishing, 2005). See also F. E. Urban, J. E. Cole and J. T. Overpeck. Influence of mean climate change on climate variability from a 155 year tropical Pacific coral record. *Nature*, **407** (2000), 989–93.

18. M. C. Taylor. *The Moment of Complexity*. (Chicago: University Press, 2001).

19. D. Harvey. *The Condition of Postmodernity*. (Oxford: Basil Blackwell, 1989).

20. A. Clark and D. J. Chalmers. The extended mind. *Analysis*, **58** (1998), 10–23. See also http://www.u.arizona.edu/chalmers/papers/extended.html. For a discussion on the history of this concept see J. Bobryk. The social construction of mind and the future of cognitive science. *Foundations of Science*, **7** (2002), 481–95.

21. See, for example, C. Handy. *The Age of Unreason*. (London: Arrow Books, 1989).

22. A. Giddens. *The Third Way: the Renewal of Social Democracy*. (London: Polity Press, 1998).

23. For an analysis of the political, social and economic impacts of the 'end of certainty' on a country like Australia, see Paul Kelly. *The End of Certainty: the Story of the 1980s*. (St Leonards, NSW: Allen and Unwin, 1992).

24. F. Fukuyama. *Trust: the Social Virtues and the Creation of Prosperity*. (New York: The Free Press, 1995).

25. A. Giddens. *The Consequences of Modernity*. (Stanford University Press, 1990).

26. P. Weingart. Science in a political environment. *EMBO Reports*, **5** (2004), S52–5.

27. J. R. Saul. *On Equilibrium*. (Toronto: Penguin Books, 2001).

28. J. Uglow. *The Lunar Men*. (London: Faber and Faber, 2002).

29. M. Janssen and M. Scheffer. Overexploitation of renewable resources by ancient societies and the role of sunk-cost effects. *Ecology and Society*, **9 (1)** (2004), 6. Available online at http://www.ecologyandsociety.org/vol9/iss1/art6.

30. F. Pryor. *Britain AD*. (London: HarperCollins, 2004).

31. See, for example, A. N. Wilson. *The Victorians*. (London: Arrow Books, 2003). A splendid discussion of the nineteenth century foundations of much of twentieth century life and values.

32. See A. R. Platt. *The First Imperative*. (Market Harborough: Matador (an imprint of Troubador Publishing), 2004). Platt sees the first imperative of life as 'to seek out and even provoke, experience, in the hope that significance will emerge' (p. 3).

33. There seem to be good arguments for evolutionary constraints on the course of human history, and on the future. See D. Penn. The evolutionary roots of our environmental problems: towards a Darwinian ecology. *Quarterly Reviews of Biology*, **78 (3)** (2003), 1–37.

34. See the recent compilation of data by A. Balmford, R. E. Green and M. Jenkins. Measuring the changing state of nature. *Trends in Ecology and Evolution*, **18** (2003), 326–30. See also data on websites from the World Watch Institute, the Millennium Ecosystem Assessment and the UN Environment Program.

35. See the reports of the Millennium Ecosystem Assessments (www.maweb.org), also D. Graham-Rowe and R. Holmes. Planet in peril. *New Scientist*, 2 April 2005, 8–11. E. Stokstad. Taking the pulse of Earth's life support systems. *Science*, **308** (2005), 41–5.

36. C. Nilsson *et al.* Fragmentation and flow regulation of the world's large river systems. *Science*, **308** (2005), 405–8.

37. In particular this debate has been stimulated by the publication of Bjorn Lomborg. *The Skeptical Environmentalist*. (Cambridge: Cambridge University Press, 2001).

38. See www.millenniumassessment.org.

39. J. A. Devine, K. D. Baker and R. L. Haedrich. Deep-sea fishes qualify as endangered. *Nature*, **439** (2006), 29.

40. E. O. Wilson. *The Future of Life*. (London: Little, Brown & Co., 2002).

41. D. Tilman *et al.* Forecasting agriculturally driven global environmental change. *Science*, **292** (2001), 281–4.

42. P. M. Vitousek *et al.* Human alteration of the global nitrogen cycle: sources and consequences. *Ecological Applications*, **7** (1997), 737–50.

43. D. Tilman *et al.* Agricultural sustainability and intensive agricultural practices. *Nature*, **418** (2002), 671–7.

44. Saul, *On Equilibrium*, p. 309. (See Note 27, above.)

45. See the discussion in J. M. Buchdahl and D. Raper. Environmental ethics and sustainable development. *Sustainable Development*, **6** (1998), 92–8.

46. B. G. Norton. Biodiversity and environmental values: in search of a universal earth ethic. *Biodiversity and Conservation*, **9** (2000), 1029–44.

47. H. Ralston III. The land ethic at the turn of the millennium. *Biodiversity and Conservation*, **9** (2000), 1045–58.

48. Ibid. See also A. Leopold. *A Sand County Almanac.* (New York: Oxford University Press, 1949).

49. N. R. Webb. Ecology and ethics. *Trends in Ecology and Evolution*, **14** (1999), 259–60. G. A. Bradshaw and M. Bekoff. Ecology and social responsibility, the re-embodiment of science. *Trends in Ecology and Evolution*, **16** (2001), 460–5.

50. P. R. Ehrlich. Human natures, nature conservation, and environmental ethics. *Bioscience*, **52** (2002), 31–43.

51. N. Cooper. Speaking and listening to nature: ethics within ecology. *Biodiversity and Conservation*, **9** (2000), 1009–27.

52. I am indebted to Bob Beeton for the origin of this idea.

53. J. S. Brashares *et al.* Bush meat hunting, wildlife declines, and fish supply in West Africa. *Science*, **306** (2004), 1180–3. W. M. Adams *et al.* Biodiversity conservation and the eradication of poverty. *Science*, **306** (2004), 1146–9.

54. C. R. Margules and R. L. Pressey. Systematic conservation planning. *Nature*, **405** (2000), 243–53. H. Doremus. Biodiversity and the challenge of saving the ordinary. *Idaho Law Review*, **38** (2002), 325–54.

55. J. Pretty and D. Smith. Social capital in biodiversity conservation. *Conservation Biology*, **18** (2003), 631–8. K. S. Bawa, R. Seidler and P. H. Raven. Reconciling conservation paradigms. *Conservation Biology*, **18** (2004), 859–60.

56. M. Chapin. A challenge to conservationists. *World-Watch*, (Nov.–Dec. 2004), 17–31. M. Shellenberger and T. Nordhaus. *The Death of Environmentalism.* (2004). 37 pp. see www.thebreakthrough.org and www.evansmcdonough.com.

57. R. B. Jackson *et al.* Water in a changing world. *Ecological Applications*, **11** (2001), 1027–45.

58. M. Jenkins. Prospects for biodiversity. *Science*, **302** (2003), 1175–7. See also the results of the Millennium Ecosystem Assessments carried out in late 2004.

59. J. W. M. La Riviere. Threats to the world's water. *Scientific American*, (September 1989), 48–55.

60. M. Falkenmark. Dilemma when entering 21st century – rapid change but lack of sense of urgency. *Water Policy*, **1** (1998), 421–36. M. Falkenmark. The greatest water problem: the inability to link environmental security, water security and food security. *Water Resources Development*, **17** (2001), 539–54.

61. See, for example, C. Kremen. Managing ecosystem services: what do we need to know about their ecology? *Ecology Letters*, **8** (2005), 468–79.

62. See, for example, the reviews of national competition policy and energy policy by the Australian Government Productivity Commission. *Review of National Competition Policy Reforms.* Productivity Commission Inquiry Report number 33 (28 Feb 2005) (Melbourne: Productivity Commission, 2005). *The Private Cost-Effectiveness of Improving Energy Efficiency.* Productivity Commission Inquiry Report number 36 (31 Aug 2005) (Melbourne: Productivity

Commission, 2005). It is also worth reading the submission of the Environment Business Association to the National Productivity Commission inquiry into national competition policy reforms, available from www.environmentbusiness.com.au.

63. H. Mooney, A. Cropper and W. Reid. Confronting the human dilemma. *Nature*, **434** (2005), 561–2.

64. The situation is not helped by the tendency of the more conservative portions of Western societies to see ecologists, 'greens' and indeed intellectuals in general as some kind of liberal 'elite'. So statements about environmental problems from these groups are instantly dismissed without addressing the actual issues at hand. See, for example, Thomas Frank. *What's the Matter with Kansas*. (New York: Metropolitan Owl Books, 2004).

65. J. Stiglitz. *Globalization and its Discontents*. (London: Penguin Books, 2002). Will Hutton. *The World We're In*. (London: Abacus, 2003).

66. A. Sen. *Development as Freedom*. (Oxford: Oxford University Press, 1999).

67. J. Stiglitz. *Making Globalization Work: the Next Steps to Global Justice*. (London: Penguin, Allen Lane, 2006).

68. D.C. Korten. *The Post-Corporate World: Life after Capitalism*. (San Francisco, CA: California Berrett-Koehler Publishers, and West Hertford, CT: Kumarian Press, 1999). D. C. Korten. *The Great Turning: from Empire to Earth Community*. (Bloomfield, CT and San Francisco, CA: Kumarian Press and Berrett-Koehlev Publishers, 2006).

2 Complexity and complex systems

The characteristics of complex adaptive systems and networks, and an introduction to emergence and emergent properties

What is emerging from the shadows is a new future, one which, instead of having dominion over nature, works with and mimics many natural functions and processes. We are beginning to focus on water recycling and reuse, just as the biosphere has been doing since time began. We are beginning to find ways of lifting water, nutrient and energy use efficiency to levels comparable to those found in natural systems; and we are beginning to recycle more raw materials and find more and more renewable energy resources. The question is: instead of security and domination, can we find a new resilience in the face of global constraints, and of complexity, change and variability? To do so will require a new approach to complexity and change and a new view of the interactions and relationships between individuals, communities and institutions that allows of greater flexibility, adaptiveness and collaboration.[1] Epistemology and science are changing also; what we know, how we know it and what we do with the knowledge we have already changed irreversibly. Not all the experiments have been, or will be, successful, but the trends are clear.

We are hedged about by sunk costs and by semiotics: the cultural baggage we carry and the signs and symbols we use to conceptualise, describe, model and manage things. Yes, even science must be concerned with semiotics – it too carries a lot of baggage and it is not as culturally and value-free as scientists would have us believe.[2] Right across the board the semiotics of culture, values, science and natural resource management are changing rapidly and we need tools to understand complexity. So it is hardly surprising that complexity theory is a field of inquiry undergoing rapid development. There is no doubt that complexity theory is very popular, but it comes in many guises. In a review in 2001, Manson attempted to define a typology of complexity theory differentiating between algorithmic complexity, deterministic complexity and, finally, aggregate complexity, in which the complexity arises from the synergies arising from the interaction of system components.[3] It is the systems that show aggregate complexity and emergence with which we shall be primarily concerned here.

One of the themes of this book will be the rising awareness of the significance of small-scale, individual actions undertaken by agents (individuals, communities, institutions) acting largely on local information (context). Actions and interactions of agents rely on information mediated by culture and connectivity. They may or may not appreciate the global context of their actions. The significance of these actions lies in the ways in which interactions between agents lead to the emergence of meso- and macro-scale system-level properties, which are not predictable from the properties of the individual agents. The recursive nature of the world in which we live is demonstrated by the fact that the emergent system-level properties of these complex systems themselves become contexts for lower-level action.

Complex adaptive systems (CAS)

The systems that have received most attention in recent times are those systems in which complex behaviour emerges from the interactions of agents, individuals or components acting on the basis of local rules and local information. In many physical and chemical systems

> complexity is associated with system-wide, self organisation to a critical point (self-organised criticality, SOC) or a bifurcation point near the 'edge of chaos'. In both cases, even the generic, random states exhibit long-range correlations.[4]

Whereas the ideal SOC systems consist of identical agents (e.g. sand grains in piles), most natural and anthropogenic systems consist of interacting sets of highly specialised and highly evolved agents (e.g. individuals and species) which show evidence of complex design and contingent (historically dependent) histories. Biological systems can evolve to an optimised state through trial and error and by swapping constituents (e.g. species)[5] over time – a mechanism very different from the thermodynamic approach to 'the edge of chaos' in physical and chemical systems. There is more to life than SOC; thus, although SOC is widely discussed in the ecological and other literatures, I lean more towards the more parsimonious explanations of Carlson and Doyle, who have been able to replicate many of the apparent statistical properties of SOC with systems that they have called Highly Optimised Tolerance (HOT) systems.[6] HOT systems have many types of interacting component and are designed for high performance in an uncertain environment. They are 'robust-yet-fragile'; that is, they are robust to designed-for perturbations and hypersensitive to unanticipated disturbances.

There is much evidence that ecosystems and other CAS are much sloppier and more loosely connected than SOC would imply, with 'kludges'[7] (see below) and other contingent structures, which show design features that are hangovers of past contexts. So although we must understand the properties and complex dynamics of the interactions of natural and man-made CAS it is not necessary to use some of the restrictive physical analogies to explain their properties. Henceforth I am going to use the more general term 'self-generated complexity' or SGC to include the observed self-organised properties of HOT and other aggregate complex systems.[8]

Physical systems may frequently be regarded as complex and may display emergent properties, but biological systems, including artefacts of human biology, psychology and sociology (financial, human, social and knowledge capitals), are indeed different. The fundamental difference lies in the non-linear and adaptive nature of the basic interactions between the differing evolved agents. For this reason biologically based CAS are sometimes referred to as Agent-based Complex Systems or ACS.[9] Biological (species; natural capital), psychological, social and cultural entities (agents, individuals; social, human and knowledge capital) interact and change their behaviour as a result, thereby leading to CAS where the system behaviour unfolds over time in a recursive manner. In CAS, context is crucial[10] and actions develop a higher-level meaning in that context. So complex is quite different from merely complicated. Relationships are important and must be seen in context. The unfolding properties of CAS are extremely difficult to predict from the behaviour of the individual isolated agents. Differing interactions and relationships in differing contexts give differing (or similar) outcomes. CAS show strong path dependence. There is an important point to be made here. The complete behaviour of the CAS arises from the pandemonium of local interactions. There is no need to invoke higher-level, structuralist rules. As Dennett[11] pointed out, there may be emergent 'cranes' to lift up system-level properties but there is no need for 'sky hooks'.

CAS have a number of important properties

First, CAS feed on variability. In a world of CAS, variability is not noise, it is signal. The pandemonium of interactions adapts both to internal, context-sensitive outcomes and to external drivers. Ecosystems respond to both biodiversity and climate change, and the interactions between them over a range of time scales; species evolve over millennia, motorists respond to traffic conditions and world fuel prices, farmers respond to local climate and world commodity prices. The resulting systems show variability at a wide range of scales and often show a spectrum of responses without displaying any single characteristic, easily identifiable periodicity. (This is precisely why there is a debate about whether Kondratiev cycles are real; technological, financial and human developments show all kinds of periodicities.) Without variability CAS would not exist.

Second, CAS are not optimal, equilibrium systems. Change is the only constant and it is not states we are interested in so much as trajectories. As they evolve over time there is much 'make do and mend'. As Dennett termed them, there are many 'kludges': entities or agents that arose in response to past demands, now being pressed into service in new contexts.[12] In many contexts we see a constrained walk through evolutionary, ecological, social and cultural space;[13] the walk is constrained by biophysical and physiological factors, by the constraints of biology and evolution, and by history and institutions.

Third, CAS are highly non-linear, as well as being adaptive and recursive. Pathways, networks and flow patterns change over time and control becomes problematic. Simple, linear systems respond to interventions in predictable and proportional ways. CAS, on the other hand, often appear arbitrary and all over the place. The same intervention in different contexts produces totally different and unexpected results, or different interventions at different times may produce the same result. This is the problem of equifinality. CAS characteristically show unpredictable fluctuations and catastrophic changes. Landslides, stock market crashes and major evolutionary extinctions have been well documented.[14] All seem to follow statistical power law distributions, with few large events and many small ones. In trying to control or manage CAS, a small nudge at a critical time may be better than a large intervention. None the less there are repeatable patterns that we can observe.

Fourth, CAS are frequently self-organised in remarkable ways. CAS show properties much like 'self-organised criticality' (SOC). Many 'SOC-like' patterns are apparently fractal – that is, they are self-similar across a range of scales – and they follow power law statistical distributions. This has two important consequences. First, in a fractal world it is very difficult to pick or define a particular scale of study, prediction or management; the systems are self-similar across scales from seconds and centimetres to decades and continents. Second, in a non-equilibrium fractal world we are not dealing with the laws of large numbers; averaging in space and time is dangerous because small-scale events can have large and long-term consequences. This means that there is a high degree of indeterminacy in all this: it is simply not possible to know all the small-scale contingent histories of individual events or to predict the outcomes that may arise from seemingly trivial happenings.

Finally, the indeterminacy and complexity of interactions in CAS, coupled with the high degree of non-linearity, mean that there always will be surprises, points of no return and hysteresis ('you can't get back by the path you came on') effects in the responses and dynamics of these systems.

Overall, the understanding and management of CAS requires a high degree of adaptability and risk management, and an acceptance that the past is no guide to the future. This is a major challenge to individuals, institutions and societies.

The view of societies, landscapes and waterscapes and ecosystems as CAS changes an entire world view. The science of ecology and natural resource management is changing away from an equilibrium view concerned with being and with the states of systems, to a much more dynamic, non-equilibrium view concerned with becoming and unfolding trajectories in complex interactions between various kinds of capital. Again, it is not system states but pathways over time with which we must be concerned. Natural systems are not homogeneous;

they are very patchy, and patch dynamics are a critical part of their form and function.[15] Much of the damage we have done to ecosystems occurred because of the imposition of human requirements for security and stability onto naturally variable systems. Because they are complex adaptive systems, ecosystems feed on and generate variability. Some of the variability is imposed through changes in climate and weather whereas some is internally generated through SGC. This world view values not averages but variability, because variability is part and parcel of ecosystem biodiversity and function. Averaging over space and time actually destroys both information and ecosystems. As might be expected from CAS, ecosystems show strong links between system structure, species identity and distribution, and may display resilience or fragility in the face of human-induced perturbations. The ecological systems that make up the critical natural capital on which we depend are robust, yet fragile, and particularly sensitive to unanticipated (anthropogenic) perturbations.

Networks

With the rise of the Internet, the World Wide Web and mobile phones, the globalisation of financial and commodity markets and intercontinental air travel, the interconnectedness of ecosystems, societies and economies is growing rapidly.[16] Information, knowledge, money and influence flow rapidly from place to place – as do people, diseases and organisms – creating unexpected change and mayhem not infrequently.[17] The changing networks of interaction and influence also show CAS properties: unpredictable fluctuations, infrequent crashes and periods of quiescence. These human networks are very similar to biological systems in that they are characteristically made up of modular architectures that are interconnected in elaborate hierarchies and layers of feedbacks. This structure appears to derive from a 'deep and necessary interplay between complexity and robustness, modularity, feedback and fragility'.[18] Network architecture and interaction patterns matter.[19]

Network architecture is an important determinant of behaviour. Networks of randomly interconnected nodes show massive phase transitions as the number of interconnecting links increases.[20] The network behaviour may suddenly jump from linear and predictable to non-linear and chaotic as the number of links is slowly increased. Detailed scrutiny of network architecture in human and biological networks is revealing that patterns of interconnection are never random. Instead of random connection patterns, many natural networks are what have been called 'small-world' nets, with many local links and fewer long-range links.[21] This is the basis of the famous 'six degrees of separation' discovered by Milgram[22] wherein it is possible to reach almost anyone in the world through about six personal links. The World Wide Web is also a good example of this kind of connectivity. Other examples include the patterns of connectedness in enzyme systems in cellular physiology and metabolism[23] and collaboration networks in science.[24] Many networks show 'scale-free' power law patterns of interconnectedness (few long links, frequent local links) quite like the power laws that describe the properties of CAS. Indeed, this appears to be a fundamental property of many natural network systems.[25] It turns out that these 'small-world' networks have remarkable properties of resilience and may have evolved to cope with the vagaries of the real world of CAS dynamics. 'Small-world' networks are highly resistant to random attack but vulnerable to targeted attack on highly connected hubs. Resilience and resistance to attack and degradation are desirable properties in a contingent world.[26]

Parallels have been drawn between SOC states, 'power law' statistical properties of networked systems and 'small-world' network architectures, but we should be careful because various types of 'power law' distribution seem to be universally observed in the dynamics of complex interacting systems: some strictly SOC, some not.[27] As Andreas Wagner has argued, the widespread presence of these statistical distributions may not necessarily be used to infer the mechanisms that generated them – and there is good evidence to assume that biological systems, with their ability to evolve and change components over time, are different from physical and chemical systems.

What we have done as the human population has grown and society has developed over the centuries, in effect, is to superimpose networks of ecological, social and economic activity – all of which have different patterns of modularity and connectedness and which operate at different scales – and we have no idea what the interconnections or overall properties of this very complex CAS are. The entire 'system of systems' has been cobbled together as we have gone along, and history has been the judge of each experiment. Some have been more successful than others and some 'kludges' have made successful transitions into new roles. Through our activities we have knocked out hubs and spokes, changed modules and altered connectivity in the natural world.

So it comes as no surprise to realise that as the human population rises and we become the most dominant and highly interconnected species the nature of the problems we face is changing rapidly. Yes, we are making progress on environmental and natural resource management issues, but as progress is made on some issues others arise in a recursive and context-sensitive way. Interactions between societies, polities and cultures are changing – a global network culture is emerging[28] – globalisation is driving the competitiveness of nations,[29] and the distribution of 'haves' and 'have-nots' is changing rapidly. Many observations have shown that the distribution of nations and enterprises in terms of wealth also follows a power law, with few very wealthy nations and many poor ones. In terms of sustainability this means we shall have to manage the growth of inequality of wealth and opportunity[30] and the growing ingenuity gap.[31] Human population growth, urbanisation and resource depletion will continue until a more sustainable future is achieved.

Emergence

The basic tenets of emergence are: first, that emergent entities arise from the coming together of lower-level modules or entities in context-sensitive interactive configurations. So CAS show emergent properties. Second, all properties of higher-level, emergent entities arise from the properties and interactions of their constituent parts. Third, emergent properties are not predictable from even exhaustive information about the properties of the lower-level entities. Fourth, emergent properties are not reducible to lower-level conditions.[32]

Emergence is something that has been the subject of debate for many years; it has given the philosophers plenty of opportunity for analysis and discussion.[33] The debate is all about the very existence of emergent entities and their predictability from the properties of their basal agents or conditions. The key conditions, which Holland identified, are non-linearity and context-sensitivity. We are concerned here with what has been called 'strong' emergence in biological and social systems.[34] With strongly non-linear and adaptive interactions between entities or agents then the emergent features of these complex interactions will not be simply predictable from the properties of the constituent agents or modules in isolation. So CAS with emergent properties show both 'upward' and 'downward' causation: the interacting modules or agents together generate the higher-level emergent entities and the emergent entities provide a context for richer forms of behaviour than would be expected from the agents alone. This is something that has given the philosophers problems. It is the non-linearity and context-sensitivity that provide the key. Context-sensitive, non-linear interactions in CAS provide rich opportunities for emergent behaviour, but only recently have attempts been made to quantify the phenomenon.[35]

If we take a view that there are many CAS in the interactions between society, the economy and the environment (between the various forms of capital) and that non-linearity is both characteristic and important in institutional and community interactions, in global market dynamics and in biology and ecology, then there are a number of things that need to be explained.

Interestingly, although they are highly dynamic and contingent systems, ecosystems do seem to generate functional constraints and repeated emergent patterns; in the process of evolutionary development under regional and global constraints, ecological systems have developed some broad similarities in growth and life forms. These are the so-called homoplasies[36] – generic similarities developed in quite different systems and situations. The existence of homoplasies would tend to indicate that there are some constraints on the way ecological systems are configured. If this is the case then it has important implications for the ways in which we might restore and redesign landscapes and waterscapes to be more sustainable. Equally, the potential existence of homoplastic structures in other types of CAS – social and economic systems, for example – would also inform our attempts to structure our affairs.

NOTES

1. W. N. Adger *et al.* Socio-ecological resilience to coastal disasters. *Science*, **309** (2005), 1036–9.
2. P. Taylor. *Unruly Complexity: Ecology, Interpretation, Engagement.* (Chicago IL: Chicago University Press, 2005).
3. S. M. Manson. Simplifying complexity: a review of complexity theory. *Geoforum*, **32** (2001), 405–14.
4. Quoted from C. Robert, J. M. Carlson and J. Doyle. Highly optimized tolerance in epidemic models incorporating local optimization and regrowth. *Physical Review E*, **63** (2001), 056122–1 to 13. See also Per Bak. *How Nature Works: the Science of Self-Organized Criticality.* (Oxford: Oxford University Press, 1997) and S. A. Kauffman. *The Origins of Order: Self-Organization and Selection in Evolution.* (Oxford: Oxford University Press, 1993).
5. A. Wagner. *Robustness and Evolvability in Living Systems.* Princeton Studies in Complexity. (Princeton, NJ: Princeton University Press, 2005).
6. J. M. Carlson and J. Doyle. Highly optimised tolerance: a mechanism for power laws in designed systems. *Physical Review E*, **60** (1999), 1412–27. J. M. Carlson and J. Doyle. Highly Optimised Tolerance: robustness and design in complex systems. *Physical Review Letters*, **84** (2000), 2529–32.
7. D. C. Dennett. *Darwin's Dangerous Idea.* (London: Allen Lane, The Penguin Press, 1995).
8. See, for example, M. P. Hassell, H. N. Comins and R. M. May. Species coexistence and self-organizing spatial dynamics. *Nature*, **370** (1994): 290–2.
9. V. Grimm *et al.* Pattern-oriented modeling of agent-based complex systems: lessons from ecology. *Science*, **310** (2005), 987–91.
10. Gregory Bateson. *Mind and Nature: a Necessary Unity.* (New York: Bantam Books, 1979).
11. Dennett, *Darwin's Dangerous Idea*, 1995. (See Note 7.)
12. Ibid.
13. N. Eldredge. *Reinventing Darwin: the Great Evolutionary Debate.* (London: Phoenix Giant/Orion Books, 1995).
14. P. Bak. *How Nature Works: the Science of Self-Organised Criticality.* (Oxford: Oxford University Press, 1997). Philip Ball. *Critical Mass; how One Thing Leads to Another.* (London: Arrow Books, 2004).
15. J. Wu and O. L. Loucks. From balance of nature to hierarchical patch dynamics: a paradigm shift in ecology. *Quarterly Reviews of Biology*, **70** (1995), 439–66.
16. R. W. Rycroft and D. E. Kash. *The Complexity Challenge: Technological Innovation for the 21st Century.* (London: Pinter, 1999).
17. Everything from 'foot and mouth' disease outbreaks in UK, to SARS and feral animals.
18. M. E. Csete and J. C. Doyle. Reverse engineering of biological complexity. *Science*, **295** (2002), 1664–9.
19. D. G. Green and S. Sadedin. Interactions matter – complexity in landscapes and ecosystems. *Ecological Complexity*, **2** (2005), 117–30.
20. M. Buchanan. *Nexus: Small-Worlds and the Groundbreaking Science of Networks.* (New York: Norton, 2002).

21. C. Song, S. Havlin and H. A. Makse. Self-similarity of complex networks. *Nature*, **433** (2005), 392–5. S. H. Strogatz. Complex systems: Romanesque networks. *Nature*, **433** (2005), 365.

22. S. Milgram. The small-world problem. *Psychology Today*, **2** (1967), 60–7.

23. E. Alm and A. P. Arkin. Biological networks. *Current Opinion in Structural Biology*, **13** (2003), 193–202.

24. M. E. J. Newman. The structure of scientific collaboration networks. *Proceedings of the National Academy of Sciences of the USA*, **98** (2001), 404–9.

25. C. Song, S. Havlin and H. A. Makse. Self-similarity of complex networks. *Nature*, **433** (2005), 392–5.

26. W. N. Adger *et al.* Socio-ecological resilience to coastal disasters. *Science*, **309** (2005), 1036–9.

27. A. Wagner, *Robustness and Evolvability in Living Systems*, p. 139. (See Note 5.)

28. M. C. Taylor. *The Moment of Complexity: Emerging Network Culture.* (Chicago, IL: Chicago University Press, 2001).

29. M. E. Porter. *The Competitive Advantage of Nations.* (New York: The Free Press, 1990).

30. A. Sen. Global doubts as global solutions. In *The Alfred Deakin Lectures: Ideas for the Future of a Civil Society.* (Sydney: ABC Books, 2001), pp. 286–98.

31. T. Homer-Dickson. *The Ingenuity Gap.* (New York: Knopf, 2000).

32. J. H. Holland. *Emergence, from Chaos to Order.* (Reading, MA: Addison Wesley, 1998), pp. 225–30.

33. See, for example, D. V. Newman. Emergence and strange attractors. *Philosophy of Science*, **63** (1996), 245–61. Jaegwon Kim. Making sense of emergence. *Philosophical Studies*, **95** (1999), 3–36.

34. Y. Bar-yam. A mathematical theory of strong emergence using multiscale variety. *Complexity*, **9** (2004), 15–24.

35. A. G. Marsh, Y. Zeng and J. Garcia-Frias. The expansion of information in ecological systems: emergence as a quantifiable state. *Ecological Informatics*, **1** (2006), 107–16.

36. S. N. Salthe. *Development and Evolution: Complexity and Change in Biology.* (Cambridge, MA: Bradford Books, MIT Press, 1993). S. Conway Morris. *Life's Solution: Inevitable Humans in a Lonely Universe.* (Cambridge: Cambridge University Press, 2003).

3   New science, new tools, new challenges

The implications of complexity for science and socio-economics; personal and institutional challenges

Viewing the world as a CAS puts an emphasis on the contingent history of the present. There are deep historical roots to all present enterprises and institutions. The enterprise of science is no different. It has a long history, which began in the sixteenth century with a change in philosophy from an Aristotelian view, seeking the underlying essences of things, towards a more practical way of knowing.[1] Concepts of nature have a similarly long history, being based around concepts of balance, unity, equilibrium and human dominion. Science is one of the cornerstones of the modern, humanist enterprise. So science is inextricably connected to an instrumentalist ethical view and has developed to its fullest extent in the context of the culture and religion of the West. In the modern era science has developed what Salthe[2] would call a Baconian, Cartesian, Newtonian, Darwinian and Comptean bias (which Salthe abbreviates as BDNDC from the first initials of Bacon, Descartes, Newton, Darwin and Compte) – being essentially realist, materialist and mechanistic, also value-free and logical – the perfect hand-maiden to the industrial revolution.

As opposed to a science of balance and equilibrium, a new science of complexity and resilience sees the world through new eyes. Instead of concentrating on linear responses to change around the equilibrium, on central tendencies, and on the average properties of data, the new science focuses instead on non-linearities, on dynamic interactions, on contexts, and on network structures and the emergent properties of the interactions of agents.[3] If we are to study the interactions of humans with the natural world we need to rethink our basic assumptions and semiotics as well as our basic philosophies and values, particularly ones in which the choices we make are constrained by global constraints.

It has been said that there is a 'new science' emerging – or a 'postmodern science' – changing from a narrow disciplinary and instrumentalist base to focus instead on larger-scale problems and engaging the community in a debate about values, purposes and outcomes.[4] Certainly there have been major changes in the enterprise of science since the early 1970s. Science is now more 'postmodern' and occupies a world in which more emphasis is placed on values, ethics and transparency. Society at large is more interested in, and concerned with, developments in science that are likely to affect the lives of the general population.[5] I do not agree with the full 'postmodern' position of ontological and epistemological relativism. Like Giddens, I prefer the term 'radicalised modernity' to the more common 'postmodernity' because I do not subscribe to the position of radical doubt that commonly goes with the full 'postmodern' view.[6] Although, as I shall show, there are some basic limitations on our ability to understand events and predict outcomes in the natural world, I do not agree that all our bases of knowledge and truth are purely contextual. I therefore argue for ontological realism but epistemological relativism. There is firm ground upon which we can stand; we simply may not always know where it is or how to get to it.[7] Indeed, it is just as Giddens argues; it is precisely because 'the universal features of truth claims force themselves upon us in an irresistible way' that we find ourselves in the present global predicament. Yes, much of the world we now live in is complex, adaptive, recursive and contextual but that does not fundamentally negate the claims and confines of reality.

There are some fundamental constraints on human actions and beliefs which arise from the laws of nature and the planet on which we evolved. What we know about those laws is still partial and uncertain. I agree with the position argued by Nancy Cartwright; this is indeed a 'dappled world' with patches of sunlight and darkness.[8] Some things we know with clarity; other things lie hidden. Our explanations and predictions will always be partial. Partly because of technological change and our expanding mind, new and more complex relationships between culture, evidence, trends and knowledge are emerging. The signs, symbols, language and concepts we employ and the systems of interpretance we use are changing.[9] This is especially so in a world of complexity and complex systems because as we find out more our entire philosophical framework will respond and change around us. There is therefore a legitimate study of the semiotics of science. Science is not now seen as a source of 'truth' but more as argument and (partial) explanation.[10] This is nowhere more so than in the whole area of catchments, hydrology, water quality and land use change, where the modelling effort has stalled because of the sheer complexity of pattern and process in space and time and the difficulty of ever knowing all the parameters and initial conditions. What is now being espoused is a philosophy that 'combines elements of instrumentalism, relativism, Bayesianism[11] and pragmatism, while allowing the realist stance that underlies much of the practice of environmental modelling as a fundamental aim'.[12]

So science is now part of the argument about sustainable futures and is part of, and engaged within, an objective and subjective debate; a debate with society in a joint enterprise to reinvent the future. This can be a very difficult place to be because it involves science and scientists in discussions about change, evidence and policy. It can place individuals in positions of advocacy in society where values are more important than 'truth'. The idea and definition of 'truth' is disputed ground. While there is a justifiable study of scientific semiotics, and epistemology is moving in the direction of a more pragmatic view of the world, none the less science does (and should) place great store on logic, objectivity and the reliance, as far as possible, on measurable, repeatable and testable statements and explanations. Other communities do clearly have differing and legitimate views about other ways of knowing and other values, but science has a unique place in terms of its willingness to test and revise hypotheses and statements about the world. There are fundamental biophysical constraints, and I shall argue that some of these are associated with SGC in the natural world. What we need is a better dialogue between the various communities of practice and ways of knowing, each recognising the culture and values of the other. This is the only ethical path.

Statements about potential constraints on human activities should be part of the dialogue, however unpopular they may be at times. There will always be a requirement in any debate for unbiased and independent advice. Science should continue to give fearless advice and 'speak truth to power', while admitting the need for dialogue over the precise nature of 'truth' and agreeing that explanations are frequently provisional. Philosophers like Kuhn have written extensively on the structure of scientific revolutions[13] and on the social nature of scientific enquiry. Science is done by people, so it is as bedevilled by culture, values, politics and greed as any other human enterprise. Nevertheless, by reason of its habit of constantly testing, refining and checking back, science has progressed hugely and has built a solid body of knowledge about the natural world. As we move into a world of complexity and surprises then the required attributes are adaptability, teamwork, collaboration and flexibility; this is a major challenge for individuals, communities and institutions.[14] Dialogue, consensus, negotiation and adaptability are the requisite skills but these raise important issues of personal and institutional sovereignty. We suffer too much from public and institutional sclerosis; our institutions, policies and planning tend to be too slow to change as new information and concepts come to hand. We are going through a period of deep social change encompassing ecology, technology, governance, social factors, politics and economics, all of which affect and have important relationships with culture, landscape and our sense of place.

Constraints and 'extremal' principles

So how do we operate social, economic and environmental policies in a world of constrained SGC? This is a non-equilibrium world subject to change, shocks and crashes as well as growth and development. Capital and resource markets require security and predictability when the natural world in which we live demands variability and change. SGC implies complexity and variability in pattern and process in space and time, but it also implies constraints. SGC systems are therefore systems that tend towards bounded solutions, and these boundaries are set by the fundamental biophysical realities within which we must live. We set social, economic and environmental policies that conflict with these biophysical realities at our peril. Recent work has shown that SOC systems tend, at the limit, towards maximum entropy solutions – or MaxEnt solutions[15] – and that this applies to all kinds of natural systems including the global climate. Under special circumstances physical systems seem to converge on various upper-bound transport principles. Biological and ecological systems (which also show SGC and HOT properties) tend towards similar limiting states characterised by maximisation of water, nutrient and energy efficiencies and use[16] through selection, interaction and evolution, and these are part of the biosphere and the global climate system.[17] (There are, if you like, 'extremal principles' that some have used as goal functions of ecosystems.[18]) Thus the SGC of the biosphere is constrained by thermodynamic and biogeochemical principles.

Carlson and Doyle showed that HOT systems are capable of better performance under evolved constraints than the more randomly generated SOC systems. HOT systems show structured high-density properties when the perturbations are restricted to designed-for (natural) perturbations. Anthropogenic change rarely, if ever, mimics these natural perturbations; this is one of the reasons for major landscape change after conversion of the natural vegetation to agricultural or urban use. The maximisation of water, nutrient or energy use (for example, maximisation of evapotranspiration might be called $MaxE_T$ solutions, by analogy to MaxEnt) arises from internal ecosystem processes during development and succession. But the attainment of $MaxE_T$ will never be perfect even in natural systems; fire, flood drought and other natural perturbation disrupt the development of ecological systems and there are always the 'frozen accidents' of evolutionary history, the contingent events with which biological systems must deal. It appears that it takes many millions of years of evolutionary history to begin to approach maximum efficiencies, and that progress is usually disrupted by climate change, geological events or human intervention. So SGC systems are not SOC and the entire natural and anthropogenic world has a problem of tracking variability and attempting to maximise efficiencies in a non-equilibrium world of change and complexity. Andreas Wagner has shown how living systems (everything from genetic architectures and codes, through biochemical networks of enzymes, to communities of organisms) can, through evolution and trial and error, come to lie in what he calls 'neutral spaces': areas in state space that are characterised by robustness, resilience and persistence over time. Indeed, he argues that living systems develop robust architectures in the face of perturbations through evolution and trial and error, precisely the kinds of solutions that were characterised as HOT solutions by Carlson and Doyle. What is important here is the recursive interaction between physics, chemistry and biology over evolutionary time.

Once we accept that this is a world of change and variability over a range of scales, and that the variability is part and parcel of the natural functioning over a range of scales (even fractal scales), then we suddenly realise that our knowledge is much more partial than it seemed. It is no longer adequate to sample occasionally and average out the results over space and time. Small-scale interaction and variability is important and may very well show emergence and larger-scale effects. Looking at the world at the wrong scale (usually too large and too infrequent, often because of our primate bias and by constraints on manpower and budgets) leads to a problem called aliasing and this, when accompanied by a basic philosophical tendency to think in terms of averages and equilibria, leads to an erroneous world view. Thus we have the problem of evidence based on partial information and of explanations based on unrepresentative, deterministic dynamical models based on averages. There is therefore a problem, not only with the evidence collected, but also with attempts at synthesis and explanation. If the small-scale disequilibrium leads to large-scale surprises then we have been modelling and managing at the wrong scales.

SGC implies fractal and other statistical 'power-law' properties and means the demise of 'phenomenalism'. By this I mean that in a world of continuous variation across a range of scales it is very hard to pick out particular phenomena to study, manage or model. This also provides real problems for the reductionist BDNDC science paradigm.[19] In particular the removal of the small-scale variability from the signals from the systems, both natural and anthropogenic, causes real difficulties in modelling and prediction, particularly because the surprise and emergence is not captured. As Cartwright has pointed out, our physical laws are *ceteris paribus* laws ('all other things being equal' laws) that are applicable in restricted circumstances, circumstances which we now realise do not cope well with natural systems with high levels of uncertainty and indeterminism. Our laws cope well with physical systems that are complicated, but less well in ecological, social and economic systems that are complex. In a world of SGC the variances in the signals show equal information and variability across all time scales so that the unexpected can always happen. This has a major impact on policy and management, which must become adaptive rather than anticipatory. In a world of partial evidence, poor predictive capacity and frequent social and cultural disagreement about what constitutes evidence, there is a real need for negotiation and an adaptive management framework.

Complexity in social and economic spheres

So a complex world view requires a total reassessment of our relationship with nature – the biosphere – and an appreciation of the complexity of the interpenetration of the biosphere and the anthroposphere because of connections between natural processes and human activities across a range of scales. Through energy, transport, water, information and other infrastructure networks we are intimately connected to the biosphere through our dependence on atmospheric composition, water flows, nutrient cycles, renewable energy sources, weather monitoring, ecosystems services and so on. Whether we like it or not the economy is a wholly owned subsidiary of the planetary environment and the situation has now become highly complex, uncertain and unpredictable. We have created a monster of our own making that is very difficult to manage. Network connections and context are now critical,[20] as is a sense of the possibilities of surprise and emergence and the way these have major implications for the indeterminate links between action and consequence.

The realisation of the complexity of the world in which we live, and the new conceptual and visualisation tools at our disposal, have led to the development of a new science and new sense of nature and society. As Mark Taylor[21] points out in his book, this is very much post 'postmodern', and certainly post 'green' in the sense of an oppositional political movement. Moving from equilibrium to non-equilibrium and from states to trajectories in a bounded world requires a much more inclusive, collaborative and negotiated view of the future. We must find a middle path between instrumentalist and objectivist values: between the 'business as usual' merchants and the environmentalists. Because we are effectively 'making it up as we go along' a mature appreciation of change, hysteresis, catastrophic impacts and irreversibility requires an adaptive and flexible approach to the potentials of pathways to good or evil. The architecture of social networks and critical infrastructure require debate and renegotiation. We already experience the power of the few over the many and the existence of 'tipping points' in history[22] when complexity and emergent properties lead to surprise. This is the contingency of history, and we live with its consequences. These issues of complexity require new conceptual and ethical tools – new sets of signs and symbols and languages – in effect a new semiotics of sustainability.

Some of these tools have been provided by the work by Gunderson and Holling,[23] and by the Resilience Alliance[24] of which they are a part. Gunderson and Holling postulate that all systems go through cyclical patterns of change: essentially growth and exploitation, and conservation or stasis, followed by release and reorganisation; and that there are panarchies or hierarchies of these linked cycles. Natural and human systems contain interacting hierarchies of social–ecological systems undergoing these cyclical patterns in which higher-level periods of growth and reconstruction influence pattern and process at lower levels. They also recognise the possibility of emergence where lower-level cycles may influence higher-level change. As a result of the influence of these cyclical patterns up and down the hierarchical chains, many social–ecological systems can operate in more than one state and there may be abrupt transitions and hysteresis effects between states.

Personal and institutional challenges

A world of SGC raises all kinds of questions about the robustness of institutions, governance and management arrangements. Sunk costs and path dependencies that lead to delays in response to environmental signals can lead to irreversible catastrophes.[25] Small management interventions may produce very large, surprising and irreversible changes in state; conversely, apparently rational decisions may lead to system collapse.[26] Risk management becomes an important consideration. These ideas are already being incorporated into the worlds of commerce and finance. The forces of globalisation are driving ever increasing trends towards efficiency and effectiveness and this, together with the realisation of unpredictability of management in the new complex environment, is driving large changes in the ways in which institutions and organisations are being run. More and more institutions are being corporatised and privatised. These changes in institutional and governance arrangements are producing consequent changes in risk management techniques. Changes to the ways we manage water resources, for example, with more privatisation of assets, water markets and trading regimes, has ensured the development of entirely new management frameworks, new intermediaries and even the use of game theory in risk management regimes.[27]

In a world of multiple choices and in multi-parameter space there are many potential ways of maximising, say, water use efficiency. These multiple solutions, which attempt to maximise things like resource use, can be called Pareto frontiers after the Italian economist who worked extensively on optimising the outcomes of multiple choices. Given the constraints of sunk costs of various kinds and the contingencies of history, the really hard question is whether we can think 'outside the historical constraints' and find a path to totally new solutions which may be far superior to the situation we are in today. How do we get from one kind of multiple resource use solution to another, especially if there are constraints and hysteresis effects to overcome? This means that real innovation in complex thinking is required, together with a set of 'what if' tools that allow us to explore new and interesting parts of the overall solution space that have not been previously explored. For example, what kinds of new land use mosaics might we envision which allow for profitable farm enterprises in a changing climate on quite different landscapes that are more sustainable and have improved biodiversity and better water quality? Rather than push for security by removing environmental variability in space and time, how do we actually exploit the natural variability on a site for increased profit and sustainability? What is the trajectory that we must take and how do we manage the transition?

As David Harvey[28] has discussed, the 'postmodern' world has seen huge changes in the reach of capital, in political geography, and in dramatic change in the scales of interaction between communities and nations, between urban and rural centres. One of the challenges of 'double democratisation' therefore is that of global decision making (and the flows of capital) versus subsidiarity; the conflict between global, national and local decision making, priorities and needs. Into this we fit the new supplies of knowledge, evidence, and performance monitoring in an era of complexity, global change and variability. There is a question of signal to noise ratios in all this welter of information and how we detect change and act on the knowledge gained. We are going through a period when there is a challenge to personal, community and institutional learning and adaptiveness.[29] As natural capital becomes limiting there is a need to build and sustain social capital and capacity. If we are to better mimic the natural world and its tendency towards the highest efficiency (e.g. $MaxE_T$) solutions, we need to strive for greater resource use efficiency in the way we do things. This is the real challenge of comprehending complexity; the ability to see future paths and possibilities and the ability to build networks and relationships and plan strategy. Above all, perhaps, the most useful skill is the ability to recognise, name and explain what is going on, and then interpret events and reveal patterns to others.

Inequality and privilege, and access to knowledge and resources, are perhaps the most important emerging issues. Democratisation and globalisation are not the same thing. The key worry is not globalisation *per se* but inequality and its management;[30] but inequality is part of the design of SGC systems in financial, economic, social and information systems, so what is the required balance of inequality and security (information access, land use mosaics, smart water and energy, economic and social goals) to obtain sustainability and what are the policy settings that give the most sustainable outcome? This is a Pareto frontier question of the highest order. This is particularly so when we consider that the focus in the modern era was on resource exploitation and profitability so that the multiple use questions were, in a way, reduced in their dimensionality by disregarding the external impacts of these practices.

Given that our knowledge and predictive capacity in the complex emerging world is inevitably going to be partial then this raises severe individual and institutional challenges. There are, as yet, few good examples of learning cultures and adaptive management. Large organisations in particular face social and cultural challenges. We can already see issues of conservatism, sclerosis and sovereignty emerging and resistance to adaptability and change. 'Speaking truth to power' can be a career-limiting move, as evidenced by the treatment of middle- and higher-level managers in governments and large corporations that do not (yet) understand the emerging challenges of complexity.[31]

In Australia social, financial and environmental policy has pushed far down the road of using market trading mechanisms for managing natural resources. A very large fraction of the total surface water resources of Australia (the 'blue' water) is traded. Water trading and other reforms were introduced by governments as a means to provide market signals to improve both financial efficiency and water use efficiency and to recover the infrastructure costs from water users. Other nations (e.g. those of Europe) use social and economic policy in different ways, providing subsidies and regulations to produce outcomes rather than markets and valuations. Economic purists argue that subsidies distort markets, but whatever the mechanisms used the policy has been to deliver both productivity and environmental gains. So there is an interpenetration of social and financial policy with natural resource management. If the requirement is to mimic the natural world and reinstate variability, how then do we operate markets in a regime of greater variability and still provide sufficient security and profitability for rural and regional communities?

There is, therefore, a focus on a new model of excellence, one that directly links learning and discovery to outcomes in a bounded network culture. A new model for science excellence is also emerging: not just excellence in science but also excellence in delivery, adoption, innovation and economic/environmental impact *and in working with and through others to achieve these ends*. This trend requires new and more complex modes of operation, changes in old (often monolithic) institutions and new modes of thought and behaviour.

It is an intriguing thought that the emergence of the complex debate outlined here might have been inevitable. With the human population rising, with globalisation, the ICT revolution and the human domination of the biosphere, perhaps this all comes together in the emergence (in the true sense) of this concept. I am not, in fact, the first to suggest this. In a paper published in 2003, Devezas and Modelski[32] argued that the evolution of the world system could be viewed as 'a cascade of multilevel, nested, and self similar, Darwinian-like processes ranging in "size" from one to over 250 generations (which) exhibits power law behaviour'. The authors see the evolution of the world system as a process of innovation and learning which shows both monotonic and cyclical behaviour (from Kondratiev cycles over two generations to much longer cycles of innovation). It seems to me that historians would hate this paper because they would argue, I am sure, that there is much more contingency and agency in the historical development of civilisations than this treatment would allow. In addition, many of the cyclical patterns identified by Devezas and Modelski are somewhat subjective and are the subject of debate. Nevertheless the basic point they make about the importance of innovation and learning over generations is, I believe, correct. There is a real need for learning about the current dilemma. I would add an extra point also. In most of the work on the social and economic development of the world system there is no mention of the environmental crisis that we now face. Devezas and Modelski argue that the emergence of the world system they define may be largely complete through social development and global connectivity, but what they do not mention is the price that we have paid for this development or the urgency of the need to rectify many global environmental issues. Even if the journey is incomplete, perhaps this is an inevitable tendency of complex societies with the requisite technology.

NOTES

1. See, for example, P. Dear. *Revolutionizing the Sciences: European Knowledge and its Ambitions, 1500–1700.* (Basingstoke: Palgrave, 2001).

2. S. N. Salthe. *Development and Evolution: Complexity and Change in Biology.* (Cambridge, MA: Bradford Books, MIT Press, 1993).

3. R. Levins and R. Lewontin. *The Dialectical Biologist.* (Cambridge, MA: Harvard University Press, 1985). W. N. Adger *et al.* Socio-ecological resilience to coastal disasters. *Science,* **309** (2005), 1036–9.

4. S. Funtowicz and J. Ravetz. Science for the post-normal age. *Futures,* **25** (1993), 735–55.

5. J. Ravetz. The challenge beyond orthodox science. *Futures,* **34** (2002), 200–3. G. C. Gallopin *et al.* Science for the 21st century: from social contract to the scientific core. *International Journal of Social Science,* **168** (2001), 219–29.

6. See A. Marshall. *The Unity of Nature: Wholeness and Disintegration in Ecology and Science.* (London: Imperial College Press, 2002).

7. N. Cartwright. *The Dappled World: a Study of the Boundaries of Science.* (Cambridge: Cambridge University Press, 1999).

8. Ibid.

9. Salthe. *Development and Evolution,* p. 169. (See Note 2.)

10. D. Deutsch. *The Fabric of Reality.* (London: Penguin Books, 1997).

11. A form of statistical analysis that is partly based on prior experience.

12. K. Beven. Towards a coherent philosophy for modelling the environment. *Proceedings of the Royal Society of London,* A**458** (2002), 1–20.

13. T. S. Kuhn. *The Structure of Scientific Revolutions,* 2nd edn (enlarged), In *Foundations of the Unity of Science,* ed. O. Neurath, R. Carnap and C. Morris, Vol. 2. (Chicago, University Press, 1970), pp. 53–272.

14. R. W. Rycroft and D. E. Kash. *The Complexity Challenge: Technological Innovation for the 21st Century.* (London: Pinter, 1999).

15. See R. Dewar. Information theory explanation of the fluctuation theorem, maximum entropy production and self-organised criticality in non-equilibrium stationary states. *Journal of Physics, A* **36** (2003), 631–41. R. Dewar. Maximum entropy production and the fluctuation theorem. Letter to the editor, *Journal of Physics, A***38** (2005), L371–81.

16. A. Wagner. *Robustness and Evolvability in Living Systems.* (Princeton, NJ: Princeton University Press, 2005).

17. See, for example, J. Whitfield. Order out of chaos. *Nature,* **436** (2005), 905–7.

18. C. Gaucherel. Influence of spatial patterns on ecological applications of extremal principles. *Ecological Modelling,* **193** (2006), 531–42.

19. D. V. Newman. Emergence and strange attractors. *Philosophy of Science,* **63** (1996), 245–61.

20. R. Dawson. *Living Networks: Leading your Company, Customers and Partners in the Hyper-connected Economy.* (London: Financial Times, Prentice Hall, Pearson Education, 2003).

21. M. C. Taylor. *The Moment of Complexity: Emerging Network Culture.* (Chicago, IL: Chicago University Press, 2001).

22. M. Gladwell. *The Tipping Point: how Little Things can make a Big Difference.* (New York: Abacus, 2001).

23. L. H. Gunderson and C. S. Holling. *Panarchy: Understanding Transformations in Human and Natural Systems.* (Washington, DC: Island Press, 2002).

24. www.resalliance.org. Taylor sees the Resilience Alliance as a development from the Adaptive Environmental Management of the 1980s in which the dynamic relationship between institutional and social factors and ecological properties are couched in the context of the new ecological ideas of non-linearity, hysteresis and trophic cascades. Peter Taylor. *Unruly Complexity: Ecology, Interpretation, Engagement*. (Chicago, IL: Chicago University Press, 2005).

25. M. Scheffer, F. Westley and W. Brock. Slow responses of societies to new problems: causes and costs. *Ecosystems*, **6** (2003), 493–502.

26. G. D. Peterson, S. R. Carpenter and W. A. Brock. Uncertainty and the management of multistate ecosystems: an apparently rational route to collapse. *Ecology*, **84** (2003), 1403–11. Jared Diamond. *Collapse*. (London: Allen Lane, Penguin Press, 2004).

27. E. Roe and M. van Eeten. Reconciling ecosystem rehabilitation and service reliability mandates in large technical systems: findings and implications of three major US ecosystem management initiatives for managing human-dominated aquatic-terrestrial systems. *Ecosystems*, **5** (2002), 509–28. E. Roe and M. van Eeten. Some recent innovations in improving ecosystem functions and service reliability. *Global Environmental Change*, **13** (2003), 155–8.

28. D. Harvey. *The Condition of Postmodernity*. (Oxford: Basil Blackwell, 1989).

29. P. M. Senge. *The Fifth Discipline; the Art and Practice of the Learning Organisation*. (Sydney: Random House, 1990).

30. A. Sen, Global doubts as global solutions. In *The Alfred Deakin Lectures: Ideas for the Future of a Civil Society*. (Sydney, ABC Books, 2001), pp. 286–98.

31. See in particular the discussion of personal career paths and vicissitudes in A. Olivier. *The Working Journey*. (Johannesburg: The Working Journey, South Africa, 2003), available from www.theworkingjourney.com.

32. T. Devezas and G. Modelski. Power law behavior and world system evolution: a millennial learning process. *Technological Forecasting and Social Change*, **70** (2003), 819–59.

4   The complexity of ecology

A changing world view within ecology

In the previous chapters I have tried to show that an explanatory framework based on complexity, emergence and uncertainty is a necessary framework to use if we are to understand our globalised and interconnected world. I have also argued that any solutions will be bounded by biophysical reality. If I have succeeded in that aim then there is a need to examine the impact of such a framework on some of the basic scientific foundations of environmental management because, as I have said, science is not totally value-free and there are many deeply contingent factors which have brought us to our present state of knowledge. The science that informs our management of natural resources and the environment is called ecology. Ecology is a curious subject, and one that is notoriously difficult to pin down. Although ecology has a long intellectual history it has only really come into vogue since the 1960s; and since then the word has come to mean almost anything to anyone.

The science of ecology attempts to understand the interactions between the organisms and processes that form the basis of what has been called the 'economy of nature'. The word 'ecology' has also been used by lobby groups and marketing gurus and on everything from soap powder to popular culture. Some insist that ecology is not a proper science at all, for the reason that controlled experiments and tests of hypotheses are so difficult to do in the natural world. Where, for example, if we are experimenting on lakes, do we find an identical copy of something like Lake Superior to use as a control? Where might we find another Murray River as a similar experimental control? We would need a duplicate planet! Nevertheless, the science of ecology, such as it is, has a strong observational base in natural history and a theoretical basis in mathematics. The science of ecology is an attempt to understand the great complexity of the natural world and to provide humans with some predictive tools. In the past 30 years or so the science of ecology has become more socially involved. In what might best be described as a parallel book to this, and taking a somewhat more sociological view than that presented here, Peter Taylor has set out the framework for an inquiry into 'unruly complexity'.[1] Taylor's framework 'integrates conceptual, contextual and reflexive angles on the practice of researchers', taking examples from 'ecology-as-social-action'. Taking the science of ecology into 'ecology-as-social-action' complicates the picture hugely because of the changing metaphors that we use to conceptualise the world and the reflexive, contextual setting of the application of that knowledge.

Intellectual foundations

Ecology has long intellectual antecedents, even if the science or the word has not been defined to the satisfaction of all concerned. McIntosh, in a history of ecology,[2] devoted an entire chapter to the concept, its roots and definition. Haeckel is credited with the first use of the word in 1866 and he provided the following definition in 1870

> By ecology we mean the body of knowledge concerning the economy of nature – the investigation of the total relations of the animal both to its inorganic and to its organic environment; including above all, its friendly and inimical relations with those animals and plants with which it comes directly or indirectly into contact – in a word, ecology is the study of all those complex interrelations referred to by Darwin as the conditions of the struggle for existence.[3]

Many others have commented that it was Darwin's fundamental insights about the struggle for existence that began the scientific study of ecology. Indeed, chapter 3 of Darwin's *Origin of Species* on the struggle for existence, and his concluding remarks about a 'tangled bank', are what would now be regarded as straightforward ecology:[4] population interactions, community structure and competition.

In Darwin's era there was a firm belief in the concept of plenitude and of the Great Chain of Being. These ideas have deep roots in the concept of the spiritual unity of the universe. Plenitude defines the desirable (and perfect) state as the one with the greatest richness of species; in short, the world is brim-full of life and the struggle for existence is continuous. In addition humankind was seen as the pinnacle of evolution with the Great Chain stretching upwards from the lowliest bacteria and protozoa all the way to us. The hand of God was seen in this design. These are very old concepts. Glacken[5] traced the roots of western ecological thinking back long before Darwin to Greek philosophy and showed how, both then and now, ecological thinking is strongly influenced by arguments from design. Glacken wrote

> I am convinced that modern ecological theory, so important in our attitude to nature and man's interferences with it, owes its origin to the design argument: The wisdom of the Creator is self evident, everything in the creation is inter-related, no living thing is useless, and all are related to one another.[6]

Following Glacken's logic, Marshall[7] pointed out that the argument from design has a number of accompanying assumptions about concepts of uniformitarianism, balance, harmony, equilibrium and the concept of life as a manifestation of order.[8] These are, of course, strongly congruent with many common semiotics of place. Furthermore, these are commonly asserted to be properties that must be tapped into for humanity to find an appropriate way of living with nature. These ideas are still current: this approach has strong resonances with the spiritual side of many modern ecological and environmental movements. Thus, perhaps largely without knowing it, ecology and much of the environmental movement has deep roots in a world of design. Whereas the ultimate subject of ecology is the entire global biosphere, a more practical approach is to define and examine various lower and discrete levels of organisation. A common view is a hierarchical arrangement. The most common hierarchical system runs up from organelle, to cell, to organ, to organism, through population to community, ecosystem and landscape, and finally to the biosphere. A theory of ecology would therefore be defined at various points in the hierarchy. The earliest attempts were made at the population and community level. Later theoretical developments – systems ecology – developed first at the ecosystem level and then at the global scale with the development of models of the biosphere. Marshall argues that these concepts have been further elaborated in systems science, and in what he calls 'Cybernetic Gigantism': in the concept of Gaia.[9] 'Systems ecology sets out to functionalise the different and separate members of the world's ecology into one great system', he writes; culminating in the vision of the entire biosphere as a single living organism. So Gaia is an echo of the Great Chain of Being in another form.

The ethics that define our relationship to the natural world differ between the two dominant value sets and world views. The essential Unitarian view would also be the utilitarian ethic: that humans have dominion over the biosphere and that the world is placed there for our sustenance and benefit. On the other hand the Deep Ecology or 'green' view is very much an objectivist ethic, valuing nature for its intrinsic worth. The two dominant sets of values are therefore in opposition while sharing a fundamentally equilibrium view of nature. There is an important point to be made here. Although it is dangerous to summarise the entire philosophy of the global environmental or 'green' movement in a few lines, it is clear that the global 'green' movement is founded upon ancient ideas of unity, harmony, balance and the spiritual value of wilderness and the natural world.[10] The 'green' movement has strong spiritual foundations.[11] In short, this is a continuation of the ancient argument from design in a modern guise but with objectivist overtones. These ideas are contrasted with the reductionist, mechanistic, utilitarian, modernist philosophy of science, industry and instrumentalist commerce, which has dominated Western thought for the past couple of hundred years. So although some of the basic beliefs are similar, the values differ greatly. The 'green' movement is therefore an oppositional movement, committed to changing the values and philosophy of the modern world. Science is such a key part of the modern world view that Appleyard's critique of science is centred on the 'severance of knowledge and value' that he argues has taken place.[12]

Natural resource management

The 'green' movement sees a continuing need to oppose the kinds of instrumental reason that John Ralston Saul exposes and so roundly criticises,[13] and the consequent resource depletion and biodiversity loss in the natural world. Wilderness and place have been frequently conflated, particularly by urban dwellers, many of whom have a strongly idealist view of nature and conservation. Nature reserves and wilderness parks are seen as places to separate the natural capital from the depredations of financial and physical capital: a separation of wilderness from the 'rest of nature'. These values are not usually shared by those who live in rural and regional areas and have to earn a living from the land through farming or forestry activities. Of necessity they tend to have a much more utilitarian view of the world. In this way there has grown up a divergence of values and culture between urban and rural communities, which bedevils debate and progress. Only a complex systems view that regards the 'rest of nature' as part and parcel of 'all of nature' will eventually move this debate forward.

As a pragmatist, I assert that conservation of wilderness and outright opposition to development and modern Western values are often necessary but insufficient. (And I do recognise that in the usual battles over development the conservationists have to win each and every battle, the developers just once.) We are too far down the development track to turn back. We have already altered landscapes, altered the regional and global stocks and flows of key materials, dammed and regulated rivers, fragmented natural habitats and reduced biodiversity. The vast majority of our landscapes and waterscapes are managed in one way or another. Unfortunately many (if not most) of the 'special' regions of the world are already so seriously changed by development, exploitation, climate change, land use change and species extinctions that mere conservation is no longer an option. We have to address the conservation, preservation and restoration of biodiversity and ecosystem services in the 'rest of nature'. We must place a higher value on the 'ordinary'. To redress the damage requires active restoration and rehabilitation and this costs money. Many farmers have said to me, 'How can I be green when I am in the red?' Analyses of the profitability of Australian farming enterprises carried out as part of the National Land and Water Resources Audit in 2001 showed, unfortunately, a familiar pattern. Large swathes of the Australian landscape are occupied by unprofitable farm enterprises,[14] and 80% of the profit is generated from less than 1% of the land area. Australia is not unusual in this respect. If commodity prices on world markets are so low that farming enterprises around the world are unprofitable, how do we expect farmers to be environmental managers as well as productive farmers? How do we therefore manage the 'rest of nature'? Many countries, including the USA and the states of the European Union (EU), resort to various kinds of agricultural subsidies or stewardship payments. Increasingly, as I shall discuss later, market activity is expanding to encompass commodities other than agricultural produce to include ecosystem services and conservation outcomes.[15]

Sustainable land management requires profitability and resources in order to make the necessary investments for restoration and conservation. There is an equal need to manage and restore agricultural and urban landscapes, which are much more heavily modified than the largely natural landscapes of parks and reserves. Furthermore, in a non-equilibrium world of emergence and constant change, it is impossible to place a fence around any area and conserve or protect it for all time: there will always be both externally and internally generated changes in ecosystems and landscapes. Everywhere is on a trajectory to somewhere, driven by complex interactions between components. It is therefore necessary to think clearly about the nature of 'the rest of nature', to attempt to find the underlying rules and mechanisms and to try to conceive practical ways to manage and restore natural landscapes and ecosystems. This is the challenge of the twenty-first century: restoring biodiversity and managing biophysical realities through the involvement of the other parts of the 'systems of systems'. We cannot ignore the impacts of global markets or the importance of local community involvement. This is a complex issue of conflicting beliefs and values, and biophysical realities.

Restoration of landscapes and rivers is going to be done by local communities. For example, the Australian dryland salinity problem is going to be fixed by farmers and graziers changing their behaviours and agricultural practices. Yes, there is a role for government to provide regulation, incentives and some investment; but the majority of the knowledge, effort and success is going to come from local groups. The decisions that rural communities take in their management of environmental and agricultural assets are based on culture and values, and on perceptions of risk and return. Social capital is critical. Success depends on having suitably sustainable management options, on learning, innovation, relationships, networks and cultural change. The difference between environmental groups and farmers lies in their perceptions of evidence, knowledge, culture, beliefs and values. There is therefore an urgent need to engage rural and urban communities – and their beliefs and value sets – and to enlist their help in restoration. This requires the exact opposite of confrontation and oppositional politics. Oppositional politics is often required to identify and raise the visibility of an issue and to 'grab people's attention'. Once that has been done, kitchen-table mentoring works better than public criticism.

The only way forward is to recognise the importance of maximising and managing multiple capitals in the landscape and the necessity of not separating the financial from the natural, the utilitarian from the objectivist, either ethically or physically. In other words, the entire landscape – people, biodiversity and productive enterprises – must become the unit of management. This concept involves rejection of 'special' wilderness places as separate from the 'ordinary' and significantly widens the definition of what constitutes ecology and what constitutes science: this is very much post normal ecology. This, of necessity, involves a much more complex set of values, cultures and ethics than is presently being demonstrated by any party; hence the need for 'lifting the level of the debate' around possible futures, and the search for alternative pathways to sustainability. Because the objectivist 'greens' tend to be an urban group in opposition to the more utilitarian rural populations this also involves capacity building on both rural and urban communities and the bringing together of a more inclusive debate. In the end these problems are only going to be solved by offering rural communities sustainable options (i.e. environmentally sound, socially acceptable and profitable options) based on justice, equity and fairness. A systems view and ethical decision making are of paramount importance. The problem with many environmental and landscape management problems is that we lack sustainable options – and this is going to require research and community consultation, working through a dialogue and an inclusive process. Science and ecology are necessary but not sufficient. So, also for a number of reasons, conservation is necessary but not sufficient. The world view, values and sense of place that we hold have a critical role to play in the way we view and manage the world. This world view has changed over time and is changing rapidly even as I write. Ideas and concepts are changing to a more complex and inclusive view, a more dynamic and challenging view – a view that I argue is going to be more sustainable in the long run, but one that is going to require a considerable change in thinking.

World views and ecological concepts

So what to do? How do we move the debate forward? How do we develop a synthetic, systems view? Do we (as some do) try to comprehend the whole in all its complexity and think of ultimate causes, or do we (as others do) take it apart for sake of convenience and simplicity and confine our studies to proximate causes at lower levels? Do we think in terms of equilibrium and balance or do we take a more dynamic and uncertain view? Once again, as so often, we face a dichotomy of views. There always have been two basic ecological approaches, representing the holistic and reductionist extremes. McIntosh identifies the two basic scientific approaches to all this complexity as 'organic' and 'mechanistic'. The organic approach is very much the Unitarian argument from

Design concerned with overarching conceptual schemes and with balance, harmony, equilibrium and ultimate causes. 'The whole exists first and its design explains the actions of the parts',[16] whereas the mechanistic approach assumes that the 'actions of individual parts of a whole are explained by known laws, and the whole is the sum of the parts and their interaction'. Basically, these are 'top-down' and 'bottom-up' approaches, which some argue are incompatible; so is there a 'Grand Canyon' down the middle of our thinking? [Readers can probably guess by now where this argument is heading – the bounded SGC view builds the bridge . . . but let us review history for a while before we come to that.]

Hengeveld and Walter[17] would argue for the Grand Canyon effect. The development of ecological thought and theory must be seen in the context of the longer-term (sometimes cyclical) developments in society at large. From its roots in the eighteenth and nineteenth centuries, ecology has always been part and parcel of the broader development of philosophy and epistemology. The theoretical development of the 'organic' approach comes from Darwin and from arguments from design. Darwin adapted an idea from Adam Smith that equilibrium could be achieved by free competition at the community level, and this set the foundation of the very common ecological principle that almost everything is explicable in terms of competition for common resources. 'Overall, he effectively transposed a complex of ideas associated with the human progressionist society to the natural environment of species, and thus settled a role for competition at the core of ecology and evolution.'[18] In the 1920s and 1930s Lotka,[19] Gause,[20] Nicholson and Bailey,[21] and Fisher[22] turned competition into the structuring force in ecological and evolutionary theory through mathematical theory. By the 1940s this was developing in conjunction with the 'modern synthesis': a conceptual and mathematical fusion of population genetics, evolutionary theory and ecology.[23] (Note that there is no mention of bounded or constrained solutions to ecological problems.)

Equilibrium population densities in animals were assumed to be reached through density-compensating mechanisms, boosting birth rates and minimising death rates at low densities and doing the reverse at high densities. Competition was seen as a key 'governor' of ecological processes, just like the governor on a steam engine.[24] An entire school of population ecology was built around this assumption.[25] Some of the key early proponents were Nicholson and Lack, who each produced seminal works[26] which became popular in the 1950s and much later. Competition was very much seen as the link between proximate (ecological) and ultimate (evolutionary) causes and was enshrined in papers by Hardin and Hutchinson on the competitive exclusion principle[27] and on 'why are there so many kinds of animals'[28] around 1960. I do not think it is an exaggeration to say that the idea of competitive equilibrium has been the basis of much, if not most, ecological theory to this day, particularly in North America. (There are recent exceptions, which we will come to later.) The equilibrium theory of competitive interactions was well developed by Tilman[29] in one of the Princeton Monographs in Population Biology, an influential series that has included a number of canonical statements of equilibrium ecological theory, notably those by MacArthur and Wilson on island biogeography[30] and by May on stability and complexity in model ecosystems.[31] So this looked like a very well-argued and complete set of founding principles for the science of ecology.

May's volume, however, opened up a debate around the relationship between complexity and stability in ecosystems. Intuitively, many students of natural history and ecology had asserted that the greater the complexity or diversity of an ecosystem, the greater its stability. In terms of the argument from Design (influential in many environmental movements), equilibrium and harmony were seen as being associated more with the diverse pristine natural systems. This assertion had been connected to Clements's successional theories, even though many had pointed out that species diversity actually declined at the climax state because of dominance, often by a small number of large tree species. May's model systems showed quite the reverse patterns: increased complexity led to reduced stability of populations and greater fragility. This paradox remained on the table for some time. We now realise that May's models suffered from the network problem discussed earlier: increased connectivity in uniform or random networks leads to chaotic behaviour. Network architecture in ecosystems is neither uniform nor random; the structure is similar to a 'small world' structure which, through a process of trial and error (and the removal of unsuccessful attempted structures) leads the system to a 'neutral domain' with particular network architectures characterised by robustness and resilience.[32] Space/time patchiness and variability in ecosystems, coupled with adaptive non-linear interactions and emergence, are also part of the explanation.

In contrast to animal ecology, which was focused very much on population statistics and theory, plant ecology became largely concerned with community structure. There is a difficulty in identifying individual plants, so counting individuals, which is easy in animals, was replaced by presence or absence of species, estimates of cover, and frequency of occurrence in defined sample areas. The theories of animal and plant ecology therefore developed differently. Nevertheless, the ideas of equilibrium and the priority of the whole were strongly developed in plant ecology quite early in the twentieth century. The concept of succession in plant ecology developed by Cowles and Clements in North America[33] and the analysis of plant associations by Braun-Blanquet in Europe had a strong holistic flavour. Clements saw plant communities and successions as 'super-organisms' with defined trajectories of growth ascending to a persistent (equilibrium) climax community. In all this there was a tendency to 'idealise' plant communities and to pigeonhole a lot of natural variability and variety into a smaller number of canonical community forms. This will become a recurrent theme in this book: the tendency of scientists to ignore or downplay the importance of natural variability in their data. Variability was seen as 'noise' to be controlled or averaged out so that the ideal forms could be found and trends discerned. The processes of colonisation, internal interaction and competition for resources drove the succession of plant communities to optimise and maximise biomass and energy flows until a stable climax was reached. These ideas were then applied to ecosystems and an ecosystem theory was developed around the flows of energy and materials. These theories of ecosystem dynamics were very much developed around the ideas of biodiversity, balance, teleology and maximisation of productivity and nutrient cycling. This became (particularly in the environmental movement) a kind of Grand Unified Theory for ecology and environmental conservation. Much of this approach has been summed up in classic textbooks by Odum and others.[34]

Just as the modern evolutionary synthesis had its origins as far back as the 1920s and before, the alternative 'mechanistic' (or autecological paradigm in Hengeveld and Walter's terminology) has equally lengthy roots. Marshall,[35] in attempting to rip the 'GUTs' or Grand Unified Theories out of ecology and environmentalism, showed that a more individualistic or mechanistic approach to ecology was first espoused by Gleason in 1926 [36] – just at the time when Clements was arguing for the opposite approach. Gleason's approach can be seen as one more concerned with proximate causes operating in the field and with a much clearer focus on what the data were telling him. Gleason's data showed that plant associations were very much individualistic and differed from place to place depending on the vagaries of immigration, colonisation and the local environment.

This is an approach familiar to many aquatic ecologists. The biodiversity of plankton is very high and there are many species contained in each millilitre of water, a situation labelled 'the paradox of the plankton' by Hutchinson.[37] My own book on phytoplankton ecology[38] took very much a 'Gleasonian' view and argued for the dominance of density-independent, non-equilibrium interactions in the plankton of lakes, rivers and the oceans. Not everyone agreed with me,[39] and it is very much a matter of degree, but there is now a large body of work showing that environmental factors and strong mixing and disturbance largely determine the distribution and abundance of plankton in surface waters. Small-scale patchiness and strong mixing, which frequently disrupt the progress towards competitive equilibrium and exclusion, seem to be a reasonable explanation of the high biodiversity of the plankton. Colin Reynolds's considerable body of work spread over many years is perhaps the best example[40] of the determining effect of light, nutrients and mixing on the occurrence of plankton in lakes.

Just as the plant ecologists were presented with the contrasting views of Clements and Gleason, the animal ecologists were also having their differences. At the same time as Lack's work on competition and density dependence was written in England, Andrewartha and Birch in Australia were taking a different view.[41] Andrewartha and Birch found that in their insect populations the greatest influence on population abundance was not density-compensating mechanisms, such as competition, but the vagaries of environment and climate. They also found strong evidence of control by proximate environmental causes.

Gleason's data on plant associations showed many different and individual patterns largely because terrestrial ecosystems are also characterised by strong spatial and temporal patterns and 'patch dynamics',[42] which are a critical part of the overall ecosystem function.[43] The Gleasonian view is that dispersal of organisms across patchy environments in space and time weakens competitive interactions and seems to produce species distributions in space and time that are largely determined (a) by the local physical and chemical environment and (b) by the regional pool of species (and a source of immigrants to a particular patch). This view argues that habitat patchiness and environmental variability serve to weaken the strength of competitive interactions and lead to a more individual view of ecology. Just as with the plankton, there are many large-scale patterns of species distributions and abundance based on latitude, energy inputs, water availability, etc.[44] For example, Mike Austin and his co-workers have shown that aspects of the physical environment (slope, aspect, temperature, water availability) are strong determinants of the distributions of *Eucalyptus* species in Australia.[45] Other work in aquatic ecosystems also shows that physical determinants of ecosystem structure are very important: Jurek Kolasa has estimated that physical factors may determine as much as 70% of the species distribution patterns in patchy systems.[46] At the regional level environmental conditions also strongly determine what species are present. Most observations of species distributions in sampling areas of various sizes also produce what are called unsaturated (or Type I) distributions,[47] i.e. there is a linear relation between local species richness and regional species richness. This is taken to be evidence of weak competitive interactions and the predominance of regional and contingent immigration in determining which species are present in particular patches of habitat.[48] Overall there is evidence for considerable environmental determination of the distributions of species and for strong local influences of immigration from the regional pool of biodiversity. This 'bottom-up' view of ecosystems is quite a different view from the more structured 'top-down' view of designed system dynamics.

This is not to say that competition and interactions between species are not occasionally important. It is a matter of degree. John Lawton goes so far as to state that 'Only at the lowest level do the core concerns of traditional community ecology come into play – the role of species interactions in winnowing out the survivors who made it through all the other big filters'. 'Viewed in this way, traditional community ecology is actually about second-, even third-order processes.'[49] None the less it is these second- and third-order processes that give us evolution and development in the long run. There is now increasing evidence that small-scale interactions between populations within patches do structure the responses to perturbations that we see. Functional traits interact within the context of environmental factors and gradients.[50] So while the overall statistical patterns of species abundances seem to be more dependent on regional immigration and environmental factors, there are underlying and important local interactions.

Bridging the gap

Hengeveld and Walter discuss the strengths and weaknesses of the two approaches to ecology and point out that, whereas the 'competitive' (organic) approach to ecology has by far the greatest theoretical development, the 'individualistic' (mechanistic) approach frequently produces data that contradict, or create difficulties for, the standard theory. The development of theoretical ecology has searched for ultimate causes in an abstract form of mathematical theory, and it has often been divorced from the practical day to day reality and complexity of the natural world. There have been problems applying abstract theory to the messy world of natural resource and environmental management. Averaging has often been used to control the 'noise' and to extract the patterns of interest. The data are always a lot 'noisier' than the models predict. When I am standing up to my hocks in someone's sewage effluent, what does theoretical ecology tell me? The problem with a theory with progressionist roots is that it does not recognise the influence of global and regional evolutionary constraints and the potential for the evolution of 'neutral zones' through SGC.

The sheer complexity of the interactions between all the species in the 'tangled bank' at a range of scales, the observed variability in space and time and the limitations of human observers has plagued us from the beginning. The theoretical (averaged) harmony and order is overlain by much 'noise' and variability, which is reflected in difficulties in field work and data gathering. The prevalence of dynamic behaviour has meant that ecology has been very good at developing abstract concepts but rather poor at developing testable theories. Rob Peters, in his critique of ecology, gave many examples of the problems with ecological theories.[51] It is indeed rather hard to do the usual kinds of scientific experiment in ecology. Experimental controls, for example, where all else is held constant while the effects of experimental treatments are examined, are usually rather hard to come by. Not only is there much small-scale variability in space and time, but how do we ever find a control for something like an ecosystem the size, say, of an ocean, a river or a large lake? This is nothing more than the recognition of the fundamental problems of dealing with uncertainty, indeterminism and ignorance, and the unique geological and climatological features of large parts of the globe. I note here again for future reference that the whole idea of trying to control 'noise' and detect change in ecological data raises some interesting issues about scientific methods and statistics.

So can we explain where all the 'noise' comes from, and is there a way to go about bridging the 'Grand Canyon'? Standing in the now dammed and regulated Colorado River, is it possible to find a way out of the chasm? One way, it seems to me, is to recognise the emergent **complexity** of the pandemonium of species and interactions and to recognise that there are issues of **connectivity** and **context** and the possibility of global and regional **constraints**. In short, the middle ground is the world of dynamic interactions within and between local patches, with emergent context at a range of scales.

NOTES

1. P. Taylor. *Unruly Complexity: Ecology, Interpretation, Engagement*. (Chicago, IL: Chicago University Press, 2005).

2. R. P. McIntosh. *The Background of Ecology, Concept and Theory*. (Cambridge: Cambridge University Press, 1985).

3. Quoted in McIntosh, *The Background of Ecology*, pp. 7–8 (see Note 2) and sourced from the translation in the frontispiece of W. C. Allee *et al. Principles of Animal Ecology*. (Philadelphia, PA: Saunders, 1949).

4. See C. Darwin, *The Origin of Species*, chapter 3, p. 57 and the beginning of the last paragraph of the book, p. 504 in the reprint of the sixth edition. (New York: The Home Library, Burt and Co., undated).

5. C. J. Glacken. *Traces on the Rhodian Shore*. (San Francisco, CA: University of California Press, 1967).

6. Glacken. *Traces on the Rhodian Shore*, p. 423. (See Note 5.) These ideas are, of course, strongly present in the widely popular ideas of Intelligent Design.

7. A. Marshall. A postmodern natural history of the world: eviscerating the GUTs from ecology and environmentalism. *Studies in the History and Philosophy of Science: Part C*, **29** (1998), 137–64.

8. Glacken, *Traces on the Rhodian Shore*, p. 708. (See Note 5.)

9. J. Lovelock. *Gaia, a New Look at Life on Earth*. (Oxford: Oxford University Press. 1979). James Lovelock. *The Ages of Gaia*. (Oxford: Oxford University Press, 1988).

10. A. Marshall. *The Unity of Nature*. (London: London Imperial College Press, 2002).

11. C. Spretnak. *The Spiritual Dimension of Green Politics*. (Santa Fe, CA: Bear, 1986).

12. B. Appleyard. *Understanding the Present*. (London: London Picador, 1992); p. 113 in a chapter entitled 'From scientific horror to the green solution'.

13. J. R. Saul. *Voltaire's Bastards*. (Toronto: Viking, Penguin Books, 1992).

14. S. A. Hajkowicz and M. D. Young (eds). *Value of Returns to Land and Water and Costs of Degradation*. Final report to the National Land and Water Resources Audit. Project 6.1. (Canberra: CSIRO Land and Water, 2002). Available from www.nlwra.gov.au.

15. H. A. Mooney, A. Cropper and W. Reid. Confronting the human dilemma. *Nature*, **434** (2005), 561–562.

16. McIntosh, *The Background of Ecology*. p. 13. (See Note 2.)

17. R. Hengeveld and G. H. Walter. The two coexisting ecological paradigms. *Acta Biotheoretica*, **47** (1999), 141–70. G. H. Walter and R. Hengeveld. The structure of the two ecological paradigms. *Acta Biotheoretica*, **48** (2000), 15–46.

18. Hengeveld and Walter. The two coexisting ecological paradigms, p. 144. (See Note 17.)

19. A. J. Lotka. *Elements of Physical Biology*. (Baltimore, MD: Williams and Wilkins, 1925).

20. G. F. Gause. *The Struggle for Existence*. (Baltimore, MD: Williams and Wilkins, 1934).

21. A. J. Nicholson and V. A. Bailey. The balance of animal populations. *Proceedings of the Zoological Society of London*, Part 3 (1935), 551–98.

22. R. A. Fisher. *The Genetical Theory of Natural Selection*. (London: Constable, 1930).

23. J. S. Huxley. *Evolution: the Modern Synthesis*. (London: George Allen and Unwin, 1942).

24. A. J. Nicholson. The role of competition in determining animal populations. *Journal of the Council of Scientific and Industrial Research*, **10** (1937), 101–6.

25. S. Kingsland. *Modelling Nature: Episodes in the History of Population Ecology*. (Chicago, IL: Chicago University Press, 1985).

26. A. J. Nicholson. The balance of animal populations. *Journal of Animal Ecology*, **2** (1933), 132–78. David Lack. *The Natural Regulation of Animal Numbers*. (Oxford: Oxford University Press, 1954).

27. G. Hardin. The competitive exclusion principle. *Science*, **131** (1960), 1292–7.

28. G. E. Hutchinson. Homage to Santa Rosalia: or why are there so many kinds of animals? *American Naturalist*, **93** (1959), 145–59.

29. D. Tilman. *Resource Competition and Community Structure*. Princeton Monographs in Population Biology, 17. (Princeton, NJ: Princeton University Press, 1982).

30. R. H. MacArthur and E. O. Wilson. *The Theory of Island Biogeography*. Princeton Monographs in Population Biology, 1. (Princeton, NJ: Princeton University Press, 1967).

31. R. M. May. *Stability and Complexity in Model Ecosystems*. Princeton Monographs in Population Biology, 6. (Princeton, NJ: Princeton University Press, 1973).

32. A. Wagner. *Robustness and Evolvability in Living Systems*. (Princeton, NJ: Princeton University Press, 2005).

33. H. C. Cowles. The causes of vegetative cycles. *Botanical Gazette*, **51** (1911), 161–83. F. E. Clements. Plant succession: an analysis of the development of vegetation. Publication No 242. (Washington: Carnegie Institute of Washington, 1916).

34. E. P. Odum. *Fundamentals of Ecology*, 3rd edn. (Philadelphia, PA: Saunders, 1971).

35. A. Marshall. A postmodern natural history of the world: eviscerating the GUTs from ecology and environmentalism. *Studies in the History and Philosophy of Science: Part C*, **29** (1998), 137–64.

36. H. A. Gleason. The individualistic concept of the plant association. *Bulletin of the Torrey Botanical Club*, **53** (1926), 1–20.

37. G. E. Hutchinson. The paradox of the plankton. *American Naturalist*, **95** (1961), 137–45.

38. G. P. Harris. *Phytoplankton Ecology*. (London: Chapman and Hall, 1986). Marshall pointed out that I had taken a Gleasonian view of ecology in this work.

39. U. Sommer (ed.) *Plankton Ecology, Succession in Plankton Communities*. (Berlin: Springer, 1989).

40. See, for example, C. S. Reynolds. *The Ecology of Phytoplankton*. (Cambridge: Cambridge University Press, 1984).

41. H. G. Andrewartha and L. C. Birch. *The Distribution and Abundance of Animals*. (Chicago, IL: Chicago University Press, 1954).

42. J. Wu and O. L. Loucks. From balance of nature to hierarchical patch dynamics: a paradigm shift in ecology. *Quarterly Review of Biology*, **70** (1995), 439–66.

43. J. Ludwig *et al. Landscape Ecology, Function and Management*. (Collingwood, Victoria: CSIRO Publishing, 1997).

44. K. J. Gaston. Global patterns in biodiversity. *Nature*, **405** (2000), 220–7.

45. M.P. Austin. An ecological perspective on biodiversity investigations – examples from Australian eucalypt forests. *Annals of the Missouri Botanical Garden*, **85** (1998), 2–17. M.P. Austin. The potential contribution of vegetation ecology to biodiversity research. *Ecography*, **22** (1999), 465–84. M.P. Austin, J.G. Pausas and A.O. Nicholls. Patterns of tree species richness in relation to environment in south-eastern New South Wales, Australia. *Australian Journal of Ecology*, **21**(1996), 154–64. J.E. Anderson *et al*. Eucalypts forming a canopy functional type in dry sclerophyll forests respond differently to environment. *Australian Journal of Botany*, **48** (2000), 759–75.

46. T.W. Therriault and J. Kolasa. Explicit links among physical stress, habitat heterogeneity and biodiversity. *Oikos*, **89** (2000), 387–91. T.W. Therriault and J. Kolasa. Physical determinants of richness, diversity, evenness and abundance in natural aquatic ecosystems. *Hydrobiologia*, **412** (1999), 123–30.

47. K.J. Gaston. Global patterns in biodiversity. (2000). (See Note 44.)

48. T.M. Blackburn and K.J. Gaston. Local avian assemblages as random draws from regional pools. *Ecography*, **24** (2001), 50–8. H.V. Cornell. Unsaturation and regional influences on species richness in ecological communities: a review of the evidence. *Ecoscience*, **6** (1999), 303–15.

49. J.H. Lawton. Are there general laws in ecology? *Oikos*, **84** (1999), 177–92.

50. B.J. McGill *et al*. Rebuilding community ecology from functional traits. *Trends in Ecology and Evolution*, **21** (2006), 178–85.

51. R.H. Peters. *A Critique for Ecology*. (Cambridge: Cambridge University Press, 1991).

5   The generation of complexity

The evidence for self-generated complexity in the natural world.

Complexity is one of those ideas where there has been considerable cross fer-
tilisation between fields and disciplines. It is very much a 'child of its time'
in terms of broader social and intellectual developments and is also another
of those ideas that has migrated from science into management-speak and
popular culture. What do we mean by complexity, and what is the difference
between the complex and the merely complicated? Complicated means what
common sense dictates: lots of interacting components or parts. The way in
which complicated systems work can be understood by taking them apart and
studying the functions of the parts, essentially a mechanistic view. Complexity, on the other hand, reveals that apparently simple sets of interacting agents
(sometimes real-life systems, sometimes modelled by equations, algorithms or
experimental designs) can produce extremely complex patterns of behaviour –
even chaos – and that there are frequently counterintuitive or surprising properties of the whole that are not found other than through the interactions of
the parts. If you take a complex system apart it loses its system-level properties.
We have good physical theories of complicated systems, but we lack good theories of causality in complex, hierarchical systems; the kinds of systems that
dominate the natural biological and human world.[1] So we are confronted,
once again, by the problem of understanding systems which show aggregate
complexity.

The properties of complex systems evolve continuously over time. This is a
world of trajectories not states. The past is not necessarily any guide to the
future because the properties of the whole lie in the non-linear interaction
of the parts; *parts which are themselves context-sensitive.* Complex systems are not
equilibrium systems and it is very difficult to study them by reductionist means.
It follows that observations of complex patterns of behaviour in space and time
are not necessarily indications of 'noise' but are more likely to be real measures
of system dynamics. I would go so far as to assert that there is no such thing
as 'noise' in these systems. What we call 'noise' is just evidence of unknown, or
unknowable, pattern and process.

There are patterns in ecosystems that we must try to explain; these explanations will be useful in management and restoration. Many of the features that
we observe in landscapes and waterscapes are an apparently emergent property,
which means that there are important context-sensitive and non-linear interactions between the parts. Species and populations in nature are not completely

disaggregated and fragmented and all is not random noise – but this is not an equilibrium world either. I differ from Marshall[2] here in that I do not agree with a totally postmodern view of ecology. There are fundamental constraints, which we must understand. A radicalised view of modernity that incorporates complexity and emergence I can agree with, but not postmodernity. Context is important, at least at times, and strong interactions between species and populations do occur. But we come back to the age-old conundrum: how much interaction is there, how important is it, and what can we explain? I accept Marshall's argument that a Unitarian view is totalising and unnecessary, and continue to lean towards a Gleasonian view. I also agree with Lawton that traditional concerns of community ecology are second- and third-order concerns in this patchy and variable world. The uncovering of complexity theory and its application to environmental issues and policies does, it seems to me, offer a middle ground which has useful attributes. This approach sits between the 'bookends' of mechanistic and Unitarian approaches, and also broadens the ethical frame to include multiple players and forms of capital, non-equilibrium properties, trajectories over time, cyclical and other patterns of abrupt change, and the exchange of materials, energy and information with the other components of the entire network of social, economic and ecological systems.

So how was complexity uncovered and how was the theory developed? The first hints of chaos came from the work of Robert May[3] on the properties of the very models of population dynamics conceived by Nicholson and Bailey and others. It turned out that these apparently simple models could produce some very complex outcomes, even chaotic solutions, if the parameters were slowly increased beyond a threshold value. This was the first hint that simple models of population dynamics could produce deterministic chaos. Further work uncovered a whole class of bifurcations and chaotic solutions revealing unexpected complexity.[4] Chaotic solutions do not converge to equilibrium; on the contrary, they diverge continuously so that very small changes (often indeterminably small changes) in the initial conditions lead to quite different outcomes. Such systems are irreversible: you cannot wind the clock backwards after a period of divergence. Chaotic solutions may take the form of strange attractors, which never repeat and whose manifolds are fractal, i.e. they show similar patterns of variability at all scales.[5] Bifurcations and sudden flips between states are also common. Analysis of the properties of many classes of ecosystem model also now shows chaotic regimes, and these appear to have some basis in reality.[6] So an analysis of both old and new ecological models indicates the widespread occurrence of chaos and highly dynamic patterns of behaviour. This provides (at least in theory) some explanation of the large amount of variability observed in natural populations. Deterministic chaos is only one form of complexity, and although ecosystems may show chaotic behaviour, deterministic systems do not show context-sensitive behaviour or emergence.

'Becoming' rather than 'being'

Whereas the Unitarian approach was concerned with equilibrium (and reversibility in a Newtonian universe), a second source of the new ideas about chaos and complexity lies in studies of systems far from equilibrium; systems that Prigogine characterises as 'becoming' rather than 'being'.[7] Early work showed that non-equilibrium thermodynamic systems also showed surprisingly complex patterns of behaviour and frequently became self-organised at macroscopic scales in quite remarkable ways. Apparently simple chemical reactions in dishes show rings, moving waves and other startling patterns, which evolve with time. Ecosystems have similar properties.[8] It was discovered that forced non-equilibrium systems could show self-organised criticality (SOC): internally generated patterns of macroscopic behaviour that emerge from small-scale processes.[9] These SOC systems (everything from chemical reactions in small dishes to earthquakes, it seems) tend to organise themselves into states that show characteristic statistical properties including inverse power law relationships. Just like the canonical sand piles of Per Bak,[10] SOC systems characteristically exhibit dynamics incorporating a few big events and large numbers of small ones. The key difference between equilibrium and non-equilibrium systems is that whereas in equilibrium systems the tendency is to assemble statistics for the distributions of equilibrium states, in non-equilibrium systems it is necessary to account for the distributions of pathways or trajectories over time. Dewar[11] shows that non-equilibrium systems, in addition to showing SOC properties, also tend to maximise entropy production so that there are some broad rules for the production of SOC states.

Simple models with complex outcomes

A third technique has revealed unexpectedly complex behaviour in model systems that again derive their complex behaviour from interactions between simple model agents. Simple computer programs, such as Conway's 'Game of Life', develop highly organised and complex evolving patterns.[12] These programs contain simple algorithms: simple rules for changing the colour of a square on a grid from black to white depending on either the pattern surrounding it or the arrangement of black and white elements in the row before. Depending on the algorithm, either very little happens or the program can produce repeating patterns, moving shapes or chaotic patterns that never repeat. Some go so far as to claim that such an algorithmic approach to computation is a new kind of science and that the complexity of the entire universe, from subatomic particles upwards, can be accounted for in this way.[13]

Another set of important results was produced by Kauffman,[14] who looked at what happened in networks of interacting points, such as a grid of interacting light bulbs. What emerged was another critical threshold, this time of inter-connectivity. Kauffman's networks produce three kinds of outcomes: a chaotic regime that is very sensitive to initial conditions, an ordered regime in which most of the interactions between points is frozen and, most interestingly, a complex transitional regime. This transitional regime, lying between order and chaos, is where islands of order lie between regions of chaotic dynamics. As Kauffman notes

> In this transition region, altering the activity of single unfrozen elements unleashes avalanches of change with a characteristic size distribution having many small and few large avalanches.[15]

We are back to the characteristic statistical properties of SOC and complex systems: inverse power laws of few large events and many small events.

But, as introduced previously, CAS that contain highly evolved and designed interacting, context-sensitive agents do not have to be strictly SOC to produce the kinds of rich dynamics and statistical properties seen in natural and artificial systems. Carlson and Doyle showed that what they called Highly Optimised Tolerance (HOT) systems can have indistinguishable dynamic statistical properties. Furthermore, Carlson and Doyle's HOT systems specifically allow for evolution, development and optimisation of the interacting agents, and produce systems that are more efficient than the more ideal, random SOC states.[16] Darwinian evolution satisfies these general properties if we think of the process of evolution as essentially algorithmic. This argument was elegantly developed by Dennett,[17] who writes that Darwin 'was offering a sceptical world what we might call a get-rich-slow scheme, a scheme for creating Design out of Chaos without the aid of Mind'.[18] In addition, Dennett had something to say about reductionism and emergence. He argued forcefully that the order and pattern that we see in the world arises from Darwin's Dangerous Idea – that of 'reductionism incarnate'[19] – the emergence (in the strict sense) of highly complex pattern and process from small-scale, local, context-sensitive interactions. The algorithmic view allows for emergent 'cranes' – structures that appear from the bottom to 'lift up' and provide a higher-level context for lower-level interactions – but not for 'skyhooks' imposed from above. So arguments from Design can be demystified. 'Good reductionists suppose that all Design can be explained without skyhooks; greedy reductionists suppose it can all be explained without cranes.'[20] I go for cranes. Dennett invented the concept of 'universal acid' that cuts through the fog of argument and provides a great clarity of view on a number of issues. We do not need skyhooks, or Unitarian or structuralist explanations, to help us account for the way the world works. The emergence of large-scale pattern and process – and 'envelope' dynamics – from small-scale context-sensitive interactions will be a recurrent theme of this book.

So by combining ideas from multiple capitals, complexity, algorithms and non-equilibrium systems can we help to bridge the 'Grand Canyon' and provide a guide to the practical people of the world? Maybe so, but these are early days. We can explain what we see in the natural world as a constrained walk through evolutionary and ecological space by evolving organisms – including humans – which interact and evolve.[21] The walk is algorithmic, wobbly and constrained by history and context: the world is contingent and certainly not fully constrained or optimal. This is not a world of 'being'. Things are constantly changing, developing and 'becoming'. Dennett uses the word 'kludges' to describe the existence of contingent organs, organisms or functions that evolved in response to one context and which frequently ended up being pressed into service in quite a different context – a Rube Goldberg device that, even though it was left over from another era, might just work in the new. Disturbance, patchiness, accident and surprise leave room for innovation and create opportunities.

So, keeping in mind the 'universal acid' and being very mindful of totalising frameworks,[22] what can we say about the natural world? Cohen and Stewart have argued that in a world of algorithmic complexity and emergence the real question is not 'where does all the complexity come from?' but 'why is there any simplicity?'[23] Cohen and Stewart coin two new terms: simplexity for the emergence of large-scale simplicities as a direct consequence of different, but similar, rules; and complicity for situations in which totally different rules converge to produce similar, large-scale structural patterns.[24] The example they quote for evolutionary complicity is flight, which has evolved several times in different major groups of animals. Each time the routes to the solutions of flight are different, using different contingent 'kludges', but nevertheless ending up with viable options.

In a paper published in 1999 I argued that the natural world may, in fact, be a lot simpler than we think.[25] After considering a number of basic propositions about the algorithmic development of ecosystems I concluded that 'buried deep within a very complex world there are some general modes of behaviour, determined by fundamental principles, which impart certain kinds of high level order and predictability'. So there does appear to be complicity in ecosystems in that there are some large-scale emergent features of ecosystems which can be observed; empirical (macro-ecological) relationships which run across many ecosystems, stoichiometric ratios, trophic interactions, functional groups, size distributions of organisms and so on.[26] These homoplastic and emergent entities are statistical entities and exhibit space/time variability, which may be useful for monitoring ecosystem structure and dynamics. Many follow the kinds of fractal and power law distributions we might expect from the operation of SGC: for example, self-similar body size distributions in insects appear to be ubiquitous at scales from several hectares to global.[27] Predictive power is limited and we shall have to live with uncertainty; nevertheless, emergent properties can be used as indicators of self-generated pattern and process.[28] As long as we recognise the limitations on our knowledge and we keep a magical container of universal acid at our side, there does seem be a bridge across the Grand Canyon, however wobbly and contingent it may be.

Evidence for complex systems properties, fractals and SGC

Adoption of the concepts of non-equilibrium thermodynamics, complexity and emergence leads to the question of whether or not ecological systems can be truly regarded as displaying self-generated complexity. Many environmental and ecological systems appear to show statistical properties similar to those expected in SGC systems. These include distributions of forest fires, population distributions, and system properties in soils and aquatic systems. But are natural landscapes really SOC or a looser form of SGC? SOC systems tend to be made up of identical and unchanging components (e.g. piles of sand and rice grains) which exist in a poised state at the 'edge of chaos'. They appear to be maximum entropy systems. There are, however, alternative theories which preserve the statistical properties of SOC systems – including power law distributions of the frequency and magnitude of events. HOT systems, for example, are made up of a diverse set of variously designed components which have undergone development and selection to maximise performance in the face of external perturbations.[29] Another key question is the strength of the local interactions in a patchy and changing world. Fully coupled thermodynamic systems do show SOC, but the natural world is much sloppier. There are fundamental constraints on the strength of local coupling in any given context because of the contingent 'kludges' or the 'frozen accidents' of history (e.g. of both evolution and immigration); because of climate variability and disturbance, drought, fire and other disasters; because of the underlying pandemonium of interactions and because of the space/time patchiness and variability generated within the systems themselves.

I believe that Andreas Wagner's ideas are relevant here. In his book on evolvability and robustness in biological systems[30] he suggests that evolved biological systems can come to occupy 'neutral spaces' in which the interaction strengths and network designs are robust to many perturbations. These dynamic spaces show many of the properties of SOC but are not strictly so. 'Kludges' and other aspects of evolved properties contribute to the successful – robust – system properties. Networks and system components show path dependencies and the 'frozen accidents' of history. It is in these 'neutral spaces' that interactions are optimised for robustness under normal conditions and only become fragile under infrequent (and not designed-for) perturbations.

One of the great challenges of observational science is how to describe and ultimately predict the behaviour of complex, extensive, poorly observed systems.

When, for example, does 'clarifying' the complexity by averaging the apparent 'noise' and making simplifying assumptions become misleading? Science has a nasty habit of making inferences from theory – and of making the data fit the theory by various kinds of statistical transformations – and theory is much more simplistic than the reality of a more broadly defined 'postnormal' ecology; of coupled environmental, social and economic systems. A review of the recent literature on the search for CAS and SGC in ecosystems reveals a relative paucity of data, much modelling and inference, and some danger of the fallacy of 'affirming the consequent'. By that I mean that there is a tendency to assume that the discovery of network structures, power laws, self-similarity and fractals in ecological data is actually evidence of SOC when, in fact, there are other ways of producing power laws than through SOC, some even simpler than invoking HOT theory.[31] Strictly speaking, ecological data should be multi-fractal rather than fractal. In many cases the data are partial and incomplete (e.g. short time series or data that describe only a restricted set of scales) so the precise definition of the distribution of the data may be hard to pin down.[32] Due care is therefore required in data interpretation and we probably need some stronger tests.[33]

So what is the evidence? To date much of the evidence comes from statistical analysis of ecological data: landscape and population statistics, size distributions, primary productivity, water quality and other measures of ecological pattern and process in space and time.[34] Ecological, geological and geographical data can be summarised by power laws, and fractal distributions are widespread.[35] Indeed, at face value there seems to be very strong evidence of self-organisation and its associated properties throughout landscapes and waterscapes.[36] The sorts of emergent properties of ecosystems that have been observed – e.g. size and biomass distributions, etc. – all show statistical properties apparently characteristic of self-organisation. Many simple, algorithmic and mathematical models of ecological processes also show similar outputs, so there is great parallelism in both data and modelling results[37] which reinforces the argument. In addition it has been argued that classes of both ecological and evolutionary models produce evidence for life existing, as Kauffman argued, at the critical boundary between stability and chaos.[38] So there is a great deal of circumstantial evidence for both CAS and SGC as being characteristic of ecological pattern and process.

There is considerable evidence for the importance of small-scale interactions and processes in determining the overall properties and dynamics of landscapes and waterscapes. Small-scale pattern and process (often dominated by simple organisms) has largely been underestimated in its importance by the dominant two-metre-tall primate on the planet, although it has a very important role to play in global dynamics. In addition there is evidence, particularly in aquatic ecosystems, of multi-fractal scaling of pattern and process over very wide ranges of time and space scales. In pelagic ecosystems multi-fractals are very powerful ways of describing the space–time distributions of organisms and water quality, where the biological and ecological processes interact within a turbulent field.[39] What this analysis shows is that there is much very small-scale variability in water quality and other aquatic data – from minutes and centimetres up – much more than we have hitherto appreciated. Given that many water bodies are turbulently mixed this might come as a surprise, but with hindsight this is not so surprising perhaps when we consider the very small size of the organisms – bacteria, algae and zooplankton – involved and the rapid reaction–diffusion reactions that occur in the turbulent field during nutrient uptake, recycling and growth.[40] Observation and modelling confirm that this is the underlying mechanism[41] and that it can be found in all water bodies so far examined: lakes, rivers, estuaries and coastal waters.

Biogeochemistry (the cycling of elements through biological, microbial and geochemical reactions) is not uniformly distributed in nature. All the action is concentrated in 'hot spots' and 'hot moments',[42] and most of the action takes place at very small scales. Microbial populations and community interactions are responsible for most of the elemental cycling in landscapes and water-scapes and they are grouped in spatially organised clumps and patches within biofilms. There is much small-scale pattern and process; the evidence points to spatially discontinuous functional groups interacting through reaction–diffusion processes.[43] Biofilms can be modelled by cellular automata models and these can account for the varying structures observed in nature. Much of the observed structural variability found in biofilms can be accounted for by sub-strate concentrations.[44] Small-scale microbial biofilms and aggregates have been found to be almost ubiquitous in nature and are responsible for many globally significant biogeochemical processes. It is now known, for example, that these kinds of small-scale, spatially structured microbial assemblages are responsible for nutrient and elemental cycling in the surface waters of the oceans.[45] New techniques of molecular genetics are being used to determine the biodiversity and functionality of these important systems at very small scales.[46] It is no over-statement to say that these small-scale, highly structured biofilms are responsible for the cycling of elements through the biosphere and are therefore critical for the long-term sustainability of the planet. The micro- really does determine the global properties of the macro-.

These interactions of reaction–diffusion relations are known to occur in ter-restrial and benthic ecosystems, and multi-fractals are also found there. These are systems in which dispersal and mortality interact with growth and repro-duction in patchy environments. Again we find space–time distributions of pop-ulations that approximate fractals or multi-fractals, and some complex relations between overall productivity and biomass and the nature of the patterns.[47] In a manner analogous to that of non-equilibrium chemical reactions, both nat-ural and model populations of animals have been found to exhibit large-scale coherence, standing waves and other coherent patterns of behaviour.[48] There is evidence of fractal-like patchiness in terrestrial systems over a very wide range of scales – from hundreds of microns upwards[49] – and those terrestrial systems are no more homogeneous than any other ecosystem examined. There is evidence for a lot of small-scale patchiness in both population dynamics and biogeochemical function, which in microbial populations in soils and sediments, just as in the aquatic realm, has major implications for the way we understand, model and predict properties of these systems. At the physiological and structural level many aspects of terrestrial plant communities may also be explained in terms of simple allometric and fractal properties of plant structure and function.[50]

In the networks of interaction within and between organisms there is also evidence of self-organised patterns of interaction. The study of networks is fundamental to many aspects of science.[51] Self-organised networks are frequently what are called 'small-world' networks with many local links and a few long linkages. Networks are made up of 'communities' associated in highly connected groups – and those groups can be groups of proteins, people or industries.[52] These networks were discovered in patterns of human contacts (the so-called 'six degrees of separation' phenomenon) and are common in many dynamical systems.[53] The patterns and maps of biochemical pathways and reactions between molecules in cells also seem to show self-organised and 'small-world' patterns.[54] It appears that homogeneity in the structure of connections in networks increases the probability of extinction events at nodes and that the structure of 'small-world' networks (lots of local links around 'hubs' and fewer longer connections) is more resistant to random attack.[55] As mentioned previously, the problem with 'small-world' networks, however, is that they are susceptible to targeted attack at nodes.[56] At the level of populations and species it has been suggested that the study of food webs provides a road map through Darwin's 'tangled bank'[57] and that self-organised food webs would tend towards robust 'small-world' and scale-free webs, which show statistical inverse power law relations. There is evidence that this is the case.[58]

What we are finding therefore is a series of large-scale macroscopic properties of organisms, populations and ecosystems (complicit properties) based on some underlying multi-fractal and apparently self-organised properties of individuals, populations and networks. These large-scale, statistical distributions have been termed 'macro-ecology'[59] or 'macro-physiology'[60] and are an active area of study. On the face of it, there is strong evidence for CAS and SGC in populations and ecological systems with widespread, even universal, occurrence of emergent and statistical properties of ecosystems based on the SGC in these systems.

Closer and more critical examination of some data sets is beginning to uncover some qualifications to this apparent success story. Ecological data sets show a strong tendency to be log-normally distributed (a log-normal statistical distribution is one that yields a normal distribution if the data are log transformed before analysis). Log-normal distributions are characteristic of every-thing from population census data to water quality data; they were 'discovered' by Preston[61] many years ago and have been largely neglected by statisticians and ecologists.[62] Robert May analysed the log-normal distribution many years ago and concluded that it probably arose from a central limit phenomenon wherein many overlapping distributions of exponentially growing populations were combined.[63] Log-normal distributions have similar skewed or 'fat-tailed' dis-tributions to power laws and may be difficult to distinguish from them. Indeed, it has recently been shown that it is possible to produce SGC-like inverse power laws from combinations of overlapping log-normal distributions.[64] It seems that ran-domly distributed, exponentially growing populations of scale insects on coffee bushes do approach power law distributions of abundance when they increase so as to fill the available 'space' (i.e. the available bushes).[65] There are devia-tions from the power law function at lower and higher abundances – the higher abundances are achieved by mutualism and predator protection by ants. Never-theless, the power law distributions appear to arise from space filling or envelope dynamics in spatially distributed systems.[66] Again there is danger of 'affirming the consequent' here and assuming that there are underlying SGC mechanisms when there are not.[67] Simplifying assumptions and ways of describing data do not necessarily provide causal explanations, but it may be that power laws do reflect the achievement of space filling behaviour by hierarchically organised and spatially distributed, patchy populations.[68]

The distributions of populations and species in space may be fractal, but some may not be. Models of fractal population distributions do not produce the species–area distributions that we usually observe.[69] (Species–area distributions are usually double log plots of the increasing numbers of species encountered in increasing sampling areas.) Detailed analysis of forest fire data shows that whereas the distributions of fires is in the form of inverse power laws (as pre-dicted by SOC theory) the actual statistics reveal that there are multiple distri-butions within the data, each with distinct ranges and break points or 'cutoffs' that relate to the control of landscape propagation at landscape scales.[70] In fact, ecological distributions should be multi-fractal (showing distinct regions or cor-relation lengths with different scaling relations rather than a single, universal one across all scales) and the interaction of disturbances with these systems through evolutionary time should produce pattern and process which, after cellular automaton-like development over time, has multiple distributions and break points. It is therefore hardly surprising that statistical patterns are not good guides to the underlying processes. Furthermore, equifinality will ensure that there are many potential routes to any system realisation. Analysis of bird population and community data also reveals that there are intermediate-scale peaks in species composition. This seems to indicate that there are specific corre-lation lengths in these populations in otherwise scale-invariant environments.[71]

Finally, recent analyses of food webs and networks of plant–animal interactions clearly show that not all of these are scale-invariant or 'small-world'; there are exceptions to the rule, which may be explicable by other mechanisms.[72]

All of this tends to indicate that whereas, overall, there are strongly SOC-like features in most ecological data, detailed analysis of these data uncovers statistical patterns that might be explicable by more simple mechanisms, such as SGC structures and HOT dynamics, evolutionary design constraints and development of communities over time, individual interactions between species, dispersal across patchy landscapes, individual contexts and multiple exponential growth of patterns of populations and species. So the jury is still out. Reflecting on some of the foregoing arguments, we have to be very careful about replacing outdated totalising theories with new ones, which will produce the same result as before but in a new guise. Certainly SOC is a popular topic at the moment and much work is being done. Overall I prefer SGC and HOT explanations to SOC explanations because of the fact that they explicitly incorporate more biological, social and cultural realism and allow for evolution, design, diversity, contingent development and resilience in the face of disturbance as well as selection for maximised throughput, efficiencies and yields.[73]

One important outcome of all this is that any understanding of ecosystems, and any predictive framework that might be employed, still has to take the strong possibility of emergent properties into account. Remember, these are non-linear, non-equilibrium systems with unfolding pathways and properties that are constantly 'becoming'. We are not dealing with the laws of averages or large numbers – these are systems in which initial conditions and divergent trajectories ensure that very small-scale, perhaps uncertain or indeterminate events determine large-scale outcomes. Models and predictive tools must either work at the level of 'macro-laws' and emergent entities[74] or be able to produce realistic emergent properties through algorithmic or other techniques.[75] Much of our statistical and modelling treatment of ecological systems achieves neither outcome.

There is growing evidence for emergent properties in ecosystems, and in coupled social–economic and ecological systems, which arise from the interaction of small-scale pattern and process but which nevertheless show a degree of 'downward causation' (i.e. the emergent entities provide context for the actions of the local agents). These properties may be reflected in some subtle changes in things such as spatial patterns which arise in ecosystems and which can control larger-scale functions.[76] There is, for example, very good evidence that semi-arid ecosystems around the world are highly efficient users of water[77] and that the vegetation and physical structure of these ecosystems shows small-scale structure and patchiness that is essential for system function.[78] The pattern and process, both of which are very patchy at small scales, are self-organised. We are beginning to change our world view from one of equilibrium and spatial homogeneity, to one of non-equilibrium trajectories and the interconnectedness of spatial mosaics at all scales. Ecosystems and landscapes can be thought of in this way.[79] Most importantly, it is water which provides the connectivity between patches and 'hot spots' of microbiological activity[80] either through molecular diffusion or through organised flow paths. This means that in some cases quite subtle changes in the SGC of ecosystems can have catastrophic effects and surprising consequences.[81] For example, the small-scale spatial distribution of microbiological 'hot spots' in the sediments of lakes and estuaries controls the macroscopic function of the water body as a whole because the closely coupled reaction–diffusion relationships between microbial assemblages in the 'hot spots' control the overall sediment metabolism. At larger scales the probability of survival or extinction of species can also be determined from the spatial patterns of relict populations.[82]

So we have come a long way in a few short years. From Unitarian, holistic equilibrium theories of ecology and individualistic, Gleasonian, non-equilibrium approaches we have moved to a middle ground of algorithmic, logically deep, non-equilibrium systems, which are based around the pandemonium of local interactions coupled across multiple spatial and temporal scales by reaction–diffusion relationships. We begin to see how the macro-scale properties of SGC systems and the 'envelope' dynamics emerge from the actions of the micro-scale. From the physical separation of financial and natural capitals we are now considering the emergent properties of multiple forms of capital interacting across scales in landscapes and waterscapes. These landscapes and waterscapes show all the characteristics of having SGC properties of high efficiencies arising from selected designs and network structures as well as emergent properties and trajectories of continuously 'becoming'. This is a revolutionary world view that will affect many of our most practical and pressing global problems.

NOTES

1. G. F. R. Ellis. Physics, complexity and causality. *Nature*, **435** (2005), 743.

2. A. Marshall. *The Unity of Nature*. (London: Imperial College Press, 2002).

3. R. M. May. Biological populations with non-overlapping generations: stable points, stable cycles and chaos. *Science*, **186** (1974), 645–7. R. M. May. Simple mathematical models with very complicated dynamics. *Nature*, **261** (1976), 459–67.

4. See, for example, J. Gleick. *Chaos: Making a New Science*. (New York: Viking, 1987).

5. B. B. Mandelbrot. *The Fractal Geometry of Nature*. Revised and updated. (New York: Freeman, 1983).

6. A. Gragnani, M. Scheffer and S. Rinaldi. Top-down control of cyanobacteria: a theoretical analysis. *American Naturalist*, **153** (1999), 59–72. J. Huisman and F. J. Weissing. Biodiversity of plankton by species oscillations and chaos. *Nature*, **402** (1999), 407–10. A. Huppert, B. Blasius and L. Stone. A model of phytoplankton blooms. *American Naturalist*, **159** (2002), 156–71. I. D. Lima, D. B. Olson and S. C. Doney. Intrinsic dynamics and stability properties of size-structured pelagic ecosystem models. *Journal of Plankton Research*, **24** (2002), 533–56.

7. I. Prigogine. *From Being to Becoming: Time and Complexity in the Physical Sciences*. (New York: Freeman and Co., 1980). I. Prigogine and I. Stengers. *Order out of Chaos: Man's new Dialogue with Nature*. (London: Heinemann, 1984).

8. M.P. Hassell, H.N. Comins and R.M. May. Species coexistence and self-organising spatial dynamics. *Nature*, **370** (1994), 290–2.

9. H.J. Jensen. *Self-organised Criticality*. (Cambridge: Cambridge University Press, 1998).

10. P. Bak. *How Nature Works: the Science of Self-organised Criticality*. (Oxford: Oxford University Press, 1997).

11. R. Dewar. Information theory explanation of the fluctuation theorem, maximum entropy production and self-organised criticality in non-equilibrium stationary states. *Journal of Physics, A***36** (2003), 631–41.

12. There are a number of accounts of Conway's game of life in the literature. See, for example, the description and diagrams in R. Rucker. *Mind Tools: the Mathematics of Information*. (London: Penguin, 1988).

13. S. Wolfram. *A New Kind of Science*. (Champaign, IL: Wolfram Media, 2002.)

14. S.A. Kauffman. *The Origins of Order: Self-organisation and Selection in Evolution*. (Oxford: Oxford University Press 1993).

15. Kauffman, *The Origins of Order*, p. 174. (See Note 14.)

16. J.M. Carlson and J. Doyle. Highly optimized tolerance: a mechanism for power laws in designed systems. *Physical Review, E***60** (1999), 1412–27. J.M. Carlson and J. Doyle. Highly optimized tolerance: robustness and design in complex systems. *Physical Review Letters*, **84** (2000), 2529–32. C. Robert, J.M. Carlson and J. Doyle. Highly optimized tolerance in epidemic models incorporating local optimization and regrowth. *Physical Review, E***63** (2001), 056122–1 to 13. D. Reynolds, J.M. Carlson and J. Doyle. Design degrees of freedom and mechanisms for complexity. *Physical Review, E***66** (2002): 016108–1 to 18.

17. D.C. Dennett. *Darwin's Dangerous Idea*. (London: Allen Lane, Penguin Press, 1994).

18. Dennett, *Darwin's Dangerous Idea*, p. 50.

19. Dennett, *Darwin's Dangerous Idea*, p. 82.

20. Dennett, *Darwin's Dangerous Idea*, p. 83.

21. Dennett, *Darwin's Dangerous Idea*. Niles Eldredge. *Reinventing Darwin, the Great Evolutionary Debate*. (London: Phoenix, 1996).

22. Even though I do not subscribe to the full postmodern critique of Marshall, I do agree that we have to be very careful of totalising or Unitarian myths and similar philosophies.

23. J. Cohen and I. Stewart. *The Collapse of Chaos*. (London: Viking Books, 1994).

24. Cohen and Stewart, *The Collapse of Chaos*, pp. 411–18.

25. G.P. Harris. This is not the end of limnology (or of science): the world may well be a lot simpler than we think. *Freshwater Biology*, **42** (1999), 689–706.

26. G.P. Harris. Predictive models in spatially and temporally variable freshwater systems. *Australian Journal of Ecology*, **23** (1998), 80–94.

27. B.J. Finlay *et al.* Self-similar patterns of nature: insect diversity at local to global scales. *Proceedings of the Royal Society* B**273** (2006): 10.1098/rspb.2006.3525.

28. G.P. Harris. Pattern, process and prediction in aquatic ecology. A limnological view of some general ecological problems. *Freshwater Biology*, **32** (1994), 143–60.

29. J.M. Carlson and J. Doyle. Highly optimised tolerance: a mechanism for power laws in designed systems. *Physical Review, E***60** (1999), 1412–27.

30. A. Wagner. *Robustness and Evolvability in Living Systems*. (Princeton, NJ: Princeton University Press, 2005).

31. A.P. Allen, B.L. Li and E.L. Charnov. Population fluctuations, power laws and mixtures of lognormal distributions. *Ecology Letters,* **4** (2001), 1–3.

32. J.M. Halley *et al.* Uses and abuses of fractal methodology in ecology. *Ecology Letters,* **7** (2004), 254–71.

33. J.J. Lennon, W.E. Kunin and S. Hartley. Fractal species distributions do not produce power-law species-area relationships. *Oikos,* **97** (2002), 378–86.

34. R.V. Sole *et al.* Criticality and scaling in evolutionary ecology. *Trends in Ecology and Evolution,* **14** (1999), 156–60. J.H. Brown *et al.* The fractal nature of nature: power laws, ecological complexity and biodiversity. *Philosophical Transactions of the Royal Society,* B**357** (2002), 619–26. B.L. Li. Fractal geometry applications in description and analysis of patch patterns and patch dynamics. *Ecological Modelling,* **132** (2000), 33–50. B.D. Malamud, G. Morein and D.L. Turcotte. Forest fires: an example of self-organized critical behaviour. *Science,* **281** (1998), 1840–2. J. Camacho and R.V. Sole. Scaling in ecological size spectra. *Europhysics Letters,* **55** (2001), 774–780.

35. V.I. Nikora, C.P. Pearson and U. Shankar. Scaling patterns in landscapes: New Zealand experience. *Landscape Ecology,* **14** (1999), 17–33. Y.N. Blagoveschensky and V.P. Samsonova. Fractal and statistical analysis of spatial distributions of Fe-Mn concretions in soddy-podsolic soils. *Geoderma,* **88** (1999), 265–82.

36. S.E. Jorgensen, H. Mejer and S.N. Nielsen. Ecosystem as self-organizing critical systems. *Ecological Modelling,* **111** (1998), 261–8.

37. J.C. Sprott, J. Bolliget and D.J. Mladenhoff. Self-organised criticality in forest-landscape evolution. *Physics Letters,* A**297** (2002), 267–71.

38. R.V. Sole, D. Alonso and A. McKane. Self-organised instability in complex ecosystems. *Philosophical Transactions of the Royal Society,* B**357** (2002), 667–81. R.V. Sole *et al.* On the fractal nature of ecological and macroevolutionary dynamics. *Fractals: Complex Geometry Patterns and Scaling in Nature and Society,* **9** (2001), 1–116.

39. L. Seuront *et al.* Universal multi-fractal analysis as a tool to characterize intermittent patterns: example of phytoplankton distribution in turbulent coastal waters. *Journal of Plankton Research,* **21** (1999), 877–923. D.I. Iudin and D.B. Gelashvily. Multi-fractality in ecological monitoring. *Nuclear Instruments and Methods in Physics Research,* A**502** (2003), 799–801. D.I. Iudin, D.B. Gelashvily and G.S. Rozenberg. Multi-fractal analysis of the species structure of biotic communities. *Doklady Biological Sciences,* **389** (2003), 143–6.

40. L. Seuront, V. Gentillhomme and Y. Lagadeuc. Small-scale nutrient patches in tidally mixed coastal waters. *Marine Ecology Progress Series,* **232** (2002), 29–44.

41. A. Pentek *et al.* Fractality, chaos, and reactions in imperfectly mixed open hydrodynamical flows. *Physica,* A**274** (1999), 120–31.

42. M.E. McClain *et al.* Biogeochemical hot spots and hot moments at the interface of terrestrial and aquatic ecosystems. *Ecosystems,* **6** (2003): 301–12.

43. See, for example, P.S. Stewart *et al.* Biofilm structural heterogeneity visualised by three microscopic methods. *Water Research,* **29** (1995), 2006–9. W. Davison, G.R. Fones and G.W. Grime. Dissolved metals in surface sediment and a microbial mat at 100 μm resolution. *Nature,* **387** (1997), 885–8.

44. J.W.T. Wimpenny and R. Colasanti. A unifying hypothesis for the structure of microbial biofilms based on cellular automaton models. *FEMS Microbiology Ecology,* **22** (1997), 1–16.

45. F. Azam. Microbial control of the ocean carbon flux: the plot thickens. *Science,* **280** (1998), 694–6. K.D. Bidle and F. Azam. Accelerated dissolution of diatom silica by marine bacterial assemblages. *Nature,* **397** (1999), 508–12.

46. F. Azam and A. Z. Worden. Microbes, molecules and marine ecosystems. *Science*, **303** (2004), 1622–4. E. M. H. Wellington, A. Berry and M. Krsek. Resolving functional diversity in relation to microbial community structure in soil: exploiting genomics and stable isotope probing. *Current Opinion in Microbiology*, **6** (2003), 295–301.

47. L. Seuront and N. Spilmont. Self-organized criticality in intertidal microphytobenthos patterns. *Physica*, A**313** (2002), 513–39. J. B. Drake and J. F. Weishampel. Multifractal analysis of canopy height measures in a longleaf pine savannah. *Forest Ecology and Management*, **128** (2000), 121–7. C. H. Flather and M. Bevers. Patchy reaction-diffusion and population abundance: the relative importance of habitat amount and arrangement. *American Naturalist*, **159** (2002), 40–56.

48. V. Kaitala, E. Ranta and P. Lundberg. Self-organised dynamics in spatially structured populations. *Proceedings of the Royal Society*, B**268** (2001), 1655–60. V. Kaitala. Travelling waves in spatial population dynamics. *Annales Zoologici Fennici*, **39** (2002), 161–71.

49. See, for example, W. Davison, G. R. Fones and G. W. Grime. Dissolved metals in surface sediment and a microbial mat at 100 μm resolution. *Nature*, **387** (1997), 885–8.

50. D. Mouillot *et al*. The fractal model: a new model to describe the species accumulation process and relative abundance distribution (RAD). *Oikos*, **90** (2000), 333–42. G. B. West, J. H. Brown and B. J. Enquist. The fourth dimension of life: fractal geometry and the allometric scaling of organisms. *Science*, **284** (1999), 1677–9.

51. S. H. Strogatz. Exploring complex networks. *Nature*, **410** (2001), 268–76.

52. G. Palla *et al*. Uncovering the overlapping community structure of complex networks in nature and society. *Nature*, **435** (2005), 814–18.

53. D. J. Watts and S. H. Strogatz. Collective dynamics of 'small-world' networks. *Nature*, **393** (1998), 440–2. See also S. Milgram. The small-world problem. *Psychology Today*, **2** (1967), 60–7.

54. H. Jeong *et al*. The large-scale organisation of metabolic networks. *Nature*, **407** (2000), 651–4. A. Wagner and D. A. Fell. The small-world inside large metabolic networks. *Proceedings of the Royal Society*, B**268** (2001), 1803–10. E. Ravasz *et al*. Hierarchical organisation of modularity in metabolic networks. *Science*, **297** (2002), 1551–5. Y. I. Wolf, G. Karev and E. V. Koonin. Scale-free networks in biology: new insights into the fundamentals of evolution? *Bioessays*, **24** (2002), 105–9.

55. R. Albert, H. Jeong and A.-L. Barbasi. Error and attack tolerance of complex networks. *Nature*, **406** (2000), 378–82.

56. F. Jordan, I. Scheuring and G. Vida. Species positions and extinction dynamics in simple food webs. *Journal of Theoretical Biology*, **215** (2002), 441–8. R. V. Sole and J. M. Montoya. Complexity and fragility in ecological networks. *Proceedings of the Royal Society*, B**268** (2001), 2039–45.

57. S. L. Pimm, J. H. Lawton and J. E. Cohen. Food web patterns and their consequences. *Nature*, **350** (1999), 669–74.

58. J. M. Montoya and R. V. Sole. Small-world patterns in food webs. *Journal of Theoretical Biology*, **214** (2002), 405–12.

59. J. H. Brown. *Macroecology*. (Chicago, IL: Chicago University Press, 1995). J. H. Brown. Macroecology: progress and prospect. *Oikos*, **87** (1999), 3–14.

60. S. L. Chown, K. J. Gaston and D. Robinson. Macrophysiology: large-scale patterns in physiological traits and their ecological implications. *Functional Ecology*, **18** (2004), 159–67.

61. F. W. Preston. The canonical distribution of commonness and rarity. *Ecology*, **43** (1962), 185–215, 410–32.

62. J. M. Halley *et al*. Uses and abuses of fractal methodology in ecology. *Ecology Letters*, **7** (2004), 254–71.

63. R. M. May. General introduction. In Ecological Stability, ed. M. B. Usher and M. H. Williamson. (London: Chapman and Hall, 1974), pp. 1–14.

64. A. P. Allen, B. L. Li and E. L. Charnov. Population fluctuations, power laws and mixtures of lognormal distributions. *Ecology Letters*, **4** (2001), 1–3.

65. J. Vandermeer and I. Perfecto. A keystone mutualism drives pattern in a power law function. *Science*, **311** (2006), 1000–2.

66. M. Pascual and F. Guichard. Criticality and disturbance in spatial ecological systems. *Trends in Ecology and Evolution*, **20** (2005), 88–95.

67. A. R. Solow. Power laws without complexity. *Ecology Letters*, **8** (2005), 361–3.

68. J. Kolasa. Complexity, system integration and susceptibility to change, biodiversity connection. *Ecological Complexity*, **2** (2005), 431–42. J. Kolasa. The community ecology perspective on variability in complex systems: the effects of hierarchy and integration. *Ecological Complexity*, **3** (2006), 71–9.

69. J. J. Lennon, W. E. Kunin and S. Hartley. Fractal species distributions do not produce power-law species-area distributions. *Oikos*, **97** (2002), 378–86.

70. C. Ricotta *et al.* Self-organised criticality of wildfires ecologically revisited. *Ecological Modelling*, **141** (2001), 307–11.

71. D. Storch, K. J. Gaston and J. Cepak. Pink landscapes, 1/f spectra of spatial environmental variability and bird community composition. *Proceedings of the Royal Society*, B**269** (2002), 1791–6.

72. D. Garlaschelli, G. Caldarelli and L. Pietronero. Universal scaling relations in food webs. *Nature*, **423** (2003), 165–8. P. Jordano, J. Bascompte and J. M. Olesen. Invariant properties in coevolutionary networks of plant-animal interactions. *Ecology Letters*, **6** (2003), 69–81.

73. D. Reynolds, J. M. Carlson and J. Doyle. Design degrees of freedom and mechanisms for complexity, *Physical Review, E***66** (2002): 016108–1 to 18.

74. G. P. Harris. Predictive models in spatially and temporally variable freshwater systems. *Australian Journal of Ecology*, **23** (1999), 80–94.

75. J. T. Wootton. Local interactions predict large-scale pattern in empirically derived cellular automata. *Nature*, **413** (2001), 841–4.

76. J. A. Ludwig, D. J. Tongway and S. G. Marsden. Stripes, bands or stipples: modelling the influence of three landscape banding patterns on resource capture and productivity in semi-arid woodlands, Australia. *Catena*, **37** (1999), 257–73.

77. M. S. Seyfried *et al.* Ecohydrological control of deep drainage in arid and semi-arid regions. *Ecology*, **86** (2005): 277–87.

78. J. A. Ludwig *et al.* Vegetation patches and runoff-erosion as interacting ecohydrological processes in semi-arid landscapes. *Ecology*, **86** (2005), 288–97.

79. M. Loreau, N. Mouquet and R. D. Holt. Meta-ecosystems: a theoretical framework for a spatial ecosystem ecology. *Ecology Letters*, **6** (2003), 673–9.

80. J. Belnap *et al.* Linkages between microbial and hydrologic processes in arid and semi-arid watersheds. *Ecology*, **86** (2005), 298–307.

81. M. Rietkerk *et al.* Self-organized patchiness and catastrophic shifts in ecosystems. *Science*, **305** (2004), 1926–9.

82. R. J. Wilson *et al.* Spatial patterns in species distributions reveal biodiversity change, *Nature*, **432** (2004): 393–6.

6 Micro-interactions and macro-constraints

How large-scale system properties arise from small- scale interactions and patch dynamics. The implications for sustainability.

If we think of landscapes and waterscapes as patterns of shifting mosaics and interactions across scales – which arise from HOT designs and from Self Generated Complexity (SGC) – what does this new world view do to our attempts to manage these systems? For a more sustainable global future and for land- and waterscape restoration to be successful there is an urgent need to better understand the complex linkages and pathways between biodiversity, land use, soil properties, hydrology and water quality because these are the dominant forces which shape our ability to manage landscapes and waterscapes sustainably. Clearly, the dominant world view has not been a raging success because evidence of landscape and waterscape degradation abounds. So something is wrong with our dominant paradigm. Progress can be made if we look at landscape and waterscape function from the perspective of small-scale pattern and process and the emergence – through SGC – of some larger, macroscopic properties. I shall argue here that what was partly wrong with the previous paradigm was the neglect of those inconveniently small scales of pattern and process (inconvenient, that is, for a two-metre primate that lives for decades) and the neglect of global and regional constraints and emergent properties. Having understood some of these processes there is a need to implement better management and restoration frameworks.

Catchments (watersheds or basins) are the natural biophysical units; water flows downhill from hill slope to estuary, connecting 'hot spots' and enabling small scale reaction–diffusion processes to occur. It is in catchments that we have made massive changes in land use for agriculture and urban development. The human population has altered catchment properties since the dawn of time to hunt and harvest resources, cut wood, grow food, control floods and provide drinking water. We have seen that there is a need for the understanding of system properties and that there is good evidence for non-equilibrium, emergent behaviour in natural systems of various kinds. Catchments are no exception. But are these systems just too hard to study? Not at all: first, I have argued that SGC systems do have larger-scale emergent statistical properties, power laws, and log-normal-like probability density functions. In the global biomes, for example, there are some strong drivers of morphological and functional convergence between species and ecological roles in biomes (homoplasies) with quite different evolutionary histories. These are the design constraints that emerge from the

CAS dynamics and the constrained SGC; the simplexic and complicit properties of Cohen and Stewart.

Conway Morris[1] has argued at some length for the existence of many homoplastic or convergent evolutionary features of organisms, even life in general. Through a process of winnowing out poor designs nature has arrived at a set of recurrent solutions to some tricky problems of resource capture and predator evasion. (These are also produced by non-equilibrium constraints on the flows of energy and materials that constrain the possibilities of design in nature. They would be the evolved and robust solutions that Wagner discusses.) There clearly are structural and functional convergences between organisms and ecosystems in various land- and waterscapes. This is the problem of development raised by Salthe,[2] who noted that it is not well explained by the usual evolutionary theories, which rely heavily on chance and contingency and on descent through modification. Certainly, as Dennett has shown,[3] there is much 'make do and mend', many 'kludges' and reliance on the frozen accidents of evolution (and we must keep our container of universal acid to hand and make sure we do not fall back on Dennett's 'sky hooks'). Nevertheless it begins to look as though there really are some constraints on how organisms do business; or constraints on what Eldredge calls the 'economics' of ecosystems.[4] In other words, if convergence in design is a general feature of organisms, ecosystems and of life in general, what might be the drivers of such features? (And remember what we are talking about here is a bottom-up, emergent, small-d design; not a top-down, structuralist or God-given Design. They are very different.) Remember, it is cranes, not sky hooks!

There is evidence that some of these constraints and design convergences emerge from the properties and functioning of constrained SGC systems. Microscopic pattern and process set in larger-scale contexts (agents acting on local information) are capable of producing macroscopic properties. There appear to be a number of higher-level properties of SGC systems that arise in response to biophysical constraints on the ways in which we might manage or restore natural landscapes. So building out of the small-scale non-equilibrium and indeterminism of SGC systems we begin to see some larger-scale patterns at the levels of growth forms, statistical distributions and emergent features (including stocks and flows of capitals), which are important for the ways in which we might plan and manage our affairs. Complexity, context and contingency produce constraints that matter. We cannot escape our evolutionary and ecological design constraints, no matter how hard we might try or might like to.

Biophysical limits to biomass and production

Notwithstanding the contingency of the non-equilibrium assemblages of ecosystems in the biosphere (oak trees in Europe, gum trees in Australia, bears in Canada, impala in Africa), there are some functional properties of biomes which are independent of species composition. There is, for example, ample evidence that the upper limit to plant biomass and production (and therefore to human affairs) is set independently of the species present by biophysical parameters such as water, rainfall, soil moisture and evaporation. In a previous chapter I noted that there is evidence that SGC systems are characterised, if not by maximum entropy solutions,[5] then certainly by high throughput and yield (the upper-bound transport principles);[6] so it is entirely possible that at large scales and in situations where there is sufficient time for the development of complementarity between functional groups in biomes then such solutions do occur. These 'envelope dynamics' require highly diverse systems with much redundancy and complementarity (and much trial and error), but they are the fundamental thermodynamic, climatological, physiological and biophysical limitations within which the human population must live.

In many respects it would seem that most basic biophysical properties of ecosystems are indeed independent of species composition; for example, the Holmes–Sinclair relation between rainfall, runoff and evapotranspiration (E_T) is independent of species composition and dependent instead on the dominant plant growth forms in the catchment.[7] Biophysical constraints appear to set upper limits on evaporation from plant communities so that over sufficiently long time periods a form of equilibrium is reached.[8] There is also evidence of large-scale convergence across biomes towards common rainfall use efficiencies: a convergence to maximal water use efficiency (WUE_{max}) in arid conditions.[9] Work over many years by Specht and others had shown that many aspects of Australian terrestrial plant communities are also set by such factors.[10] Thus the overall fluxes of 'green' water in the biosphere – the evaporative fluxes of water that sustain life and provide essential ecosystem services – are set by some high-level properties of ecological systems. There is empirical evidence for a kind of 'extremal principle' similar to the MaxEnt solutions to non-equilibrium systems discussed earlier. The global water and energy fluxes that are parts of the global climate system (and which themselves seem to adhere to MaxEnt principles) are therefore global constraints, which are partly controlled by small-scale SGC in the ecosystems on the planetary surface. We do also know, however, that these properties take a long time to establish – often requiring evolutionary time scales – so that disturbances at shorter time scales can lead to reduced efficiencies. Clearing forests and converting land to other uses removes the self-organised properties of landscapes and their coupled waterscapes and leads rapidly to reduced WUE. There is empirical evidence for a similar kind of extremal principle in the response of ecosystems to nutrient loadings. The Vollenweider response of lakes to phosphorus loadings has been well known for decades. Lakes approach an upper bound of algal biomass (in the form of the photosynthetic pigment chlorophyll a) when phosphorus is added to lakes; this relationship has been used as a means of managing nutrient loads.[11] Similarly, marine[12] and terrestrial[13] ecosystems respond in repeatable ways when 'titrated' with nitrogen. There are critical loading thresholds, beyond which ecosystem damage is noticeable.

Work by Enquist and West and others has shown the importance of some simple structuring relationships between plant structure and function so that, for example, total water flux through terrestrial plants is largely independent of species composition across a wide range of plant functional types and sizes.[14] These fractal scaling relationships seem to hold across as wide a range of scales of physiology and organisation as they do across scales of spatial and temporal variability. Brian Enquist argues that the principle of minimal energy dissipation in the transport of fluid through space-filling, fractal-like networks is central to the scaling of animal and plant form and function from cells to ecosystems;[15] similar scale-invariant approaches are now being applied to water and energy fluxes at landscape scales.[16] There is therefore evidence for what might be regarded as 'space filling' maximum entropy (MaxEnt) or maximum evapotranspiration (MaxE$_T$) solutions emerging from the SGC properties of organisms in landscapes and ecosystems. 'Envelope' or extremal solutions require long time scales to develop in terrestrial systems (long time periods to allow for the immigration of a diverse group of plant species) and are also dependent on high biodiversity and much functional complementarity between groups of organisms. By processing water, energy and nutrient flows with high efficiency (e.g. the 'green' water flows from natural ecosystems) the ecosystems that cover the surface of the planet are a part of the global climate system.[17] In planktonic ecosystems time scales are shorter because of the rapid growth rates of the organisms (one day doubling times are common) and the very high biodiversity of surface waters. Spatial patterning and patch dynamics also seem to be part and parcel of these states.[18]

So out of contingent evolutionary history and the vagaries of immigration and the extinction of species some general overall relations appear, which relate energy and nutrient supply and use efficiencies to the life forms of the various biomes. These in turn are related to climate and geography. So we may possibly argue that out of some of the fundamental physiological properties of organisms and their relationships to the environment some high-level structuring forces emerge. These forces are the fundamental constraints on the way in which we might manage landscapes or alter land use. These solutions to the basic problems of survival in plants are ancient and fundamental. Some of these basic processes, like photosynthesis, only evolved once and we are stuck with the single solution.[19] It appears that the structure of higher plant and animal cells was produced by fusion and symbiosis of previous simpler organisms: another wonderful example of 'kludges' and the contingency of evolutionary history. We are very much the prisoners of 'frozen accidents' of the past and path dependencies which are also constrained by thermodynamics, energy and water fluxes. At the macroscopic scale these emergent evolutionary and thermodynamic constraints apply to all forms of life.

Competition or neutral theories of ecology?

The high efficiencies and $MaxE_T$ solutions seen in ecosystem properties seem to depend on high taxonomic and functional biodiversity. If anything, functional diversity appears to be the more important determinant of efficient ecosystem function.[20] But there remains a series of questions about how the high local taxonomic and functional diversity is achieved and maintained. After all, some tropical forests achieve local diversities as high as 300 tree species per hectare. What are the interactions between species at the local level and how can we build diverse function into landscapes? According to the standard equilibrium view, competition should ensure competitive exclusion[21] and diversity should reduce as ecosystems develop and competition proceeds. The standard view of ecology focuses on niche differentiation and competition as the major structuring forces of ecosystems. According to this view the only mechanism for coexistence is for the species to differ in their habitat or resource requirements – they must have different niches – and that habitat diversity permits coexistence. The contrary view is that species do not have strongly differing habitat or resource requirements, the environment may be uniform and that coexistence merely arises from dispersal over time into the same area. This contrary 'neutral' view is regarded by many as heretical.

The big debate in recent years has, however, been around 'neutral' models. A number of people have developed 'neutral' models of species distributions in landscapes; so called because they make none of the usual equilibrium assumptions about the nature of ecological interactions between species and rely instead merely on the balance of birth, death, migration and speciation in ecologically equivalent organisms.[22] Although these models have generated some controversy, they have now been thoroughly tested in a variety of ecosystems and their predictions are remarkably consistent and impressive.[23] Stephen Hubbell is the doyen of this approach. Hubbell's work was only ever intended to include single trophic levels (e.g. trees) on homogeneous tracts of land; however, others have developed equally simple models of biodiversity for patchy and non-homogeneous environments which are equally powerful in their predictions. These models use body size distributions and fractal resource distributions to make good predictions about biodiversity in plants and animals.[24]

So how good is the neutral theory? Pattern is not a good proxy or test for process; nevertheless, there is strong evidence for niche differentiation and frequency-dependent selection at small scales.[25] Wootton has attempted to separate pattern and process and has shown that although neutral theory can predict the overall relative abundance of species on rocky shores it cannot properly predict the detailed processes involved.[26] He wrote

> . . . species differences seem to be essential elements in generating the structure and dynamics of this intertidal community. Hence, accurate prediction of the system response to external impacts requires an accounting of variation in species interactions, and is not primarily determined by global abundance patterns.

So simple models and regionally dependent immigration can predict some of the overall statistical distributions of abundance but cannot predict the detailed assemblages or responses to perturbations. This conclusion has been confirmed by Morris, who worked on the assembly of communities of small boreal mammals,[27] and by Graves and Rahbek, who looked at the distribution of birds across the whole of South America.[28] Lawton was correct. The regional distribution of species provides the immigrants, and the local heterogeneity and disturbance regime of the environment (often at small scales) modulates the survival and interactions between the species that arrive.[29] So there are important local interactions and contingent trajectories of immigration and community development, which are important determinants of the response to disturbance and change.[30] A mix of processes best explains the patterns and processes involved in the assembly of communities of animals and plants in Darwin's 'tangled bank', namely regional biodiversity, dispersal, environmental factors, stochastic effects including drift, and local competitive interactions.[31] None the less there is a focus on small-scale pattern and process as determinants of the interactions between organisms and as determinants of the responses to the history of perturbations at each site.

Patch dynamics

So why do physiological and forms of 'neutral' explanations provide such powerful tools? Environmental factors are generally important determinants of ecosystem structure. Close examination of data from all kinds of ecosystems reveals that both aquatic and terrestrial ecosystems are characterised both by temporal fluctuations and by strong spatial patterns and 'patch dynamics'.[32] Dispersal of organisms across patchy environments weakens competitive interactions and seems to produce species distributions in space and time that are largely determined (a) by the regional pool of species (and a source of immigrants to a particular patch) and (b) by the local physical and chemical environment where the organisms end up. As Walter and Hengeveld have argued, habitat patchiness and environmental variability serve to weaken the strength of competitive interactions and lead to a more individual view of ecology – one in which environmental factors play a more important role than competitive interactions. Pacala and Levin have shown that spatial heterogeneity is easily produced through stochastic processes and limited dispersal. Small-scale spatial segregation – which is common in many communities – totally changes the equilibrium ecological 'mean field' theories and outcomes.[33] Simulations of community patch dynamics show no equilibrial states and instead display long-term stochastically driven fluctuations. Add back the local interactions within patches and we obtain a very complex world view which, albeit dependent on small-scale interactions, may nevertheless show emergent properties such as complicit homoplasies and features of SGC.[34] The patch dynamics of aquatic and terrestrial ecosystems are a critical part of the overall functional dynamics. They are not just incidental but are part and parcel of the dynamics – structure, function and fluctuation in time and space are intertwined in these self-organised and non-equilibrium systems.[35] 'Patchy' ecology is quite different from the 'mean field' theory and includes many situations in which small-scale stochastic effects drive the large-scale dynamics of ecosystems. Spatial and temporal patchiness and transient interactions can lead to an 'emergent neutrality' and also to self-organised community structures. Thus a view of ecology that emphasises dispersal and 'patchy' processes can easily lead to the kinds of distribution we observe, even though the fundamental processes are those of traditional ecological theories.[36]

Patchy and dynamic systems lead to highly diverse communities in both aquatic and terrestrial systems. Indeed, this seems to be the explanation for the paradoxical biodiversity of planktonic communities: the water is not as well mixed as we might have thought. Many communities of micro-organisms seem to exhibit quasi-fractal distributions in space/time. In addition to the plankton communities discussed earlier there is similar evidence from soil bacteria[37] and from intertidal communities of microscopic algae.[38] Again it seems to be true that the best evidence of SGC comes from communities of micro-organisms, which are strongly coupled to their environments through reaction–diffusion interactions over small distances. It certainly seems to be true that ubiquitous organisms are strongly coupled to their environments through reaction–diffusion relations (i.e. the amount of resource is important) whereas when the coverage of species falls below 30%–50% of the environment then it is not so much the amount of resource that is critical, but rather the spatial arrangement.[39] At lower percentage covers the spatial arrangement of resource patches becomes more important, as species must migrate and play 'hopscotch' from patch to patch. Thus we might expect there to be varying degrees of self-organisation depending on the spatial arrangement of resources from place to place and the abundance of the populations and communities concerned. It is certainly true that patch dynamics control much of the ecology we see, and it is also true that when we change land use and regulate rivers we alter the spatial and temporal arrangement of resources and interactions between species in curious and complex ways that we simply do not understand. Herein lies one of the most fundamental and complex aspects of the uniqueness of place.

Stoichiometry

There are other constraints on the functioning of landscapes and water-scapes which are relevant to understanding the ways in which we might manage or mismanage them. Ecological stoichiometry is the ratio of elements in the composition of (in this case) an organic molecule, an organism or an ecosystem component (biomass, detritus, etc.). Thus ecological stoichiometry is mostly concerned with the ratios and elemental cycling of the major and minor biologically important elements: hydrogen, oxygen, carbon, nitrogen, phosphorus, silicon, iron and sulphur. The study of ecological stoichiometry has recently undergone a transformation with the publication of a major work of synthesis by Sterner and Elser.[40] Much of what needs to be said is contained in that work; nevertheless there are some key points of relevance here. Analysis and synthesis of the ratios and cycling of major elements in landscapes and ecosystems reveals that the patterns of behaviour we see at this level are in essence the products of the physiological properties of the major functional groups of macro- and micro-biota in the system concerned.[41] Thus the stoichiometry of the major elements is controlled by the same kinds of processes as discussed above: individuals and physiology rule. The fact that the Redfield ratio[42] (an atomic ratio of $105\,C : 15\,N : 1\,P$) is so commonly found in the ratios of carbon : nitrogen : phosphorus in natural waters and landscapes is merely a reflection of the ubiquity of micro-organisms and the fact that the Redfield ratio is the average composition of those elements in bacteria and microscopic plants. Sterner and Elser point out that the elemental composition of plants and animals is quite different: plants tend to be more variable and flexible, whereas animals tend to have relatively fixed stoichiometric ratios of the major elements, which vary between the major phylogenetic groups. Thus the ways in which organisms influence the cycling of elements in ecosystems, and which elements tend to become limiting, are frequently determined by evolutionary history and the differing identity of major groups. Furthermore, Sterner and Elser traced the ratios exhibited by many organisms back to their fundamental biochemical makeup in terms of RNA, DNA and other key macromolecules. Once again we are seeing evidence of the evolutionary history of organisms played out in real time through their elemental requirements and, in the case of stoichiometry, we have a direct link across scales between the biochemistry of fundamental macromolecules, the resulting physiology of the organisms and the dynamics of ecosystem we observe and must manage. Micro-biology, physiology and small-scale pattern and process determine the macroscopic properties of ecosystems, landscapes and waterscapes.

It is now known that trophic (food chain) interactions within ecosystems are critically determined by the inputs and outputs of the major chemical elements mediated through the physiological activities of the major organisms and functional groups (e.g. plants, animals, bacteria, fungi). When these activities are combined with the evolutionary history of terrestrial, freshwater and marine systems and the fundamental differences between these systems in terms of their geochemistry, then it is possible to explain most of the broad patterns of nutrient limitation and ecosystem biogeochemistry. For example there are big differences between marine and freshwater ecosystems both in terms of many of the dominant species of animals and plants (which have evolutionary explanations) and in terms of the nature of the major limiting nutrient elements (which can be explained by differences in biology and geochemistry).[43] This is yet another example of the ways in which the deep structure in ecosystems determines much of the dynamics that we see – and in addition to its being a constraint on biological processes, it is also a constraint on human actions and policy.

Given that the basic stoichiometry of living organisms appears to be the major determinant of soil nutrient stocks in most places, it is perhaps not surprising that the nutrient ratios of catchment exports closely follow the proportions found in living organisms.[44] Stoichiometric arguments can now be made to better understand the linkages between ecosystems in landscapes and waterscapes, and the ways in which elements are cycled and transformed. Recent work has focused on the linkages between populations, communities and ecosystems and the ways in which stoichiometric linkages can lead to both stability and instability.[45] Work is also progressing to understand the ways in which 'hot spots' are linked across boundaries in landscapes where cascading disturbances may be transmitted within terrestrial and aquatic systems.[46]

Biodiversity

Observations of species distributions in sampling areas of various sizes frequently produce what are called unsaturated distributions,[47] i.e. when the biodiversity of smaller areas is compared with the biodiversity of regions there is a linear relation between species number and area. In effect what this seems to mean is that it is possible to keep on adding species without competitive or other interactions intervening. (Remember the standard ecological idea of plenitude: that the world is brim full of life. Clearly, if it is possible to keep on adding species then plenitude does not hold. This is why the distributions are called unsaturated.) The ability to keep on adding species may be taken as evidence of the predominance of regional and contingent immigration in patchy environments.[48] Trophic interactions in food chains are also powerful structuring processes but again some relatively simple models can produce highly realistic results.[49] Even in patchy and dynamic environments there clearly are some competitive interactions that structure community processes.[50] It is also evident that community assembly rules can be found, so that when food chains are assembled in differing orders the result can be quite different;[51] none the less, competition and trophic interactions can be weakened by organisms playing 'hopscotch' across patchy environments. It is difficult to determine causality, and pattern may not be a reliable guide to process because various kinds of species interactions and differing relations between scales of diversity (at patch, local and regional scales) can produce similar results.[52] Notwithstanding the practical and theoretical objections to simple neutral models (after all, they do fly in the face of the standard Unitarian ecological assumptions), the overall impression that emerges is that there is considerable descriptive power in ecosystem models that incorporate allometry, physiology and biophysical environmental conditions.[53] Despite the apparent complexity of the natural world, it certainly seems to be possible to explain many aspects of the overall biodiversity and functioning of both terrestrial and aquatic ecosystems (and many of the emergent properties of these ecosystems) by means of simple physiological and algorithmic models which show, overall, the properties of SGC systems.

Implications for sustainability and development

What all this means is that when biodiversity and the physiological and stoichiometric constraints of macro- and micro-organisms are added to patch dynamics and the existence of 'hot spots' and small-scale reaction–diffusion interactions, two major features emerge through the processes of SGC. First, there are upper bounds to the rates at which materials and energy can be processed by ecosystems. These form the 'speed bumps' on the road of human technological advance and resource use. They constrain our attempts at sustainable development. If the natural turnover rates of energy and materials in the biosphere are exceeded then regional and global stocks and flows are distorted and ecosystem perturbations ensue. Approach to, and compliance with, these constraints is measured both by the analysis of stocks and flows of energy and materials (through the analysis of the biogeochemistry of urban areas and ecosystems)[54] and by the more usual measures of ecosystem health and condition (extent of native vegetation, biodiversity measures). Second, when left to their own devices natural systems approach these upper bounds through processes of evolution, immigration, interaction and selection so that 'envelope dynamics' appear. Approach to the envelope boundary takes time and natural perturbations (fire, flood and other extreme events) disturb the approach to the upper bounds, so the process is rarely complete. Nevertheless these properties of natural systems form a kind of Pareto frontier where resource use is maximised – they are the robust 'neutral spaces' that complex natural systems of many kinds approach over time – and they also constrain human endeavours. Thus in a recursive process of interaction within the biosphere life has evolved to both constrain, and be constrained by, the global cycling of energy and materials. Without the cybernetic overtones and building from small-scale 'hot spots' and interactions (without Dennett's 'sky hooks', and merely by using 'cranes'), this is Gaia.[55] Human ambitions cannot override the workings of the planet on which we evolved.

NOTES

1. S. Conway Morris. *Life's Solution: Inevitable Humans in a Lonely Universe*. (Cambridge: Cambridge University Press, 2003).

2. S. N. Salthe. *Development and Evolution: Complexity and Change in Biology*. (Cambridge, MA: Bradford Books, MIT Press, 1993).

3. D. C. Dennett. *Darwin's Dangerous Idea*. (London: Allen Lane, Penguin Press, 1995).

4. N. Eldredge. *Reinventing Darwin, the Great Evolutionary Debate*. (London: Phoenix, Orion Books 1996).

5. R. Dewar. Information theory explanation of the fluctuation theorem, maximum entropy production and self-organised criticality in non-equilibrium stationary states. *Journal of Physics, A***36** (2003), 631–41.

6. R. Dewar. Maximum entropy production and the fluctuation theorem. Letter to the Editor. *Journal of Physics, A***38** (2005), L371–81.

7. J. W. Holmes and J. A. Sinclair. Water yield from some afforested catchments in Victoria. *Hydrology and Water Resources Symposium*. (Griffith University, Brisbane, Australia: Institution of Engineers, 1986). L. Zhang, W. R. Dawes and G. R. Walker. Predicting the effect of vegetation changes on catchment average water balance. (Melbourne: Cooperative Research Centre for Catchment Hydrology, 1999). Technical Report 9/99.

8. T. J. Hatton, G. D. Salvucci and H. I. Wu. Eagleson's optimality theory of an ecohydrological equilibrium: quo vadis? *Functional Ecology*, **11** (1997), 665–74.

9. T. E. Huxman *et al.* Convergence across biomes to a common rain-use efficiency. *Nature*, **429** (2004), 651–4.

10. R. L. Specht and A. Specht. *Australian Plant Communities: Dynamics of Structure, Growth and Biodiversity*. (Oxford: Oxford University Press, 1999).

11. R. A. Vollenweider. Scientific fundamentals of the eutrophication of lakes and flowing waters with particular reference to nitrogen and phosphorus as factors in eutrophication. (Paris: OECD, 1968). Technical Report DAS/SCI/68.27, 182 pp.

12. K. R. Hinga, H. Jeon and N. F. Lewis. Marine eutrophication review. NOAA Coastal Ocean Program, Decision Analysis Series No. 4, (Silver Springs, MD: US Dept. of Commerce, NOAA Coastal Ocean Office, 1995). 120 pp.

13. J. R. Kelly and S. A. Levin. A comparison of aquatic and terrestrial nutrient cycling and production processes in natural ecosystems, with reference to ecological concepts of relevance to some waste disposal issues. In *The Role of the Oceans as a Waste Disposal Option*. ed. G. Kullenberg. (Amsterdam: D. Reidel, 1986), pp. 165–203.

14. B. J. Enquist, J. H. Brown and G. B. West. Allometric scaling of plant energetics and population density. *Nature*, **395** (1998), 163–5. B. J. Enquist *et al.* Allometric scaling of production and life-history variation in vascular plants. *Nature*, **401** (1999), 907–91. B. J. Enquist and K. J. Niklas. Invariant scaling relations across tree-dominated communities. *Nature*, **410** (2001), 655–60.

G. B. West, J. H. Brown and B. J. Enquist. A general model for the origin of allometric scaling laws in biology. *Science*, **276** (1997), 122–6. G. B. West, J. H. Brown and B. J. Enquist. A general model for the structure and allometry of plant vascular systems. *Nature*, **400** (1999), 664–7. K. J. Niklas and B. J. Enquist. Invariant scaling relationships for interspecific plant biomass production rates and body size. *Proceedings of the National Academy of Sciences USA*, **98** (2001), 2922–7.

15. B. J. Enquist. Universal scaling in tree and vascular plant allometry: toward a general quantitative theory linking plant form and function from cells to ecosystems. *Tree Physiology*, **22** (2002), 1045–64.

16. B. T. Milne, V. K. Gupta and C. Restrepo. A scale invariant coupling of plants, water, energy and terrain. *Ecoscience*, **9** (2002), 191–9. V. O. Sadras. Influence of size of rainfall events on water driven processes – I: Water budget of wheat crops in south-eastern Australia. *Australian Journal of Agricultural Research*, **54** (2003), 341–51.

17. See, for example, J. Whitfield. Order out of chaos. *Nature*, **436** (2005), 905–7.

18. C. Gaucherel. Influence of spatial patterns on ecological applications of extremal principles. *Ecological Modelling*, **193** (2006), 531–42.

19. Conway Morris, *Life's Solution*, pp. 106–11. (See Note 1.)

20. D. A. Heemsbergen *et al.* Biodiversity effects on soil processes explained by interspecific functional dissimilarity. *Science*, **306** (2004), 1019–20.

21. J. Silvertown. Plant coexistence and the niche. *Trends in Ecology and Evolution*, **19** (2004), 605–11.

22. S. P. Hubbell. *The Unified Neutral Theory of Biodiversity and Biogeography*. Monographs in Population Biology 32. (Princeton, NJ: Princeton University Press, 2001). G. Bell. Ecology – neutral macroecology. *Science*, **293** (2001), 2413–18.

23. See B. J. McGill. A test of the unified neutral theory of biodiversity. *Nature*, **422** (2003), 881–5. J. Harte. Tail of death and resurrection. *Nature*, **424** (2003), 1006–7. I. Volkov *et al.* Neutral theory and relative species abundance in ecology. *Nature*, **424** (2003), 1035–7. J. S. Clark and J. S. McClachlan. Stability of forest biodiversity. *Nature*, **423** (2003), 635–8. I. Volkov *et al.* The stability of forest biodiversity. *Nature*, **427** (2004), 696.

24. M. E. Ritchie and H. Olff. Spatial scaling laws yield a synthetic theory of biodiversity. *Nature*, **400** (1999), 557–60. J. P. Haskell, M. E. Ritchie and H. Olff. Fractal geometry predicts varying body size scaling relationships for mammal and bird home ranges. *Nature*, **418** (2002), 527–30.

25. C. Wills *et al.* Non-random processes maintain diversity in tropical forests. *Science*, **311** (2006), 527–31.

26. J. T. Wootton. Field parameterization and experimental test of the neutral theory of biodiversity. *Nature*, **433** (2005), 309–12.

27. D. W. Morris. On the roles of time, space and habitat in a boreal small mammal assemblage: predictably stochastic assembly. *Oikos*, **109** (2005), 223–38.

28. G. R. Graves and C. Rahbek. Source pool geometry and the assembly of continental avifaunas. *Proceedings of the National Academy of Sciences, USA*, **102** (2005), 7871–6. See also A. Ostling. Neutral theory tested by birds. *Nature*, **436** (2005), 635–6.

29. D. Storch, P. A. Marquet and K. J. Gaston. Untangling the tangled bank. *Science*, **307** (2005), 684–6.

30. J. M. Pandolfi. Corals fail test of neutrality. *Nature*, **440** (2006), 35–6. M. Dornelas, S. M. Connolly and T. P. Hughes. Coral reef diversity refutes the neutral theory of biodiversity. *Nature*, **440** (2006), 80–2.

31. W. Ulrich. Species co-occurrences and neutral models: J. M. Diamond's assembly rules. *Oikos*, **93** (2004), 603–9.

32. J. Wu and O. L. Loucks. From balance of nature to hierarchical patch dynamics: a paradigm shift in ecology. *Quarterly Review of Biology*, **70** (1995), 439–66.

33. S. W. Pacala and S. A. Levin. Biologically generated spatial pattern and the coexistence of competing species. In *Spatial Ecology: the Role of Space in Population Dynamics and Interspecific Interactions*, ed. D. Tilman and P. Kareiva. (Princeton, NJ: Princeton University Press, 1998), pp. 204–32.

34. M. L. Cadenasso, S. T. A. Pickett and J. M. Grove. Dimensions of ecosystem complexity: heterogeneity, connectivity and history. *Ecological Complexity*, **3** (2006):1–12.

35. J. Ludwig *et al*. *Landscape Ecology, Function and Management*. (Collingwood, Victoria: CSIRO Publishing, 1997).

36. J. M. Chase Towards a really unified theory for metacommunities. *Functional Ecology*, **19** (2005), 182–6. D. Gravel *et al*. Reconciling niche and neutrality: the continuum hypothesis. *Ecology Letters*, **9** (2006), 399–409. R. D. Holt. Emergent neutrality. *Trends in Ecology and Evolution*, **21** (2006), 531–4. M. Scheffer and E. H. van Ness. Self-organized similarity: the evolutionary emergence of groups of similar species. *Proceedings of the National Academy of Sciences, USA*, **103** (2006), 6230–5.

37. I. M. Young and J. W. Crawford. Interactions and self-organisation in the soil-microbe complex. *Science*, **304** (2004), 1634–7.

38. L. Seuront and N. Spilmont. Self-organised criticality in intertidal microphytobenthos patch patterns. *Physica, A***313** (2002), 513–39.

39. C. H. Flather and M. Bevers. Patchy reaction-diffusion and population abundance: the relative importance of habitat amount and arrangement. *American Naturalist*, **159** (2002), 40–56.

40. R. W. Sterner and J. J. Elser. *Ecological Stoichiometry: the Biology of Elements from Molecules to the Biosphere*. (Princeton, NJ: Princeton University Press, 2002).

41. G. P. Harris. Comparison of the biogeochemistry of lakes and estuaries: ecosystem processes, functional groups, hysteresis effects and interactions between macro- and microbiology. *Marine and Freshwater Research*, **50** (1999), 791–811.

42. The Redfield ratio is the ratio of C:N:P in the deep ocean (approx. 105C:15N:1P by atoms) and reflects the decomposition and regeneration of those elements in oceanic systems. See A. C. Redfield. The biological control of chemical factors in the environment. *American Scientist*, **46** (1958), 205–22. This ratio is common in ecological systems because of the ubiquity of bacterial decomposition.

43. G. P. Harris. Comparison of the biogeochemistry of lakes and estuaries. (See Note 41.)

44. G. P. Harris. The biogeochemistry of nitrogen and phosphorus in Australian catchments, rivers and estuaries: effects of land use and flow regulation and comparisons with global patterns. *Marine and Freshwater Research*, **52** (2001), 139–49.

45. S. J. Moe *et al*. Recent advances in ecological stoichiometry: insights for population and community ecology. *Oikos*, **109** (2005), 29–39.

46. R. Ptacnik *et al*. Applications of ecological stoichiometry for sustainable acquisition of ecosystem services. *Oikos*, **109** (2005), 52–62.

47. K. J. Gaston. Global patterns in biodiversity. *Nature*, **405** (2000), 220–7.

48. H. V. Cornell. Unsaturation and regional influences on species richness in ecological communities: a review of the evidence. *Ecoscience*, **6** (1999), 303–15. J. W. Fox, J. McGrady-Steed and O. L. Petchey. Testing for local species saturation with non-independent regional

species pools. *Ecology Letters*, **3** (2000), 198–206. T. M. Blackburn and K. J. Gaston. Linking patterns in macroecology. *Journal of Animal Ecology*, **70** (2001), 338–52.

49. R. J. Williams and N. D. Martinez. Simple rules yield complex food webs. *Nature*, **404** (2000), 180–3.

50. A. J. Symstad *et al.* Species loss and ecosystem functioning: effects of species identity and community composition. *Oikos*, **81** (1998), 389–97.

51. T. Fukami and P. J. Morin. Productivity-biodiversity relationships depend on the history of community assembly. *Nature*, **424** (2003), 423–6.

52. J. B. Shurin *et al.* Local and regional zooplankton species richness: a scale independent test for saturation. *Ecology*, **81** (2000), 3062–73. M. Loreau. Are communities saturated? On the relationship between alpha, beta and gamma diversity. *Ecology Letters*, **3** (2000), 73–6. S. Bartha and P. Ittzes. Local richness-species pool ratio: a consequence of the species-area relationship. *Folia Geobotanica*, **36** (2001), 9–23. R. J. Whittaker, K. J. Willis and R. Field. Scale and species richness: towards a general, hierarchical theory of species diversity. *Journal of Biogeography*, **28** (2001), 453–70.

53. G. P. Harris. This is not the end of limnology (or of science): the world may well be a lot simpler than we think. *Freshwater Biology*, **42** (1999), 689–706.

54. J. P. Kaye *et al.* A distinct urban biogeochemistry? *Trends in Ecology and Evolution*, **21** (2006), 192–9.

55. The concept of Gaia, first developed by James Lovelock in *Gaia: a New Look at Life on Earth* (Oxford: Oxford University Press, 1979), became shrouded in all kinds of mystical overtones (Dennett's 'sky hooks' if you like). It was even suggested by some that the planet was some form of sentient being. Such suggestions are unnecessary: well-known processes of ecology and evolution operating at local scales can easily account for the properties of the biosphere.

7   A sense of place

The anthropocentric view of landscape: historical and cultural overtones

All of us have a deep sense of 'place' built around landscape, ecology and biogeography. Something deep in the human psyche identifies with particular aspects of landscape; not just the obvious 'look and feel' but also very subtle features of the light, the sounds and the smell.[1] What we see and feel is an emergent whole, the product of many interacting aspects of pattern and process ranging over many time and space scales. All of us carry culturally determined values and a deep familiarity with a set of signs and symbols – with a set of semiotics. In many cases this is a reflection of the environment in which we grew up; there are evidently many early influences on our sense of place. Whatever the reason, whether learned or more deeply engrained, a sense of place is important to all of us and we build mental and landscape models of our preferences through culture, art, architecture, agriculture and urban planning and development. All around the world as development proceeds we simply make the landscape conform to our sense of place and values.

Dustin Penn has written a long piece on the use of evolutionary explanations of the present environmental crisis.[2] He argues that the human species has a long history of causing environmental problems. The 'Noble Savage' was no more sustainable than we are now; there were just fewer of us and we had less technological power and assistance. Penn argues that this behaviour, and our inability to think of the future and of intergenerational equity, is based around necessary evolutionary constraints, which drove survival in uncertain environments in the past. Short-term thinking clearly paid off in the past. Some may see this as a form of biological determinism, something which has been the subject of vitriolic debate;[3] nevertheless, I begin to see the rise of evolutionary explanations that inform the present situation. Penn concludes

> I suggest that integrating evolutionary perspectives into the environmental sciences will help to break down the artificial barriers that continue to divide the biological and social sciences, which unfortunately obstruct our ability to understand ourselves and effectively address our environmental problems.

As Don Wayne has shown, there is a set of semiotics – the semiotics of place[4] – that crop up time and time again in everything from poetry to architecture and landscape design. We have a preference for particular scales: road widths, building sizes and urban landscapes are a case in point.[5] Many cultures have long used huge statues, large city squares and massive buildings built to dwarf the human scale and embody religious and secular power, permanence and dominance over the populace.[6] The designs of built artefacts are, however, peculiar to the more highly developed agrarian and urban cultures. A sense of place can also be embodied in art, story and song. The sense of place we have imposed on the landscape is built from generations of tinkering – individual small decisions which, when taken together, become a set of landscape semiotics and functions. We have discounted the cumulative impact of many small-scale decisions and actions, and ignored the fact that regional and global constraints exist. This strong sense of place is also closely allied to a rather poor sense of deep time: although we all appreciate place in the here and now, we are not so good at appreciating the historical components. What we see in our landscapes is frequently much older than we think. We fail to notice creeping change and landscape degradation; we fail to notice cumulative impacts, presuming instead that the present state of affairs is the norm. As a result, we fail to see landscape degradation until it hits us in the face and we frequently fail to distinguish between the natural and the created landscapes. Even those 'park-like' landscapes of Australia which the early settlers so eagerly identified with were the product of millennia of patch burning. They were an Aboriginal creation.[7]

A sense of place is both formed by and part of our culture and memory, and both change over time. As Schama writes in *Landscape and Memory* '. . . landscape is the work of the mind. Its scenery is built up as much from strata of memory as from layers of rock'. There is a recursive dialogue between us and our environment, but our memories and our evolutionary legacy can be faulty and lead us into danger. Our institutions are also built from, and even physically sited near, memories and long residues of culture and past needs.[8] Any review of Victorian history, for example, will quickly show the extent to which we are still dependent on ideas, cultures, values and norms developed in the nineteenth century.[9] Our social structures and institutions provide resilience and persistence in a time of change – they are also part of our cultural 'deep time' – so they are both a blessing and a curse. Institutions provide resilience in times of change, but are often incapable of rapid change when it is most needed.[10] Redman and Kinzig[11] see great opportunities for collaboration between archaeology and ecology in analysing the periods of development and change in human societies, and also see parallels between cyclical patterns in ecology and society with those in economics. Jared Diamond has written at length about the collapse of past civilisations and has given many examples of the close linkages between ecological and social developments.[12] Ronald Wright has taken a similar approach.[13]

In a world of ever-increasing connectivity between the biosphere and the anthroposphere, and in a world of patchy and discontinuous change, one of the key problems is knowing what is the appropriate 'early warning' indicator of change, at what scale is it likely to present itself (in a world of CAS it may initially be a small signal among what appears to be a lot of noise) and what, then, is the appropriate social or institutional response. Even if we can identify the requisite signal of interest, in a non-equilibrium world, what lags in perception, decision and response can be tolerated? What are the necessary institutions that must be established or removed? These are questions that have particular relevance in the context of the growing possibility of global climate change. Redman and Kinzig document examples from the archaeological record where past human societies, because of investment in infrastructure and institutions and high 'sunk' costs, were unable to respond to changing climates, drought and landscape salinisation. Diamond and Wright have documented similar cases of social collapse because of inappropriate social and economic strategies, environmental failure and degradation. There are important parallels and lessons for our present predicament in the study of sustainability and 'deep time'.

Ecosystems in which the human species is a central agent have been called 'human ecosystems'.[14] They have some remarkable properties, largely because of the human constraints on the information flows to and from the biosphere and the anthroposphere. Many of the basic textbooks of ecology ignore the issue of information flows between the human and natural worlds, whereas in our new situation of human domination of the biosphere everything that exchanges information within the coupled social, economic and ecological system is within the purview of a more broadly defined discipline. Similarly, the community development literature is more focused on the social and economic factors, tending to discount environmental linkages. Belief systems, culture, fetishes and memory – many linked to the semiotics of particular places or values – have frequently disrupted or canalised information flows so as to make them maladaptive to changing times and conditions. Bateson[15] was the first to see human families and communities as part of an interactive context, but clearly there are times when belief systems and other cultural constructs can distort or cloud the messages coming from the surrounding environment. Culture, history and values filter and condition the responses of individuals or local communities to their environments. The landscapes we have built have been built through deeply recursive interactions over centuries and millennia. They are the ultimate meso- and macro-scale realisations of micro-scale decision making and they are set in larger, pre-existing global contexts.

Biogeography: evolution and climate

In every respect the entire planetary history and ecology of the planet is a large-scale, long-term working out of a complex adaptive system and we have been major players in the outcome for a very long time. We have both influenced, and been influenced by, the changing face of the planet. Evolution has left the planet with a contingent pattern of biodiversity: its biogeography. Some continents have oaks, some have gum trees. Some continents developed large populations of grazing ungulates; others are populated by marsupial grazers that hop. These differences are a function of chance, contingent evolutionary history, geographical isolation and past continental movements. What we now see is a planet with a very uneven distribution of biodiversity and one that has decided 'hot spots' requiring special attention for preservation and conservation. The 'hot spots' arose because of the particular evolutionary history of the continents and islands, modulated by geology, geography, climate and geomorphology. Myers and co-workers have identified 25 biodiversity 'hot spots' around the globe, which contain 44% of all species of vascular plant and 35% of species in four major vertebrate groups on a mere 1.4% of the land area.[16] Clearly, these 'hot spots' are priorities for conservation efforts.

Although preservation of biodiversity 'hot spots' and protection of the world's last 'great wild places' is obviously required, overall this strategy of biodiversity protection has not been hugely successful. Many of the iconic sites in World Heritage Areas and national parks are protected for cultural and historical reasons and preservation of a particular sense of place. Although there are many heroic success stories (e.g. the wolf in North America) we are still losing biodiversity overall and many of even the largest protected areas are not sustainable. This really places greater emphasis on the preservation and even restoration of biodiversity in that part of nature where humans and nature coexist: 'the rest of nature' as it has been called. Chapin has criticised the 'hot spots' doctrine as it is formulated by some of the big environmental NGOs because of the way in which 'hot spots' can focus effort on the preservation of natural capital to the detriment of human and social capital.[17] Sustainability requires a balanced account consisting of all forms of capital. So much of the world is now cleared for agriculture and for urban development that even a small benefit from such a large area would be a major outcome. These areas require people – knowledge, human and social capital – to manage them.

Even the shape of and arrangement of particular continents had an effect on regional patterns of biodiversity. Both Jared Diamond and Tim Flannery[18] have discussed the evolutionary history of continental flora and fauna and have shown in detail how the evolutionary history and ecology of the flora and fauna and the cultural and economic development of human populations has depended on the vagaries of migration pathways, space and resources at various latitudes. The impact of continental drift on the present flora and fauna of the continents is very noticeable, with the species composition of major groups differing on the various continents depending on evolutionary histories and on isolation and subsequent contact. The final (modern) patterns of distribution of animal and plant groups (e.g. mammals and angiosperms) display major groupings and discontinuities, showing clearly that the present has been shaped by the past. The mammalian fauna of the Arctic, North Temperate and Oriental regions show great similarities due to frequent contact over the millennia. Endemicity in the Nearctic and Palaearctic regions is low (3%–13%) whereas the geographical isolation of Neotropical South America and Australasia has led to much higher endemicity (47%–91%).[19]

Evolutionary history is one factor. Looking at the global vegetation, it is also possible to see how the basic structure of the vegetation in various places has been determined by climate. A number of the early botanical explorers, including von Humboldt, noticed that similar broad functional and structural types of vegetation occurred in different parts of the world under similar climate regimes. Even though the actual taxonomy and evolutionary history of the species was different in different places they remarked on the overall similarity of structure of vegetation in, for example, deserts, heathlands, grasslands and forests. The vegetation structure in different regions was classified by Raunkiaer,[20] who grouped vegetation into a variety of life forms dependent on the structure of the plants and protection of the growing point. The concept of global biomes developed out of these large-scale distributions of plant functional types: the biomes are the largest global vegetation and ecosystem units. The global biomes experience similar climatic regimes and have similar vegetation structures.[21] In addition, they contain species with similar life histories and appear to have similar sensitivities to disturbance and human impacts. Together these produce ensemble properties: homoplastic stocks and flows of energy and materials. Here we begin to see direct evidence of large-scale biophysical constraints on the design and functioning of organisms across the globe.

So as a result of evolutionary history and climate what we are left with is a very uneven distribution of biodiversity on the planet. This is not a static distribution. The distribution of biomes across the surface of the planet is in a continuous state of flux and has changed dramatically in the postglacial period. Sometimes the changes were very rapid, as in the period about 11 000 years ago when the last ice age ended.[22] The postglacial history of the planetary biomes can be traced through palaeoecological data such as fossil material and pollen distributions. These show quite clearly, for example, that what we now regard as the normal distribution of deciduous and coniferous forest in the northern hemisphere changed totally from the glacial maximum to the present as the climate warmed.[23] Pollen data can be used to map past biomes and the distributions of plant functional groups; these data can then be linked to climate modelling scenarios to validate large-scale models of climate change and biome distributions.[24] Further evidence of the changing distributions of biomes and plant communities and path dependencies in the postglacial period can be gleaned from genetic data. The structure of present-day forests in the northern Europe shows strong genetic evidence of reinvasion from glacial refuges in the south[25] and of later introductions. This can have major consequences in the modern era. The surviving English elms, for example, once iconic trees of the English landscape and now decimated by Dutch elm disease imported in the 1970s, show clear effects of relatively recent human introduction. The landscape appears to be dominated now by a single clone introduced by the Romans some 2000 years ago.[26] The existence of a single genotype explains its uniform susceptibility to the fungus.

All the present patterns of biodiversity show these patterns of contingent historical events and accidents. The present flora and fauna of North America, for example, has been shown to be a legacy of a whole series of cosmic, geological and evolutionary events. The present ecological state of North America can be traced all the way back to its beginnings 65 million years ago with a meteorite impact at the end of the Cretaceous period.[27] The present-day flora and fauna of Australia is also very much a function of contingent evolutionary history, geography, geomorphology and climate change. In a series of books Mary White has similarly traced the geological and ecological history of the Australian continent through 'deep time', from the evolution of the Gondwana flora about 400 million years ago, through the break up of the super-continent and ice-ages to the present.[28] The continent has become inexorably drier over time, changing slowly from the dominance of rainforest to become a fire dominated desert. Mary White shows how the present-day sustainability crisis in Australia is inextricably linked to the poor soils and arid climate of this very old continent, exacerbated by an incorrect sense of place on the part of European settlers.[29]

Global biomes and 'green' water

Water is the lifeblood of the planet. Before the human population grew to its present size, and before we began to have a major impact on many aspects of the biosphere, the global water cycle supported the natural biomes of the planet and there was a close coupling between the climate, the structure and function of the biomes, and the cycling of water and other materials. Water connects all forms of life and by cycling water through the biosphere and its biomes this planet has been recycling water since time immemorial. So water recycling is not a new idea. As humans we tend to focus on the world's terrestrial freshwater resource – the water in rivers, lakes and streams – but this is only a small portion of the total global water supply; most of the water on Earth is either salty or inaccessible. About 97.5% of the world's water is in the oceans (*c.* 1 380 000 000 cubic kilometres, km^3) whereas only 2.5% (or about 35 000 000 km^3) is freshwater. Of the freshwater resource of the Earth, 68.9% is tied up in snow and ice, 29.9% is fresh groundwater and only 0.26% is in lakes and rivers. Every year the planet turns over about 577 000 km^3 of water, made up of evaporative fluxes from the oceans (503 000 km^3) and from the land (74 000 km^3). Estimates vary[30] but the total runoff in rivers is about 42 000 km^3 per year. This is derived from the difference between the rainfall ($110\,000\,\text{km}^3$) and evaporative fluxes over the land and a small component of direct groundwater flow to the ocean.[31] The residence times of water in the various planetary pools vary enormously: whereas the water in the oceans is replaced by the hydrological cycle every 2500 years, it takes about 10 000 years to turn over the ice in the polar ice caps and the permafrost. Water cycling through the soil, lakes and rivers turns over much more rapidly. Lakes replace their water every 17 years, soil moisture is replaced every year, and water in the rivers has a residence time of merely 16 days. Water vapour in the atmosphere has a residence time of only 8 days. So our sense of place has caused us to focus on a very small and transient part of the whole picture, and as the dominant global species we have changed the overall phenology of water availability in rivers and streams to suit our needs for security and agricultural production.

The entire biosphere is sustained by the flows of freshwater around and through the planet. These flows of rainfall and evaporation have been called 'green' water flows and they support the biodiversity and function of the terrestrial biomes, with about $70\,000\,\text{km}^3$ per annum of water vapour being released by the terrestrial biosphere.[32] The 'green' water flows not only supply the world's rain-fed agriculture but also maintain the great bulk of the global terrestrial ecosystems. Thus the global ecosystem services that Costanza et al.[33] deduced were so valuable are maintained by the 'green' water flows. Our human sense of place has tended to ignore the 'green' water flows and instead focus merely on the freshwater in lakes, rivers and streams; the so called 'blue' water flows. Shiklomanov estimated the total 'blue water' withdrawal as $3790\,\text{km}^3$ per year and the total consumption at $2070\,\text{km}^3$ per year, or 61% of withdrawals. Since the earliest times we have always been inveterate tinkerers with these 'blue' water flows, building dams, aqueducts, irrigations systems and diversions to ensure security and constancy of supply. Human use presently comes to about 5%–7% of the total runoff; not, it might seem, a very large proportion. However, in many regions we are already using more water than the world can sustainably provide; most accessible rivers are now dammed or regulated.[34] To make matters worse, water is unevenly distributed in space and time. Some countries (e.g. Canada, Ireland) have abundant water supplies whereas others (e.g. Kuwait) have almost none. Drought and floods are common, and interannual climate variability is a major issue. Countries like India and Bangladesh suffer highly seasonal and interannually variable rainfall, with the annual monsoon varying greatly from year to year. Many countries around the world face severe water stress in the next fifty years[35] and in countries like Australia water restrictions during periods of drought are already the cause of major fluctuations in economic performance. Because of the close linkage between security of supply, economic performance and public health, huge efforts have been made all across the globe to provide security of supply. Since the dawn of history human populations have engineered the environment to provide water supplies for irrigation and for drinking, and we have constantly striven to reduce the natural variability of water supply in space and time. Dams are the standard solution but now, with natural supplies over-committed and climate change beginning to influence both 'green' water flows and runoff, energy-intensive solutions – such as desalination – are being proposed to continue the security of supply for urban areas.

The increase in dams world wide in the past fifty years has resulted in most of the major rivers on Earth being dammed and regulated, so that 60% of the global river basins are now seriously affected. Many major rivers (e.g. Colorado River, Yellow River, Murray–Darling) no longer flow to the sea during dry periods. Dams provide security of supply for urban and agricultural development but changes in the river hydrology have major ecological implications. Despite our best efforts to dam, regulate and tame the 'blue' water supplies over the years, vast numbers of people on this planet still have inadequate access to potable water and water for sanitation: 2.4 billion at the last count, and the number is likely to rise over time. This is partly because the human population is as unevenly distributed across the face of the planet as is the water, and the distributions are also almost always the inverse of one another. Countries rich in 'blue' water resources tend to be thinly populated and vice versa.

Water is extremely valuable. Irrigation water is much more valuable than rain water because it is a secure and dependable supply. Irrigated agriculture uses 2–3 times the water of rain-fed agriculture but the profits may be as much as 15 times higher.[36] About 70% of all the water extracted for human use goes to agriculture and irrigation, and the ecosystem services provided by freshwater ecosystems have been valued at about twice the value of the global gross national product. Unfortunately the huge global demand on water supplies is leading to reductions in flows, habitat fragmentation and rapid extinction of freshwater biota.[37] Indeed, freshwater biodiversity is declining more rapidly than that in any other major group of ecosystems owing to loss of connectivity between populations because of dams, barriers and weirs, regulation of flows and extraction of water, overfishing and pollution of various kinds. Tragically, because most of this is going on underwater, it is not so widely appreciated by most human populations. Clearing of forests and other lands, habitat fragmentation and loss of terrestrial biodiversity leads to degradation of catchments and water quality. By flowing across, under and through the landscape, water is the compound that links many of the processes in landscapes and waterscapes. Terrestrial and aquatic systems are closely linked – much more closely that we have realised – so that management actions for land and water are interrelated in very complex ways.

The imposition of constancy on natural systems that require variability causes particular problems for systems that are naturally non-linear, non-equilibrium CAS. Problems are caused through the human need for security of supply and constancy of flow. Attempts are being made to address this by the restoration of what are called environmental flows, but even now the focus is largely on annual average flows rather than the particular distribution of floods and low-flow periods with a more natural character. Gravity ensures that almost all the 'blue' water runs to the sea (the exception being so-called endorheic catchments, which have no outlet and where the water is finally lost through evaporation) so that estuaries are the receiving waters of all our urban and agricultural land use effects.

By ignoring the 'green' water fluxes we have very much underestimated the impact of land use change on the overall water budget of the continents; and it should be remembered that the 'green' water flows are important structuring elements in the biogeography of the continents. It is the magnitude and seasonality of the 'green' water flows – the climate and hydrological cycle drivers – which are largely responsible for the life forms of Raunkiaer, the homoplastic structures of the vegetation that occur in similar climatological regions around the globe. Changing the close link between vegetation cover and type and the 'green' water flows has major ramifications. For example, Gordon et al.[38] recently calculated that as a result of land clearing over the past two hundred years in Australia the total water vapour flows from the continent have decreased by about 10%. Annual average precipitation (which is, admittedly, highly variable from year to year) is about 3314 km^3 per year.[39] In the 1780s, before the advent of western agriculture and land clearing, the total water vapour flux was of the order of 3440 km^3 per year – within the limits of error, very similar to the rainfall. River flows from the continent are of the order of 360 km^3 per year, only about 10% of the rainfall.[40] Much of the runoff from Australia arises in tropical catchments during the monsoon season, so the water is not where the people are and the runoff is restricted to a short period in mid-summer. As a result only about 100 km^3 per year can really be used economically.[41] Large areas of the centre of the continent are endorheic catchments where there is no runoff to the ocean. By the 1980s, as a result of land use change, the estimated water vapour fluxes from the continent were down to 3100 km^3 per year.[42] So something like 340 km^3 of water vapour flows has been diverted from the atmosphere. This may not seem much, and may be thought of as down in the statistical noise given the interannual variability in rainfall and evaporation. The reduction in water vapour fluxes is, however, of the same order of magnitude as the annual continental runoff, five times the total Australian water diversions of about 69 km^3 per year and about 17 times the total water consumed; at about 20 km^3 per year. So while we continue to argue over the 20 km^3 used annually (and the politics of water in Australia is an increasingly tough game) more than 340 km^3 of water is flowing through different routes each year.

The ultimate challenge – the integrated management of a human-dominated planet – is going to be a very complex task. Falkenmark has rightly called attention to a growing sense of crisis in the world's water supply because of our inability to effectively link environmental security, water security and food security.[43] Because of a range of cultural, historical and other values (and institutional fragmentation) insufficient attention has been paid to the fact that all forms of water (solid, liquid and vapour) are the lifeblood of the biosphere and that disturbances to the entire hydrological cycle are placing global security at risk. We are now appropriating about one third of the total production of the biosphere for human use[44] (actually 31%–32%) so land use conversion will have large-scale impacts on the global hydrological cycle. Only in recent years have we attempted to address the linkages between water vapour flows, agricultural food production and terrestrial ecosystem services.[45] Falkenmark writes:

> Both land/water linkages and water/ecosystem linkages will have to be properly entered into an integrated and catchment-based land/water/ecosystem approach. The goal has to meet both societal needs and environmental sustainability conditions.

This is one of the major challenges of sustainability in the twenty-first century. The major security threats include water quality deterioration, water constraints and food insecurity risks, and river depletion. Falkenmark has called for a sense of urgency about water management and has identified a set of crucial policy measures to be set in place over the next 20 years.[46] These include:

- Conflict aversion through water sharing strategies
- Pollution aversion through proper waste management and cessation of landscape scale leaching
- Aversion of land fertility decline
- Aversion of urban water supply collapses
- Aversion of human health impacts through poor sanitation
- Aversion of crop failures and inferior crop yields

Above all Falkenmark identifies the great complexity of the challenge: to integrate a variety of land and water use practices as we modify global elemental cycles and increasingly push into more marginal lands,[47] to improve water use efficiency so as to improve food production to meet the needs of population growth,[48] to cope with the probability of increased water stress as a result of climate change,[49] and to do this in an integrated manner so as to achieve a more sustainable outcome. The real challenge behind all this is a challenge to capacity and capability.

Human history: biogeography and blitzkrieg?

The contingent evolutionary history and biogeography of the planet is a basic driver of subsequent human history. The landscapes in which we set our settlements, enterprises and agriculture are different around the world. The link between the biogeographical setting and the development of human populations in various places on the globe has been thoroughly discussed by Jared Diamond in his book *Guns, Germs and Steel*.[50] Diamond shows that the history of the human race varies from place to place on the planet, not because of racial differences but because of fundamental difference in the environment, natural resources and the evolutionary history. Some places were endowed with a diversity of easily domesticated stock, some were not; some were endowed with native grasses that could be bred for seed production, some were not. Some places enjoyed equable climates; others were plagued with strong interannual climate variability. Some regions were therefore able to develop hunter–gatherer societies and agriculture before others, and so had a head start. The varying resource base for human settlement and cultural development led Paul Colinvaux to propose a biological or ecological theory of history.[51] There is therefore some strong evidence of the impact of biogeography, climate and geography on the course of human history. Collapses have occurred in the past because of environmental and climatological forces.[52]

This is not to say that we have been totally dependent on our surroundings. There is also strong evidence of human impacts on the natural biomes and on the biodiversity of the planet. We have, on occasion, lived off our natural capital to the detriment of both ecosystems and sustainability. A number of authors have documented the demise of the megafauna of continents and islands soon after the arrival of man in the past 50 000–60 000 years.[53] There is a debate about whether or not people have been directly responsible for the extinctions of the megafauna in all cases. Tim Flannery is one of those who believe that a human 'blitzkrieg' is responsible for the elimination of many species of large mammal and bird around the world, and he is supported by others,[54] especially by E. O. Wilson.[55] Certainly the story in New Zealand and many other Pacific islands is clear: there is a strong case for overharvesting and exploitation of the native flightless birds.[56] On the continents there are arguments about dates, migration paths and the coincidence of artefacts and sites.[57] Nevertheless, recent dating of burial sites in Australia at 46 000 years ago seems to be strong evidence of major anthropogenic impacts very soon after the arrival on humans on the continent of Australia.[58] A simulation of the arrival of humans on the North American continent 13 000 years ago produces similar results.[59] Whatever the reason, overkill, climate and habitat change, disease or the introduction of pests and domestic animals (or any combination of the above), the sudden decline of large numbers of Pleistocene megafauna upon the arrival of people on continents and islands is striking.

Taken at face value these observations would tend to suggest that the impacts of the human population on the biodiversity of the planet have long been quite marked. Perhaps we could go so far as to conclude that the evidence indicates that lack of impact in many cases was more a result of low population densities and low resource use than lack of intent.[60] This is not to deny that there are many cultural practices in indigenous peoples that ensure wise and sustainable resource use. Nevertheless, the 'wisdom of the ancients' may not be as applicable to our present predicament as some would like to suggest. At the very least the context of modern times is very different and demands different institutional and personal responses.

Reviews of the causes of land use and land cover change have shown just how complex the interactions are between population growth, poverty, economic opportunity and institutional factors.[61] Studies of the relationships between populations and land cover changes in East and Sub-Saharan Africa show that there are deep historical footprints in the contemporary land use systems. Whereas colonial forestry systems are often perceived to be the major determinants of present-day land use patterns, it is clear that these patterns merely reinforced much older precolonial patterns.[62] There are complex social, cultural, economic and ecological processes at work, which make simple explanations redundant. Interactions across multiple and nested scales of space and time are coupled to complex social and institutional forces which determine access to a range of resources.[63] Strong regional differences in geomorphology, climate and biogeography introduce further complexities, particularly when these are set in the globalised world of markets, finance and economics.[64] As the human population has risen and land clearing, agriculture, urban development and water and resource extraction have proceeded apace we are seeing a second wave of biodiversity loss. E. O. Wilson has written eloquently about this loss and its potential impacts.[65] This loss is due both to direct resource utilisation and to habitat destruction and fragmentation. Having removed the Pleistocene megafauna and the flightless birds, we are now turning our attention to other smaller terrestrial species. Part of the problem is not simply habitat loss and fragmentation; there are more subtle forces at work.

Because part of the spatial patterning of landscapes is self-generated and therefore an emergent property of landscapes, breaking up the landscape into fragments smaller than the emergent self-generated structure makes it impossible for the natural fluctuations and interactions between species to occur. As Hassell, Comins and May wrote

> if habitat destruction were to bring the community below its critical spatial size (which, being a collective property of the system, is not easily inferred from the movements of individuals), we would expect the system to collapse.[66]

The complex interaction in space and time between the scales of ecological, social and economic systems produces some highly complex and surprising results. The effects can be seen not just on the land. Myers and Worm have recently shown that there has been a similar removal of the marine megafauna through overfishing. The biomass of large predatory fish species in the world ocean is now about 10% of its pre-industrial level.[67] We have not paid enough attention to the huge shifts in baselines that have occurred, and major ecological changes have gone unrecognised.[68] We have simply forgotten what the oceans used to be like. What we now regard as the normal state of the oceans has been severely perturbed by the removal of top predators.

David Western has summarised the impact of humans on ecosystems and has categorised these broadly into intended and unintended changes (but also recognises the 'murky dividing line' between the two).[69] Intended changes were designed to improve food supplies, provisions, safety and comfort, and perhaps to construct 'humanscapes' (landscapes to suit our 'savannah' origins). Western points out that many of the unintended changes in human-modified ecosystems are very similar to the kinds of density-dependent impacts seen in ecosystems as a result of high population densities of other species. Perhaps there is nothing very special about the impacts of large numbers of the human animal. If we live off our natural capital, human-dominated ecosystems lose biodiversity, suffer altered size distributions (particularly the loss of the megafauna) and show major changes in spatial patterning and network structure through fragmentation, homogenisation and changes to the disturbance regime. These complex changes have unintended consequences.[70]

We have replaced some of what we have lost. There is a long history of deliberate and accidental introductions of species, which go back to Roman times and even further. Domestic animals, mice, rats and weeds have followed the human migrations around the planet. In the early days of Western colonisation there were even organised committees to oversee the introduction of foxes, rabbits, birds, fish, crops and garden plants from Europe to the far-flung corners of the world. As the human population has become more mobile in recent decades, so also have many other species. We are now moving species around the planet on aircraft, on ships and attached to our feet through seeds, various kinds of propagules and even adult animals and plants. So as some of the endemic biodiversity of the globe has declined it has been replaced by a more homogeneous collection of successful feral species: dogs, pigs, rats, foxes, cats, rabbits, starlings, sparrows, Indian mynah birds, zebra mussels, *Tilapia* and carp, to name but a few. Islands, like Hawaii for example, have suffered particularly badly from extinctions of endemic species and their replacement by feral introductions. Recent syntheses of work in the Pacific Islands have documented the introduction of new species as well as the elimination of native species through predation and land use change. To piece together the story this work required the synthesis of archaeological, cultural, historical, social, linguistic and genetic data from a wide range of sites.[71]

The boundaries between the great biogeographic regions are beginning to blur. As long ago as the 1950s Elton[72] noted the breakdown of species distributions on either side of Wallace's line as a result of the movement of species through commerce. What is now emerging is a new 'homogecene' or a 'New Pangea'[73] in which the bio-distinctiveness of regions is declining. Olden *et al.*[74] list studies of the homogenisation of communities of marine algae, higher plants, insects, mussels and snails, fish, amphibians, reptiles, birds and mammals and have concluded that the consequences of the homogenisation of biodiversity will include trophic (food chain) effects as predators are removed and their biodiversity homogenised, as well as increased susceptibility of ecological communities to further invasions by new species. There is also good evidence of rapid hybridisation and interbreeding between the native and exotic species. Thus the course of evolution is also being influenced. E. O. Wilson and many others have argued cogently for a major conservation effort to prevent further extinctions and to return the biosphere to a more balanced state.

Biodiversity is not just animals and plants or charismatic megaflora and megafauna. Biodiversity is function. Biodiversity provides valuable ecosystem services – such as recycling 'green' water, controlling runoff, recycling nutrients, ensuring soil fertility – and ensures the smooth functioning of the biosphere.[75] Causing extinctions and moving other species around is altering the biospheric function as well as its aesthetic appeal in complex and unexpected ways. There is emerging evidence that land use change and loss of biodiversity can change the global climate through alterations in evaporation rates and runoff.[76] I like to think of this as a process of changing the rivets in a ship while at sea: dropping some over the side in the process and moving others around to fill in gaps. It would be different if we actually understood the full consequences of our actions. How long, I wonder, will the ship stay afloat?

NOTES

1. S. Schama. *Landscape and Memory.* (London: HarperCollins, 1995). G. Seddon. *Landprints: Reflections on Place and Landscape.* (Cambridge: Cambridge University Press, 1997). Also see the discussion in G. Seddon. *Sense of Place: a Response to Environment, the Swan Coastal Plain.* (Nedlands, WA.: University of Western Australia Press, 1972).

2. D. Penn. The evolutionary roots of our environmental problems: towards a Darwinian ecology. *Quarterly Reviews of Biology,* **78** (3) (2003), 1–37.

3. For example, the debate around the publication of E. O. Wilson. *Sociobiology.* (Cambridge, MA: Harvard University Press, 1975).

4. D. E. Wayne. *Penshurst, the Semiotics of Place and the Poetics of History.* (Madison, WI: The University of Wisconsin Press, 1984).

5. Seddon, *Landprints: Reflections on Place and Landscape.* (See Note 1.)

6. But remember Ozymandias, King of Kings. Diamond also chose this poem as a preface to his book. J. Diamond. *Collapse.* (London: Allen Lane, Penguin Press, 2004).

7. T. Bonyhady. *The Colonial Earth.* (Melbourne: Melbourne University Press, 2000).

8. F. Pryor. *Britain AD*. (London: HarperCollins, 2004).

9. A. N. Wilson. *The Victorians*. (London: Arrow Books, 2003).

10. M. Scheffer, F. Westley and W. Brock. Slow response of societies to new problems: causes and costs. *Ecosystems*, **6** (2003), 493–502.

11. C. L. Redman and A. P. Kinzig. Resilience of past landscapes: resilience theory, society and the Longue Duree. *Conservation Ecology*, 7(1): 14 (2003). See http://www.consecol.org/vol7/iss1/art14.

12. Diamond, *Collapse*. (See Note 6.)

13. R. Wright. *A Short History of Progress*. (Melbourne: Text Publishing, 2004).

14. J. R. Stepp *et al*. Remarkable properties of human ecosystems. *Conservation Ecology*, **7**: 11 (2003). See http://www.consecol.org/vol7/iss3/art11.

15. G. Bateson. *Steps to an Ecology of Mind*. (St Albans: Paladin, 1973).

16. N. Myers *et al*. Biodiversity hotspots for conservation priorities. *Nature*, **403** (2000), 853–8.

17. M. Chapin. A challenge to conservationists. *World Watch*, Nov–Dec 2004, pp. 17–31.

18. J. Diamond. *Guns, Germs and Steel*. (New York: Norton, 1997). T. F. Flannery. *The Eternal Frontier: an Ecological History of North America and its Peoples*. (New York: Atlantic Monthly Press, 2001).

19. C. B. Cox and P. Moore. *Biogeography, an Ecological and Evolutionary Approach*, 3rd edn. (New York: Halsted Press, Wiley, 1980), p. 171.

20. C. Raunkiaer. *The Life Form of Plants*. (Oxford: Oxford University Press, 1934).

21. R. H. Whittaker. *Communities and Ecosystems*, 2nd edn. (New York: Macmillan, 1975).

22. See E. Post. *Trends in Ecology and Evolution*, **18** (2003), 551.

23. I. C. Prentice *et al*. Reconstructing biomes from palaeo-ecological data: a general method and its application to European pollen data at 0 and 6 ka. *Climate Dynamics*, **12** (1996), 185–94.

24. J. W. Williams, R. L. Summers and T. Webb. Applying plant functional types to construct biome maps from Eastern North America pollen data: comparisons with model results. *Quaternary Science Reviews*, **17** (1998), 607–27.

25. R. J. Petit *et al*. Chloroplast DNA variation in European white oaks – phylogeography and patterns of diversity based on data from over 2600 populations. *Forest Ecology and Management*, **156** (2002), 5–26. There are a number of other papers on the genetics of European forest species in that issue.

26. L. Gil *et al*. English elm is a 2000-year-old Roman clone. *Nature*, **431** (2004), 1053.

27. Flannery, *The Eternal Frontier*. (See Note 18.)

28. M. White. *The Greening of Gondwana*. (Kenthurst, NSW: Kangaroo Press, 1986). M. White. *After the Greening*. (Kenthurst, NSW: Kangaroo Press, 1994).

29. M. White. *Listen, our Land is Crying*. (Kenthurst, NSW: Kangaroo Press, 1986).

30. I. A. Shiklomanov. *World Water Resources at the Beginning of the 21st Century*. (Geneva: IHP UNESCO, 2000). Shiklomanov estimated an annual river flow of $42\,600\,km^3$. C. J. Vorosmarty *et al*. Global water resources: vulnerability from climate change and population growth. *Science*, **289** (2000), 284–8. Vorosmarty *et al*. estimated annual river flows to be $39\,300\,km^3$. See also H. L. F. Saeijs and M. J. van Berkel. Global water crisis: the major issue of the 21st century, a growing and explosive problem. *European Water Pollution Control Journal*, **5** (1995). 26–40. See also T. Oki *et al*. Global assessment of current water resources using total runoff integrating pathways. *Hydrological Sciences – Journal des Sciences Hydrologiques*, **46** (2001), 983–95. Using a different method, Oki *et al*. obtained an estimate of total runoff about 20% less than the other authors.

31. I. A. Shiklomanov (2000). (See Note 30.)

32. J. Rockstrom and L. Gordon. Assessment of green water flows to sustain the major biomes of the world: implications for future ecohydrological landscape management. *Physics and Chemistry of the Earth (B)*, **26** (2001), 843–51. These authors estimated the annual average evapotranspiration of the world's biomes to be $63\,200\,km^3$ with maximum and minimum values between $79\,900$ and $47\,600\,km^3$ per year. Total human green water dependence was estimated to be $69\,800\,km^3$ and total water vapour flow from the continental ecosystems was estimated at $71\,300\,km^3$ per year.

33. R. Costanza *et al*. The value of the world's ecosystem services and natural capital. *Nature*, **387** (1997), 253–60.

34. C. Revenga *et al*. *Watersheds of the World: Ecological Value and Vulnerability*. (Washington, DC: World Resources Institute and Worldwatch Institute, 1998). N. Johnson, C. Revenga and J. Echeverria. Managing water for people and nature. *Science*, **292** (2001), 1071–2.

35. J. S. Wallace. Increasing agricultural water use efficiency to meet future food production. *Agriculture, Ecosystems and Environment*, **82** (2000), 105–19.

36. W. Meyer, personal communication: data from the Murray–Darling Basin in Australia.

37. A. Balmford, R. E. Green and M. Jenkins. Measuring the changing state of nature. *Trends in Ecology and Evolution*, **18** (2003), 326–30.

38. L. Gordon, M. Dunlop and B. Foran. Land cover change and water vapour flows: learning from Australia. *Philosophical Transactions of the Royal Society of London*, B, **358** (2003), 1973–84.

39. M. I. L'vovich. *World Water Resources and their Future*. (Chelsea, MI: LithoCrafters Inc, 1979) had obtained a similar figure of $3390\,km^3$ per year.

40. Figures for the Murray–Darling Basin show similarly low runoff in comparison to rainfall. Over the Basin the median rainfall is estimated to be $250\,km^3$ per year and the runoff about $23\,km^3$ per year. Thanks to evaporation as the Murray River wends its way to the sea, the median annual flow through the Murray River mouth is a mere $11.88\,km^3$. In the late 1980s and early 1990s, when extractions were capped, the annual extractions from the Murray River totalled about $10.7\,km^3$ – hence the concern about environmental flows in the river!

41. Australian Academy of Technological Science and Engineering. *Water and the Australian Economy*. (Melbourne: ATSE, 1999).

42. Again, L'vovich's (1979) estimates were similar for the 1970s at $3028\,km^3$ per year. (See Note 39.)

43. M. Falkenmark. The greatest water problem: the inability to link environmental security, water security and food security. *Water Resources Development*, **17** (2001), 539–54.

44. S. Rojstaczer, S. M. Sterling and N. J. Moore. Human appropriation of photosynthesis products. *Science*, **294** (2001), 2549–52.

45. J. Rockstrom *et al*. Linkages among water vapour flows, food production and terrestrial ecosystem services. *Conservation Ecology*, **3** (2) (1999), 5. http://www.consecol.org/vol3/iss2/art5.

46. M. Falkenmark. Dilemma when entering 21st century – rapid change but lack of sense of urgency. *Water Policy*, **1** (1998), 421–36.

47. D. Tilman *et al*. Forecasting agriculturally driven global environmental change. *Science*, **292** (2001), 281–4. P. A. Matson *et al*. Agricultural intensification and ecosystem properties. *Science*, **277** (1997), 504–9.

48. J. S. Wallace. Increasing agricultural water use efficiency to meet future food production. *Agriculture, Ecosystems and Environment*, **82** (2000), 105–19. J. S. Wallace and P. J. Gregory. Water resources and their use in food production systems. *Aquatic Sciences*, **64** (2002), 363–75.

49. C.J. Vorosmarty *et al.* Global water resources: vulnerability from climate change and population growth. *Science*, **289** (2000), 284–8.

50. Diamond, *Guns, Germs and Steel*. (See Note 18.)

51. Paul Colinvaux. *The Fates of Nations: a Biological Theory of History*. (New York: Simon and Schuster, 1980).

52. Diamond, *Collapse*. Ronald Wright, *A Short History of Progress*. (See Notes 6 and 13).

53. See, for example, T.F. Flannery. *The Future Eaters: an Ecological History of the Australasian Lands and Peoples*. (Melbourne: Reed Press, 1994).

54. These ideas were first espoused by P.S. Martin in the 1960s. See Flannery, ibid. on North American and Australian palaeo-history. See also Jared Diamond. *The Third Chimpanzee: the Evolution and Future of the Human Animal*. (New York: HarperCollins, 1992). Also reviewed in D. Penn. The evolutionary roots of our environmental problems: toward a Darwinian ecology. *The Quarterly Review of Biology*, **78** (2003), 1–37. See also D.A. Burney and T.F. Flannery. Fifty millennia of catastrophic extinctions after human contact. *Trends in Ecology and Evolution*, **20** (2005), 395–401.

55. E.O. Wilson. *The Future of Life*. (New York: Abacus, 2003).

56. A. Anderson. *Prodigious Birds*. (Cambridge: Cambridge University Press, 1989).

57. See, for example, D.K. Grayson and D.J. Meltzer. A requiem for North American overkill. *Journal of Archaeological Science*, **30** (2003), 585–93.

58. R.G. Roberts *et al.* New ages for the last Australian megafauna: continent wide extinction about 46,000 years ago. *Science*, **292** (2001), 1888–92, also T.F. Flannery. *Country*. (Melbourne: Text Publishing, 2004).

59. J. Alroy. A multispecies overkill simulation of the end-Pleistocene megafaunal mass extinction. *Science*, **292** (2001), 1893–6.

60. D. Penn. The evolutionary roots of our environmental problems: toward a Darwinian ecology. *The Quarterly Review of Biology*, **78** (2003), 1–37.

61. E.F. Lambin *et al.* The causes of land-use and land-cover change: moving beyond the myths. *Global Environmental Change*, **11** (2001), 261–9.

62. D.A. Wardell, A. Reenberg and C. Tottrup. Historical footprints in contemporary land use systems: forest cover changes in savannah woodlands in the Sudano-Sahelian zone. *Global Environmental Change*, **13** (2003), 235–54.

63. S.P.J. Batterbury and A.J. Bebbington. Environmental histories: access to resources and landscape change: an introduction. *Land Degradation and Development*, **10** (1999), 279–89.

64. S.P.J. Batterbury and A. Warren. The African Sahel 25 years after the great drought: assessing progress and moving towards new agendas and approaches. *Global Environmental Change*, **11** (2001), 1–8.

65. See E.O. Wilson. *Consilience: the Unity of Knowledge*. (New York: Knopf, 1998). E.O. Wilson. *The Future of Life*. (London: Little, Brown, 2002).

66. M.P. Hassell, H.N. Comins and R.M. May. Species co-existence and self-organising spatial dynamics. *Nature*, **370** (1994), 290–2.

67. R.A. Myers and B. Worm. Rapid worldwide depletion of predatory fish communities. *Nature*, **423** (2003), 280–3. B. Worm *et al.* Global patterns of predator diversity in the open oceans. *Science*, **309** (2005), 1365–9.

68. J.K. Baum and R.A. Myers. Shifting baselines and the decline of pelagic sharks in the Gulf of Mexico. *Ecology Letters*, **7** (2004), 135–45.

69. D. Western. Human-modified ecosystems and future evolution. *Proceedings of the National Academy of Sciences, USA*, **98** (2004), 5458–65.

70. These lists of human impacts on ecosystems are similar to those listed by Jared Diamond, *Collapse*. (See Note 6.)

71. M. E. Hurles *et al.* Untangling oceanic settlement: the edge of the knowable. *Trends in Ecology and Evolution*, **18** (2003), 531–40.

72. C. S. Elton. *The Ecology of Invasions by Animals and Plants.* (Chicago, IL: Chicago University Press, 1958).

73. M. L. Rozenzweig. The four questions: what does the introduction of exotic species do to diversity. *Evolutionary and Ecological Research*, **3** (2001), 361–7.

74. J. D. Olden *et al.* Ecological and evolutionary consequences of biotic homogenisation. *Trends in Ecology and Evolution*, **19** (2004), 18–24.

75. C. Kremen. Managing ecosystem services: what do we need to know about their ecology? *Ecology Letters*, **8** (2005), 468–79.

76. D. Schröter *et al.* Ecosystem service supply and vulnerability to global change in Europe. *Science*, **310** (2005), 1333–7.

8 Created landscapes and our changing sense of place

The surprising effects that complex interactions can produce in our created landscapes.

Given the large human population and its global spread, we must accept that the landscapes that most of us grew up in and which we might regard as 'normal' – at least those that contribute to our strong sense of place – are largely created by human hands.[1] George Seddon writes:

> The sum of the distinctive characters in a given area, whether 'natural' or man-made, can be called a 'landscape'. But although they have a physical substrate, landscapes are also a cultural construct. The ways in which we read them, talk about them, perceive them, work them over, use them, evaluate them functionally, aesthetically, morally: these are all informed by our culture.[2]

Landscapes are not static entities and require constant effort to maintain. It is a sobering thought to realise that many iconic places have been created by people through cultural practices, village and urban development, agriculture and industry. There are few pristine places remaining on this planet. There are a set of semiotics of place – varying with landscape, culture and memory – which condition our language, norms and management actions. The entire English landscape is a created entity, maintained by agriculture: by arable and pastoral farming. There is an underlying set of established metaphors in the English rural and domestic landscape concerning style, design and history and the way these relate the topography to the house and the garden. Don Wayne has called these historical semiotics.[3]

The English landscape – that cultural and agricultural icon that attracts tourists from around the world – is a fascinating and well documented example of the complexity of landscape interactions between the patterns of human settlements, agricultural enterprise and ecology. Agriculture, settlement patterns, culture and ecology are all undergoing rapid change at the present time, so the English landscape is a microcosm of many factors at work in postmodern landscapes. It is an excellent example of dramatic changes in our relationship with ancient landscapes. It is also a classic case of changing interactions between processes acting at a range of scales – all of which were brought to a head by the outbreak of foot and mouth disease in 2001. That disease outbreak showed just how complex and surprising the interactions between society, the rural landscape and economy, and the broader national and global economy have become in a time when complexity and connectivity are increasing rapidly.

The postglacial history of the British flora was summarised by Godwin in his magisterial work *The History of the British Flora*.[4] Development of the English landscape as we presently know it began after the last ice age about 10 000 years ago with the slow redevelopment of deciduous forest. Not all of England was glaciated at the height of the last glaciation; the maximum extent of the ice fell on a line roughly from the Severn River across to Essex. Some small mountain areas in south central Ireland also probably remained unglaciated. In very general terms, as the warming preceded birch (*Betula* sp.) was replaced by pine (*Pinus* sp.) and hazel (*Corylus* sp.) and then mixed oak–elm forest (*Quercus–Ulmus* sp.). So, across most of the country, the basic raw material, the geomorphology and forest composition, is postglacial. Early hominids had been present in Britain from the Lower Palaeolithic era, some 500 000 years ago, but populations were small, perhaps no more than 5000, and they eventually disappeared. Human populations reappeared and grew soon after the retreat of the ice and were well established by 7500 years ago. Very roughly, the population of Britain might have been around 100 000 people by 5000–6000 years ago. About 5000 years ago the first influence of people on the landscape is detected in the sudden decline in elm pollen. This 'pollen decline', as it is called, seems to indicate more widespread clearing and early farming activity by Neolithic people and, perhaps, either the influence of disease or the feeding of animals on elm tree leaves (or both). Whatever the mechanism, the 'pollen decline' is a widespread feature of pollen assemblages in fen[5] and lake sediments[6] from this time throughout the British Isles. Simultaneously there is an increase in pollen from grasses, weeds and other species that grow in clearings and disturbed ground. The Late Neolithic period is the time of the construction of the spectacular barrows, henges and stone circles. Pryor argues for great cultural continuity from the Neolithic, through the Bronze and Iron Ages into more modern times when Celtic, Roman, Viking and Saxon cultures all washed across the landscape, leaving traces of their pasts in the remains of hill forts, villas, hamlets, villages and place names. In this landscape everything is usually much older than you think.[7]

As you drive along the motorways you can see signs saying 'Beautiful Britain, brought to you by British agriculture' – this is literally true. The characteristic English landscape of field and village, of coppice and hedgerow, which is so loved by tourists from around the world, has been designed and remade many times by the changing face of agriculture and the associated social and economic changes. As Hoskins notes

> it is a matter of geology, topography, climate, and the historical facts of land ownership, even to obscure customs of inheritance . . . Climate plays an obvious part over the centuries, chiefly in the form of water. . . Within these physical limits, men and women have fashioned the local scene according to their needs.[8]

Geology and soil type changes rapidly across the British Isles, as does the climate. Rocks are older in the west, where it is wetter, and younger in the east, where it is drier.[9] Agriculture follows the climate and soils, being largely pastoral in the west and arable in the east.

The features that dominate the tourist view of England are the settlements and their boundaries, the hedges, banks and ditches. The medieval open-field landscape was enclosed at different times in different places. The hedges of the west are old, some of them the boundaries of very early settlements, protection against the surrounding 'wastes'. The west-country enclosures were built early on, as far back as the thirteenth century. They were originally designed as a means to conveniently divide up the landscape for the management of herds of sheep and cattle: a small flock or herd in each few acres of land.[10] These landscapes of hedgerows and coppice – often called 'bocage' landscapes – are now critical for the maintenance of agricultural production, landscape function, water quality and biodiversity.[11] They are equally critical for aesthetic values, tourism and other off-farm revenues, which have become increasingly important sources of income in rural areas.[12] Hedgerows act as windbreaks and control the hydrology of these agricultural landscapes by slowing runoff and containing erosion; furthermore, they act as corridors for the migration of woodland species and as refuges for butterflies.[13] In the east of England, where the boundaries are relics of Parliamentary Acts of Enclosure, they are much more modern, dating mostly from the period between 1750 and 1850. Over 2.5 million acres of open land were carefully replanned during this period and miles of straight hawthorn hedges were planted. 'On the open field arable it was a total revolution in the landscape.'[14] People's worlds were transformed within their lifetimes. Species composition and biodiversity were also affected because of the widespread planting of ash (*Fraxinus*), sycamore (*Acer*) and holly (*Ilex*) along with the oak and hawthorn (*Crataegus*). Now the hedges are vital for the preservation of everything from water quality to biodiversity because of the way they act as barriers to overland flow and provide refuges for wildlife in an otherwise cultivated landscape. The advent of changing farming practices after World War II, and particularly the introduction of greater extensification and intensification through mechanisation, led to the removal of the hedgerows across large areas, with subsequent impacts on hydrology, water quality and biodiversity.[15] In addition, land use change from pasture to arable, together with the spreading of animal manures on fields as fertiliser, resulted in increased phosphorus exports and nutrient enrichment of receiving waters.[16]

Settlement patterns also reflect the geology, climate and past social and economic forces. Villages tend to be larger and surrounded by arable fields in the east because of the greater fertility and profitability obtained. In the west, particularly in upland areas, smaller hamlets and isolated farms are scattered across the largely pastoral landscape. These are broad generalisations, and exceptions can be found based around local variations in the geology and climate; never-theless, in broad terms the patterns are clear. Much of the social and economic evolution of the English landscape is also tied up with transport networks, which have also changed over time; from prehistoric trackways, to Roman roads, turn-pikes and coaching routes, to railways, main roads and motorways.[17] Settle-ments, villages and early towns grew or declined depending on whether or not they were on ancient frequented tracks, main coach routes or railways. Villages that were once important have almost disappeared and many once fine country houses have crumbled into ruin; other minor centres suddenly expanded with the coming of rail. The overall message is clear: the present iconic landscape is a product of postglacial geomorphology and more than a thousand years of human tinkering.

What the extensification and intensification of agriculture has done in England in the past thirty or forty years is to bring about spectacular changes in water quality and biodiversity. Surface and groundwater quality in the British Isles has been degraded by human and agricultural wastes and by fertiliser usage. Very few rivers do not have one or more point-source sewage discharges in their catchments; phosphorus and nitrogen concentrations in most rivers are higher than acceptable standards.[18] It is now well documented that large areas of the British Isles are leaking phosphorus almost uncontrollably, owing to the large amount of animal wastes that have been disposed of on land for many years. The case of Northern Ireland is particularly well studied because of the long-term record of water quality in Lough Neagh, the water supply for Belfast.[19] As a result of eutrophication by rising phosphorus concentrations in the rivers feeding the Lough, the abundance of algal blooms in Lough Neagh is slowly but surely rising. Lough Neagh was cleaned up once before when the eutrophication problem was largely from point-source sewage inflows. Phosphorus removal turned that problem around. The problem now is much more insidious and difficult to address because of the huge phosphorus surpluses in surface soils in catchments all across the British Isles. Spreading manures on pastures leads to increased export of dissolved reactive phosphorus because of rapid surface flows after heavy rain.[20]

The mechanisation and the intensification of agriculture in the past 30 years or more have led to dramatic declines in the populations of British farmland birds since the 1970s. Many species have declined in abundance by more than 50% in 30 years (e.g. skylark, song thrush, bullfinch) and some have decreased by as much as 90% (partridge, corn bunting, tree sparrow). Remarkably, common British birds such as the starling and house sparrow are also now in decline.[21] Many farm birds appear to have declined in abundance because of the removal of habitat and through farming practices that have resulted in a lack of feed in winter fields in arable areas. Populations of raptors such as buzzards have increased as a result of restrictions on the use of pesticides; other species, such as the stone curlew, have responded well to targeted conservation measures. Simultaneously other populations, some of exotic introduced species like Canada geese, have also shown large increases so that the bird populations in England have changed markedly in living memory. What I see when I visit England now is not what I saw when bird-watching in Devon as a child.

In addition to reductions in biodiversity and water quality, other indicators of rural sustainability in England indicate that the socioeconomic basis of the rural society is also at risk. UK government surveys show that as many as 50% of farm enterprises are not financially viable. Total rural employment has declined in the past thirty years and many, if not most, farm enterprises are now supported by off-farm and other sources of income. Forty per cent of farms sold in the past few years have been sold to those with little or no interest in farming *per se*, and large areas of rural UK are highly dependent on tourism revenues. So although agriculture has made and still maintains the landscape, it is now tourism that is the primary source of income for sustainable rural communities.

The 2001 outbreak of foot and mouth disease

Foot and mouth disease (FMD) is a very highly contagious, but rarely fatal disease of cattle, sheep and pigs, which has been known for hundreds of years. The disease is caused by a virus, one of a number of types of picornavirus, which are widespread around the world. The virus is spread between infected animals very easily (particularly by pigs, which exhale many more virus particles than other animals)[22] and by other vectors such as animal products, milk, meat, swill and the wind. Although mortality is low except in young animals, morbidity is high; in many places where FMD is widespread and endemic the effects of the disease, largely lameness, reduced weight gain and reduced milk production, are an accepted part of farming economics. For many years the UK and most of Europe has had a policy of stamping out the disease by immediately culling infected animals so that a disease-free status has been maintained apart from occasional outbreaks. The UK outbreak was from a Pan-Asian type O strain of the virus, which had seemingly originated in India some ten years before.[23] FMD produces only mild clinical symptoms in sheep and goats and unfortunately this type O strain of the virus was practically silent in sheep, so that diagnosis was difficult and in many cases it was not detected until other animals (cattle and pigs) were infected by the sheep. The 2001 disease outbreak was the largest outbreak of the disease so far recorded anywhere in the world (at least in terms of the numbers of animals killed) and the total cost was more than £9 million.

The disease outbreak was focused around the wetter pastoral areas of NW England and SW Scotland, SW England and the Welsh Borders where livestock densities were highest. Other smaller outbreaks were scattered across the countryside. The virus apparently thrives in cool and moist conditions; conditions found in those parts of the UK in the early part of the year.

The outbreak of foot and mouth disease in 2001 revealed all kinds of changes in farming practices and shortcomings in policy and regulation in the UK. Major changes to the industry had been instituted over the previous few decades which predisposed the country to a major disease outbreak. Basically, neither the agribusiness industry nor the government agencies had realised the extent to which the complexity of the national livestock scene had increased. FMD was first diagnosed in pigs at an abattoir in Brentwood, Essex, on 19 February 2001. The disease spread very rapidly, so rapidly that the epidemic was out of control before the usual practice of culling both infected animals and their immediate contacts could become effective. (Indeed, the disease spread so rapidly that the usually accepted source, a small pig-rearing operation in Northumberland, may not in fact be the source, because infected animals appeared around this time in France and they had been shipped prior to this date from Wales.)[24] The structure of the European livestock market, perverse incentives and payments from the EU Common Agriculture Policy all distorted the market, encouraged long-range transport of animals to markets and to abattoirs, 'Bed and Breakfasting' of animals to ensure higher capitage payments, and various nefarious transfers of animals from country to country to collect higher price premiums and tax windfalls. All this meant that animals were rapidly moved around the country, often overnight, and that the disease was out of control before it was first diagnosed. It has been estimated that 24 000 potentially infected animals were moved before the UK government established exclusion zones and that there may have been as many as 100 infected sites by the time the presence of the disease was first confirmed.[25] It became apparent that infected animals were quickly moved through six markets in England and one in Wales as well as various dealers before restrictions on movement were put in place.[26] Infected animals were quickly found in Cumbria, Wales and Devon. What made matters worse was the fact that the numbers of cattle markets and abattoirs in England had been dropping rapidly in the previous decades because of economies of scale, the effects of market domination by the big supermarket chains and new EU health and animal welfare regulations. In 1940 there were 554 English livestock auction markets. By 1981 the number had fallen to 312 and by 1992 only 246 remained. By 1998 there were only 173 markets dealing in prime stock.[27] Animals were being moved longer and longer distances to market. So regulation and market structures, together with the trend towards intensification of agriculture leading to fewer, larger herds, meant that the situation was predisposed to higher infection rates within herds and more rapid spread of the disease.[28] Increased connectivity, market complexity and the practice of live exports led to a more rapid spread of the disease: a 'tipping point' was reached.[29]

Modelling of the epidemic also revealed a number of new factors.[30] First, as might now be expected, the modellers found that the regulatory agencies were underestimating the spatial transmission kernel: the relationship between the location of an infected property and the drop-off in probability of spread of the disease with distance. Indeed, it seems that the Ministry of Agriculture, Fisheries and Food (MAFF) underestimated the rate of spread of the disease by about a factor of two. The epidemic was travelling further and faster than expected and the landscape mosaic was also critical. The number of disaggregated land parcels on each farm was significantly correlated with the risk of FMD infection because of the requirement for greater movement of stock and farm equipment between parcels to work the land. Land disaggregation is high in Cumbria and low in Devon, so FMD infection rates were higher in Cumbria than in Devon and the epidemic was eradicated much sooner in Devon (31 May 2001) than in Cumbria (12 September 2001).[31] The modelling also showed that, because of the sheer scale of the outbreak, government agencies failed to succeed in the stated policy of culling the infected animals and 'stamping out' the disease within 24 h on infected properties and within 48 h on contiguous properties. This also led to the further spread of the disease.

What the outbreak of foot and mouth disease in 2001 suddenly revealed was that when large areas of the British Isles were placed under quarantine the losses were not primarily in agriculture but in tourism. After government compensation was paid to farmers for stock losses, the net loss to agriculture was of the order of £0.5 billion, whereas the financial losses in tourism were of the order of £5 bn – about £3 bn in direct costs and about £2 bn in indirect costs.[32] The sense of place turned out to be a shared space and the problem was not solely, or even primarily, an agricultural problem. As in other parts of the world, the terms of trade for livestock farming in counties like Cumbria has been falling for many years, and returns on capital were as low as 1%. In Cumbria the FMD outbreak caused a 60% fall in revenue from traditional farm enterprises, a 17% reduction in earnings from other more diversified activities and a 15% fall in salaries from off-farm employment.[33] The net result of traumatised communities and financial losses will take years to work out but there is evidence that rural farming communities in the affected areas will diversify into a wider range of activities in the coming years, including more sources of off-farm income, tourism, agri-environment schemes and other opportunities for rural development. In any event greater resilience and community capacity is the goal for these communities.

So the FMD outbreak is a case study in complexity, 'tipping points' and the unintended consequences of market forces and regulatory policy played out in a landscape that was the result of long-term historical tinkering. The ability to control the outbreak was partly determined by subtle local and historical land use patterns. Given that there was insufficient realisation of the overall situation and how the risk profile for FMD and other consequences was changing, one lesson to be learned must be that more complete and sophisticated risk management tools are required and these tools must be kept up to date. It is clear that the regulatory agencies were not sufficiently aware of the full picture in the industry and had not fully analysed the risks involved. Equally important is the fact that the industry clearly regarded the compensation in the event of a disease outbreak as a public good, so the risks were not internalised by the industry and the rural community. The FMD outbreak is a classic case study of how a sense of place can become 'misplaced' through encountering a 'tipping point' and how risks can slowly increase through external, even global, interactions to the point where catastrophic change ensues. It is also an excellent example of the interaction between process and pattern, of how the spatial pattern of land tenure and land use can influence the course of events and how institutional factors control responses. There is considerable resilience and conservatism in these communities, so many of the farmers who lived through the outbreak will pick up the pieces and return to past farming practices.[34] None the less the FMD outbreak will, in many cases, speed up diversification and increase the resilience of rural communities to future change.

What has arisen following the FMD outbreak is the establishment of a major interdisciplinary research programme – the Rural Economy and Land Use Programme (RELU) – to study the possibilities for innovative supply chains, new social and economic outcomes and a more sustainable land use pattern. This is precisely the kind of 'postnormal' science programme now being developed. It will place major drivers on the research community in the UK to work more effectively in teams, to focus on outcomes and to dovetail their research efforts more effectively into the rural community. As if this was not a big enough task, the promulgation by the European Commission of the Water Framework Directive – which directs member states to return their surface water quality to 'good' ecological condition – will also drive the science, policy and management communities to focus their efforts around innovative solutions to these landscape-scale problems.

Urban landscapes

In his book *Emergence* Steven Johnson uses cities as a classic example of self-organised, emergent systems.[35] Since the earliest towns and cities emerged in the Middle East they have been built from the 'bottom up' by people, and neighbourhoods have survived for thousands of years – often despite the best efforts of Princes, Lords of the Manor and city planners to impose more rational or utopian solutions! The literature on urban planning and design is enormous and it is not possible to do justice to it here. The point I want to make is that cities may be seen as complex adaptive systems, with city development follow-ing a hugely complex series of interactions between people, climate, geography, natural resources, trade routes, built infrastructure (physical capital, e.g. water supply, sanitation and transport services) and social and economic forces, includ-ing warfare. Cities are fluid, negotiated and highly complex spatial hybrids.[36] Johnson quotes examples of neighbourhoods that have survived for centuries while wars raged and the physical infrastructure of the surrounding city was rebuilt many times over. So cities are also deeply contingent and historically determined entities, which show properties of complex adaptive systems. Since the earliest towns and cities of Mesopotamia around the fourth millennium BC, cities have developed through a series of interactions between necessity and the semiotics of the built spaces and places. Cities and their architecture respond to social, economic and intellectual developments also. The semiotics of the planned, rational, modernist cities are being replaced by the more chaotic world of postmodern pastiche.[37]

Since the conceptualisation of the city as a self-organising system in the 1990s[38] much urban modelling has been done by using cellular automata and other algorithmic approaches.[39] The rules for urban planning and management are, of necessity, becoming more complex and integrative taking into account all forms of capital – natural, social, physical and financial – and their inter-actions in a spatially patterned mosaic.[40] This can be done by using 'top-down' approaches but is probably better done through 'bottom-up' agent-based and cellular automaton approaches. It has not gone unnoticed in the ecological lit-erature that, although cities are built environments that arise from human adap-tations to the natural environment, nevertheless their hierarchical and patchy structures and interactions in space and time closely mirror the 'patch dynam-ics' of natural systems.[41] The realisation that 'patch dynamics' fundamentally change an equilibrium view of the world has been a paradigm shift in both disciplines.

Evidence for cities as self-organising systems has come from the analysis of size distributions and the growth of cities over time. Much has been written about this aspect of urban development ever since Zipf[42] noted that statistical distributions of city size showed a particular form of the power law distribu-tion. Zipf's law states that a plot of city-size distributions takes the form of a linear power law plot in which the number of cities of size S or larger is inversely proportional to S, so that doubling the size of the city reduces the frequency of occurrence by one half. The existence of such a fractal scaling dis-tribution has generated a lot of work and many papers since it was first noted.[43] If this law holds across a wide range of city sizes then this distribution is scale-independent and therefore fractal. It could therefore be taken as evidence of some self-organised behaviour in the whole. Zipf proposed that this law arose from a hierarchy of time-minimising constraints. It has been proposed that Zipf's law is a special case of information theory in which these non-equilibrium, self-organising systems 'use' the external interactions with the larger (national or global) systems to control their internal order.[44] Others have proposed less complex explanations for the occurrence of the Zipf law, involving sampling at random intervals from a distribution of settlement sizes in which individual settlements may spawn new settlements at any time with equal probability, and where each obeys a stochastic version of simple exponential growth.[45] A similar model in which settlements disappeared when they shrank below a certain minimal size also rapidly converged on a Zipf law result.[46] Not all city size patterns follow the Zipf law precisely. As we might expect, some cities do show the impact of large-scale planning decisions. Regional data sets can show multi-modal patterns and, with data from structures within cities (e.g. roads, city blocks), also show other exponents and non-linearity.[47]

Our urban centres have huge ecological footprints, much greater than their present area. They draw resources from a large surrounding feeder area and from around the world.[48] In the design and construction of our urban areas we have used an almost universal set of signs and symbols – the semiotics of modernism and postmodernism[49] – so we have huge 'sunk costs' and investments in infrastructure, networks and constraints that are associated with particular technologies and design concepts. As we become more and more an urban society we are constrained culturally, visually and institutionally by our sense of place all around the world. In this respect they are the products of western modernism and are only sustainable with large subsidies of energy, materials and food. Although the fabric of many cities is ancient, much of our present urban infrastructure, especially sanitation and water supply infrastructure, comes to us (with a few embellishments) from the nineteenth century. Some of the basic ideas about water supply and sanitation infrastructure are Roman in origin; security of supply has been the major driver of water infrastructure for thousands of years. Much of that infrastructure is now in trouble because of environmental impacts.

Population growth and rapid urbanisation in the Third World has led to the unplanned growth of major conurbations in which many of the basic infrastructure investments were made in colonial times. In cities like Alexandria and Jakarta the sewage systems were constructed to cope with between 0.5 and 1.0 million people.[50] The populations now exceed 4 million and 10 million, respectively. Urban growth is leading to de-ruralisation of many regions and countries through the disparity in income and opportunity in rural and urban areas.[51] Promotion of investment in physical capital has led to underinvestment in human, social and natural capital and this has resulted in economic stagnation, social inequities and environmental destruction.[52]

Our sense of place requires updating and modifying, not least because the appreciation of complexity, self-organisation and network interactions is dramatically changing our view of the way the world works and how it might be better managed. The complexity of the interactions between all forms and values of capital is now being appreciated, as are the ways in which complex, adaptive and non-linear interactions can produce surprising and unplanned outcomes.

Overlapping mosaics and landscape function

What the example of the English landscape and urban development shows is that any one sense of place is, in fact, a set of overlapping values and decisions taken for contingent historical and often local reasons. Furthermore the resulting landscape is a set of overlapping scales of pattern and process:

- Scales of geology, climate and geomorphology, of soils, hydrology, bio-geography and ecology
- Scales of human settlement and agriculture, of enterprises and institutions of various kinds and of finance and capital
- Scales of governance and regulation, from village to nation
- Scales of transport and communication, both local, national and (in some cases) international

All this is wrapped up in the one sense of place, which we hold dear. Each of these sets of patterns and processes has its own intrinsic scales which, as we shall see, vary from the minute to the planetary. What we have done is to slap these patterns and processes over the top of one another without any real idea of what we are doing. To make matters worse we are changing the entire context through globalisation and subsidiarity even as we try to understand and manage the complexities of the interactions and the resulting outcomes. While there has been a recursive dialogue between ourselves and the landscape it has not been based on a sound understanding of both 'deep time' in the sense of the history of the place, and 'wide time' in the sense of the present operation of pattern and process, of system thinking.

NOTES

1. This is well discussed by G. Seddon. *Landprints: Reflections on Place and Landscape*. (Cambridge: Cambridge University Press, 1997).
2. Seddon, *Landprints*, p. xv. (See Note 1.)
3. D. Wayne. *Penshurst; the Semiotics of Place and the Poetics of History*. (Madison, WI: University of Wisconsin Press, 1984).
4. H. Godwin. *The History of the British Flora*, 2nd edn. (Cambridge: Cambridge University Press, 1975).
5. H. Godwin. *Fenland: its Ancient Past and Uncertain Future*. (Cambridge: Cambridge University Press, 1978).
6. See, for example, W. A. Watts. The Holocene vegetation of the Burren, Western Ireland, *Lake Sediments and Environmental History*, ed. E. Y. Haworth and J. W. G. Lund (Leicester: Leicester University Press, 1984), pp. 359–76.

7. F. Pryor. *Britain BC: Life in Britain and Ireland Before the Romans*. (London: HarperCollins, 2003).

8. W. G. Hoskins. *English Landscapes*. (London: BBC, 1973), pp. 5–6.

9. For an approachable account of British geology and the first map thereof, see S. Winchester. *The Map that Changed the World: William Smith and the Birth of Modern Geology*. (New York: HarperCollins, 2001).

10. See W. G. Hoskins. *The Making of the English Landscape*. (London: Book Club Associates, 1955), also W. G. Hoskins. *One Man's England*. (London: BBC, 1978).

11. J. Baudry, R. G. H. Bunce and F. Burel. Hedgerows: an international perspective on their origin, function and management. *Journal of Environmental Management*, **60** (2000), 7–22.

12. F. Burel and J. Baudry. Social, aesthetic and ecological aspects of hedgerows in rural landscapes as a framework for greenways. *Landscape and Urban Planning*, **33** (1995), 327–40.

13. A. Ouin and F. Burel. Influence of herbaceous elements on butterfly diversity in hedgerow agricultural landscapes. *Agriculture, Ecosystems and Environment*, **93** (2002), 45–53.

14. Hoskins, *English Landscapes*, p. 78. (See Note 8.)

15. R. H. G. Jongman. Homogenisation and fragmentation of the European landscape: ecological consequences and solution. *Landscape and Urban Planning*, **58** (2002), 211–21.

16. R. H. Foy and S. D. Lennox. Evidence for a delayed response of riverine phosphorus exports from increasing agricultural catchment pressures in the Lough Neagh catchment. *Limnology and Oceanography*, **51** (1, part 2) (2006), 655–63.

17. See for example the chapters on 'Roads and Tracks', by Robert Groves (pp. 182–203) and 'Railways' by Michael Evans (pp. 204–24) in *Dartmoor; a New Study*, ed. Crispin Gill, (Newton Abbot, Devon: David and Charles, Circa 1971).

18. See the maps of surface water quality posted annually on the website of the UK Environment Agency.

19. R. H. Foy and A. E. Bailey-Watts. Observations on the spatial and temporal variation in the phosphorus status of lakes in the British Isles. *Soil Use and Management*, **14** (1998), 131–38 (June 1998 supplement, Phosphorus, agriculture and water quality). Also S. I. Heaney *et al.* Impacts of agriculture on aquatic systems: lessons learnt and new unknowns in Northern Ireland. *Marine and Freshwater Research*, **52** (2001), 151–63. R. H. Foy, S. D. Lennox and C. E. Gibson. Changing perspectives on the importance of urban phosphorus inputs as the cause of nutrient enrichment in Lough Neagh. *The Science of the Total Environment*, **310** (2003), 87–90.

20. R. H. Foy and S. D. Lennox. Evidence for a delayed response of riverine phosphorus exports from increasing agricultural catchment pressures in the Lough Neagh catchment. *Limnology and Oceanography*, **51** (1, part 2) (2006), 655–63.

21. See the annual *State of the UK's Birds* reports posted annually on the website of the Royal Society for the Protection of Birds. Bird populations are particularly well documented in the UK because of a set of standard annual censuses that have been carried out since about 1970. Birds are also the iconic biodiversity in the English landscape and are watched by large numbers of amateur ornithologists.

22. C. Barclay. *Foot and mouth disease*. Research Paper 01/35, (London: Science and Environment Section, House of Commons Library, 27 March 2001).

23. G. Davies. The foot and mouth disease (FMD) epidemic in the United Kingdom 2001. *Comparative Immunology, Microbiology and Infectious Diseases*, **25** (2002), 331–43.

24. D. Campbell and R. Lee, *The foot and mouth outbreak 2001: lessons not yet learned*. 27 pp. D. Campbell, and R. Lee. '*Carnage by computer*': the blackboard economics of the 2001 foot and mouth epidemic. 54 pp. D. Campbell and R. Lee. *Culling by numbers: blackboard economics and foot and*

mouth disease control. 15 pp. Papers published by The ESRC Centre for Business Relationships, Accountability, Sustainability and Society, Cardiff University. See http://www.fmd.brass.cf. ac.uk.

25. Campbell and Lee, *Carnage by computer*, p. 12. (See Note 24.)

26. Davies, The foot and mouth disease (FMD) epidemic in the United Kingdom 2001, p. 332. (See Note 23.)

27. Quoted from the first paragraph of J. Wright *et al*. The effect of local livestock population changes on auction market viability – a spatial analysis. *Journal of Rural Studies*, **18** (2002), 477–83.

28. In the 1967 FMD outbreak in the UK, infection rates were dependent on herd size: less than 1% of herds of fewer than 10 cows were infected, whereas 29% of herds with over 80 cows became infected. Para 3.15 in *Infectious diseases of livestock*. (London: The Royal Society, 2002). Inquiry chaired by Sir Brian Follett.

29. M. Gladwell. *The Tipping Point*. (London: Abacus, 2000).

30. R. R. Kao. The role of mathematical modelling in the control of the 2001 FMD epidemic in the UK. *Trends in Microbiology*, **10** (2002), 279–86. N. M. Ferguson, C. A. Donnelly and R. M. Anderson. Transmission intensity and impact of control policies on the foot and mouth epidemic in Great Britain. *Nature*, **413** (2001), 542–8. M. J. Keeling *et al*. Dynamics of the 2001 foot and mouth epidemic: stochastic dispersal in a heterogeneous landscape. *Science*, **294** (2001), 813–17.

31. J. W. Wilesmith *et al*. Spatio-temporal epidemiology of foot-and-mouth disease in two counties of Great Britain in 2001. *Preventive Veterinary Medicine*, **61** (2003), 157–70.

32. A. Scott, M. Christie and P. Midmore. Impact of the 2001 foot-and-mouth disease outbreak in Britain: implications for rural studies. *Journal of Rural Studies*, **20** (2004), 1–14.

33. J. Franks *et al*. The impact of foot and mouth disease on farm businesses in Cumbria. *Land Use Policy*, **20** (2003), 159–68.

34. Ibid.

35. S. Johnson. *Emergence*. (London: Allen Lane, The Penguin Press, 2001).

36. W. Medd and S. Marvin. Complexity and spatiality: regions, networks and fluids in sustainable water management. In *Managing the Complex: Philosophy, Theory and Applications*. A volume in the series Managing the Complex. (London: The Information Age Publishing Inc., 2004), pp. 491–502.

37. F. Jameson. *Postmodernism, or, the Cultural Logic of Late Capitalism*. (London and New York: Verso, 1991).

38. See, for example, J. Portugali. Self-organizing cities. *Futures*, **29** (1997), 353–80. J. Portugali. Notions concerning the nature of world urbanization. In *Contemporary Perspectives on Urbanization*, ed. F. J. C. Amos, L. S. Bourne and J. Portugali. *Progress in Planning*, **46** (1996), 145–62.

39. See, for example, Y. Liu and S. R. Phinn. Modelling urban development with cellular automata incorporating fuzzy-set approaches. *Computers, Environment and Urban Systems*, **27** (2003), 637–58 and references therein.

40. J. Rotmans, M. van Asselt and P. Vellinga. An integrated planning tool for sustainable cities. *Environmental Impact Assessment Review*, **20** (2000), 265–76.

41. K. M. Bessey. Structure and dynamics in an urban landscape: towards a multiscale view. *Ecosystems*, **5** (2002), 360–75. J. Wu and O. L. Loucks. From balance of nature to hierarchical patch dynamics: a paradigm shift in ecology. *Quarterly Reviews of Biology*, **70** (1995), 439–66.

42. G. K. Zipf. *Human Behaviour and the Principle of Least Effort: an Introduction to Human Ecology.* (Cambridge, MA: Addison-Wesley, 1949).

43. G. R. Carroll. National city size distributions: what do we know after 67 years of research? *Progress in Human Geography*, **6** (1982), 1–43.

44. Y. Dover. A short account of a connection of power laws to the information entropy. *Physica, A***334** (2004), 591–9.

45. W. J. Reed. The Pareto, Zipf and other power laws. *Economics Letters*, **74** (2001), 15–19.

46. A. Blank and S. Solomon. Power laws in cities, populations, financial markets and internet sites (scaling in systems with a variable number of components). *Physica, A***287** (2000), 279–88.

47. R. Carvalho and A. Penn. Scaling and universality in the micro-structure of urban space. *Physica, A***332** (2004), 539–47. Y. M. Ioannides and H. G. Overman. Zipf's law for cities: an empirical examination. *Regional Science and Urban Economics*, **33** (2003), 127–37.

48. W. Rees and M. Wackernagel. Urban ecological footprints: why cities cannot be sustainable – and why they are a key to sustainability. *Environmental Impact Assessment Review*, **16** (1996), 223–48.

49. Jameson, *Postmodernism.* (See Note 37.)

50. O. Varis and L. Somlyody. Global urbanization and urban water: can sustainability be afforded? *Water Science and Technology*, **35** (1997), 21–32.

51. T. M. Aide and H. R. Grau. Globalisation, migration and Latin American ecosystems. *Science*, **305** (2004), 1915–16.

52. See, for example, R. Lopez. The policy roots of socioeconomic stagnation and environmental implosion: Latin America. *World Development*, **31** (2003), 259–80.

9 Catchment form and function

The interaction of landscapes and waterscapes: how micro-scale pattern and process can impact on macro-scale properties.

It has been known for some time that land use change has major impacts on catchment behaviour and hydrology, and on the water quality in rivers and estuaries.[1] Natural landscapes, dominated as they are by largely undisturbed ecosystems responding to biophysical constraints, are characterised by high biodiversity, high nutrient and water use efficiencies and what I have called MaxEnt and $MaxE_T$ solutions arising from SGC or HOT designs. These are the robust 'neutral domain' solutions arrived at by long periods of selection through trial and error. In forested systems it may take as long as a few hundred years for the ecosystem to fully develop in terms of the maturity of individual trees and the overall biodiversity; even then there is constant change as patches form and close through disturbance, death and reinvasion.[2] After major disturbance (fire, flood, windthrow, logging, etc.) ecosystems go through a rebuilding sequence of invasion and development. Overall productivity is high in early successional stages but at maturity there is a balance between production and decomposition. This aspect of ecology has been well studied since the early days of ecological investigation.[3] Given time for the development of ecosystems with high biodiversity and maturity (efficient energy and nutrient cycling) then it is clear that production through photosynthesis becomes largely balanced by decomposition and respiration and that internal nutrient recycling is very efficient so that nutrient exports are small. In what has become a classic study of forest biogeochemistry at Hubbard Brook in New Hampshire, Likens and Bormann[4] showed that any disturbance to the mature ecosystem (in this case clear felling) immediately altered the hydrology, erosion rates and nutrient export from catchments, rendering the streams flows more flashy and turbid. Subsequent recovery is slow and depends on the regrowth of the trees.

In terms of hydrology it can be said that in general 'trees are trees'. Other than differences between major growth forms (e.g. deciduous versus evergreen) species differences seem to matter less than overall changes in leaf area and standing crop. Using data from many catchments, the work of Holmes and Sinclair (and later that of Zhang and others)[5] showed that, as forests are cleared, and the evaporation rate and water use efficiency of the tree cover is eliminated, then stream flows increase. (Stream flows are very much determined by the balance of rainfall and evaporation from catchments.) Replanting and regrowth of catchments eventually replaces the standing crop of the trees and the associated leaf area, so that after about 25–40 years when the tree canopy is just lifting off the ground and the growth and evaporation rates of the trees are maximal then stream flows decrease by as much as 25%–60%.[6] In forestry operations in catchments it is usual to develop a mosaic of forest coups of varying age so that stream flows will be a function of time since the last forest harvest and the positions of patches of trees of various ages. In this way stream flows out of catchments that are logged may show complex variability over time scales of many decades to centuries. This has major implications for the aquatic life in the streams as well as for water yields for human use. There is much subtlety in the interaction between tree growth and other mechanisms for the retention and recycling of nutrients within ecosystems. Although stream water exports of nutrients from catchments decline after regrowth of the trees, even severe winters may be enough to cause exports to increase.[7] There is much complexity that we still do not understand.

Over postglacial scales of the order of 10 000 years (and these are the time scales that most European and North American ecologists are familiar with) soil fertility is largely determined by the weathering of cations and other nutrients from the underlying rock. Streams draining catchments in peri- and postglacial regions show changes in chemistry over time that are closely related to soil and ecosystem development because there is a close relationship between soil formation and water quality.[8] Postglacial soils are productive; the streams that drain them therefore tend to be rich in cations and nutrients. Over much longer time scales (>200 000 years) in humid tropical and subtropical regions, weathering products are washed from the soils and the ecosystems become increasingly dependent on atmospheric sources of anions and cations.[9] Rivers and streams draining old tropical and subtropical catchments therefore tend to be more dilute and, perhaps because of higher rates of denitrification in warmer soils and ground waters, relatively poor in nitrogen.

Although the ability of ecosystems to control and efficiently recycle the flows of energy and materials across the landscape is impressive (and indicates a large degree of biotic dominance over such processes) it is not perfect. Natural disturbances and climate variability, even climate change, are sufficient to compromise the effectiveness of the internal compensation and recycling mechanisms. Fire, for example, totally alters catchment water and nutrient balances for long periods until the vegetation regrows. The addition of fertilisers to partly cleared catch-ments with cropping leads to increased exports of nitrogen and phosphorus in streams. Human interference with the cycling of materials within the biosphere is now overriding the natural mechanisms: we have introduced major perturbations to the cycling of carbon, sulphur, nitrogen and other elements.[10] Carbon emissions are leading to an increase in carbon dioxide in the atmosphere; sulphur and nitrogen emissions and fertiliser use are causing acid rain, catchment exports of nutrients and enrichment of surface waters. In the global nitrogen cycle, annual emissions of nitrogen oxides from the burning of fossil fuels and the use of fertilisers now rival the natural rate of cycling of this ele-ment. In the late 1990s the effects of nitrogen fertiliser applications, fossil fuel burning and the growth of leguminous crops were estimated to deposit around 140 Tg of nitrogen[11] onto terrestrial landscapes each year, compared with esti-mates of the natural terrestrial nitrogen cycle at about 35 Tg N per year. We have therefore increased the rate of nitrogen cycling in global landscapes by a factor of four since before the agricultural and industrial revolutions. At local scales emissions may exceed the natural cycling rate by as much as an order of magnitude.[12] This increase in the rate of nitrogen cycling has contributed to the acidification of soils, lakes and rivers, caused loss of soil nutrients, increased the rate of movement of nitrogen from catchments to coastal waters and accelerated the loss of terrestrial and marine biodiversity.[13] A nitrogen deposition threshold of about 10–15 kg per hectare per year exists for many terrestrial and marine ecosystems. Above this threshold changes in species composition and ecological function can be expected. Many global 'hot spots' of biodiversity are particularly at risk from nitrogen deposition and acidification as a result of the developing industrialisation of the third world.[14]

As noted above, catchment hydrology changes when clearing occurs. Both runoff and groundwater recharge increase, so that groundwater recharge under agricultural crops or grazed pasture is much larger than that under forest. For example, rates of groundwater recharge and downstream transport of materi-als have increased dramatically since Western agriculture was introduced in Australia. This appears to be due to a reduction in the leaf area of the veg-etation and therefore a decrease in evapotranspiration.[15] Compared with that observed under native bush, groundwater recharge in Australia has increased by at least an order of magnitude, and erosion and sediment transport to coastal waters have increased by at least one to two orders of magnitude.[16] As I argued earlier, the disturbance to the 'green' water flux by land use change rivals the entire 'blue' water fluxes in rivers at continental scales. We have almost totally neglected the role of the biosphere in the controls on 'green' water flows and the role we have played in altering those through global land use change and increases in atmospheric CO_2. We have altered the global hydrological balance through industrialisation, land use change, agriculture, habitat fragmentation and reductions in biodiversity. After accounting for land use and vegetation changes, deforestation and climate change, Gedney et al. were still able to iden-tify a direct CO_2 effect on runoff.[17]

Conversion of land use to agriculture or grazing also commonly results in soil erosion and gullying and increased downstream transport of nutrients and suspended particulate material.[18] This is widely documented and known to be a general phenomenon.[19] A survey of data from lakes around the world by Kira shows that as forests are cleared and the area of farmland in the drainage basins of lakes increases then suspended solids concentrations in the water increase.

The palaeolimnological record recovered from sediment cores in lakes shows that all around the world the development of land clearing and agriculture over the past few hundred years has had major impacts on the nutrient status and ecology of lakes. Increased turbidity, nutrient enrichment and algal blooms are now frequently encountered. A developing sense of place has altered the nutrient status of lakes in catchments. In addition, as populations in the catchments increase so do the concentrations of total nitrogen and phosphorus in the water.[20] Clearing of native vegetation and conversion of land use to agriculture has also resulted in higher mobility of major ions (Cl^-, SO_4^{2-}, Na^+, K^+, Ca^{2+}) and salinisation of soils and catchments in many arid and subtropical environments: loss of biodiversity and function ensures that water moves more quickly and that major elements are less tightly held. These effects are now well documented and are widespread in Australia.[21]

There is now good evidence for a close coupling between the state of the terrestrial ecosystems and water quality.[22] Land use, soil conditions and the state of ecosystem development are reflected in the water quality of streams draining catchments. Likens and Bormann showed many years ago that nutrient and cation exports increased dramatically in clear-felled catchments.[23] Exports from forested catchments are dominated by organic forms of carbon, nitrogen and phosphorus.[24] Around the world nutrient exports from agricultural and deforested catchments have increased with greater delivery of C, N and P to coastal waters.[25] The overall ratio of C, N and P discharged from catchments is now in roughly Redfield proportions (106 C : 15 N : 1 P by atoms); despite large variations in flow, the average ratio is quite stable. This is indicative of the fact that washout of nutrients from decay and decomposition in the soil is a significant source of nutrients and cations.[26] Microbial processes in soils determine the stoichiometry of exports. The metabolism of rivers and lakes is subsidised by imports of organic carbon from their catchments, so that most oligotrophic rivers and lakes are net heterotrophic and release carbon dioxide to the atmosphere.[27] Only productive nutrient-enriched lakes and rivers act as carbon sinks. Thus exports of dissolved organic carbon (DOC) and nutrients from soils act as important links between land and water.

Concentrations of nitrate and ammonia are usually small in rivers draining forested catchments.[28] This is a common observation worldwide. The explanation for this lies in the close coupling of root uptake and microbial cycling of N in forest soils.[29] In agricultural soils, reduction in biodiversity and the addition of fertiliser leads to an uncoupling of microbial recycling and plant uptake. Soil nitrate and ammonia concentrations increase in fragmented and agricultural ecosystems and washout to rivers becomes greater. Nitrogen may be flushed out of soils by fluctuating water tables and soil moisture levels.[30] One certain influence on N exports is the density of cattle and sheep in the catchment. The recycling of C, N and P in terrestrial and freshwater ecosystems is dependent on the abundance and size of the dominant producers and consumers in the ecosystems.[31]

The observed relationships between catchment clearing and exports of nutrients and major ions are decidedly non-linear. All the available observations indicate that the export of nutrients and major ions remains low as long as less than about 50% of the catchment is cleared of native forest.[32] Once the clearing exceeds 50% of the catchment, horizontal and vertical movement of water through and across the landscape increases sharply and nutrient exports increase exponentially. This is consistent with information coming from percolation models of reaction–diffusion relations in patchy landscapes and waterscapes, where 'hot spots' of activity are linked by biological and physical processes. In addition to increased loads of total N and P (TN and TP) sourced from cleared and agricultural land, the forms of N and P are changed so as to also proportionally increase the loads of available forms of dissolved inorganic N and P (DIN and DIP), thus rendering them more biologically available.[33] This appears to be because of a change from predominantly fungal decomposition under trees and forest cover to dominance by bacteria under crops. The rates of turnover of nitrogen and phosphorus are controlled by bacterial metabolism and rates of decomposition appear to be much higher in cleared land.

Conversion of land use to urban development drastically alters the hydrology and nutrient export characteristics of catchments. First, the construction of impervious surfaces (roofs, driveways, pavements and roads) causes greatly increased runoff. Whereas soils in catchments take time to wet up after rain (as much as 25–50 mm of rain may need to fall before runoff occurs from a dry vegetated catchment), roofs and roads shed water almost instantly so that storm runoff from urban areas occurs quickly and in large volumes. Indeed, calculations of the water balance of cities show that they are net exporters of water,[34] but the storm flows are usually regarded as a nuisance to be shed as quickly as possible rather than as a resource. Similar observations have been made in urban catchments compared to more vegetated catchments: exports of TN and TP rise exponentially with increasing population density, and as the exports increase more and more of the TN and TP exports are in available forms.[35] Thus urban areas shed large volumes of water rapidly after rain. The runoff is usually contaminated with nutrients, pathogens from sewer overflows, and toxic substances washed off from roads and industrial areas. The biogeochemistry of urban areas is significantly different from that of rural areas.[36]

Spatial patterns, small-scale patch dynamics and macroscopic catchment function

Runoff from catchments is never uniform. Water runs first off impervious and saturated regions while soaking into vegetated areas with good soil structure. Quick flows are surface flows; inter-flows and base flows come later through infiltration and interaction with the shallow and deeper ground waters. Pathways of surface and inter- and base flows differ and are spatially and temporally disjunct; indeed, the pathways that connect the catchment to the stream channel may be narrow and very specific. Each catchment has a specific detail of place, with some regions of the catchment rapidly and completely connected to the channel and others more or less totally isolated except under extreme rainfall conditions. This uniqueness of place makes it difficult to model and predict precisely what will happen in each case when land uses are changed.[37]

Land use change, from native woodland ecosystems to crops or pastoral systems, changes many aspects of the small-scale spatial patterning and patchiness of landscapes. Ludwig et al.[38] gave an excellent example of the importance of species-specific spatial patterning in arid zone landscapes. The entire functioning of these landscapes depends on the spatial patterns created idiosyncratically by the dominant species. The dominant open woodland species of the Australian arid zone (e.g. tussock grasses and mulga, Acacia aneura) are highly patterned in unmodified bush so that runoff and run-on zones are separated. Infiltration is highest under the mulga, where the deep roots create networks of cracks and fissures in the soil which are called macropores. Clearing and ploughing or trampling destroys these macropore networks, rapidly decreasing the rate of infiltration of water and increasing runoff.[39] Land use change at large scales alters biodiversity through habitat fragmentation, but it also changes the small-scale patterning and functioning of landscapes.

It has recently been discovered that one of the ways in which plants cope with small-scale spatial and temporal patchiness in the supply of nutrients in soils is through differences in root architecture. Highly branched (dichotomous) root systems have quite different nutrient uptake characteristics from root systems with a more sparsely branched (herringbone) pattern. Nutrient uptake efficiencies depend on the spatial and temporal patchiness of the resource in the soil – the transitory nature of the resource – as well as the root architecture itself.[40] So growth strategies and the performance of the plants respond to the leaching environment of water and nutrient movement around the roots. Macrofauna in the soil (moles, earthworms) create preferential flow pathways in temperate soils. Other dominant types of species in tropical landscapes, such as termites, also create macropores and increase infiltration.

Land clearing and the removal of deep-rooted perennials have been shown to commonly lead to reduced infiltration and increased runoff. Deep-rooted perennials also create macropores and preferential flow pathways through cracks and old root channels that penetrate deep into the soil, thereby connecting surface flows, interflows and shallow groundwaters. Forested and woodland catchments have higher infiltration rates than cleared catchments so that surface runoff and sheet flow are greater after clearing. Fire regimes also influence runoff characteristics. There is a tendency for cleared catchments to have more imper-meable areas and higher water tables (because of increased recharge) so that they have larger areas that are quickly wetted up during rain. Even depressions in forest catchments were relatively permeable so that runoff was delayed and reduced in magnitude. Sources of increased nutrient loads to rivers are spatially distinct; the importance of saturated areas in catchments is well known because they lead to increased surface flows and higher runoff.[41]

Macropores have been shown to be very important in providing preferential flow pathways for infiltration and through-flow, thus connecting soil processes and nutrients to water quality in receiving waters. Infiltration is higher and deep drainage more rapid in soils with greater numbers of macropores, and the numbers of macropores decrease under tillage.[42] There are numerous literature accounts of the effect of macropores in ensuring rapid and effective connection between soil chemistry and water quality.[43] Large differences in the water qual-ity of streams can be observed, depending on whether the water came from fast overland flow pathways or slower, shallow groundwater influences.[44] The combi-nation of geomorphology, soil and vegetation development leads to patchiness in the hydrological and biogeochemical properties of catchments. Catchments are not homogeneous; instead the connectivity between the land and the water is uneven, with 'hot spots' contributing disproportionate amounts of sediment and nutrients to the river. These 'critical source areas' or 'hydro-chemical response units' are the areas from which material is preferentially sourced.[45] Critical source areas depend on slope, soil characteristics, vegetation type and proximity to the stream. In rainforest systems the rapid surface flows tend to be more dilute in nutrients than the slower pathways that are connected to shallow perched water tables.[46] In urban and agricultural catchments, however, the more rapid pulses of surface sheet flows are usually more concentrated than some of the slower base flow components because they contain eroded materials, various pol-lutants and higher concentrations of fertilisers and animal wastes. Areas that preferentially wet up after rain may be important sources of quick flows to the channel. These areas may be important regions for investment and management when catchment remediation programmes are established. The fact that there are numerous occasions when regional remediation strategies do not lead to larger-scale benefits is a clear indication that we have not identified the critical source areas in all cases.

Catchments as fractal generators

Only in recent years have we begun to realise that the connection between catchment land use, hydrology and water quality is much more complex than we thought. Although there is an intimate connection between land use and water quality, new work shows that these systems are highly heterogeneous at very small scales, a finding that has fundamental importance for our ability to model and predict the outcomes of our actions. So what is the observational basis for this statement? Studies in the Plynlimon catchment in Wales by Colin Neal and his co-workers have been going on for more than 30 years. The data reveal a 'highly heterogeneous system that barely conforms with current understanding of hydrology'.[47] In 2000, Kirchner *et al.* studied detailed time series of chloride in rainfall and stream flows at Plynlimon and showed that although the rainfall and chloride series were 'white noise' (i.e. they exhibited equal amounts of variability across all frequencies analysed) the distribution of variability of the chloride signal in the stream scaled as $1/f$ (i.e. the variability was proportional to wavelength) up to a scale of a few months.[48] So the travel time distribution of the chloride coming out of the catchment showed fractal properties. Further analyses of these data have used spectral analysis techniques to describe the retardation of chloride in the catchment as it flows through the highly heterogeneous flow pathways in the soil.[49] The hydrology of the Plynlimon catchment has a few paradoxical properties,[50] such as the apparently rapid mobilisation of 'old' water from storage in the soil after rain (thus producing the damped response of the chloride signal in the stream compared with that of the rainfall) and also the variable chemistry of the 'old' water (i.e. not all 'old' water is the same, so it must come from different places by different routes). Kirchner called for a search for a unified theory of catchment hydrology and geochemistry which would resolve such paradoxes but the explanation probably lies much more in the uniqueness of place and in detailed interactions over time between catchment wetting and drying and between surface and ground waters as they discharge to the stream.[51] It is clear that there are a series of processes at work here, including the connection of 'hot spots' in the catchment soils and groundwater to the stream by a fractal distribution of flow pathways. Once again we see that the macroscopic properties of the catchment are determined by processes that run across a range of scales and produce outputs that are quite different from the inputs.

NOTES

1. See, for example, G. P. Harris. Biogeochemistry of nitrogen and phosphorus in Australian catchments, rivers and estuaries: effects of land use and flow regulation and comparisons with global patterns. *Marine and Freshwater Research*, **52** (2001), 139–49. G. P. Harris. *A nutrient dynamics model for Australian waterways – Land use, catchment biogeochemistry and water quality in Australian rivers.* Technical report for Commonwealth Department of Environment and Heritage, State of Environment Reporting Group Canberra, 2002. See http://www.ea.gov.au/soe/techpapers/nutrient-dynamics/index.html.
2. This can now be studied by computer models of forest growth and development, such as SORTIE, which take into account the interactions of individual tree growth, patch dynamics and the overall species composition. See, for example, D. K. Coates *et al.* Use of a spatially

explicit individual-tree model (SORTIE/BC) to explore the implications of patchiness in structurally complex forests. *Forest Ecology and Management*, **186** (2003), 297–310.

3. See, for example, chapter, 9 in E. P. Odum. *Fundamentals of Ecology*, 3rd edn. (Philadelphia, PA: Saunders and Co., 1971). The canonical old field succession is not perhaps the best example of ecosystem development because it does begin with a fully developed soil matrix and a resident seed bank; nevertheless the developmental sequence after disturbance of woodland is well documented.

4. G. E. Likens and F. H. Bormann. *Biogeochemistry of a Forested Ecosystem*, 2nd edn. (New York: Springer-Verlag, 1995).

5. L. Zhang, W. R. Dawes and G. R. Walker. *Predicting the effect of vegetation changes on catchment average water balance*. Technical Report 9/99 (Melbourne, Cooperative Research Centre for Catchment Hydrology, 1999). L. Zhang, W. R. Dawes and G. R. Walker. Response of mean annual evapotranspiration to vegetation changes at catchment scale. *Water Resources Research*, **37** (2001), 701–8.

6. R. B. Jackson *et al*. Trading water for carbon with biological carbon sequestration. *Science*, **310** (2005), 1944–7.

7. G. E. Likens. Ecosystems; energetics and biogeochemistry. In *A New Century of Biology*, ed. W. J. Kress and G. W. Barrett. (Washington, DC: Smithsonian Institution Press, 2001), pp. 53–88.

8. D. R. Engstrom *et al*. Chemical and biological trends during lake evolution in recently deglaciated terrain. *Nature*, **408** (2000), 161–6.

9. O. A. Chadwick *et al*. Changing sources of nutrients during four million years of ecosystem development. *Nature*, **397** (1999), 491–7.

10. The anthropogenic impact on the global cycles of the major elements has been well described by Vaclav Smil. *Cycles of Life: Civilization and the Biosphere*. (New York: Scientific American Library, 1997).

11. A teragram (Tg) is 10^{12} grams or one million metric tonnes.

12. P. M. Vitousek *et al*. Human alteration of the global nitrogen cycle: sources and consequences. *Ecological Applications*, **7** (1997), 737–50. Also P. M. Vitousek *et al*. *Human Alteration of the Global Nitrogen Cycle: Causes and Consequences*. Issues in Ecology 1. (Washington DC: Ecological Society of America, Spring 1997.)

13. R. W. Howarth *et al*. Regional nitrogen budgets and riverine N & P fluxes for the drainages to the North Atlantic Ocean: natural and human influences. *Biogeochemistry*, **35** (1996), 75–139.

14. G. K. Phoenix *et al*. Atmospheric nitrogen deposition in world biodiversity hotspots: the need for a greater global perspective in assessing N deposition impacts. *Global Change Biology*, **12** (2006), 470–6.

15. L. Zhang *et al*. *Recharge estimations in the Liverpool Plains (NSW) for input into groundwater models*. Technical Report 10/97. (Canberra: CSIRO land and Water, 1997).

16. R. J. Wasson, L. J. Olive and C. J. Rosewell. Rates of erosion and sediment transport in Australia. *International Association of Hydrological Sciences*, Publication **236** (1996), 139–48.

17. N. Gedney *et al*. Detection of a direct carbon dioxide effect in continental runoff records. *Nature*, **439** (2006), 835–8. D. Matthews. The water cycle freshens up. *Nature*, **439** (2006), 793–4.

18. G. P. Harris. Biogeochemistry of nitrogen and phosphorus in Australian catchments, rivers and estuaries: effects of land use and flow regulation and comparisons with global patterns. *Marine and Freshwater Research*, **52** (2001), 139–49. I. P. Prosser *et al*. Large scale patterns of erosion and sediment transport in river networks, with examples from Australia. *Marine and Freshwater Research*, **52** (2001), 81–99.

19. N. F. Caraco. Influence of human populations on P transfers to aquatic systems: a regional scale study using large rivers. In *Phosphorus in the Global Environment*, SCOPE 54, ed. H. Tiessen. (Chichester: John Wiley and Sons, 1995), pp. 235–44. N. Caraco and J. J. Cole. Regional export of C, N, P and sediment: what river data tell us about key controlling variables. In *Integrating Hydrology, Ecosystem Dynamics and Biogeochemistry in Complex Landscapes*, ed. J. D. Tenhunen and P. Kabat. (New York: John Wiley and Sons, 1999), pp. 239–53. N. F. Caraco and J. J. Cole. Human influence on nitrogen export: a comparison of mesic and xeric catchments. *Marine and Freshwater Research*, **52** (2001), 119–25.

20. T. Kira. (1991) State of the environments of world lakes – from the survey of ILEC/UNEP. In *Proceedings of the Symposium on Water Resources Management*. (Otsu, Japan: UNEP and ILEC, Nov 1991), pp. 48–54.

21. I. D. Jolly *et al.* Historical stream salinity trends and catchment salt balances in the Murray-Darling Basin, Australia. *Marine and Freshwater Research*, **52** (2001), 53–63.

22. D. R. Engstrom *et al.* Chemical and biological trends during lake evolution in recently deglaciated terrain. *Nature*, **408** (2000), 161–6.

23. G. E. Likens and F. H. Bormann. Linkages between terrestrial and aquatic ecosystems. *Bioscience*, **24** (1974), 447–56. G. E. Likens and F. H. Bormann. *Biogeochemistry of a Forested Ecosystem*. (New York: Springer, 1995).

24. S. S. Perakis and L. O. Hedin. Nitrogen loss from unpolluted South American forests mainly via dissolved organic compounds. *Nature*, **415** (2002), 416–19.

25. D. Justic *et al.* Changes in the nutrient structure of river dominated waters: stoichiometric nutrient balance and is consequences. *Estuarine Coastal and Shelf Science*, **40** (1995), 339–56.

26. D. Markewitz *et al.* Control of stream cation concentrations in stream waters by surface soil processes in an Amazonian watershed. *Nature*, **410** (2001), 802–5.

27. P. A. del Giorgio and R. H. Peters. Balance between phytoplankton production and plankton respiration in lakes. *Canadian Journal of Fisheries and Aquatic Science*, **50** (1993), 282–9. P. A. del Giorgio and R. H. Peters. Patterns in planktonic P:R ratios in lakes: influence of lake trophy and dissolved organic carbon. *Limnology and Oceanography*, **39** (1994), 772–87.

28. D. W. Flinn, L. J. Bren and P. Hopmans. Soluble nutrient inputs from rain and outputs in stream water from small forested catchments. *Australian Forestry*, **42** (1979), 39–49.

29. S. S. Perakis and L. O. Hedin. Fluxes and fates of nitrogen in soil of an unpolluted old-growth temperate forest, Southern Chile. *Ecology*, **82** (2001), 2245–60.

30. I. F. Creed *et al.* Regulation of nitrate-N release from temperate forests: a test of the N flushing hypothesis. *Water Resources Research*, **32** (1996), 3337–54. I. F. Creed and L. E. Band. Export of nitrogen from catchments within a temperate forest – evidence for a unifying mechanism regulated by variable source area dynamics. *Water Resources Research*, **34** (1998), 3105–20.

31. J. J. Elser *et al.* Organism size, life history and N:P stoichiometry. *BioScience*, **46** (1996), 674–84. J. J. Elser *et al.* Nutritional constraints in terrestrial and freshwater food webs. *Nature*, **408** (2000), 578–80. J. J. Elser and J. Urabe. The stoichiometry of consumer-driven nutrient recycling: theory, observations and consequences. *Ecology*, **80** (1999), 735–51.

32. G. Bott. (1993) *Relationships between the extent of conventional broad-scale agriculture and stream phosphorus concentration and phosphorus export in south-west Western Australia*. Office of Catchment Management, Perth, Western Australia, Discussion paper No. 2, March 1993, 22pp. B. Eyre, P. Pepperell and P. Davies. Budgets for Australian estuarine systems: Queensland and New South Wales tropical and subtropical systems. In *Australasian Estuarine*

Systems: Carbon, Nitrogen and Phosphorus Fluxes, ed. S. V. Smith and C. J. Crossland. LOICZ Reports and Studies, 12. (Texel, The Netherlands: LOICZ IPO, 1999), pp. 9–17.

33. N. F. Caraco and J. J. Cole. Human influence on nitrogen export: a comparison of mesic and xeric catchments. *Marine and Freshwater Research*, **52** (2001), 119–25.

34. V. G. Mitchell, T. A. McMahon and R. G. Mein. Components of the total water balance of an urban catchment. *Environmental Management*, **32** (2003), 735–46.

35. See, for example, C. Ferguson, J. Long and M. Simeoni. *Stormwater Monitoring Project, 1994 Annual Report*. Report 95/49. (Sydney: Australian Water Technologies, 1995). M. Simeoni *et al.* *Stormwater Monitoring Report, 1993 Annual Report*. Report 94/93. (Sydney: Australian Water Technologies, 1994).

36. J. P. Kaye *et al.* A distinct urban biogeochemistry? *Trends in Ecology and Evolution*, **21** (2006), 192–9.

37. K. J. Beven. Uniqueness of place and process representations in hydrological modelling. *Hydrology and Earth System Sciences*, **4** (2000), 203–13.

38. J. A. Ludwig, D. J. Tongway and S. G. Marsden. Stripes, bands or stipples: modelling the influence of three landscape banding patterns on resource capture and productivity in semi-arid woodlands, Australia. *Catena*, **37** (1999), 257–73. J. A. Ludwig *et al.* Vegetation patches and runoff-erosion as interacting ecohydrological processes in semi-arid landscapes. *Ecology*, **86** (2005), 288–97.

39. R. S. B. Greene. Soil physical properties in three geomorphic zones in a semi-arid mulga woodland. *Australian Journal of Soil Research*, **30** (1992), 55–69.

40. V. Dunbabin, Z. Rengel and A. J. Diggle. Simulating form and function of root systems: efficiency of nitrate uptake is dependent on root system architecture and the spatial and temporal variability of nitrate supply. *Functional Ecology*, **18** (2004), 204–11. V. Dunbabin, A. Diggle and Z. Rengel. Is there an optimal root architecture for nitrate capture in leaching environments? *Plant, Cell and Environment*, **26** (2003), 835–44.

41. H. B. Pionke, W. J. Gburek and A. N. Sharpley. Critical source area controls on water quality in an agricultural watershed located in the Chesapeake Basin. *Ecological Engineering*, **14** (2000), 325–35.

42. D. McGarry, B. J. Bridge and B. J. Radford. Contrasting soil physical properties after zero and traditional tillage of an alluvial soil in the semi-arid tropics. *Soil and Tillage Research*, **53** (2000), 105–15.

43. J. W. Cox *et al.* Mobility of phosphorus through intact soil cores collected from the Adelaide Hills, South Australia. *Australian Journal of Soil Research*, **38** (2000), 973–90. A. L. Heathwaite and R. M. Dils. Characterising phosphorus loss in surface and subsurface hydrological pathways. *Science of the Total Environment*, **251** (2000), 523–38. M. F. Pampolino, T. Urushiyama and R. Hatano. Detection of nitrate leaching through bypass flow using pan lysimeter, suction cup and resin capsule. *Soil Science and Plant Nutrition*, **46** (2000), 703–11.

44. L. A., McKergow *et al.* Before and after riparian management: sediment and nutrient exports from a small agricultural catchment, Western Australia. *Journal of Hydrology*, **270** (2003), 253–72.

45. W.-A. Flugel. Combining GIS with regional hydrological modelling using hydrological response units (HRUs): an application from Germany. *Mathematics and Computers in Simulation*, **43** (1997), 297–304. A. L. Heathwaite, P. F. Quinn and C. J. M. Hewett. Modelling and managing critical source areas of diffuse pollution from agricultural land using flow connectivity simulation. *Journal of Hydrology*, **304** (2005), 446–61.

46. H. Elsenbeer, A. West and M. Bonell. Hydrologic pathways and storm flow hydrochemistry at South Creek, north-east Queensland. *Journal of Hydrology*, **162** (1994), 1–21.
47. C. Neal. A view of water quality from the Plynlimon watershed. *Hydrology and Earth System Sciences*, **1** (1997), 743–53.
48. J. W. Kirchner, X. Feng and C. Neal. Fractal stream chemistry and its implications for contaminant transport in catchments. *Nature*, **403** (2000), 524–7.
49. J. W. Kirchner, X. Feng and C. Neal. Catchment-scale advection and dispersal as a mechanism for fractal scaling in stream tracer concentrations. *Journal of Hydrology*, **254** (2001), 82–101. X. Feng, J. W. Kirchner and C. Neal. Measuring catchment-scale retardation using spectral analysis of reactive and passive tracer time series. *Journal of Hydrology*, **292** (2004), 296–307.
50. J. W. Kirchner. A double paradox in catchment hydrology and geochemistry. *Hydrological Processes*, **17** (2003), 871–4.
51. K. Bishop *et al.* Resolving the double paradox of rapidly mobilized old water with highly variable responses in runoff chemistry. *Hydrological Processes*, **18** (2004), 185–9.

10   Catchment loads: ecosystem impacts

Human interference in catchment and the ecosystem responses: titrating ecosystems with nutrients. Non-linear responses and thresholds.

Despite the fractal properties of the linkages between catchments and rivers, the tendency in almost all the work on land use and nutrient loads to receiving waters has been to use large-scale and long-term averages of water quality data collected in rivers and streams to assess downstream impacts. This is partly because of two fundamental biases and misconceptions: first, that the usual regime of weekly or more infrequent sampling is sufficient, and second, that the observed variability in the data is just noise, which can be averaged and dealt with statistically. Recent analysis of high-frequency data from rivers, lakes and coastal waters (and by high-frequency I mean data collected daily or even more frequently than that – down to minutes in some cases) indicates that both these basic assumptions are false.[1] The data are not just 'noisy', there is information there, and weekly or less frequent sampling does not resolve the true scales of pattern and process. In short, catchments have fractal flow paths and these produce fractal distributions of patches of water flowing down rivers and into receiving waters. The species that characterise both terrestrial and aquatic ecosystems interact to both produce and exploit these fractal patterns; they are part and parcel of the reaction–diffusion relationships between organisms at small scales. When these dynamics are coupled with the internal dynamics of SGC in the aquatic ecosystems themselves the result is some very complex dynamics, which can be seen in the data. Despite the limitations of the data and the way in which they are dealt with statistically there are, nevertheless, some well-known examples of whole-ecosystem responses to anthropogenic change.

Titrating ecosystems with nutrients: ecosystem responses

The process of nutrient enrichment of rivers, lakes and coastal waters, otherwise known as eutrophication, has been well studied since the pioneering work of Vollenweider in the Organization for Economic Cooperation and Development (OECD) studies of the 1960s.[2] What Vollenweider set out to do was not to study the response of a particular lake to nutrient addition in detail (increased phosphorus loadings from effluent discharge was a particular problem at the time), but rather to study the effects of such loadings across a large number of lakes to see if there were generic empirical responses. What he found was that there were indeed such generic empirical relations between phosphorus loads and a large number of ecosystem components. When nutrients are added to lakes a whole series of changes take place which can be largely explained by changes to the nutrient cycling regimes within the plankton community at the bottom of the food chain, followed by repercussions up the chain to influence fish and other animal communities.[3] What Vollenweider invented was a form of empirical ecology in which correlations and regressions between various high-level ecosystem parameters (biomass at particular trophic levels, size distributions, light penetration underwater, sediment oxygen concentrations, etc.) were used as measures of system state that could be related to management actions. Phosphorus loads to lakes were reduced by both catchment management and improved waste water treatment (P removal) using Vollenweider's regression as a guide and to set target loads. This approach was highly successful although it was criticised at the time as being short on specific explanations for the precise causes, particularly by those steeped in the limnological tradition of detailed work on specific taxonomic groups. Nevertheless the approach was rapidly and widely adopted by managers and was the basis of major successes in controlling the eutrophication of lakes and the improvement of surface water quality throughout the world.

What Vollenweider recognised from the outset was that any prediction of the response of the lake or water body to an alteration in the nutrient load would have to be a statistical statement. As we might expect, an ensemble of lakes exhibits a range of responses to a particular level of nutrient loading because of a whole series of factors: morphometry, freshwater inflows, flushing time, species composition, climate forcing, contingent history and internal dynamics. So for any given nutrient load the only statement that could be made was that there was a probability that the lake fell into a given category and that changing the load increased or decreased the risk of algal blooms occurring by a given amount. High-level ecological predictions (e.g. probability of some concentration of total algal biomass in surface waters) could be made with more confidence than more detailed predictions (e.g. precisely which species of algae would form the blooms). Despite this limitation, water quality managers around the world found the relationships easy to use.

Aquatic ecosystems loaded with nutrients display a form of 'envelope dynamics' which is analogous to an 'extremal' MaxEnt state. This can be regarded as a kind of 'space filling' behaviour arising from high biodiversity and self-organisation across and between trophic levels, which, I argue, arises from SGC and approaches to upper-bound nutrient use efficiencies (a kind of maximal nutrient use efficiency akin to the maximal water use efficiencies discussed earlier). Phytoplankton do display both log-normal and power law distributions characteristic of space filling and patchily distributed populations. At low nutrient loads the biomass of plankton algae in the water is limited by the available stock of nutrients. Nutrient turnover rates can be very high in surface waters, so growth, grazing and recycling rates may be high even though the biomass is low. As the stock of nutrients is increased then the biomass of algae increases and the size distribution changes to larger, slower-growing species that are lost more through sedimentation than by grazing. This has the effect of throwing more and more of the production down to the sediments, eventually leading to rapid decomposition and anoxia. Both in the water column and in the sediment the role of micro-scale patchiness and microbial activity is critical to the overall system function. The biomass of algae rises until most of the available light in the water column is absorbed by photosynthetic pigments and the algal community becomes light-limited. Through these mechanisms – driven largely by physiological processes and subsequent food chain interactions – the overall ecosystem 'envelope' is filled by a diverse range of species, functional groups and food chain components. There is high biodiversity in the plankton of both lakes and the oceans and it seems that the small-scale, multi-fractal space/time patchiness of these systems discussed above is the reason for the very high biodiversity and for the space-filling, 'envelope dynamics'. Even though there is less predictability than for the overall biomass of algae, the particular species of plankton that occurs in any given lake and season is, to a degree, predictable on the basis of a relatively small number of driving parameters: nutrient concentrations and loads, light climate, temperature, mixing, etc. Reynolds has done more than most to provide a predictive framework in this regard.[4]

There have been two major areas of controversy in this field and they have both been about the relative strengths of external drivers on ecosystem responses (nutrient loads, climate) versus internal ecosystem dynamics (competitive interactions and system dynamics at the level of food chains).[5] I hardly need to point out that this is just the same debate as we have encountered previously: that between essentially Unitarian and mechanistic (Gleasonian) world views.

The first area of controversy has been debate around the roles of competition in structuring the planktonic community (the strengths of interactions debate). Again, this is not an 'either/or' debate. There is good evidence that the patchiness and disturbed nature of surface waters is such as to ensure the disruption of competitive exclusion so that the primary drivers of the occurrence of many species are essentially physiological and environmental (if it were otherwise then Reynolds's predictive framework, which is able to predict the dominant species of planktonic algae likely to occur in a variety of lake types, would not work). This is the Gleasonian view.[6] Certainly (as discussed previously) there is very good evidence that the planktonic environmental is multi-fractal with variability across a wide range of scales.[7] This is not to deny, however, that there are times and places when competitive interactions and resource depletion are important factors. So the observed outcome is a balance between disturbance, patchiness and interspecific interactions and competition for resources.[8] Nevertheless the multi-fractal nature of the pelagic environment, the ubiquitous involvement of microbial processes and the regular disturbance at a range of scales by wind and tide ensure high taxonomic and functional biodiversity, and 'envelope' dynamics. Clearly, resource constraints and stoichiometry do play a role at some level.

What I find quite fascinating is the fact that in both marine and freshwater ecosystems the overall system performance and dynamics is well explained by the evolutionary, biochemical and physiological constraints of the major species and functional groups involved. In particular, the major groups of grazing zooplankton – which differ markedly between marine and freshwater ecosystems – have quite different requirements for N and P, and that, together with the differences between macro-algae (seaweeds) and freshwater aquatic macrophytes, serves to structure the dynamics of these two systems. When coupled with the differing chemistries of marine and freshwaters, and the microbial reactions to those chemistries, it is possible to explain the fact that freshwaters are largely phosphorus-limited whereas marine waters are largely nitrogen-limited. Evolutionary history, biochemistry and physiology, together with elemental stoichiometry, can explain a lot of what we see.[9] Similarly, a large amount of cross-scale multi-fractal variability and upper-bound nutrient use efficiencies leads to large-scale, predictable, macroscopic properties in these systems.

This is an excellent example of the micro-scale interactions producing meso-scale ecosystem properties and emergent 'extremal' constraints, which recursively set the context for the smaller-scale processes and interactions. In many ways the world in which we humans live is the complex and recursive world of meso-scale ecosystems, landscapes and waterscapes. In a paper in 1999 I argued that many features of the ecology of aquatic systems could be explained in terms of some simple propositions. These propositions related the ensemble properties of aquatic ecosystems to the physiology and population dynamics of the major species and functional groups found in those aquatic ecosystems.[10] I then elaborated on this approach to explain features of the biogeochemistry of rivers, lakes and estuaries.[11] When nutrient loads to estuaries increase, seagrasses are replaced by macrophytic algae and, finally, by phytoplankton blooms – and the systems do not recover easily.[12] Lakes, estuaries and coastal embayments show strong hysteresis effects when subjected to increased nutrient loads; by hysteresis I mean that the system enters a degraded state (poor water quality, loss of biodiversity, algal blooms) and we find that 'you can't get back from here'. Restoration proves very difficult because of a series of non-linear interactions between the aquatic plants, the algae and microbial processes in the sediments.[13] Simple models of these systems show that the strong hysteresis effects have their origin in the physiological responses of the major functional groups in these ecosystems. In short, simple models can have some very complex and realistic properties and a study of 'ecosystem physiology' can explain much.

The second area of controversy in the response of water bodies to nutrient loading has been the extent to which it is possible to use food chain interactions – and particularly changes in the grazing pressure on the nuisance algal blooms that form in response to nutrient loads – as a means of controlling these blooms rather than (or in addition to) changing the nutrient load. In a situation where catchment land use and the nutrient loading is difficult to reduce (in an urban area, for example), is it possible to stock the lake with fish to suppress the algal blooms by other means? In these food chain or trophic interactions there is certainly evidence of an ability to modify grazing pressure on the algae and so alter the observed empirical relationships between nutrient loads and algal biomass. This has been a controversial topic because, although there have now been many experimental manipulations of food chains in lakes (by adding or removing larger predatory fish, for example) the results of such manipulations, at least in the early days, were not as clear cut as we might have wished. Now, however, after numerous experiments the picture is becoming clearer.[14] What the manipulation of food chains in lakes usually does is to introduce large predatory fish into lakes. What this does is to reduce the populations of smaller fish, which eat the grazing zooplankton, allowing zooplankton populations to rise so that they can graze down the (nuisance) algal blooms. The food chain interactions in lakes are reinforced by the fact that, when predation on the zooplankton is reduced, populations of larger cladocerans tend to reappear. These larger *Daphnia* are very efficient grazers of algae.[15] These kinds of manipulations in lakes can have long-term impacts on algal bloom abundance[16] and they do often lead to major shifts in the population structure of the predatory fish by producing small numbers of gigantic, cannibalistic predators within the lakes.[17] There are many complexities in the lake manipulation experiments, not least because of the fact that the dominant nutrient recycling pathways and the overall stoichiometry of the food chain is altered by the changes in the dominant organisms. Furthermore there is recent evidence of information flow through the release and exchange of 'infochemicals' between trophic levels; chemicals that can influence the growth strategies and grazing susceptibility of organisms.[18]

Trophic cascades

'Top-down' food chain interactions or 'trophic cascades' turn out to be almost a universal phenomenon.[19] It appears that the cascades in lakes are probably the strongest known; certainly they are stronger than those found in the oceans or on land.[20] Nevertheless, cascades in the oceans have also been discovered, resulting in completely restructured food webs and dominance by previously uncommon species.[21] Despite the fact they may be weaker than those in aquatic systems, we now know, for example, that there are a number of examples of 'top-down' control in terrestrial systems. Changing predator numbers in Arctic tundra systems has a major effect on plant damage and plant cover. The abundance of voles is up to five times higher in areas without predators.[22] Equally, the absence of predators on small forested islands in tropical South American hydro-power reservoirs causes excessive grazing to occur, leading to a kind of ecological meltdown when predators are absent.[23] As I have discussed previously, habitat fragmentation reduces biodiversity, particularly of larger predators, so that predator abundance and diversity is reduced in smaller habitat fragments. Reduced predator diversity increases the strength of cascades through reductions in the diversity of alternative food chain paths.[24] Changing predator abundance has a strong effect on grazing animals in the East African savannah: small grazing animals have many predators, whereas large grazing ungulates (above *c.* 150 kg in mass) have few predators. Small prey therefore tends to be (top-down) predator-limited whereas larger animals tend to be (bottom-up) food-limited.[25] Changing the spatial patterns and abundance of predators in these ecosystems has strong effects on the abundance and limitation mechanisms of their prey. Analysis of a number of experimental manipulations of ecosystems led Boris Worm and his co-workers to conclude that the effects of 'top-down' (predator) manipulations and 'bottom-up' (nutrient) enrichments were usually interactive and synergistic.[26] Of course, this is the most usual pattern of human interventions in ecosystems: we have commonly both increased nutrient availability through agriculture, fertiliser use, runoff, etc. and reduced the number of larger predators through hunting and habitat fragmentation. These effects cannot be managed in isolation.

In one of the best known examples of predator reintroduction – the reintroduction of wolves to Yellowstone National Park – increasing predation on the elk by the wolves has allowed trees such as willow, aspen and cottonwood to recover in ways not seen for generations.[27] The almost universal identification of trophic cascades in ecosystems means that there is a second very important set of process that determine biodiversity and ecosystem function, namely the effects of predation on herbivores and the effects of grazing on plants and other primary producers. This idea was suggested by Hairston and his co-workers in 1960 – the famous Hairston, Smith and Slobodkin (or HSS) paper[28] – in which it was suggested that the world is green because predators control the numbers of herbivores, so allowing the plants to grow more luxuriantly. So the removal of top predators from ecosystems (e.g. wolves in North America, pike and other large fish in freshwaters and the oceans),[29] which is a very common effect of human intervention in ecosystems around the globe, has major impacts on ecosystem biodiversity and function.[30] Furthermore, habitat fragmentation also influences the outcomes of such trophic perturbations through its interaction with range size and the spatial distribution of such things as refuges and nest sites.[31]

So the global removal of the Pleistocene megafauna, largely by human hands, had massive and unexpected impacts on the structure and function of global ecosystems. We have been living off natural capital for some time. The ongoing overexploitation of terrestrial and marine ecosystems tends to preferentially remove the larger mammalian predators (larger than 3 kg).[32] The ecosystems we know today are very much modified compared with even 50–100 years ago.[33] This is yet another example of our poor memory of 'deep time' and long-term change letting us down. The fragmented and largely predator-free landscapes and waterscapes we are familiar with today are but ciphers of their former selves. Vegetation structure and dynamics have been greatly altered in all parts of the globe.[34] The success of predator reintroductions and the recovery of large mammal populations in parts of Europe have led to calls for a systematic 'rewilding' of the continents, including plans to reintroduce large Pleistocene herbivores and predators to North America.[35] Unfortunately, 'rewilding' can only take place with species analogous to those that originally occurred on the continents – the original species are long since extinct.

In catchments both fire and erosion can cause long-term state shifts that can be difficult to reverse. In arid savannahs, fire regimes and overgrazing can cause switches between states dominated by either grasses or woody shrubs.[36] Australian plant successions may also suffer irreversible damage if clearing is accompanied by erosion and loss of soil nutrients.[37] Interestingly, new evidence seems to indicate that savannah systems have water-limited regimes as well as regimes in which state shifts and hysteresis effects are visible.[38] In African savannahs, woody cover rises linearly with mean annual precipitation up to a value of 650 mm; below this value woody cover is constrained by water availability and small trees and grasses coexist. Above this threshold savannahs are 'unstable' systems in which canopy closure is possible and combinations of fire and grazing are necessary for the coexistence of trees and grasses. So the system dynamics and the presence, or not, of hysteresis effects is dependent on moisture availability. There is good evidence for multiple stable states and for strong hysteresis effects in ecosystems as a result of the removal of top predators – the effects of trophic cascades of various kinds. These occur in both aquatic and terrestrial systems.[39]

There is growing evidence of strong hysteresis at landscape scales associated with interactions between the physiology of the dominant organisms and the timing of climate events.[40] This has very important implications for climate change. In a world of CAS and SGC, landscape-scale responses are not influenced by changes in means and long-term trends, but by subtle changes in phenology: the length and timing of changes in climate variability. There is good evidence that this has been important in the past and that points of no return occur as thresholds and step functions.[41] SGC and HOT systems are resilient to designed-for perturbations but very sensitive to unexpected change. For this reason there have been catastrophic changes in past environments caused by management decisions taken in good faith. Surprise and hysteresis are facts of life – they have had major impacts on the past course of human affairs.[42]

What is now required is a fusion of knowledge about aquatic ecosystem impacts with information about the relationships between terrestrial biodiversity, trophic cascades, ecosystem function and biogeochemistry so that some useful explanations of the complex linkages between terrestrial and aquatic systems may be achieved. In effect what is required is a definition of what Richard Vollenweider called 'catchment physiology' or the ways in which the ensemble properties of the constituent species and patch distributions together make up the catchment response. We can expect that preferential flow pathways and reaction–diffusion reactions within and between 'hot spots' will ensure that small-scale pattern and process will have significant macro-scale impacts. 'Catchment physiology' is presumed to be the sum of the physiological activities of the constituent species in the catchment together with any food chain dynamics and complexity. We can expect there to be some emergent properties that arise from the complex spatial and temporal interactions of the species in fragmented landscapes, the changing hydrology, stoichiometric constraints and the recycling of nutrients between producers and consumers. Further complexities arise from the altered species composition both above and below the water. An excellent example is the effect of double trophic cascades within and between aquatic and terrestrial ecosystems.[43] Changing fish populations in streams and lakes can change pollination success in nearby terrestrial plants through a complex web of predation both in the water and in the air. Fish prey on dragonfly larvae underwater and the adult dragonflies prey on pollinating insects on land nearby.

Ecosystem impacts: complexity, hysteresis effects and non-linear responses

Before the clearing of the land for agriculture and urban development, catchments around the world were largely dominated by deep-rooted perennial plants that had evolved a diverse range of functional types. There were also populations of Pleistocene megafauna that browsed on the vegetation and recycled biomass and nutrients. The plants were highly efficient users of the available water, and a long-term quasi-equilibrium had developed perturbed on occasion by natural disasters and disturbances of various kinds. There is good evidence for the development of ecosystems which, as far as possible, maximised water use. In addition there was close coupling of nutrient cycling and uptake, which had arisen because of the complementarity of functional groups.[44] We have replaced this dominant land use type with a meso-scale mosaic of much less efficient agricultural and urban ecosystems that lack large predators, and leak water and nutrients because of reduced biodiversity and reduced water use efficiency and nutrient recycling. (Across the globe there is a trend towards the destruction of the larger organisms that provide the three-dimensional structures of ecosystems and their replacement with much simpler, microbially dominated systems. This has been termed the 'slippery slope to slime'.[45]) On land we have made major changes to fire regimes and made consequent changes to the dominant vegetation types. The hydrological balance has been disturbed and the balance between evaporation, recharge and runoff has been changed; this is a common observation in catchments around the world.[46] Water quality in lakes and rivers reflects the dominant land use in their catchments and we see widespread degradation. If we are to preserve water quality and our lakes and estuaries, the challenge is to replace what function we can.

How much of the original landscape function must we replace? The data clearly show that once 50% of the original native Australian bush is removed then the hydrological and nutrient fluxes from catchments are disturbed enough to greatly increase exports. Even removing 20%–30% of the forest cover in American watersheds gives a 10% chance of increasing nutrient exports to the median level of predominantly agricultural or urban catchments,[47] so large-scale landscape restoration is required. Replacing the three-dimensional structure of ecosystems is critical. Predator removal and habitat fragmentation leads to changes in herbivore populations. Wildlife management in this situation is a complex task of managing habitat mosaics and the availability of fodder and water. Culling may be required to replace predation. Given the range of possible agricultural crops (without developing totally new perennial crops), the only practical way to replace landscape function is to replace it in the form of mosaics of annual and perennial plants, patches of remnant native ecosystems surrounded by farmland. The question is then: to what extent is this possible, and to what extent can a mosaic of different land uses contain biodiversity, hydrology and nutrient fluxes at landscape scales?

Connectivity between the catchment and the river is a key factor. We do know that riparian strips even a few metres wide reduce N exports from cleared land quite effectively.[48] Riparian zones 10–20 m wide reduce N exports by 60%–80%. Restoration of riparian vegetation also tends to protect stream banks and reduce erosion.[49] Reduction of riparian strips in agriculture contributes greatly to catchment exports, particularly in areas where row crops are grown. Given that inputs of nutrients to rivers are largely sourced from riparian vegetation there are very good arguments for ensuring that wide riparian strips, dominated by native vegetation, are replaced along riverbanks. Of course, water extraction leading to drastic changes in river flow patterns is also a factor that will make it difficult to restore large amounts of the original riparian native vegetation. Control of extractions and the restoration of the original land use and environmental flow patterns – including the longer-term interannual variability – is a key requirement for effective river management.[50] Mosaics containing constructed or natural wetlands can also be used to intercept surface flows and their associated nutrient loads to streams. Mosaics containing forest patches will also serve to reduce sheet flows and catchment exports, but will change the overall balance of rainfall and evapotranspiration. Once again it is important to stress that replacing the river flows is not just a matter of replacing annual average flows, it will be necessary to pay attention to the natural regime of flow variability from daily to interannual scales. This is a particular challenge when it is remembered that most rivers around the world are regulated and that the engineering structures have been placed there to reduce the impact of flood and drought. In short, we have set the entire system up to reduce flow variability and to provide security; now we have to rethink the way we manage catchments and river systems to return at least some of the patterns of natural variability and biodiversity.

For a number of reasons it appears that mosaics of larger blocks of native vegetation interspersed with pastoral and cropping land would be better than the same proportion of catchments divided into smaller fragments. As long as grazing is controlled, biodiversity and ecosystem function are both improved in larger fragments and, if strategically placed so as to control and intercept runoff from farmlands, these larger fragments would also control connectivity to the river channels. Larger fragments have more species and more complete biophysical function. There are therefore some complex non-linear interactions between the landscape pattern, the precise manner of the fragmentation and the landscape function.

If we are to protect water quality and landscape function then we need not only to build biodiversity in habitat fragments but also to restore the biophysical functioning and biogeochemistry of the mosaics of land uses in catchments.[51] A closer approach to 'extremal' envelope properties is required. We need to pay more attention to soil biodiversity and function and the effects of particular functional groups of organisms, including the bacteria and fungi. This will require an appreciation of landscape function at all scales: from micro-scale reaction–diffusion linkages, micro-biota and macro-pores, through the meso-scale interactions between patches of different land uses, to the emergent biophysical properties of entire catchments. The existence of the small-scale reaction–diffusion relationships, which recursively both exist within a patchy structure and at the same time are partly responsible for its generation, are presumably what, at evolutionary time scales, lead to homoplastic structures and functions in landscapes and ecosystems. There is therefore an emergent property of the interaction between the climate and the physiology of organisms and between the spatial arrangement and connectivity between ecosystem fragments at landscape scales. Climate influences survival strategies through stoichiometry and physiology. Clearing changes patchiness and subtly alters landscape function. This is the essence of landscape ecology,[52] in which it is explicitly recognised that structure is important in the longer-term dynamics of landscapes.[53]

NOTES

1. G. P. Harris and A. L. Heathwaite. Inadmissible evidence: knowledge and prediction in land and waterscapes. *Journal of Hydrology*, **304** (2005), 3–19.

2. R. A. Vollenweider. *Scientific fundamentals of the eutrophication of lakes and flowing waters with particular reference to nitrogen and phosphorus as factors in eutrophication.* Technical Report DAS/SCI/68.27, 182pp. (Paris: OECD, 1968).

3. For a review of much of this literature and further references see G. P. Harris. Pattern, process and prediction in aquatic ecology. A limnological view of some general ecological problems. *Freshwater Biology*, **32** (1994): 143–60.

4. See, for example, C. S. Reynolds. *The Ecology of Freshwater Phytoplankton*. (Cambridge: Cambridge University Press, 1984).

5. G. P. Harris. This is not the end of limnology (or of science): the world may well be a lot simpler than we think. *Freshwater Biology*, **42** (1999), 689–706.

6. As adopted by G. P. Harris. *Phytoplankton Ecology*. (London: Chapman and Hall, 1986).

7. L. Seuront *et al*. Universal multi-fractal analysis as a tool to characterize intermittent patterns: example of phytoplankton distribution in turbulent coastal waters. *Journal of Plankton Research*, **21** (1999), 877–923.

8. See the discussion in G. P. Harris. This is not the end of limnology (or of science): the world may well be a lot simpler than we think. *Freshwater Biology*, **42** (1999), 689–706.

9. R. W. Sterner and J. J. Elser. *Ecological Stoichiometry: the Biology of Elements from Molecules to the Biosphere*. (Princeton, NJ: Princeton University Press, 2002). G. P. Harris. Comparison of the biogeochemistry of lakes and estuaries: ecosystem processes, functional groups, hysteresis effects and interactions between macro- and microbiology. *Marine and Freshwater Research*, **50** (1999), 791–811.

10. G. P. Harris. This is not the end of limnology (or of science). (See Note 5.)

11. G. P. Harris. Comparison of the biogeochemistry of lakes and estuaries: ecosystem processes, functional groups, hysteresis effects and interactions between macro- and microbiology. *Marine and Freshwater Research*, **50** (1999), 791–811.

12. G. P. Harris. Algal biomass and biogeochemistry in catchments and aquatic ecosystems: scaling of processes, models and empirical tests. *Hydrobiologia*, **349** (1997), 19–26. G. P. Harris. Predictive models in spatially and temporally variable freshwater systems. *Australian Journal of Ecology*, **23** (1998), 80–94. G. P. Harris. Comparison of the biogeochemistry of lakes and estuaries: ecosystem processes, functional groups, hysteresis effects and interactions between macro- and microbiology. *Marine and Freshwater Research*, **50** (1999), 791–811. G. P. Harris. The response of Australasian estuaries and coastal embayments to increased nutrient loadings and changes in hydrology. In *Australasian Estuarine Systems: Carbon, Nitrogen and Phosphorus Fluxes*. LOICZ Reports and Studies No. 12, ed. S. V. Smith and C. J. Crossland. (Texel, The Netherlands: LOICZ IPO, 1999), pp. 112–24. G. P. Harris. Biogeochemistry of nitrogen and phosphorus in Australian catchments, rivers and estuaries: effects of land use and flow regulation and comparisons with global patterns. *Marine and Freshwater Research*, **52** (2001), 139–49. G. Harris *et al*. *Port Phillip Bay Environmental Study: Final Report*. (Dickson, ACT: CSIRO, 1996).

13. R. Muradian. Ecological thresholds: a survey. *Ecological Economics*, **38** (2001), 7–24. M. Scheffer. *Ecology of Shallow Lakes*. (London: Chapman and Hall, 1998). M. Scheffer *et al*. Alternative equilibria in shallow lakes. *Trends in Ecology and Evolution*, **8** (1993), 275–9. M. Scheffer *et al*. Catastrophic shifts in ecosystems. *Nature*, **413** (2001), 591–6.

14. M. T. Brett and C. R. Goldman. A meta-analysis of the freshwater trophic cascade. *Proceedings of the National Academy of Sciences, USA*, **93** (1996), 7723–6. J. B. Shurin *et al*. A cross-ecosystem comparison of the strength of trophic cascades. *Ecology Letters*, **5** (2002), 785–91.

15. V. Matveev. Testing predictions of the lake food web theory on pelagic communities in Australian reservoirs. *Oikos*, **100** (2003), 149–61.

16. W. Bell, W. E. Neill and D. Schluter. The effect of temporal scale on the outcome of trophic cascade experiments. *Oecologia*, **134** (2003), 578–86.

17. L. Persson *et al.* Gigantic cannibals driving whole-lake cascade. *Proceedings of the National Academy of Sciences, USA,* **100** (2003), 4035–9.

18. M. Vos *et al.* Infochemicals structure marine, terrestrial and freshwater food webs: implications for ecological informatics. *Ecological Informatics,* **1** (2006), 23–32.

19. M. L. Pace *et al.* Trophic cascades revealed in diverse ecosystems. *Trends in Ecology and Evolution,* **14** (1999), 483–8. M. Scheffer, S. Carpenter and B. de Young. Cascading effects of overfishing marine systems. *Trends in Ecology and Evolution,* **20** (2005), 579–81.

20. J. B. Shurin *et al.* A cross-ecosystem comparison of the strength of trophic cascades. *Ecology Letters,* **5** (2002), 785–91.

21. K. T. Frank *et al.* Trophic cascades in a formerly cod-dominated ecosystem. *Science,* **308** (2005), 1621–3.

22. P. A. Hamback *et al.* Predators indirectly protect tundra plants by reducing herbivore abundance. *Oikos,* **106** (2004), 85–92.

23. J. Terborgh *et al.* Ecological meltdown in predator-free forest fragments. *Science,* **294** (2001), 1923–6.

24. D. L. Finke and R. F. Denno. Predator diversity dampens trophic cascades. *Nature,* **429** (2004), 407–10.

25. A. R. E. Sinclair, S. Mduma and J. S. Brashares. Patterns of predation in a diverse predator-prey system. *Nature,* **425** (2003), 288–90.

26. B. Worm *et al.* Consumer versus resource control of species diversity and ecosystem functioning. *Nature,* **417** (2002), 848–50.

27. W. J. Ripple *et al.* Trophic cascades among wolves, elk and aspen on Yellowstone National Park's northern range. *Biological Conservation,* **102** (2001), 227–34. W. J. Ripple and R. L. Beschta. Wolf reintroduction, predation risk, and cottonwood recovery in Yellowstone National Park. *Forest Ecology and Management,* **184** (2003), 299–313. W. J. Ripple and R. L. Beschta. Wolves, elk, willows, and trophic cascades in the upper Gallatin Range of South-western Montana, USA. *Forest Ecology and Management,* **200** (2004), 161–81.

28. N. G. Hairston, Jr., F. E. Smith and L. B. Slobodkin. Community structure, population control and competition. *American Naturalist,* **44** (1960), 421–5.

29. R. A. Myers and B. Worm. Rapid worldwide depletion of predatory fish communities. *Nature,* **423** (2003), 280–3. J. K. Baum and R. A. Myers. Shifting baselines and the decline of pelagic sharks in the Gulf of Mexico. *Ecology Letters,* **7** (2004), 135–45.

30. J. Terborgh *et al.* Vegetation dynamics of predator-free land-bridge islands. *Journal of Ecology,* **94** (2006), 253–63.

31. M. A. Patten and D. T. Bolger. Variation in top down control of avian reproductive success across a fragmentation gradient. *Oikos,* **101** (2003), 479–88.

32. M. Cardillo *et al.* Multiple causes of high extinction risk in large mammal species. *Science,* **309** (2005), 1239–41.

33. J. B. C. Jackson. What was natural in the coastal oceans? *Proceedings of the National Academy of Sciences, USA* **98** (2001), 5411–18.

34. J. Terborgh *et al.* Ecological meltdown in predator-free forest fragments. *Science,* **294** (2001), 1923–6.

35. J. Donlan *et al.* Re-wilding North America. *Nature,* **436** (2005), 913–14.

36. A. J. Ash *et al.* Building grass castles: integrating ecology and the management of Australia's tropical tall grass rangelands. *Rangelands Journal,* **19** (1997), 123–44. J. M. Anderies, M. A. Janssen and B. H. Walker. Grazing management, resilience, and the dynamics of a fire-driven

rangelands system. *Ecosystems*, **5** (2002), 23–44. M. A. Janssen, J. M. Anderies and B. H. Walker. Robust strategies for managing rangelands with multiple stable attractors. *Journal of Environmental Economics and Management*, **47** (2004), 140–62.

37. J. Walker *et al.* The influence of landscape age in influencing landscape health. *Ecosystem Health*, **7** (2001), 7–14.

38. M. Sankaran *et al.* Determinants of woody cover in African savannas. *Nature*, **438** (2005), 846–9.

39. M. Scheffer *et al.* Catastrophic shifts in ecosystems. *Nature*, **413** (2001), 591–6. S. R. Carpenter (ed.). *Complex Interactions in Lake Communities*. (Berlin: Springer-Verlag, 1988). M. Scheffer. *Ecology of Shallow Lakes*, (1998). (See Note 13.)

40. T. C. Jennerjahn *et al.* Asynchronous terrestrial and marine signals of climate change during Heinrich events. *Science*, **306** (2004), 2236–9.

41. M. Maslin. Ecological versus climatic thresholds. *Science*, **306** (2004), 2197–8.

42. J. Diamond. *Collapse*. (London: Allen Lane, The Penguin Press, 2004).

43. T. M. Knight *et al.* Trophic cascades across ecosystems. *Nature*, **437** (2005), 880–3.

44. M. Loreau. Ecosystem development explained by competition within and between material cycles. *Proceedings of the Royal Society*, B**265** (1998), 33–8.

45. J. M. Pandolfi *et al.* Global trajectories of the long-term decline of coral reef ecosystems. *Science*, **301** (2003), 955–8. J. M. Pandolfi *et al.* Are US coral reefs on the slippery slope to slime? *Science*, **307** (2005), 1725–6.

46. X. B. Wu, T. L. Thurow and S. G. Whisenant. Fragmentation and change in hydrologic function of Tiger Bush landscapes, south-west Niger. *Journal of Ecology*, **88** (2000), 790–800.

47. J. D. Wickham *et al.* Land cover as a framework for assessing risk of water pollution. *Journal of the American Water Resources Association*, **36** (2000), 1417–22.

48. P. E. Davies and M. Nelson. Relationships between riparian buffer strip widths and the effects of logging on stream habitat, invertebrate community composition and fish abundance. *Australian Journal of Marine and Freshwater Research*, **45** (1994), 1298–305. L. B. M. Vought *et al.* Nutrient retention in riparian ecotones. *Ambio*, **23** (1994), 342–8.

49. L. A. McKergow *et al.* Before and after riparian management: sediment and nutrient exports from a small agricultural catchment, Western Australia. *Journal of Hydrology*, **270** (2003), 253–72. L. A. McKergow *et al.* Performance of grass and eucalyptus riparian buffers in a pasture catchment, Western Australia. Part 1: Riparian hydrology; Part 2: Water quality. *Hydrological Processes*, **20** (2006), 2309–26, 2327–46.

50. J. T. Puckridge *et al.* Flow variability and the ecology of large rivers. *Marine and Freshwater Research*, **49** (1998), 55–72. J. T. Puckridge, K. F. Walker and J. F. Costelloe. Hydrological persistence and the ecology of dryland rivers. *Regulated Rivers – Research and Management*, **16** (2000), 385–402.

51. R. J. Hobbs and S. R. Morton. Moving from descriptive to predictive ecology. *Agroforestry Systems*, **45** (1999), 43–55.

52. R. Barbault. Biodiversity dynamics: from population and community ecology approaches to a landscape ecology point of view. *Landscape and Urban Planning*, **31** (1995), 89–98.

53. H. H. Shugart. Importance of structure in the longer-term dynamics of landscapes. *Journal of Geophysical Research – Atmospheres*, **105 (D15)** (2000), 20065–75.

11 Change detection, monitoring and prediction

The implications of the new paradigms for monitoring and prediction: new techniques for modelling ecosystems.

If we are trying to understand pattern and process in the natural world, if we are trying to determine what we know and whether change has occurred, and if we are trying to figure out what to do about it, then unfortunately we can only rely on samples to provide the evidence – snapshots of reality. We collect data in various ways, usually at our convenience: often weekly, almost never on Mondays or Fridays, and rarely for more than a couple of years because of the tenure of governments, programmes, grants and graduate students. We do have some new technologies that will revolutionise our understanding of environmental pattern and process. From satellites and spacecraft we can image the entire globe and from various automatic sensors we can obtain time series of data from the depths of the oceans. Nevertheless, we are forced to infer pattern and process and to take decisions based on parlous sources of information. Surprisingly, perhaps, as the global environmental problems grow, we are actually collecting fewer data in some cases than we were a decade ago because of smaller governments, reduced funding, de-skilling and cuts to government programmes. We are flying almost blind while arguing endlessly about the course we are on and not looking out for hazards and risks up ahead.

As I showed in previous chapters, ecosystems are complex entities that show dynamic behaviour and spatial and temporal heterogeneity, discontinuities and multiple equilibria at a range of scales.[1] They display many of the properties attributed to CAS and show multi-fractal scaling and SGC or HOT designs.[2] Many properties of landscapes show power law distributions of properties and fractal-like variability across a wide range of temporal and spatial scales.[3] Aquatic ecosystems and their catchments are particularly useful as model ecological systems because of the wide range of spatial and temporal scales encountered: from the large and slow (kilometres to decades) in catchments to the small and fast (micrometres to seconds) in the water. Catchments appear to have fractal properties, with stream networks showing self-similar or self-affine properties.[4] In addition, the concentrations of elements in stream flow show $1/f$ scaling properties and memories of events at all scales.[5] With variability showing self-similar properties across many scales it is difficult to define entities and gather effective data. The little we know about catchments and their receiving waters shows that there are significant periodicities in climatological drivers of these systems at interannual, seasonal, 40–50 day, 5–10 day and diurnal scales.[6]

Much of the higher-frequency end of the spectrum is very poorly understood because a lot of the data we collect are collected weekly at best, and often more infrequently than that. So the first preconception that we need to change is the idea that ecosystems, particularly catchments, rivers and estuaries, are equilibrium systems. Disequilibrium occurs over a range of scales. We are beginning to obtain a handle on some of the climate variability, but hitherto we have never appreciated the importance of small-scale disequilibrium on our world view. It really does matter when we collect data, and we must match the scales of data collection to the predominant scales and processes in the ecosystems we are studying; to do anything else results in seriously undersampled systems, aliased data and a lack of descriptive power. There is therefore a need for optimised sampling designs to maximise returns and minimise cost. Recognising that our knowledge is partial and that any evidence upon which policy and management action is based is partial, there is an urgent need for tools through which we can move forward, take action, monitor progress and learn from our experiences.[7] Data-gathering networks provide a baseline of information but 'missing variables, low resolution, inadequate duration, temporal and spatial gaps, and declining coverage are pervasive limitations'.[8]

Statistics makes quite stringent demands on the data it treats. The theory makes a large number of assumptions about the structure of the data and is unable to deal effectively with data that break those assumptions. Statistical analysis should only be applied to data that are 'white noise', i.e. with mean and variance independent and constant over time, data that are normally distributed, and data within which the correlations and generating functions are additive and do not change over time. Variance about the mean is supposed to be due to random variation, which is uncorrelated to the mean. Environmental data break just about all these assumptions. The data are usually not normally distributed, so various transformations have to be applied. As I have stated, environmental data are most often log-normally or power law distributed, so a logarithmic transformation is usually applied before analysis. Consequent to the characteristic log-normal data distributions, there are usually correlations between the means and variances in environmental data, and these usually change over time as well. Time series analysis (which was originally developed for data like those obtained in electrical engineering and physics) is hard to apply to ecological data because the means and variances change over time and there are epochs in the data when the sign and character of the generating functions and correlations changes during the run of the data.[9]

So attempts are made to glean environmental information and evidence about change from data that are noisy, sparse in space and time and in which the structure is not readily amenable to statistical analysis. It is not surprising to learn therefore that an entire industry has grown up around this topic. Many handbooks and manuals have been written about the collection and analysis of environmental data.[10] Basically, a large amount of time has been spent controlling variability in the data – and making it amenable to the restrictions of statistical analysis – rather than trying to understand it. Much time has been spent on the assumption that somewhere, buried amidst all the supposedly random noise, is a signal, if only we could find it.

We therefore have problems dealing with inference and risk. Epistemology, sampling, statistics and hypothesis testing are all related to the ways in which we deal with uncertainty and manage risk. Mark Burgman has written about these issues in an EcoEssay for the National Center for Ecological Analysis and Synthesis.[11] The problem seems to be that people are biased and optimistic in their approach to decision making and they also tend to think they know more than they really do. Science is part of the problem because it is an essential part of the decision-making process. Burgman lists some of the symptoms of a 'scientific disease' as: technical myopia, professional paranoia (and, I would guess, a degree of hubris and instrumental reason too), overoptimism, overconfidence and denial of linguistic uncertainty. Not only is there usually a degree of epistemic uncertainty in environmental matters, there is also much linguistic uncertainty: terms are often vague and there is little agreement in the 'sense giving and sense receiving'[12] that communities of various kinds share. Statistical techniques are very much concerned with the testing of null hypotheses, i.e. with minimising Type I errors. We tend to assume that people are not guilty until proven otherwise. But there are clearly problems with scientific hypothesis testing and inference in the environmental realm. Burgman calls this 'a curious, one sided logic' and finds fault with the logical tools we rely on to deal with evidence and make inferences.

The noise in environmental data isn't noise

As it turns out, what we thought was noise in environmental data isn't actually noise. Analysis of numerous data sets from freshwater, coastal and oceanic systems shows a number of consistent phenomena:[13]

- All water quality data sets show strong and changing internal correlations over short time and space scales
- These correlation patterns occur at all scales examined, from data collected at scales of minutes to weeks
- These correlations do not arise from random variations in the data sets: the data are consistently non-random as long as the sampling interval is short enough to resolve the true dynamics (i.e. the data are not aliased)
- The water quality data sets show evidence of multi-fractal variability and power law statistics

- Aliasing is a severe problem in the most common forms of weekly (or even fortnightly or monthly) water quality data sets.

As discussed previously, the uncertainty and indeterminism in these data most probably arise from small scale reaction–diffusion interactions within catchments, in throughflow and runoff, and between biological and chemical processes at small scales. Others[14] have recently noted the prevalent and importance of small-scale variability in water quality data and have offered similar explanations. Seuront *et al.* suggested that

> the observed small-scale nutrient patches [in coastal waters – my addition] could be the result of complex interactions between hydrodynamic conditions, biological processes related to phytoplankton populations, and the productive efficiency of bacterial populations.

In effect, what we are seeing is the result of much small-scale coupling between growth, nutrient uptake and recycling in discrete patches of water. Even if we conceptually understand the nature of the fundamental processes involved and can model this (e.g. interactions between nutrient uptake, growth, grazing and nutrient recycling for any given set of interacting species), we cannot know the initial conditions or the precise species composition of each patch of water or flow path. From microns to continental scales, there is contingency and indeterminism brought about by the vagaries of dispersal and environmental heterogeneity. Different processes come to predominate at different levels in the hierarchy and 'more is (indeed) different'.[15] Whereas biogeochemistry sums processes across spatial and temporal scales by looking at entities such as watersheds, at very small scales microbial processes are patchy and contingent[16] and riverine nutrient inputs come from small-scale interactions between the landscape and the river.[17] The importance of small-scale variability has previously been underestimated. Effectively there is evidence of indeterminism and uncertainty across a range of scales from the climatological to the microbial and therefore no true base for our theorising. Together these new results may be taken as evidence of SGC in the interaction of physical, chemical and biological processes in catchments and runoff. There is a growing literature that studies the emergence of large-scale patterns from small-scale interactions in ecosystems.[18] This discussion of catchments and water quality is but more evidence of those kinds of phenomena.

Ecological explanation and prediction

Much ecological prediction is based on complicated computer models of environmental systems. These dynamical simulation models are large sets of differential equations describing ecological processes, major functional groups and their interactions. Dynamical simulation models of many ecosystems, including aquatic ecosystems, are little changed since the work of Riley *et al.* in 1949.[19] The approach has been widely used to assist with practical management problems and ecological restoration programmes: for example, the Great Lakes models of Scavia, Thomann and Di Toro[20] were the basis of the phosphorus reduction programmes in the Great Lakes in the 1970s, and the Port Phillip Bay model of Murray and Parslow[21] was the basis of the recommendations about nutrient loading reductions in that coastal lagoon in the 1990s. Many other examples could be quoted. There are, for example, many frequently used models that attempt to link land use to hydrology and water quality. The selection of the processes modelled is based on experience and the 'state of the art' at the time. These models can be used heuristically to synthesize knowledge and to guide further data collection and experimentation, or they can be used to directly predict the outcomes of management action and other forms of human intervention. Either way they form the basis of explanations of ecological pattern and process. The explanations and predictions are, however, fraught with problems; the models seem able to reproduce some of the central tendencies (some of the 'dominant modes' of the systems in question) but do not capture the fine-scale dynamics of the systems.

The models we produce are merely metaphors of reality; they are laden with semiotics and with cultural, sociological and theoretical baggage.[22] Nevertheless, the predominant scientific paradigm is one in which we are encouraged to write down all that we think is important about the processes in question and then, in accordance with Popper's philosophical framework, place our best hypotheses at risk. So we do this. The models are both calibrated and then validated as best they may be by using observed data. No attempt is made to represent all the species or interactions in the models, relying instead on a 'lumped' representation of the ecosystem and its constituent species. The models represent noisy, non-equilibrium systems, characterised by variability at a wide range of temporal and spatial sales. The 'boxes' in the dynamical models do not usually explicitly define simplexic or complicit emergent (or even fungible) entities. The representations of biological and ecological components and interactions in the models are based on experience, fashion and convenience: for example, the phytoplankton box in aquatic models is very often defined by the biomass of all species measured by chlorophyll a, the concentration of the major photosynthetic pigment in the water. The commonest aquatic ecosystem models contain what is called an NPZ model, combining nutrients, phytoplankton and zooplankton and their interactions. Some models may have some simple size fractionation (into small and large fractions perhaps, because of their differing growth rates, nutrient uptake kinetics and fates) but no attempt is usually made to represent the 200–300 species present in the community. Recent developments of the NPZ models have included functional groups of phytoplankton instead of size fractions in an attempt to garner more realism.[23] Nevertheless there is an ongoing debate about the adequacy, complexity, structure and parameterisation of such models.[24] In all models deterministic equations replace fractal, probabilistic and contingent distributions. Models with varying parameterisations and structures display differing properties depending on whether they are run to steady state or as perturbed solutions. So the models are diagrammatic at best, highly averaged and strongly scale-dependent. They remain abstractions from reality.

As I have argued, the data used in attempts to calibrate and validate such models are also partial and noisy. Any set of ecological data is a sample from the normal spatial and temporal variability encountered in natural systems. Most ecological data are therefore aliased: they are, in effect, sparse samples, which are unrepresentative of the full spectrum of natural variability.[25] Thus we have the problem of evidence based on partial information and of explanations based on unrepresentative, sketchy, deterministic dynamical models. Since the early days there have been worries over the philosophical basis of dynamical simulation modelling[26] and the ability to calibrate and validate such models.[27] There is always much hand-waving and lack of rigour in comparisons between water quality data and model outputs (usually in the form of visual comparison of time series plots of data and model predictions). There is insufficient objective statistical analysis of model bias and the fit to the data. Of course, an ability to fit the data does not, in itself, make any definitive statement about the adequacy of the model structure or its parameterisation. There 'may be more than one set of parameterisations and more than one set of parameter values that can give equally acceptable predictions of the observational data available'. This is the problem of non-uniqueness, or equifinality, and it has fundamental and practical implications.[28]

One thing that has become clear in recent years is that the predictive properties of simulation models are related to their structure (in terms of the network of links). This insight has emerged from graph and network theory.[29] Thus the ability of dynamical simulation models to predict ecological outcomes is a function of the level of abstraction and the supposed network of key interactions, all of which are abstractions from a much more complex natural entity. Dynamical models rarely have the kind of network structure seen in real world networks, which are usually hierarchical and scale-free.[30] In fact the properties of many real world networks (and their models) seem to be more dependent on the network (or model) structure than on the different types of interaction functions. The overall structure is usually more important then the precise nature of the interactions[31] – even simple 'on-off' functions work adequately in many cases – so getting the model structure correct is critically important. Differing models, with differing structures, may well give quite different dynamical behaviour, but are the data sufficient to distinguish between the various models? There is certainly growing evidence for much structural error in environmental simulation models. As we learn more about the natural world we are seeing increasing problems with this aspect of modelling.[32] The trouble is, it is impossible to estimate the true structural error in a model without actually knowing the 'real' model structure – and this is usually unknown. Therefore all that actually can be done is to estimate the relative structural error through simplification or complexification of an existing model.[33] Now that we know that the real world is quasi-fractal in space and time (across a wide range of scales) the very act of applying an existing model, say, at a larger scale by increasing grid sizes and time steps to cover a larger area, automatically engenders changes in the fundamental structural errors involved. One counterintuitive result from analyses of data, parameter and structural errors in a phosphorus model for a river in the UK was that, in the presence of noise in the data and structural errors in the model, adding more data at higher frequency did not improve model calibration.[34] In short, if the model has structural errors no amount of calibration data will improve the situation. So even though it is now possible to use electrodes *in situ* and other high-frequency sampling equipment to collect more data, more frequently, if the model is structurally flawed then the calibration and prediction errors remain.

Simulation models are only capable of modelling the central tendencies in the data, not the actual small-scale variability.[35] What the small-scale dynamics also shows is that fractal variability and non-linearity at small scales may be sufficient to render the predictions of simulation models unsafe at larger scales or higher levels. Clearly, there are fundamental limitations to our ability to measure and predict the contingent variability in catchments, rivers and estuaries. We know that stochastic events can lead to hysteresis effects and non-linear state shifts in natural ecosystems.[36] Any predictions should therefore be probabilistic and hedged about with uncertainty. Furthermore, small-scale events – including the time history of particular bodies of water and the occurrence of individual species, things that we would like to know – are inherently unpredictable.[37] Observations bear out this assertion. Magnusson *et al.*[38] showed that the temporal unfolding of a suite of properties from a group of 'similar' lakes was unpredictable; Reynolds had the same problems with attempts at ecosystem scale 'controls' in large enclosures.[39]

Parameterisation and data availability

The debate about parameterisation and data availability has been the subject of much discussion in the hydrological literature.[40] In fact, Beven preferred the term prophecy to prediction! The problems of scale, missing data and the lack of inclusion of key processes have also been discussed,[41] as has the issue of partial and incomplete data, which, together with the problems of climate variability and prediction, means that there are some fundamental problems with calibration, validation and prediction. The usual approach for parameter estimation in data-sparse situations is to define a 'lumped' parameter at large scale, effectively removing the bias in model predictions by defining an 'effective parameter'. Beven has, however, criticised this approach on the basis that the data are often insufficient to constrain the chosen parameter values.[42] This approach also suffers from the problem of fundamental indeterminacy described above as well as an incommensurability problem in that it might not be possible to either obtain the necessary data at the scale the model requires or run the model at the scale at which the data can be collected.[43]

This is not just an academic debate. With water resources becoming more scarce and valuable there is growing interest within hydrology about predictive ability in ungauged basins. The situation is bad enough when attempting to model in relatively data-rich situations, let alone in ungauged catchments. As Sivapalan *et al.* wrote, 'we are still nowhere near solving the problems related to arbitrary model structures and the a priori estimation of parameters that hamper predictions'.[44] The Prediction in Ungauged Basins (PUB) initiative intends to seek general frameworks that might allow for a predictive ability in data-poor contexts.[45] Some rebel at the thought of incoherence and uncertainty, and cling to the hope that among all the process complexities in catchments there might be 'common threads, concepts or patterns that transcend the range of scales we are dealing with'.[46] The problem is, as we have discussed, the uniqueness of place that defies generalisations across space and time.[47] There is uniqueness in a number of categories. There is uniqueness in the point data that are collected from empirically fractal distributions of parameters of interest in these self-organising or HOT systems. There is uniqueness in the model residuals that arise from the comparison of the models with the actual performance of self-organising or HOT systems, which are all on trajectories of change. Again the usual frequentist statistical assumptions of stochasticity are violated. There is uniqueness in the necessary model parameters for any particular place and there is uniqueness in the mapping of the particular landscape into model space. There is enormous spatial uncertainty in all ecological and catchment models.[48] There is a need for sensitivity and uncertainty analyses, error budgets – even neutral models as benchmarks; even so it simply may not be possible to identify a 'behavioural' model for any particular place of interest. The necessary 'behavioural' model or models may be scattered throughout the entire multi-dimensional 'model-space' of all possible structures and parameters and most of the models identified may not be 'behavioural' at all.

Keith Beven, who has spent most of his working life building models of catchment hydrology, has, in recent years, done a series of detailed analyses of his models using rigorous statistical validation techniques. He has developed what he has called the GLUE methodology – generalised likelihood uncertainty estimation – to attempt to identify the few 'behavioural' models for any given situation.[49] The reason that GLUE was developed was to answer questions about the choice of model structure and parameters in catchment hydrology models and to better define the potential errors involved in parameter estimation. What GLUE does is to use a form of uniform Monte Carlo simulation to explore the 'model space' of parameter values for each model structure. Random sets of parameter values are generated uniformly within the total 'model space' and the results assessed to see if the resulting model run is 'behavioural'. GLUE is capable of producing cumulative likelihood distributions for key parameters within the 'behavioural' space of the model; the problem is that many of these are flat right across the state space of reasonable parameter values! GLUE shows that there are many partly 'behavioural' models and sometimes no fully 'behavioural' models, and that it is often impossible to decide between a suite of more or less 'acceptable' models of hydrological and environmental systems, all of which have different structures. This is nothing more than the problem of equifinality writ large. Beven has concluded a recent 'manifesto for the equifinality thesis' with the following challenges and research questions.[50]

- How to define 'effective observational error' for cases where the observations and the (non-linear) predictions are not commensurate variables, even if they have the same name
- How to define the limits of acceptability for model predictions in any given application
- How to separate the effects of input errors and structural errors
- How to ensure efficiency in search model parameter spaces
- How to estimate changes in 'behavioural' parameter sets when attempting to simulate new places or as catchment characteristics change over time
- How to reduce the dimensionality of models to reduce the potential for equifinality and increase robustness
- How to present to the user the resulting uncertainties as conditional probabilities of outcomes and to explain the dependence on the assumptions used

These certainly include some challenging research problems and explicitly recognise the need for a kind of pragmatic realism in modelling these coupled physical/environmental systems.[51] Omlin and Reichert have advocated the use of Bayesian statistics (a form of statistical analysis that admits the inclusion of prior knowledge as a way to condition the outcome of the analysis) for the identification of 'behavioural' models. Unfortunately these techniques are computationally intensive because (as with GLUE) they require the exploration of the model space with Monte Carlo simulation techniques and, in poorly identified models, may require averaging the results of predictions based on many model structures.[52] Prior knowledge can improve the problem of model identification but the fundamental issues remain.

I need to make it clear at this point that the kinds of problems identified by Beven and others in catchment and hydrological modelling are perhaps the worst case of equifinality found in environmental modelling. But they are not confined to hydrology; ecological models suffer from the same problems. Over-fitted ecological models abound.[53] Purely physical models of atmospheric processes, fluid physics and hydrodynamics, while also being scale-dependent and having to deal with difficult issues of turbulence, scaling and effective parameters, nevertheless are better validated and calibrated than their environmental and ecological counterparts. Indeed, hydrodynamic models of lakes and models of ocean and atmospheric circulation can show considerable skill. There are still problems with parameterisation of small, sub-grid scale, processes such as clouds and individual rainfall events. Progress is being made in 'downscaling' from the coarser grids of the global circulation models to actual rainfall distributions and other predictions of practical relevance to hydrological and ecological work. The real difficulties arise when these purely physical transport models – including aspects of the global hydrological cycles – are coupled to models of the biosphere, with all its recursive, non-linear interactions. For example, attempts to build physically based 'soil–vegetation–atmosphere transfer' (SVAT) models are bedevilled by the same kinds of problems as the hydrological models because of the difficulties in parameterisation and model structure definition given the disparities between the scales of the models and the scales of the heterogeneity in the vegetation and landscapes.[54] The modelling of the global biosphere – a form of Earth System Science – will be discussed more fully in a later chapter.

Models of receiving waters

A better understanding of the relationships between land use change, hydrology and nutrient exports is important because of the non-linearities and hysteresis effects present in these systems, not just in the catchments but also in the receiving waters. We continue to be surprised on occasion. What the models must reproduce is not just the annual average flows but also the frequency and magnitude of flood events and the effects of land use change on these events. Models of the emergent simplicities of ecosystems are widely used in ecosystem impact models of receiving waters: lakes, estuaries and coastal waters.[55] By 'chunking up' the ecosystem function into non-linear interactions between large combined functional groups – nutrients, plankton, macrophytes, macroalgae, sediment microbiology – we have had some success in providing what are essentially physiological explanations of ecosystem dynamics. The models do, for example, reproduce some of the observed large-scale empirical responses of these ecosystems to increased nutrient loads. Only the central tendencies can be predicted, however, not the true dynamics of the systems, and then only at the level of broad functional groups. Nevertheless, there is hope therefore that, despite the pessimism, there are some simple underlying rules that can be understood and explained and that in terrestrial, as in aquatic ecosystems, the world may indeed be 'simpler than we think'.[56]

Estuarine and coastal systems are strongly non-linear in their response to nutrient loads; the resulting hysteresis is common. Once pushed from a seagrass-dominated state to a phytoplankton-dominated state, recovery is difficult. Shallow lakes show very similar state shifts[57] and there is at least anecdotal evidence for a similar response in Australian rivers.[58] The systems responses are produced by the highly non-linear physiological interactions between the dominant functional groups close to bifurcation points. It has been suggested that one of the causes in the shift between states is the interaction of noise in the inputs and model parameters with the occurrence of unstable system dynamics close to the bifurcation points. It is possible that, just like the models, ecosystems also show particular sensitivity to noise in input parameters around points close to chaotic bifurcations and that this is one of the mechanisms responsible for the sudden hysteretic shifts in state.[59]

There are important and subtle differences in the model responses when nutrient loads are either modelled as smooth functions of time or are strongly pulsed (as in nature). Estuarine and coastal ecosystems appear to be highly sensitive to changes in the frequency and magnitude of pulsed inputs of sediment and nutrients, and this is precisely what has been changed by anthropogenic changes in the catchments.[60] Changing the frequency and magnitude of nutrient loading events, while keeping the annual average load constant, produces major changes in the biomass of the dominant functional groups in estuarine models. Strongly pulsed and infrequent loading events lead to dominance by phytoplankton. Rivers are also highly sensitive to changes in their flow regimes. Degradation in water quality (and dominance by phytoplankton) seems to be more probable and severe in situations where nutrient loads are increased and where there are prolonged periods of low flushing or stagnation – this is precisely analogous to the estuarine response. This has a direct bearing on the environmental flows debate in rivers: the ecosystem response is a function not just of the changes in the annual flows in rivers but also of the frequency and magnitude of floods, often over periods of years.[61]

Spatial and temporal emergence

The high-level physiological and biophysical constraints form the backdrop of much smaller-scale pattern and process. Dynamical simulation models do not adequately represent the spatial and temporal emergence and the temporal unfolding that is so critical for the function of catchments and receiving waters. Spatially explicit models of individual dispersal, growth and death show the emergence of large-scale patterns[62] and provide evidence of self-organisation in landscapes and waterscapes. Patch dynamics are critical in terrestrial habitats where dispersal rates may be slow, whereas temporal and spatial dynamics are dominant in fluid environments because they are linked through the processes of fluid mechanics and turbulence. Catchments where landscapes and waterscapes meet are combinations of both sets of scales and processes, and we have much to learn about the precise mechanisms and scales involved.[63] The landscape mosaic and the way in which it changes over time owing to natural and anthropogenic forces are key aspects of our sense of individual 'place'. We know enough now to realise that the precise details of the spatial and temporal arrangement of landscape units – our sense of 'place' – is a key determinant of landscape and waterscape function. Neither landscapes nor waterscapes are equilibrium systems; both show evidence of long-term change and self-organisation in response to climatological and other factors. We also know that these systems are primarily responsive to extreme events, which can structure responses for years, even decades, afterwards. Even simple estuarine models respond in strongly non-linear ways to the frequency and magnitude of pulsed nutrient inputs.[64] Catchment exports do follow a central tendency of Redfield ratios, but these ratios must now be seen as emergent properties of much small-scale pattern and process.[65] As we have seen, the long-term changes in hydrology and nutrient exports from catchments undergoing land use change are functions of interactions at all scales, from large-scale, long-term climatological and land use change to the smallest scales of soil microstructure.

Changes to land use in catchments not only change the annual averaged nutrient loads to rivers and estuaries but also change flood frequencies and the frequency and magnitude of events. The function of the entire entity is a result of many smaller-scale interactions and therefore prediction is limited except in terms of central tendencies and statistical properties at a fairly high level. Throughout this process of building models it is necessary to remind ourselves that ecosystems are in many ways irreducibly complex, that knowledge of key parameters will be lacking and that the necessary data will not always be available at the correct scales.[66] Omniscience is rare and hubris is to be avoided at all costs, a point made by David Berlinski in his wonderfully pungent critique of ecosystem modelling and all its faults.[67]

A further complication arises from the fact that the underlying stochastic drivers of ecosystems as well as the pandemonium of internal dynamics and coupling through reaction–diffusion relations leads to the biodiversity that we observe,[68] and we know that the biodiversity controls the overall function, often in idiosyncratic ways.[69] Although there are some overall patterns of response, dynamical simulation models do not predict the dynamics, emergence, contingency and biodiversity of real world systems. The fundamental question that now needs to be answered is 'how often do the small-scale contingency, indeterminacy, non-linearity and the cross-correlations that have been revealed engender surprises at higher levels so as to render predictions of central tendencies unsafe?' We simply do not know.

Overall the development of these highly parameterised 'top-down' models of catchment hydrology will, it seems, remain a highly subjective exercise in which fashion, judgement and group-think within the scientific community will continue to play key roles. Not all agree with Beven's pessimistic analysis, although it is clear from the arguments presented here that there will remain much irreducible uncertainty and use of incommensurate data and predictions. Modelling catchments is a risky and uncertain business and the predictions so produced must be seen in the light of that fact. The time is ripe for new observations and models: new evidence of the coupling of land use change to water quality will be produced, new explanations will become possible, and this will have an effect on 'evidence-based' policy development and management techniques.[70]

Alternatives to standard simulation modelling techniques

There are alternatives to the usual dynamical simulation modelling techniques. Instead of building large, over-parameterised models of catchments and ecosystems (models that are almost impossible to validate) it is possible to use the data to objectively determine the most parsimonious models. These data-based modelling (DBM) techniques have been shown to produce much simpler, but more robust, models of these complex systems.[71] The DBM technique is designed to objectively define the most powerful and lowest-order non-linear models of complex systems in ways that explain as much of the variability in the data as possible. (Håkanson's analysis of lake and estuarine simulation models showed that the optimal number of variables (compartments) was small: fewer than five in most cases.[72] If the models were more complex than this then the uncertainty in the predictions increased sharply.) DBM explicitly recognises that not all of the input variability will be explicable by the model; it merely attempts to account for as much as possible by using the most parsimonious explanation. As such it attempts to overcome the problems of over-parameterisation and the associated questions of model identifiability. DBM can be coupled with other techniques, that also acknowledge that ecological and environmental time series do show non-linearity and epochs of changing correlations and relationships between parameters. Extensions of the DBM techniques include data mining techniques and various kinds of Bayesian statistical addition to determine system structures and bring prior information to the table.[73] The developing discipline of ecoinformatics aims to use data mining and other techniques to reveal ecological relations in partial and complex data. Analysis of data by using pattern recognition techniques can also include the use of neural networks.[74]

These new statistical and modelling techniques directly address the issues of 'lumping' processes and parameters, of missing and incommensurate parameters, of lack of data and indeterminacy discussed above. In essence, the data define the most parsimonious model. New techniques of time-varying parameter (TVP) analysis have begun to reveal much new information in water quality data and form the basis of new explanations.[75] In addition the new objective TVP techniques directly address the non-stationarity and other problems in ecological data. These techniques also go the heart of the 'theory' versus 'data' problem of Fox Keller[76] and lead to new approaches to biological systems which rely more on reality than some predetermined theoretical framework, with all its epistemological shortcomings. Surprises occur when these models are used.

Individual- and agent-based modelling (IBM and ABM)

Unlike the usual style of dynamical simulation models that sit squarely with the mainstream of ecological theory and practice, Individual-Based Models (IBM), which are based on the interactions of individuals and do not reply on 'chunked' properties or even population statistics, were seen from the beginning as a new practical and theoretical departure.[77] IBMs track the fate of interacting individuals so they do not predict equilibrium populations over time. Uchmanski and Grimm found that various IBMs could be classified on the basis of four categories: (i) the degree to which the individual's life cycle is represented, (ii) the degree to which the spatial and temporal dynamics of food, habitat and resources are taken into account, (iii) the use, or not, of natural population sizes, (iv) the extent of variability between individuals of the same age. Narrowly defined 'true' IBMs should fit each of those categories. Not all do. In other words, not all IBMs are totally realistic because of limitations of conceptual development, ecological knowledge and computer power. Even IBMs are approximations to reality. Nevertheless they reproduce aspects of ecological reality that are quite different from dynamical models.

IBMs build on the 'patch dynamics' concepts discussed earlier and attempt to describe the dynamics of individuals interacting in space and time in heterogeneous habitats. Narrowly defined IBMs do not produce a 'balance of nature'; neither do they produce 'stable' ecosystem dynamics. These models do not lend themselves to grand, unifying 'top-down' ecological theories, but instead produce long-term trajectories of ecosystem change, just as we observe in nature.[78] They also predict chaotic or oscillatory behaviour at various scales and 'extinctions' in model space may occur. To those schooled in the classical equilibrium ecological theory these 'bottom-up' models are an anathema. Some consider that the technical difficulties and the enormous knowledge requirements render this approach difficult to impossible,[79] but there have been notable successes, particularly in the simulation of forest dynamics.[80] The simulation of forest dynamics by tracking individual tree stems and their interactions with neighbours over time was begun in the 1970s with the FOREST[81] model, and continued with SORTIE.[82] Further development has taken place with various Geographical Information System (GIS)-based forest models,[83] which can be interfaced with other kinds of landscape-scale models of disturbance and succession. Because of the limitations of computer power there are usually some trade-offs between spatial and temporal resolution or the size of the forest stand that can be simulated. The addition of a forest growth and yield component further stretched the computational resources. Recent work has found new ways of increasing computational efficiency by representing patch dynamics without the need for a grid, by treating both individuals and patches as computational objects.[84] One problem with these models is that they usually assume constant climate regimes, and they are very sensitive to changing climate parameterisations. Indeed, they are so sensitive to climate change that the kinds of outputs produced by global circulation models are insufficiently precise to be able to drive adequate simulations.[85] As we shall discuss later, climate change is a serious issue to be faced.

The conceptual similarity of CAS and SGC and the fundamental properties of IBM models has been pointed out in the literature.[86] To be fully realistic and representative of CAS, IBMs would need to have large numbers of individuals and types of individual, sophisticated and realistic individual strategies, rich, non-linear interactions and the potential to display emergent properties. Few, if any, IBMs as yet do this. Nevertheless developments are moving in that direction and there have been recent attempts to quantify the emergent properties of IBMs.[87] These properties of IBMs seem to be strongly related to the spatial interactions contained in the models.[88] Modelling of global biogeochemistry by using IBMs does produce results quite different from those of the more usual equilibrium models discussed above. Small-scale stochastic processes at the community level – for example, the generation of gaps in forest canopies by the death of individual trees – causes very different dynamics. IBMs of regional forest dynamics 'illustrate the importance of fine scale heterogeneity in governing large scale ecosystem function, showing how population and community-level processes influence ecosystem composition and structure, patterns of aboveground carbon accumulation, and net ecosystem production'.[89]

Agent-based modelling (ABM) has been developed in recent years in an attempt to include some of the recursive, non-linear features of complex adaptive systems. In ABM, as the name implies, the agents in the models (communities, actors, individuals) change their responses to physical and environmental factors according to the contingencies of past history and the present social context. Hare and Deadman reviewed the taxonomy of a suite of agent-based simulation models and showed how the heritage of ABM can be traced to (a) individual-based disaggregated models, (b) artificial-life simulation and (c) multi-agent simulations in which the agents are autonomous, social, communicative, reactive and goal-driven.[90] These models are therefore capable of displaying new modes of behaviour that feed back onto the trajectories of change in the coupled system. For example, the case of the multiple states of rangelands ecosystems discussed in the last chapter (where the grassland and shrub-dominated states are reached by combinations of fire regimes and grazing pressure) has been simulated by using ABM.[91] Janssen, Walker and others examined the cost of managing under uncertainty and compared the outcomes of various regulatory and free market management strategies. Uncertainty in rainfall reduced overall profitability by about one third compared with the optimal solution. According to the model, with perfect information the best financial and ecological outcomes were achieved by strongly fluctuating stocking densities and frequent burning to remove the shrubs. Free market solutions coupled with learning and adaptive management performed better than 'conservation' pastoralist strategies. A further modelling effort using a genetic algorithm identified the most robust strategy, which more than doubled the expected returns.[92] ABM is still in its infancy and suffers from a number of shortcomings at the present time; agents tend to be small in number, heuristic rules tend to be simple and the modelling of scale-dependent interactions is still in its infancy. Nevertheless, combinations of ABM with artificial neural networks, genetic algorithms or other forms of evolutionary computation do promise to provide a means to move beyond the usual problems of models with fixed structures and rigidly specified interactions and equations.[93] These models are already being employed in the simulation of lake responses to nutrient loads.[94]

Individual- and agent-based models are difficult to calibrate and validate because of the complexity of their outputs. Nevertheless, recent models are becoming sufficiently complex that they are beginning to reproduce some of the features of agent-based complex systems (ACS). Work has begun to focus on the validation of these models via the patterns they produce. The idea is that higher-level patterns of behaviour are 'defining characteristics of a system and often, therefore, indicators of essential underlying processes and structures'.[95] Therefore the multiple patterns observed in natural systems may be used to guide model development. This is, in effect, once again an attempt to use the emergent properties of CAS and ACS to guide model development but, in this case, the models are being built strictly 'bottom-up' rather than the more traditional 'top-down' approach. Despite the complexity this approach has been used to 'inverse model' observed patterns and to choose parameter sets that reproduce the observed patterns of natural behaviour. This approach can therefore be used to constrain parameter choices and values in the model.

NOTES

1. J. Wu and O. L. Loucks. From balance of nature to hierarchical patch dynamics: a paradigm shift in ecology. *Quarterly Review of Biology*, **70** (1995), 439–66. R. V. O'Neill. Recovery in complex ecosystems. *Journal of Aquatic Ecosystem Stress and Recovery*, **6** (1999), 181–7.

2. J. M. Carlson and J. Doyle. Highly optimised tolerance: a mechanism for power laws in designed systems. *Physical Review, E***60** (1999), 1412–27. J. C. Sprott, J. Bolliger and D. J. Mladenhoff. Self-organised criticality in forest-landscape evolution. *Physics Letters, A***297** (2002), 267–71.

3. C. Lohle and B.-L. Li. Statistical properties of ecological and geologic fractals. *Ecological Modelling*, **85** (1996): 271–84. R. V. Sole *et al.* Criticality and scaling in evolutionary ecology. *Trends in Ecology and Evolution*, **14** (1999), 156–60. B.-L. Li. Fractal geometry applications in description and analysis of patch patterns and patch dynamics. *Ecological Modelling*, **132** (2000), 33–50. J. H. Brown *et al.* The fractal nature of nature: power laws, ecological complexity and biodiversity. *Philosophical Transactions of the Royal Society of London*, B**357** (2002), 619–26.

4. M. Veltri, P. Veltri and M. Maiolo. On the fractal description of natural channel networks. *Journal of Hydrology*, **187** (1996), 137–44. P. Claps, M. Fiorentino and G. Oliveto. Informational entropy of fractal river networks. *Journal of Hydrology*, **187** (1996), 145–56. D. J. Schuller, A. R. Rao and G. D. Jeong. Fractal characteristics of dense stream networks. *Journal of Hydrology*, **243** (2001), 1–16.

5. J. W. Kirchner, X. Feng and C. Neal. Fractal stream chemistry and its implications for contaminant transport in catchments. *Nature*, **403** (2000), 524–7.

6. G. P. Harris. Temporal and spatial scales in phytoplankton ecology: Mechanisms, methods, models and management. *Canadian Journal of Fisheries and Aquatic Science*, **37** (1980), 877–900. G. P. Harris. Time series analysis of water quality data from Lake Ontario: implications for the measurement of water quality in large and small lakes. *Freshwater Biology*, **18** (1987), 389–403. G. P. Harris. Pattern, process and prediction in aquatic ecology – a limnological view of some general ecological problems. *Freshwater Biology*, **32** (1994), 143–60. G. P. Harris and G. Baxter. Interannual variability in phytoplankton biomass and species composition in a subtropical reservoir. *Freshwater Biology*, **35** (1996), 545–60. G. P. Harris *et al.* Interannual variability in climate and fisheries in Tasmania. *Nature*, **333** (1988), 754–7.

7. D. Haag and M. Kaupenjohann. Parameters, prediction, post-normal science and the precautionary principle – a roadmap for modeling for decision-making. *Ecological Modelling*, **144** (2001), 45–60.

8. J. S. Clark *et al.* Ecological forecasts: an emerging imperative. *Science*, **293** (2001), 657–60.

9. See, for example, G. P. Harris. Time series analysis of water quality data from Lake Ontario: implications for the measurement of water quality in large and small lakes. *Freshwater Biology*, **18** (1987), 389–403. G. P. Harris and A. M. Trimbee. Phytoplankton population dynamics of a small reservoir: physical/biological coupling and the time scales of community change. *Journal of Plankton Research*, **8** (1986), 1011–25.

10. See, for example, R. H. Green. *Sampling Design and Statistical Methods for Environmental Biologists*. (New York: Wiley Interscience, 1979). See also B. F. J. Manly. *Statistics for Environmental Science and Management*. (London: Chapman and Hall, 2001).

11. M. Burgman. *Remedies for the scientific disease*. EcoEssay Series Number 4. (Santa Barbara, CA: National Center for Ecological Analysis and Synthesis, 2002). (http://www.nceas.ucsb.edu).

12. M. Polyani. *Knowing and Being*. (London: Routledge and Kegan Paul, 1969).

13. G. P. Harris and A. L. Heathwaite. Inadmissible evidence: knowledge and prediction in land and waterscapes. *Journal of Hydrology*, **304** (2005), 3–19.

14. V. Hatje, K. Rae and G. F. Birch. Trace metal and total suspended solids concentrations in freshwater: the importance of small-scale temporal variation. *Journal of Environmental Monitoring*, **3** (2001), 251–6. L. Seuront, V. Gentilhomme and Y. Lagadeuc. Small-scale nutrient patches in tidally mixed coastal waters. *Marine Ecology Progress Series*, **232** (2002), 29–44.

15. P. W. Anderson. More is different. *Science*, **177** (1972), 393–6.

16. W. Davison, G. R. Fones and G. W. Grime. Dissolved metals in surface sediment and a microbial mat at 100 μm resolution. *Nature*, **387** (1997), 885–8.

17. R. B. Alexander, R. A. Smith and G. E. Schwarz. Effect of stream channel size on the delivery of nitrogen to the Gulf of Mexico. *Nature*, **403** (2000), 758–61.

18. O. N. Bjornstad *et al.* Waves of Larch Budmoth outbreaks in the European Alps. *Science*, **298** (2002), 1020–3. J. T. Wootton. Local interactions predict large-scale pattern in empirically derived cellular automata. *Nature*, **413** (2001), 841–4.

19. G. A. Riley, H. Stommel and D. F. Bumpus. Quantitative ecology of the plankton of the western North Atlantic. *Bulletin of the Bingham Oceanographic College*, **12** (1949), 1–169.

20. R. V. Thomann *et al. Mathematical modelling of phytoplankton in Lake Ontario. 1. Model development and verification.* EPA 660/3–75–005. (Corvallis, OR: US Environmental Protection Agency, 1975). R. V. Thomann *et al. Mathematical modelling of phytoplankton in Lake Ontario. 2. Simulations using lake 1 model.* EPA 660/3–76–065. (Corvallis, OR: US Environmental Protection Agency, 1976).

21. G. P. Harris *et al. Port Phillip Bay Environmental Study: Final Report.* (Dickson, ACT: CSIRO, 1996). A. G. Murray and J. S. Parslow. Modelling of nutrient impacts in Port Phillip Bay – a semi-enclosed marine Australian ecosystem. *Marine and Freshwater Research*, **50** (1999), 597–611. A. G. Murray and J. S. Parslow. The analysis of alternative formulations in a simple model of a coastal ecosystem. *Ecological Modelling*, **119** (1999), 149–66.

22. P. Taylor. *Unruly Complexity: Ecology, Interpretation, Engagement.* (Chicago, IL: Chicago University Press, 2005).

23. T. R. Anderson. Plankton functional type modelling: running before we can walk? *Journal of Plankton Research*, **27** (2005), 1073–81.

24. K. J. Flynn. Castles built on sand: dysfunctionality in plankton models and the inadequacy of dialogue between biologists and modelers. *Journal of Plankton Research*, **27** (2005), 1205–10.

25. Clark *et al. Ecological Forecasts*, 2001. (See Note 8.)

26. D. Berlinski. *On Systems Analysis: an Essay Concerning the Limitations of some Mathematical Models in the Social, Political and Biological Sciences.* (Boston, MA: MIT Press, 1976).

27. N. Orekes, K. Shrader-Frechette and K. Belitz. Verification, validation and confirmation of numerical models in the earth sciences. *Science*, **263** (1994), 641–6.

28. K. J. Beven. On model uncertainty, risk and decision making. *Hydrological Processes*, **14** (2000), 2605–6. V. Klemes. Dilettantism in hydrology: transition or destiny. *Water Resources Research*, **22** (1986), 177S–88S. E. J. Rykiel. Testing ecological models: the meaning of validation. *Ecological Modelling*, **90** (1996), 229–44.

29. M. Buchanan. *Nexus, Small-worlds and the Groundbreaking Science of Networks.* (New York: Norton, 2002).

30. E. Ravasz *et al.* Hierarchical organization of modularity in metabolic networks. *Science*, **297** (2002), 1551–5.

31. S. Bornholdt. Less is more in modeling large genetic networks. *Science*, **310** (2005), 449–51.

32. G. van Straten. Models for water quality management: the problem of structural change. *Water Science and Technology*, **37** (1998), 103–11.

33. M.J.W. Jansen. Prediction error through modelling concepts and uncertainty from basic data. *Nutrient Cycling in Agroecosystems*, **50** (1998), 247–53.

34. N.R. McIntyre and H.S. Wheater. Calibration of an in-river phosphorus model: prior evaluation of data needs and model uncertainty. *Journal of Hydrology*, **290** (2004), 100–16.

35. G.P. Harris. Predictive models in spatially and temporally variable freshwater systems. *Australian Journal of Ecology*, **23** (1998), 80–94. G.P. Harris. This is not the end of limnology (or of science): the world may well be a lot simpler than we think. *Freshwater Biology*, **42** (1999), 689–706.

36. C.-H. Hsieh *et al.* Distinguishing random environmental fluctuations from ecological catastrophes for the North Pacific Ocean. *Nature*, **435** (2005), 336–40.

37. G.P. Harris. Pattern, process and prediction in aquatic ecology – a limnological view of some general ecological problems. *Freshwater Biology*, **32** (1994), 143–60.

38. J.J. Magnusson, B.J. Benson and T.K. Kratz. Temporal changes in the limnology of a suite of lakes in Wisconsin, USA. *Freshwater Biology*, **23** (1990), 145–59.

39. C.S. Reynolds. Experimental manipulations of the phytoplankton periodicity in large limnetic enclosures in Blelham Tarn, English Lake District. *Hydrobiologia*, **138** (1986), 43–64.

40. K.J. Beven. Changing ideas in hydrology – the case of physically-based models. *Journal of Hydrology*, **105** (1989), 157–72. K.J. Beven. Prophecy, reality and uncertainty in distributed hydrological modelling. *Advances in Water Resources*, **16** (1993), 41–51. K.M. Loague and R.A. Freeze. A comparison of rainfall-runoff modelling techniques on small upland catchments. *Water Resources Research*, **21** (1985), 229–48.

41. M. Haus. Ecosystem modelling: science or technology? *Journal of Hydrology*, **116** (1990), 25–33.

42. Beven, *Advances in Water Resources*, (1993). (See Note 40.)

43. K.J. Beven. Does an interagency meeting in Washington imply uncertainty? *Hydrological Processes*, **18** (2004), 1747–50.

44. M. Sivapalan *et al.* Downward approach to hydrological prediction. *Hydrological Processes*, **17** (2003), 2101–11.

45. I.G. Littlewood *et al.* The role of 'top-down' modelling for Prediction in Ungauged Basins (PUB). *Hydrological Processes*, **17** (2003), 1673–9.

46. M. Sivapalan. Process complexity at hillslope scale, process simplicity at the watershed scale: is there a connection? *Hydrological Processes*, **17** (2003), 1037–41.

47. K.J. Beven. Uniqueness of place and process representations in hydrological modelling. *Hydrology and Earth System Sciences*, **4** (2000), 203–13.

48. H.I. Jager and A.W. King. Spatial uncertainty and ecological models. *Ecosystems*, **7** (2004), 841–7.

49. K.J. Beven and A.M. Binley. The future of distributed models: model calibration and uncertainty prediction. *Hydrological Processes*, **6** (1992), 279–98.

50. K.J. Beven. A manifesto for the equifinality thesis. *Journal of Hydrology*, **320** (2006), 18–36.

51. K.J. Beven. Towards a coherent philosophy for modelling the environment. *Proceedings of the Royal Society of London, A***458** (2002), 1–20.

52. P. Reichert and M. Omlin. On the usefulness of over parameterized ecological models. *Ecological Modelling*, **95** (1997), 289–99. M. Omlin and P. Reichert. A comparison of techniques for the estimation of model prediction uncertainty. *Ecological Modelling*, **115** (1999), 45–59.

53. L.R. Ginsburg and C.X.J. Jensen. Rules of thumb for judging ecological theories. *Trends in Ecology and Evolution*, **19** (2003), 121–6.

54. K. Schultz and K. J. Beven. Data-supported robust parameterisations in land surface-atmosphere flux predictions: towards a top-down approach. *Hydrological Processes*, **17** (2003), 2259–77.

55. G. P. Harris. Predictive models in spatially and temporally variable freshwater systems. *Australian Journal of Ecology*, **23** (1998), 80–94.

56. G. P. Harris. This is not the end of limnology (or of science): the world may well be a lot simpler than we think. *Freshwater Biology*, **42** (1999), 689–706.

57. S. R. Carpenter (ed.). *Complex Interactions in Lake Communities*. (New York: Springer-Verlag, 1988). M. Scheffer. *Shallow Lakes*. (London: Chapman and Hall, 1998). M. Scheffer *et al.* Catastrophic shifts in ecosystems. *Nature*, **413** (2001), 591–6.

58. G. P. Harris. *A nutrient dynamics model for Australian waterways – Land use, catchment biogeochemistry and water quality in Australian rivers*. (2002). http://www.ea.gov.au/soe/techpapers/nutrient-dynamics/index.html.

59. E. H. van Ness and M. Scheffer. Alternative attractors may boost uncertainty and sensitivity in ecological models. *Ecological Modelling*, **159** (2003), 117–24.

60. I. Webster and G. P. Harris. Anthropogenic impacts on the ecosystems of coastal lagoons – fundamental processes and management. *Marine and Freshwater Research*, **55** (2003), 67–78.

61. J. T. Puckridge *et al.* Flow variability and the ecology of large rivers. *Marine and Freshwater Research*, **49** (1998), 55–72.

62. O. P. Judson. The rise of the individual-based model in ecology. *Trends in Ecology and Evolution*, **9** (1994), 9–14.

63. G. P. Harris and A. L. Heathwaite. Inadmissible evidence: knowledge and prediction in land and waterscapes. *Journal of Hydrology*, **304** (2004), 3–19.

64. I. Webster and G. P. Harris. Anthropogenic impacts on the ecosystems of coastal lagoons – fundamental processes and management. *Marine and Freshwater Research*, **55** (2003), 67–78.

65. G. P. Harris. The biogeochemistry of nitrogen and phosphorus in Australian catchments, rivers and estuaries: effects of land use and flow regulation and comparisons with global patterns. *Marine and Freshwater Research*, **52** (2001), 139–49. G. P. Harris. *Simple rules underlie the complex and non–linear dynamics of terrestrial and aquatic ecosystems: implications for catchment biogeochemistry and modelling*. Technical report no. 11/02. (Canberra, ACT: CSIRO Land and Water, 2002). http://www.clw.csiro.au/publications/technical2002.

66. R. V. O'Neill. Recovery in complex ecosystems. *Journal of Aquatic Ecosystem Stress and Recovery*, **6** (1999), 181–7.

67. Berlinski, *On Systems Analysis*. (See Note 26.)

68. A. Gragnani, M. Scheffer and S. Rinaldi. Top-down control of cyanobacteria: a theoretical analysis. *American Naturalist*, **153** (1999), 59–72. J. Huisman and F. J. Weissing. Biodiversity of plankton by species oscillations and chaos. *Nature*, **402** (1999), 407–10. A. Huppert, B. Blasius, and L. Stone. A model of phytoplankton blooms. *American Naturalist*, **159** (2002), 156–71. I. D. Lima, D. B. Olson and S. C. Doney. Intrinsic dynamics and stability properties of size-structured pelagic ecosystem models. *Journal of Plankton Research*, **24** (2002), 533–56.

69. M. C. Emmerson *et al.* Consistent patterns and idiosyncratic effects of biodiversity in marine systems. *Nature*, **411** (2001), 73–7.

70. D. Haag and M. Kaupenjohann. Parameters, prediction, post-normal science and the precautionary principle – a roadmap for modeling for decision-making. *Ecological Modelling*, **144** (2001), 45–60.

71. P. C. Young, S. Parkinson and M. J. Lees. Simplicity out of complexity: Occam's razor revisited. *Journal of Applied Statistics*, **23** (1996), 165–210. P. C. Young. Data-based mechanistic modelling

of environmental, ecological, economic and engineering systems. *Environmental Modelling and Software*, **13** (1998), 105–22. K. Schultz and K. J. Beven. Data-supported robust parameterisations in land surface-atmosphere flux predictions: towards a top-down approach. *Hydrological Processes*, **17** (2003), 2259–77. P. C. Young and H. Garnier. Identification and estimation of continuous-time, data-based mechanistic (DBM) models for environmental systems. *Environmental Modelling and Software*, **21** (2006), 1055–72.

72. L. Håkanson. Optimal size of predictive models. *Ecological Modelling*, **78** (1995), 195–204.

73. E. N. Bui, B. L. Hendersen and K. Viergever. Knowledge discovery from models of soil properties developed through data mining. *Ecological Modelling*, **191** (2006), 431–46. G. B. Arhonditsis *et al.* Exploring ecological patterns with structural equation modelling and Bayesian analysis. *Ecological Modelling*, **192** (2006), 385–409.

74. J. D. Olden, N. L. Poff and B. P. Bledsoe. Incorporating ecological knowledge into ecoinformatics: an example of modeling hierarchically structured aquatic communities with neural networks. *Ecological Informatics*, **1** (2006), 33–42.

75. P. C. Young. Non-stationary time series analysis and forecasting. *Progress in Environmental Science*, **1** (1999), 3–48.

76. E. Fox Keller. *Making Sense of Life: Explaining Biological Development with Models, Metaphors and Machines.* (Cambridge, MA: Harvard University Press, 2002).

77. M. A. Huston, D. de Angelis and W. Post. New computer models unify ecological theory. *Bioscience*, **38** (1988), 682–91. J. Uchmanski and V. Grimm Individual based modeling in ecology; what makes a difference? *Trends in Ecology and Evolution*, **11** (1996), 437–41.

78. V. Grimm. Ten years of individual-based modeling in ecology: what have we learned and what could we learn in the future? *Ecological Modelling*, **115** (1999), 129–48.

79. A. Lomnicki. Individual-based models and the individual-based approach to population ecology. *Ecological Modelling*, **115** (1999), 191–8.

80. For a thorough review of the development of these types of models, see H. H. Shugart. *A Theory of Forest Dynamics. The Ecological Implications of Forest Succession Models.* (Berlin: Springer-Verlag, 1984).

81. A. R. Ek and R. A. Monserud. *FOREST: a computer model for the growth and reproduction of mixed forest stands.* Research paper A 2635. (University of Madison, Wisconsin, College of Agriculture and Life Science, 1974).

82. S. W. Pacala, C. D. Canham and J. A. Silander, Jr. Forest models defined by field measurements. I. The design of a northeastern forest simulator. *Canadian Journal of Forestry Research*, **23** (1993), 1980–8.

83. D. J. Mladenhoff. LANDIS and forest landscape models. *Ecological Modelling*, **180** (2004), 7–19.

84. L. Bian. The representation of the environment in the context of individual-based modelling. *Ecological Modelling*, **159** (2003), 259–76.

85. A. Fischlin, H. Bugmann and D. Gyalistras. Sensitivity of a forest ecosystem model to climate parameterisation schemes. *Environmental Pollution*, **87** (1995), 267–82.

86. S. F. Railsback. Concepts from complex adaptive systems as a framework for individual-based modelling. *Ecological Modelling*, **139** (2001), 47–62.

87. B. Breckling *et al.* Emergent properties in individual-based ecological models – introducing case studies in an ecosystem research context. *Ecological Modelling*, **186** (2005), 376–88. H. Reuter *et al.* The concepts of emergent and collective properties in individual-based models – summary and outlook of the Bornhöved case studies. *Ecological Modelling*, **186** (2005), 489–501.

88. A.G. Marsh, Y. Zheng, and J. Garcia-Frias. The expansion of information in ecological systems: emergence as a quantifiable state. *Ecological Informatics*, **1** (2006), 107–16.

89. P.R. Moorcroft, G.C. Hurtt and S.W. Pacala. A method for scaling vegetation dynamics: the ecosystem demography model (ED). *Ecological Monographs*, **71** (2001) 557–86.

90. M. Hare and P. Deadman. Further towards a taxonomy of agent-based simulation models in environmental management. *Mathematics and Computers in Simulation*, **64** (2004), 25–40.

91. J.M. Anderies, M.A. Janssen and B.H. Walker. Grazing management, resilience, and the dynamics of a fire-driven rangelands system. *Ecosystems*, **5** (2002), 23–44. M.A. Janssen *et al*. An adaptive agent model for analysing co-evolution of management and policies in a complex rangeland system. *Ecological Modelling*, **131** (2000), 249–68.

92. M.A. Janssen, J.M. Anderies and B.H. Walker. Robust strategies for managing rangelands with multiple stable attractors. *Journal of Environmental Economics and Management*, **47** (2004), 140–62.

93. F. Recknagel. Simulation of aquatic food webs and species interactions by adaptive agents embodied with evolutionary computation: a conceptual framework. *Ecological Modelling*, **170** (2003), 291–302.

94. M. Janssen and S.R. Carpenter. Managing the resilience of lakes: a multi-agent modelling approach. *Conservation Ecology*, **3**(2) (2004), 15. On line at http://www.consecol.org/vol3/iss2/art15.

95. V. Grimm *et al*. Pattern-oriented modeling of agent-based complex systems: lessons from ecology. *Science*, **310** (2005), 987–91.

12 Evidence, uncertainty and risk

Provisional theories of risk and uncertainty: 'wicked' meso-scale problems and a new kind of science

Recognising that all knowledge is partial at best we are left with a variety of trade offs – none of our predictions is going to be foolproof. We continue to seek ways and means of making predictions about the world which provide useful guidance for actions and investment. The fact that the knowledge upon which we base our investments is noisy and incomplete at best does not alter the fact that investments still have to be made. This is a significant problem for regional and catchment-based management authorities. Subsidiarity is pushing decision making down to these bodies and they must cope with the lack of good data as best they can. In a world of 'becoming', of climate change and climate variability, even with new technologies it is going to be difficult to design and complete adequate performance monitoring after management interventions. Across the worlds of science, the community and the psychology of individuals there is a growing appreciation of increased complexity, recursive interaction and the importance of context.[1] Science is developing concepts of complex adaptive systems, emergence and fractals but, in practice, data gathering in the field is not keeping up with the conceptual revolution. The emphasis here is on a more fluid and evolving epistemology built around becoming rather than being, on process rather than structure and on change rather than stasis. In the ecological context the philosophy is moving away from Grand Unifying Theories such as Clementsian succession and competition to a raft of neutral and statistical models, which listen more closely to the data. Nevertheless the data are still partial and incomplete (infrequent in space and time, and with a tendency to be limited to pattern rather than both pattern and process) so there is more work yet to be done.

The challenge of managing 'multiple capitals' is going to be to set the biophysical data into a socioeconomic framework and find ways to trade off the various interactions. Any new biophysical data sets will have to be integrated with other partial and incomplete data sets, including data from various kinds of incommensurate variables, especially social and economic data and expert opinion. This problem of transdisciplinary data fusion does nothing to decrease the problems of uncertainty and risk. Interactions between the biosphere and the anthroposphere add to the level of complexity and the possibilities of SGC. All of the above places more and more emphasis on the need for adaptive management. Anticipatory strategies are very risky in a world of SGC and surprise. Once we recognise that we live in a world of uncertainty, that our knowledge is partial and that our predictive powers are limited, then there is a real need for institutional agility and rapid feedback from knowledge to response.

Uncertainty and risk

So despite our best efforts at eliminating uncertainty with the latest computing and intellectual firepower, doubt and risk remain; indeed, I argue that they are fundamental and always will remain. The recursive world of social, ecological and economic systems is highly uncertain. Knowledge always will be incomplete and theories partial. This is the human and the biophysical condition. We are beyond risk into a regional of indeterminacy. Healy[2] (quoting Wynne) uses the following classification:

- Risk: the system behaviour is known and probabilities of particular outcomes can be assigned
- Uncertainty: the system parameters are not known and probabilities cannot be assigned
- Indeterminacy: causal chains, networks and processes are open and defy prediction.
- Ignorance: what is not known is not known

In many environmental matters we are beyond risk: the situation is usually at least uncertain or indeterminate. Once science is no longer seen to be a superior form of knowledge with special access to a higher form of rationality, and trust is broken because of sense mismatches and suspicion of instrumentalism, then communication within extended peer communities often breaks down. Communication of risk is a complex area in itself; the various communities may have quite different perceptions of how risk is perceived and communicated.[3] In a world of uncertainty, indeterminacy and ignorance the players in the 'magic circle' – the keepers of multiple capitals including business, science, policy, the community and the media – must trust each other and share many values.[4] Building trust and keeping it is a key factor in successful conflict resolution.

In the last twenty years risk management and communication has become a major global industry. There is a huge literature on the subject. Most Western countries have in place regulatory frameworks and guidelines to codify and assist with the processes of risk assessment and management.[5] When people think of risk assessment *per se* they tend to think of environmental toxicology, i.e. the exposure of people and other organisms to pesticides, toxicants and other chemicals of concern. All techniques use various forms of modelling to help define the problem or the stressor, assess the actions or chemicals of concern (hazard characterisation), determine pathways of exposure or linkages from action to impact and define the dose–response relationships, and characterise the risks associated with the expected outcomes. The kinds of catchment modelling discussed above are a form of risk assessment based on deterministic modelling – after all, the reason for doing a lot of it is to understand the effects of landscape change on hydrology and to be able to manage water resources better. In addition, the huge effort that has been put into environmental impact (or effects) statements (EIS or EES statements) for major engineering and other projects is also a form of risk assessment on engineering works and their likely impacts.

By now we should be able to predict some of the major issues and problems with risk assessments. There will be a need to carefully define the stressors, the spatial and temporal scales of interest, the ecosystems and levels of organisation affected and the potential outcomes. There is a real need to define the appropriate level of detail required in any particular case.[6] Choices between simple (e.g. screening-level risk assessments) and the more complex assessments require a thorough understanding of:[7]

- Scale and complexity and the possibility of the presence of incommensurate parameters and predictions (as with catchment modelling)
- The identification and selection of end points (as in the eutrophication of lakes)
- Exposure characterisation (bioavailability in the case of toxicants, again a function of microbial interactions, solution chemistry and other factors)
- Stressor–response relationships (as with nutrient loadings to lakes and estuaries and including the possibility of non-linearity)
- Ecosystem recovery times and restoration possibility (and the possibility of hysteresis effects)
- Ecological significance (and the values that are placed on the various assets at risk)
- Uncertainties (in theory, data, parameters and model structures, other non-linearity, etc.)
- Biological stressors (introduced species, ecological interactions, genetically modified organisms)

There is also a real need to look at the synergies between risks to ecosystems because of higher-level interactions. For example, and an example with which I am presently familiar, the proposed dredging of a large coastal lagoon presents risks to the ecosystem through the spread of turbid plumes, reductions in light under water, damage to seagrasses and macro-algae, smothering of sediments and damage to benthic ecosystems, reductions in sediment denitrification rates, and the spread of toxicants from harbours and drains. Assessing the risk of the project to each potential impact in isolation of the interactions and synergies will not give an overall risk assessment for the project and the resulting EIS will be flawed.

Rather than provide (another) review of risk assessment methods here, I wish rather to provide an overview of some of the larger trends in this subject, because what seems to be happening is what we might expect. At the outset the analysis of risk was left to experts who undertook risk assessments largely with a view to obtaining technology or risk acceptance by the public. The entire exercise was about 'aligning public views with those held by the experts regarding the acceptability or otherwise of a particular hazard'.[8] This approach smacks of the whole approach to the public understanding of science: it's just that people do not understand, and all we had to do was to close the knowledge gap between the experts and the lay public. The scientists discounted the existence of social and other factors in assessing acceptable risks. Not surprisingly this did little to generate trust or acceptance and as access to information has become more widespread through the Web and the Internet the situation has merely got worse.

Through the 1980s and 1990s, public trust was increasingly eroded and suspicions grew that the risk management and EIS process was seriously flawed. So the focus now is on a much more thorough and involved dialogue process to build trust and engender a much greater level of understanding around risk, justice, equity, procedural fairness and values.[9] This requires the establishment of a 'magic circle' of interested parties and raises issues about the ability of all parties to deal with complexity, surprise, scientific uncertainties and the values and beliefs of others. Many are now arguing for the open acknowledgement of uncertainties to increase the credibility of the communicators and for a community discourse around these difficult issues.[10] One of the problems that we face is that there are varying perceptions of risks and in many cases risks are assessed on a number of incommensurate scales: human health, life expectancy, toxicological impacts, biodiversity loss and water quality, to name but a few. Risk is not a monolithic concept but a mental construct that allows for prediction of future hazards and facilitates risk reduction measures.[11] Risk is a multi-dimensional, subjective and value-laden concept involving uncertainties in knowledge and much contextual baggage.[12] As with other fields of endeavour, we have moved from an initial stance of scientific dominance and certainty to a much more negotiated space involving uncertainty, doubt, social justice and value-laden concepts.[13]

Nassim Taleb strongly argues that we actually know much less than we think. He defines two categories of randomness. 'Type one' randomness complies with the usual kinds of statistical assumptions – white noise, Gaussian distributions, stationarity – and provides situations in which averages mean something. On the other hand, he argues, more and more of the situations we now encounter in coupled socioeconomic and environmental systems are what he calls 'type two' randomness in which we do not know (or cannot define) the distributions; means and variances change over time, generating functions switch sign, and rare and catastrophic events are so rare and catastrophic as to be unrecorded and/or quite unpredictable. This is a state of complexity and uncertainty quite unlike a state of uniformitarianism. Agent-based or individual-based systems, such as those discussed in this book, characteristically produce this kind of 'type two' randomness. Prediction under these circumstances is a matter of chance.[14] Taleb calls these unpredictable events 'black swans' because no amount of examination of white swans would have prepared the first Australian explorers for their first sight of a black one! In papers on his website, Taleb discusses a continuum of system properties, which range from 'type one' – in which the usual statistical constraints and definitions do apply – to 'type two' systems in which fractal and power law properties of agent-based complex systems lead to pink or red spectra and the appearance of 'fat tails' of rare and unpredictable events. Taleb argues that we often fool ourselves into thinking that events are more predictable than they really are and that risks are actually contained when they are not. Most of the situations described in this book fall into the 'type two' classification; the tools we develop and the techniques we adopt – like the co-production of knowledge and adaptive management – often fail because we underestimate the risks. Taleb argues that we have a quite dire track record of predicting 'black swans'.

Provisional theories of context and ignorance

Michael Smithson[15] has discussed the topic of dealing with uncertainty, indeterminism and ignorance at some length. He points out that although we have many and good theories of knowledge we are short on theories of ignorance. New techniques of decision making under uncertainty need to be developed.[16] Nassim Taleb would surely agree. The commonly used theories of frequentist probability make the usual strong assumptions about the statistical distributions of data, about stationarity and normality, as well as the ability of past events to make statements about the future. We are trying to move down the track of developing tools to cope with more uncertain systems, but we have a long way to go. Moving away from purely frequentist statistics into statistical techniques that include prior knowledge is increasingly becoming common practice (Bayesian statistics), as is the use of techniques that include belief and categorical data (Dempster–Shafer logic and other frameworks). In other words, statistical practice is catching up with demands for more complex techniques that cope with uncertain worlds. Nevertheless, none has moved as far as Taleb suggests is necessary.

Bayesian statistical techniques are becoming more and more common as we appreciate the uncertainties associated with either overfitting and failing to validate complex models, or sticking with simple models that oversimplify the complexities of complex adaptive systems. Hierarchical Bayesian models can accommodate both sources of uncertainty and estimation errors as well as internally generated variability in the form of both known and unknown processes; as such they can accommodate complexity in its various forms.[17] As yet the general understanding of Bayesian statistics is not as well developed as that of the usual frequentist statistics, so more needs to be done to develop the techniques as well as 'user-friendly' software. There are some good examples in the literature of the use of simple Bayesian methods, which employ a good deal of pragmatism and practicality.

One good example of the use of simple Bayesian techniques is the management of nutrient loads to lakes and estuaries in the USA developed by Reckhow and others. Environmental Protection Agency regulations to clean up lakes in the USA require the definition of Total Maximum Daily Loads of nutrients (TMDLs) for as many as 40 000 lakes. Reckhow and his collaborators understood all the issues discussed above concerning model parameterisations, prediction errors and uncertainty.[18] Indeed, these issues have been well understood since the early days of lake modelling, more than twenty years ago. The issues were well known to those modelling the Great Lakes in the late 1970s and early 1980s; in a review article in 1987 Beck reviewed the sources of uncertainty in water quality modelling, coming to many of the same conclusions we have reached here.[19] This did nothing, however, to prevent the proliferation of complex dynamical simulation models for the prediction and management of water quality in lakes and estuaries and their use by regulatory agencies in subsequent years. (I have been as guilty as any: a testament, I think, to the hegemony of the scientific method and the strength of the frequentist statistical paradigm.) Many of the water quality models constructed to manage receiving waters are too complex to be comprehended by lay persons and so have only been used by experts – and not all of those have fully comprehended the uncertainties involved. There seems to be an inverse relation between model complexity and widespread use by all members of the community. This has not engendered trust between the scientific and lay communities. So in an explicit attempt to move on beyond the uncertainties associated with complex deterministic water quality models, and to find a technique that was simpler and could be used more effectively in a community dialogue process, Reckhow and others turned to Bayesian nets and probabilistic approaches, to explicitly recognise and learn from the uncertainties involved.[20] Bayesian nets are simple representations of the linkages between key processes and understandings that determine chosen outcomes. At each step of the chain prior information is included in the form of Bayesian priors, to aid the processes of determining the probability of an outcome. All except the initial conditions are therefore conditional probabilities; each step of the network is conditioned by knowledge about prior associations or dependencies.

The diagrammatic Bayesian nets display the key dependencies.[21] This approach has been thoroughly tested in the Neuse River estuary in North Carolina[22] and has been shown to be no better or worse in its ability to predict algal biomass in the estuary than a complex dynamical model of the same system.[23] More importantly, because of their simplicity and ease of comprehension these Bayesian nets have proved very useful in stakeholder dialogues and community consultation.[24]

Wicked meso-scale problems and a new kind of science: beyond 'sweet reason'

So moves are afoot to find simpler modelling techniques that explicitly recognise the uncertainties of our ecological predictions and which can be used by a broader church of experts, agency managers and concerned citizens. Because of spatial and temporal variability, partial and incomplete knowledge, incommensurate variables and values, and complex adaptive interactions between these 'systems of systems' we are dealing with a totally new class of problem in terms of difficulty. They are the kinds of problems that Dovers[25] has called 'wicked problems' – problems that are characterised by:

- Deepened and variable temporal scales
- Broadened and variable spatial scales
- Possible ecological limits to human activities
- Often, irreversible and/or cumulative impacts
- Complexity within problems, and connectivity between problems
- Pervasive risk and uncertainty
- Poor information base for many processes
- Important assets not traded and thus not valued economically
- New ethical dimensions (rights of other species, future generations)
- Systemic problem causes, rooted in patterns of production and consumption, settlement and governance
- Insufficiently developed and/or contested theories, methods and techniques
- Poorly defined policy and property rights and responsibilities
- Public/private costs and benefits difficult to separate
- Demands and justification for broad community participation in policy discussion and formulation
- Sheer novelty as a recently defined policy field

As Dovers notes

> these problem attributes, especially when encountered in combination, give some meaning and tractability to the widespread perception and common claim that sustainability problems are particularly difficult.[26]

All such problems require a new approach on the part of individuals and institutions, one that encompasses the ability to respond to change and complexity, and an ability to participate in a recursive debate between the worlds of science, policy, commerce and the broader community.

Wicked meso-scale interactive problems call for a new kind of science. It is a science that Gibbons *et al.* have called Mode II science or 'science in the context of its application'.[27] I argue here that what is going to be required is what might be called Mode III science: science that is done in the context of its application *but which also influences the context and application through engagement in a contextual and recursive debate*. Knowledge is indeed an agent of change, but change will only be achieved if science works *with and through various forms of natural, human and social capital to achieve outcomes*. Mode III science is transdisciplinary and deeply recursive and is an explicit acknowledgement *that reason is not a sufficient guide to our actions*.

Achieving outcomes requires the establishment of a collaborative 'magic circle':[28] a creative collaboration linking the worlds of science, governance, industry, the media and the community.[29] To do this requires an understanding of ethics, values and context. All players need to be engaged in systems thinking; weighing and judging their knowledge, needs and actions in a collaborative context. This is not easy to achieve and there are few experienced players of such games.[30] Most scientists are trained to just solve problems, and they usually pick simple, soluble problems. Careers in science are not built on failure to solve problems. Nor are they built on activism and community liaison skills. New systems thinking skills are going to be required. Systems thinking cuts to the very heart of epistemology and context. What is it we know? How do we know it? What is the associated value set and accompanying assumptions? Who else shares our view? What can we do with the knowledge we have? These questions raise important issues about our ability to observe and recognise what is going on – environmentally, socially and culturally – to name and understand actions and behaviours, and to use the knowledge to predict and achieve outcomes. The new world requires an inquiry into the nature and use of evidence.

If we are trying to achieve desirable outcomes, such as the conservation of biodiversity and ecosystem function, increased water use efficiency or a reduction in forest clearing, then there is a need to lift the level of the debate and to empower the actors in the 'magic circle'. Simultaneously, in the recursive world of debate and changing contexts, science becomes less the source of truth and more a form of partial evidence to be negotiated and used in argument and explanation. Both knowledge and ignorance need to be recognised.[31] These are not new ideas. Anthony Giddens wrote about the consequences of modernity more than ten years ago and scientists like Buzz Holling have been speaking and writing about adaptive management[32] for about thirty years. The uptake of these ideas has been slow. The reasons for this we will have to explore, but they probably lie at the intersection of philosophy, risk management, sociology and psychology: outside the normal realms of science. Although the 'magic circle' can bring players together and stimulate debate, there must be suitable receptors.

In many ways science has not helped itself: assertions of priority in ways of knowing strike some as hubristic. The global scientific enterprise has put much emphasis on the search for truth and ultimate causes through reductionism: pulling systems apart and studying the components in isolation, controlling variability and using statistical techniques to extract averages, correlations and trends through time. Much of what might be regarded as systems dynamics was seen as noise to be controlled and, as far as possible, eliminated. Interactions were assumed to be linear, close to equilibrium and time-reversible in a Newtonian universe. True, biological and ecological data were known to be much noisier than physical and chemical data, but the basic scientific method was to let theory have primacy and to allow the data to be used to test theory. Perhaps because of the evident complexity and the noisy data that resulted, the status of theory in ecology has long been questioned.[33] Now ideas are changing, particularly in biology, and the data are being allowed to speak for themselves.[34] The basic philosophy is changing to be more open to the complex interactions between parts and to expect emergent properties from complex wholes.[35] We have learned to expect non-linearity and irreversibility. Much of what we see in biology and ecology cannot be explained by dissection. This includes seeing science as part of, and engaged with, society.

Science is changing, however. What has been going on in a number of disciplines in recent years has been an intellectual acceptance and understanding of the complexity of the natural world and of the need for systems thinking, both within science and without. Much new science is what might be called multi-disciplinary or transdisciplinary. In order to tackle many of the emerging environmental problems we face around the globe we need teams of specialists drawn from many disciplines, and many of the real challenges lie at the interstices between traditional disciplines. So to find solutions to some of our problems we will need to find systems solutions, which engage all players and parties in a collaborative venture.[36] None should underestimate the challenge of bringing teams of scientists together, let alone achieving engagement and collaboration with the broader community!

A 'postnormal' science?

Again, this is not a new idea. As long ago as 1958 Gregory Bateson wrote of a 'science that had, as yet, no satisfactory name'[37] when discussing the recursive debate between science and society. Bateson's work is only now being rediscovered in some key disciplines[38] but its emphasis on systems dynamics and social context forms the basis of what might now be called 'postnormal' science. 'Postnormal' science is the term used by Ravetz and others[39] to describe the kind of complex, value-laden, socially engaged science we are discussing here. In the context of 'postnormal' science, and sustainability science in particular, Gallopin *et al.* define complexity in terms of the multiplicity of legitimate perspectives, non-linearity, emergence, self-organisation and multiplicity of scales: in short, Dovers' 'wicked problems'. The factors that particularly impinge on the science of complexity, they claim, are the complexities of physical reality (self-organisation, emergence and uncertainty) combined with the need to consider a plurality of epistemologies and intentionalities. As opposed to traditional applied science, which occupies a space where the decision stakes, risks and systems uncertainties are low, 'postnormal' science occupies a space characterised by high decision stakes and systems uncertainties. Pertinent recent examples would be the debate over genetically modified organisms in agriculture and foods, the BSE outbreak in the UK, the future of irrigation and the rivers in the Murray–Darling Basin, and numerous other environmental issues. In these debates beliefs, values and ethics are paramount, as is distrust of the more 'normal' kinds of scientific instrumentalism.

Marshall[40] has provided a thorough criticism of science and has sought to deconstruct much of what we have come to believe in ecology over the last two hundred years. Science is deeply rooted in our systems of beliefs about the world, particularly a tendency to believe in holistic, Unitarian frameworks with strong religious overtones. O'Connor[41] sees 'postnormal' science as moving away from more traditional and ethical stances where a focus on universal theory and knowledge based on simple axioms is thought to be able to be integrated into a single, internally consistent grand conceptual framework. (Perhaps a classic example would be the search for a Grand Unified Theory of cosmology.) This approach very much sees knowledge in instrumental terms. 'Postnormal' science instead occupies a space characterised by a plurality of perspectives, which cannot be integrated into a single coherent framework. Various valid perspectives coexist in a recursive debate. Knowledge is obtained through a series of collaborative dialogues involving trust, respect and recognition of the validity of other perspectives and values. There is usually no single 'correct' answer. What O'Connor calls 'dialogical, complex reconciliations' requires careful attention to language and rhetoric so that argument and explanation become paramount. Much listening is required by all parties. In the approach to achieving outcomes we are confronted by issues around what Polanyi called 'sense giving and sense receiving':[42] paying careful attention to what is said, how it is being said and the messages received. Communities with different perspectives and value sets rarely use identical words to mean the same things. Lines of communication and trust may therefore be broken unwittingly if the sense that is intended to be given is not what is received. Building trust in uncertain areas requires careful, deliberative and inclusive processes to be established.

NOTES

1. G. Bateson. *Steps to an Ecology of Mind*. (St Albans, Herts: Paladin, 1973). Alan Marshall. *The Unity of Nature*. (London: Imperial College Press, 2002).

2. S. Healy. Extended peer communities and the ascendance of post-normal politics. *Futures*, **31** (1999), 655–69. B. Wynne. Uncertainty and environmental learning: reconceiving science and policy in the preventive paradigm. *Global Environmental change*, **2** (1992), 111–27.

3. M. Smithson. *Ignorance and Uncertainty: Emerging Paradigms*. (New York: Springer-Verlag, 1989).

4. Clearly, building trust and aligning values between groups within society is a highly politicized process. See, for example, Thomas Frank. *What's the Matter with Kansas?* (New York: Metropolitan Owl Books, 2004).

5. See, for example, L. S. McCarty and M. Power. Approaches to developing risk management objectives: an analysis of international strategies. *Environmental Science and Policy*, **3** (2000), 311–19. R. E. Kwiatkowski. The role of risk assessment and risk management in environmental assessment. *Envirometrics*, **9** (1998), 587–98.

6. R. A. Hill *et al.* Level of detail in ecological risk assessments. *Marine Pollution Bulletin*, **40** (2000), 471–7.

7. J. H. Gentile *et al.* Ecological risk assessment: a scientific perspective. *Journal of Hazardous Materials*, **35** (1993), 241–53.

8. L. Frewer. The public and effective risk communication. *Toxicology Letters*, **149** (2004), 391–7.

9. G. H. Eduljee. Trends in risk assessment and risk management. *Science of the Total Environment*, **249** (2000), 13–23.

10. J. Corburn. Environmental justice, local knowledge, and risk: the discourse of a community-based cumulative exposure assessment. *Environmental Management*, **29** (2002), 451–66.

11. O. Renn. Perception of risks. *Toxicology Letters*, **149** (2004), 405–13.

12. P. Slovic. The risk game. *Journal of Hazardous Materials*, **86** (2001), 17–24.

13. The situation is made more complex by the politicization of intellectual endeavours by a supposedly liberal 'elite'. See, for example, Frank, *What's the Matter with Kansas?* (See Note 4.)

14. M. Bond. You can't predict life's black swans. An interview with Nassim Nicholas Taleb. *New Scientist*, No. 2558, 1 July 2006, 50–1. N. N. Taleb. *Fooled by Randomness: the Hidden Role of Chance in Life and in the Markets*, 2nd edn. (New York: Texere, 2004).

15. M. Smithson. *Ignorance and Uncertainty: Emerging Paradigms*. (New York: Springer-Verlag, 1989).

16. New theories of decision making under uncertainty are being developed. See, for example, Y. Ben-Haim. *Information-gap Decision Theory: Decisions under Severe Uncertainty*. (San Diego, CA: Academic Press, 2006). See also D. R. Fox *et al.* An info-gap approach to power and sample size calculations. *Envirometrics*, **17** (2006), 1–15.

17. J. S. Clark. Why environmental scientists are becoming Bayesians. *Ecology Letters*, **8** (2005), 2–14.

18. K. H. Reckhow. Water quality simulation modelling and uncertainty analysis for risk assessment and decision making. *Ecological Modelling*, **72** (1994), 1–20. Also N. N. Taleb's website: www.fooledbyramdomness.com.

19. M. B. Beck. Water quality modelling: a review of the analysis of uncertainty. *Water Resources Research*, **23** (1987), 1393–442.

20. M. E. Borsuk, C. A. Stow and K. H. Reckhow. Predicting the frequency of water quality standard violations: and probabilistic approach for TMDL development. *Environmental Science and Technology*, **36** (2002), 2109–15. W. W. Walker, Jr. Consideration of variability and uncertainty

in phosphorus total maximum daily loads for lakes. *Journal of Water Resources Planning and Management, ASCE*, **129** (4) (2003), 337–44 (July/August 2003).

21. K. H. Reckhow. Water quality prediction and probability network models. *Canadian Journal of Fisheries and Aquatic Science*, **56** (1999), 1150–8.

22. M. E. Borsuk, C. A. Stow and K. H. Reckhow. Integrated approach to total maximum daily load development for Neuse River estuary using Bayesian probability network model (Neu-BERN). *Journal of Water Resources Planning and Management, ASCE*, **129** (2003), 271–82 (July/August 2003).

23. C. A. Stow *et al.* Comparison of estuarine water quality models for total maximum daily load development in Neuse River estuary. *Journal of Water Resources Planning and Management, ASCE*, **129** (2003), 307–14 (July/August 2003).

24. M. Borsuk *et al.* Stakeholder values and scientific modelling in the Neuse River watershed. *Group Decision and Negotiation*, **10** (2001), 355–73.

25. S. R. Dovers. Sustainability; demands on policy. *Journal of Public Policy*, **16** (1997), 303–18.

26. R. D. Connor and S. R. Dovers. *Institutional change and learning for sustainable development.* Working paper 2002/1. (Canberra: Centre for Resource and Environmental Studies, Australian National University, 2002): www.cres.anu.edu.au/outputs/.

27. M. Gibbons *et al. The New Production of Knowledge, the Dynamics of Science and Research in Contemporary Societies*. (London: Sage, 1994).

28. J. Burgess. Public understanding of environmental change. Paper presented at the International Conference *Detecting Environmental Change*. University of London, 17–20 July 2001; J. Burgess *et al. Local Outreach*. R&D Technical Report, SWCON 204. ESRU Dept. of Geography, University of London, (Bristol, UK: Environment Agency, 2001). See also Vera John-Steiner. *Creative Collaboration*. (Oxford: Oxford University Press, 2000). R. W. Rycroft and D. E. Kash. *The Complexity Challenge: Technological Innovation for the 21st Century*. (London: Pinter, 1999).

29. P. Taylor. *Unruly Complexity: Ecology, Interpretation, Engagement*. (Chicago, IL: Chicago University Press, 2005). Taylor describes this kind of science-in-action as 'heterogeneously constructed'.

30. The entire debate is usually highly politicized. See, for example, Frank, *What's the matter with Kansas?* (See Note 4.)

31. D. Deutsch. *The Fabric of Reality*. (London: Allen Lane, The Penguin Press, 1997). See also Smithson, *Ignorance and Uncertainty*. (See Note 3.)

32. C. S. Holling. *Adaptive Environmental Assessment and Management*. (New York: Wiley, 1978).

33. R. H. Peters. *A Critique for Ecology*. (Cambridge: Cambridge University Press, 1991).

34. E. Fox Keller. *Making Sense of Life*. (Cambridge, MA: Harvard University Press, 2002).

35. Stuart Kauffman, for example, has opened up new fields by studying the emergence of self-organisation and adaptation in models of complex biological systems. See also S. A. Kauffman. *The Origins of Order*. (Oxford: Oxford University Press, 1993).

36. Taylor. *Unruly Complexity*. (See Note 29.)

37. G. Bateson. *Naven, a Survey of the Problems Suggested by a Composite Picture of a New Guinea Tribe Drawn from Three Points of View*. (California: Stanford University Press, 1958). Bateson is quoted in S. S. Tognetti. Science in a double bind: Gregory Bateson and the origins of post-normal science. *Futures*, **31** (1999), 689–703.

38. H. Wardle. Gregory Bateson's lost world: the anthropology of Haddon and Rivers continued and deflected. *Journal of the History of Behavioural Sciences*, **35** (1999), 379–89. L. B. Edwards and G. G. Jaros. Psychology, a discipline with a structure-based history and a process-based future. *Journal of Social and Evolutionary Systems*, **18** (1995), 67–85.

39. J. Ravetz. What is post-normal science. *Futures*, **31** (1999), 647–53. The content of that entire issue of *Futures* was taken up with a series of papers on postnormal science and its development. See also G. C. Gallopin *et al.* Science for the twenty-first century: from social contract to the scientific core. *International Journal of Social Science*, **168** (2001), 219–29, also posted to www.sustainabilityscience.org, June 2002.

40. A. Marshall. *The Unity of Science*. (London: Imperial College Press, 2003).

41. M. O'Connor. Dialogue and debate in a post-normal practice of science: a reflexion. *Futures*, **31** (1999), 671–87.

42. M. Polanyi. *Knowing and Being*. (London: Routledge and Kegan Paul, 1969).

13 Modified landscapes: biodiversity

Anthropogenic change and biodiversity: landscape ecology in fragmented landscapes, biodiversity and function.

So far we have looked at the philosophical basis of our ecological knowledge, the problems that our new understanding of ecological and environmental complexity bring, and the state of knowledge with respect to landscape function and habitat fragmentation. Along the way we have discussed some of the environmental problems wrought by our modern global society and made particular reference to the importance of water. We live in a world of constant change, of complexity, uncertainty and risk, at least some of which is brought about by the emergence of events driven by hitherto unrecognised small-scale interactions. We suffer from the tyranny of the small writ large.

Now we must begin to turn to the question 'so what can we do about all this'. The first step must be a discussion about the nature and functioning of the landscapes we have modified and created: what might be called the 'rest of nature', because most of the planet is now modified by human activity in one way or another. Our modern agricultural and urban landscapes have been constructed over long time periods, sometimes millennia. As we saw previously in the discussion of the English landscape, little by little the native vegetation and ecosystems have been modified, cleared and replaced by human tinkering; everything is indeed much older than we think. We now have huge cultural, intellectual, institutional and infrastructure investments, 'sunk costs' if you like, that constrain our actions and our ability to radically change what we do. What do we know about the broader patterns of landscape behaviour? What has happened to our attempts to construct or manage landscapes?

Landscape ecology

Landscape ecology is the discipline that studies the aesthetics, function and management of landscapes as mosaics of pattern and process. This discipline attempts to deal with landscapes at the scale of smaller catchments and paddocks – the scales of lived places. This is a much more difficult scale to tackle because of the details of individual places. The first papers in this area were published in the late 1980s. Landscape ecology deals with the interplay of pattern and process in heterogeneous landscapes[1] and although Turner's original article was subtitled 'the effect of pattern on process', I agree with Hobbs[2] that with our recursive view of complexity we should now stress the interplay between the two in space and time over a range of scales. All landscapes are simultaneously complex adaptive systems and networks of interacting pattern and process. You cannot consider one without the other. It is the networks of interactions that can reveal much about how landscapes (and waterscapes) work. Through the interplay of pattern and process there is considerable evidence of emergent statistical and macroscopic properties.

Landscape ecology has tended to focus rather too much on the classification, modelling and analysis of landscape pattern. As with the detection of ecological interactions in communities, it seems that we tend to get hung up on the description of patterns rather than the analysis of the underlying processes that generate those patterns. In a self-organised world, where the pattern arises from internal recursive interactions, knowledge of the pattern alone is insufficient to explain what is going on, and certainly an insufficient predictor of impending change. Knowledge of process and the scales of disturbance and recovery are required also.[3] Certainly landscape ecology has the potential to be central to the solution of many of the pressing problems we all face at landscape scales although, to achieve this, some transdisciplinary science and integration across scales and disciplines is going to be required (even, for example, between landscape ecology and spatial economics).[4] What we are going to need is more 'joined-up thinking' about the subtleties and complexities of multiple capitals and their interactions in mosaics across a wide range of scales.[5]

I would be the first to admit that when dealing with landscape scales we are dealing with one of the most intractable problems and some of the most difficult of all scales. Solutions for many of our most pressing environmental problems are going to be sought at the meso-scales, which lie in that ghastly zone between plots and paddocks and the larger scales of regional and global models. It is here that the surprises and interactions of complex adaptive systems lie. It is here that we see the interplay of environmental, social and economic forces; and it is here that we are going to begin to 'do something about all this'.

The literature abounds with papers on debates about appropriate statistical tools and metrics for landscape ecology.[6] Indeed, there are so many possible measures of spatial pattern that there have even been numerous meta-analyses of the relationships between various measures.[7] Different measures of patchiness give different results at different scales; perhaps because of this, there has also been a move towards the use of spectral or fractal measures of habitat fragmentation.[8] Either way one of the problems is that as land use change proceeds most measures do not produce monotonic relationships with fragmentation. For example, during clearing, as the landscape changes from uniform forest to uniform arable land many measures change in complex and non-linear ways;[9] gaps grow and patches shrink so measures of spatial dimensions are complex.

Species in fragmented landscapes

From the earliest development of landscape ecology there has been an interest in trying to model patch distributions and the spread of species across fragmented landscapes. Many different models have been used but the canonical development was done by using simple neutral and percolation models.[10] Others have used graph theory to look at connectivity along edges and at nodes.[11] These models revealed that there are, apparently, critical thresholds for the movement of species across patterned landscapes. These thresholds arise from the non-linear interactions of scale-dependent processes and the degree of fragmentation. As fragmentation proceeds, and the landscape becomes disconnected into more and more smaller patches of suitable habitat, then landscape connectivity in the models (the function relating spatial contiguity of habitat and the ability of species to move across the grid) may undergo abrupt changes. This is analogous to the properties of randomly connected networks (also modelled by percolation theory) and the abrupt changes in their properties that occur as connectivity gradually increases. Many simple grid-based models (analogous in many ways to cellular automaton models) produce this kind of threshold behaviour; many do so at the point where about 20%–40% of the original 'favourable' habitat is left in the grid. Newer versions of these models use fractal landscapes.[12] So there are strong echoes of various kinds of complex systems theory here also and there are, as might be expected, parallels in the conceptual development.

The significance of the possibility of thresholds for clearing was not lost on the conservation biology community. These kinds of results quickly became enshrined in 'rules of thumb' for ensuring the preservation of species in fragmented landscapes. For example, Fahrig[13] recommended that a threshold value of 20% of the original habitat should be preserved to ensure population persistence. If this was done, she argued, then species persistence in fragmented landscapes was ensured. Unfortunately, more modelling has only clouded the issue, with new work revealing that many factors influence the persistence and survival of populations in fragmented landscapes and that threshold values from 2% to over 90% may be found.[14] The situation became even more complex when models revealed that representing the landscape as a continuous function of habitat suitability, rather than a binary representation, gave quite different results and showed that dispersal across continuously graded landscapes was much easier.[15] The binary view of habitat is clearly too simplistic.[16]

So what do we make of all this? What do the data show? Unfortunately the results of habitat fragmentation experiments show that the patterns of the distribution of species across fragmented landscapes do not follow the theoretical predictions.[17] Overall, the results were very mixed.[18] Whereas some[19] insist that the problem lies in confusion and the lack of definition of the fragmentation metrics, others[20] see the problems much more as being fundamental and arising from the properties of complex adaptive systems. Fragmentation of ecosystems produces a number of responses, not the least in time. Snapshots of an evolving relationship between fragmentation and biodiversity are likely to produce some temporally complex outcomes and there are quite likely to be surprises and points of no return. Resource availability will change over time as the fragmentation proceeds and as the biophysical environment changes, so there is a real need to understand the temporal and spatial dynamics of the effects of land use change and habitat fragmentation as well as the relationships between pattern and process.

Many of the models discussed above were neutral models of patchiness and dispersal. Plotnick and Gardner[21] have written a more general model of species interactions in fragmented landscapes, which does include some of the concepts from equilibrium ecology, including competition and niche overlap. By incorporating more complexity in process and interaction the model is analogous to a very complex cellular automaton model, one with an ability to simulate the interactions of up to 20 species. This model produced much more complex outcomes depending on disturbance frequencies, habitat characteristics over time, and species-specific differences in fecundity and dispersal. Furthermore, the model showed the importance of initial conditions (including contingent spatial distributions of populations and resources), the temporal unfolding of interactions between land use change and population distributions, and even reversals in outcomes depending on the trajectory of development. In short, the model was realistic and complex and showed long-term dynamical behaviour dependent on the initial conditions for up to 200 simulated years. These outputs share similarities with other attempts to increase the realism of models relating the processes of establishment, competition for resources and trophic interactions.[22] All show highly complex non-linear behaviour and path-dependent dynamics over long time periods. Hassell, Comins and May showed a decade ago that there are self organised patterns of community structure in landscapes and that fragmentation of the landscape into patches smaller than the characteristic size of the self-organised structures caused landscape collapse.[23] In addition, Krummel and co-workers showed that some of the most complex interactions in landscapes occur at a point where fractal dimensions change: at a point between predominantly human determination of patterns at small scales and topographic determination at large scales.[24]

More recent work has shown that ecological interactions in landscapes and waterscapes can produce memory effects, which may actually be reinforced by disturbance.[25] These effects will interact with non-linear community-level assembly rules and food-chain interactions (trophic cascades) to produce surprising results when species are added or deleted in spatially disaggregated landscapes and waterscapes.[26] Ecosystem function is determined by some complex interactions between the biodiversity, spatial patterning and functional roles of species, which change across scales as species are gained or lost. Land use change and clearing also alters the context of the interactions and therefore the solutions that are seen as a result. Add to this the recent work on the very complex and emergent properties of networks of connected species and populations as revealed by using graph theory,[27] and we begin to realise that what we are dealing with is a deeply complex and recursive network of local interactions, which produces a set of ensemble properties at landscape and waterscape scales. These properties are very difficult to predict when ecosystems are fragmented or perturbed. This is the day-to-day reality of what have been called meso-scale 'middle number' systems: systems that have too few interacting components to have macro-ecological statistical properties (large number systems, e.g. gas laws) but too many recursively interacting components to be simply predictable.[28] This is, indeed, the world of day-to-day living, of complexity, uncertainty and 'wicked' problems.

Biodiversity and ecosystem function

If some simple functions of physiology and nutrient stoichiometry underlie and determine the overall response of ecosystems in terms of water balance and nutrient cycling, and the patch dynamics of land- and waterscapes influence the overall function, then these factors are important determinants of the responses we are likely to see when we alter patchiness by clearing catchments or changing land use. Sustainability is therefore constrained by some basic evolved properties of organisms; the ways in which these give rise to higher-level properties through interactions across scales are critical. Models and observations indicate that, for example, in the relatively arid Australian landscape climate, water availability and temperature have an overall role in determining the structure of plant communities across the landscape.[29] The native Australian bush is both biologically diverse and a highly efficient user of water and resources.[30] Land clearing and deforestation fragments the native bush, reduces biodiversity and destroys the original patchiness and hydrological equilibrium. Reduction in leaf area and water use efficiency leads to disruption of the hydrological balance and increases in runoff and infiltration.[31] The frequency and magnitude of peaks in runoff changes and nutrient exports increase.[32] Thus biodiversity on the land controls hydrological function through the functional complementarity of the species and determines the balance of the 'green' and 'blue' water flows. Patchiness plays a key role in all this.

So what happens when we artificially change habitat patchiness? After all, this is a pervasive human influence in catchments all across the globe. All the models and observations of habitat fragmentation indicate that as the patch size of fragments of intact ecosystems is reduced then overall species number and abundance declines. Biodiversity is lower in fragmented landscapes.[33] Intuitively this must be true in situations where immigration becomes less likely as patches become more and more isolated, and where mortality rates increase owing to disturbance within patches. One further factor that reduces biodiversity in terrestrial systems is the reduction in habitat complexity that occurs in smaller patches due to grazing, logging, removal of dead wood, etc. A similar phenomenon can occur in rivers and lakes when habitats are simplified by the removal of dead trees and other riparian vegetation, and when connectivity between river reaches is reduced by dams and weirs and by the straightening and 'improvement' of river reaches. Predators and species requiring complex habitats show proportionally greater reductions in abundance in smaller fragments.[34] As biodiversity declines in fragments then ecosystem function will be compromised. Many studies now show that reduction in biodiversity leads to reduced biomass, productivity and nutrient use by plants.[35] Both large-scale experiments[36] and meta-analyses[37] reveal statistically significant relations between biodiversity and a number of aspects of ecosystem function. Because function appears to saturate, some have therefore argued that to preserve ecosystem function it is not essential to preserve all the original, unfragmented regional biodiversity,[38] but Tilman and his co-workers have demonstrated that the longer plot scale experiments are run, the more ecosystem function continues to improve with species number.

Most importantly, perhaps, it is not just reduction in species number and biodiversity that is important; it is reduction in the number of functional groups (e.g. in plants: annuals, perennials, deep- and shallow-rooted, differing flowering times, etc.) that compromises ecosystem function.[39] Overall, reductions in plant biodiversity lead to increases in nutrient concentrations in soils, less efficient use of soil nutrients and lower productivity and the export of nutrients from catchments in streams draining cleared areas. Although there are some individual and idiosyncratic effects of particular species on ecosystem function,[40] Wardle and his co-workers discovered precisely the expected relationships between a number of aspects of nutrient dynamics in small vegetated islands and variations in the sizes of those fragments.[41] Soil nutrient concentrations in particular are higher in smaller patches with fewer species. Forests normally cycle nutrients very efficiently[42] (this is why nutrient concentrations are usually low in streams draining old growth forests) but detailed work by Durka *et al.* showed that reductions in the growth rates of trees led to increased nitrate leaching from woodland soils.[43] Tilman also showed the same effect from reduced biodiversity in artificially manipulated plots. Higher nutrient exports and enrichment of receiving waters are to be expected when habitat fragmentation occurs and biodiversity is reduced. Fragmentation alters the hydrological connection between the land and the water and allows larger amounts of nutrients to move. It also moves the system away from the upper-bound properties of complex, non-equilibrium systems that show MaxEnt-like characteristics.

Functional complementarity is important for the overall hydrological balance and efficient cycling of nutrients in ecosystems. Reductions in functional complementarity disrupt the $MaxE_T$ and MaxWUE (water use efficiency) properties of diverse systems. For example, Pate and Bell have done some of the most complete work on functional complementarity in Australian woodland ecosystems.[44] They dug up and categorised the root systems of the main species in the *Banksia prionotes* woodlands of Western Australia. Species grew at different times of the year and had various rooting depths and distributions. Pate and Bell showed that the functional complementarity between the various rooting strategies was responsible for the high water use efficiency in these woodlands. I have already discussed the importance of root architecture in controlling nutrient use efficiencies (NUE). Differing root branching patterns perform quite differently depending on the spatial and temporal patchiness in nutrient supply in soils.[45] Thus one of the reasons for the approximation to MaxWUE and MaxNUE in terrestrial ecosystems lies in the long-term approach to maximal functional diversity as immigration proceeds, but it does require evolutionary time scales to produce the maximal response. Replacement of these highly diverse plant communities by a single agricultural crop with a uniform growth form and physiology reduces water and nutrient use efficiency and increases groundwater recharge after rainfall. The hydrological impacts of land clearing for agriculture in Australia have been well documented for about 100 years.[46] The resulting groundwater rise and the mobilisation of salt have caused, and are causing, severe and widespread problems: salinisation of the landscape has resulted. Irrigation makes matters worse. This has been a universal observation as agriculture has spread into arid lands around the world.

What we have been doing ever since we began to clear landscapes, fragment habitats and harvest the larger species from ecosystems is to reduce and remove structure. Throughout the world, ecosystems are being shifted from highly three-dimensionally structured systems to much simpler systems: forests are being cut down, larger ecosystem engineers are being removed, reefs and stands of aquatic plants are being eliminated. At the same time we are adding nutrients to these systems from fertiliser use and industrial waste disposal so that enrichment and structural simplifications are going hand in hand. This is influencing everything from the prevalence of bacterial populations to nutrient and water use efficiencies.

Biodiversity and land use planning

If we are going to be able to manage the conflicting requirement of many different land uses and also include the restoration of biodiversity as one

of the tasks, then we require land use planning tools that allow us to determine the suitability of various land types and take into account a variety of
trade-offs and preferences. There are now a variety of tools that allow us to
do this task. None of these are perfect because of the difficulties of predicting
what will succeed where, but none the less progress is being made.[47] Reserve
selection and planning is aided by tools that use various kinds of geographic
information system (GIS) overlain by topographic, climate, geological and soils
information. These are combined with knowledge of the regional biogeography
and the nature of the local species pool. From empirical relations of the types
discussed earlier (between the occurrence of species and slope, aspect, moisture, temperature, soil types, etc.) it is possible to predict where species might
preferentially occur and hence where the biodiversity 'hot spots' might be. The
location of these areas can then be used to ensure that key communities and
representative areas are included in the reserve design. Initially these techniques
were used as a means of separating out natural capital from the other forms of
capital in the shape of nature reserves. However, further trade-offs are possible
with competing land uses using techniques that can balance a variety of preferences and include forestry, agriculture and urban development. For example,
a Land Use Planning and Information System (LUPIS) can be combined in a GIS
with biodiversity measures of various kinds to provide a basis for a dialogue
over broader planning possibilities.[48] What these tools produce is a set of potential land use planning scenarios, which can be set so as to maximise various
values (production, forestry, biodiversity) based on empirical data, expert rules
and other information. The maps produced are then the basis for discussion
among the community and decision makers. Because of the partial nature of
ecological and other information, and the general lack of firm rules for land use
planning, the discipline has evolved to use a mixture of information sources in
various kinds of multi-criterion analyses and dialogues. We shall see later how
these tools have been developed further to include social and economic data
and preferences to form the basis of means to plan for multiple outcomes and
find ways to balance multiple capitals.

In the United Kingdom under the auspices of the Department of Environment,
Food and Rural Affairs the old system of EU farm subsidies is being replaced by
a system of stewardship payments. In order to obtain the payments farmers are
required to plan and carry out works which, among other things, conserve biodiversity, control erosion, improve water quality and protect heritage and cultural
values. If certain thresholds are met then payments for these services are made.[49]
The entry-level plan requires farmers to submit a map of their property showing
proposed improvements. Each of these proposed works is given a weighted set of
points towards a required total. What points awarded for each action effectively
do is to weight and value the outcomes of the proposed works; works given

high weights towards the total are evidently favoured and predicted to produce greatly improved outcomes and services. In the higher-level scheme the farmer is required to identify key priority features of his or her farm landscape and submit a farm environment plan that contains 'a detailed assessment of the historical, landscape and conservation value of the land' together with plans to manage these key features.[50] The higher-level scheme requires more specialised knowledge from the farmer (the ability to identify rare and threatened plants, for example) and can be tailored to suit regional priorities. The higher-level scheme places emphasis on such ecological assets as habitats for breeding wading birds, historic buildings, upland hay meadows, vulnerable soils, ponds, ancient trees and traditional orchards. Together with a handbook for entry-level organic farming stewardship, the DEFRA programmes provide a comprehensive method of achieving improved environmental, cultural and landscape outcomes. What is interesting is that the UK environmental stewardship scheme does not seem to have been developed with great consultation with the farming community. It has been delivered as a national incentive scheme but does not, from the outset, work closely with the farming community to achieve a dialogue about a jointly designed landscape. The stewardship payments are delivered as set of cash incentives rather than the more complex consultative process of the Australian programme, which also uses market-based instruments as signals and incentives.

The outcomes of the EU agri-environment schemes have been extensively reviewed by David Kleijn and his colleagues in Holland. The results, which have proved to be controversial,[51] are mixed: some benefit has been achieved for common species and plants but rarer species, including birds, have shown little increase.[52] Part of the analysis problem seems to be methodological: baseline data are frequently missing so controlled 'before and after' sampling cannot be compared. In addition, it may be that these schemes have not yet existed for long enough to show large benefits. Whatever the reason, debate has broken out about methodological and practical aspects of the programme.[53] Certainly, many are unhappy that so little appears to have been achieved; these results have caused the entire programme to be questioned and policies reviewed. Another part of the problem lies in the ways in which farmers allocate land to the schemes. If the farmers allocated poorer or more distant fields to such schemes then it is possible that they contained less biodiversity to begin with. Kleijn and Sutherland wrote

> Our impression from the literature, discussions with researchers, extension officers and farmers, and from visiting a wide range of schemes is that agri-environment schemes are most effective when they provide the finances that enable farmers or conservationists to

carry out measures that they feel positive about. Schemes that are considered financially beneficial but an inconvenience and with little support, feedback, encouragement or inspection are much less likely to provide gains. Thus, we have observed many situations where the land managers care about the outcome and tune their management of the agri-environment scheme to benefit biodiversity. Conversely, we have observed many other situations where an agri-environment scheme is clearly considered a financially beneficial inconvenience and carried out in the minimal manner possible, without regard to the outcome.[54]

Thus there needs to be support and encouragement, and strong signals and incentives need to be provided to ensure enthusiastic adoption and the desired outcome. It would be better if the programme were co-produced through greater involvement of farmers and land managers. Whatever the outcome, it is imperative that we do more of these retrospective analyses of programme performance and outcomes. This is all part of learning and adaptive management. In all probability these analyses will tell us a lot about ecological pattern and process as well as socioeconomic policy options. We just have to be prepared for occasional failures, and remember that they are actually learning opportunities.

NOTES

1. G. Merriam. Landscape dynamics in farmland. *Trends in Ecology and Evolution*, **3** (1988) 16–20. M. G. Turner. Landscape ecology: the effect of pattern on process. *Annual Reviews of Ecology and Systematics*, **20** (1989), 171–97.

2. R. Hobbs. Future landscapes and the future of landscape ecology. *Landscape and Urban Planning*, **37** (1997), 1–9.

3. M. Pascual and F. Guichard. Criticality and disturbance in spatial ecological systems. *Trends in Ecology and Evolution*, **20** (2005), 88–95.

4. J. E. Vermaat *et al.* Aggregation and the matching of scales in spatial economics and landscape ecology: empirical evidence and prospects for integration. *Ecological Economics*, **52** (2005), 229–37.

5. H. T. Murphy and J. Lovett-Doust. Context and connectivity in plant populations and landscape mosaics: does the matrix matter? *Oikos*, **105** (2004), 3–14.

6. M. G. Turner and R. H. Gardner. *Quantitative Methods in Landscape Ecology*. (New York: Springer-Verlag, 1991). Or more recently see B.-L. Li and S. Archer. Weighted mean patch size: a robust index for quantifying landscape structure. *Ecological Modelling*, **102** (1997), 353–61. M. K. Trani and R. H. Giles. An analysis of deforestation: metrics used to describe pattern change. *Forest Ecology and Management*, **114** (1999), 459–70. A. Lausch and F. Herzog. Applicability of landscape metrics for the monitoring of landscape change: issues of scale, resolution and interpretability. *Ecological Indicators*, **2** (2002), 3–15.

7. K. H. Riitters *et al.* A factor analysis of landscape pattern and structure metrics. *Landscape Ecology*, **10** (1995), 23–39. D. H. Cain, K. Riitters and K. Orvis. A multi-scale analysis of landscape statistics. *Landscape Ecology*, **12** (1997), 199–212.

8. T. H. Keitt. Spectral representation of neutral landscapes. *Landscape Ecology*, **15** (2000), 479–93. H. Olff and M. E. Ritchie. Fragmented nature: consequences for biodiversity. *Landscape and Urban Planning*, **58** (2002), 83–92.

9. Trani and Giles, *Forest Ecology and Management* (1999). (See Note 6.)

10. R. H. Gardner *et al.* Neutral models for the analysis of broad scale landscape pattern. *Landscape Ecology*, **1** (1987), 19–28. R. H. Gardner *et al.* Quantifying scale-dependent effects of animal movement with simple percolation models. *Landscape Ecology*, **3** (1989), 217–27.

11. A. G. Bunn, D. L. Urban and T. H. Keitt. Landscape connectivity: a conservation application of graph theory. *Journal of Environmental Management*, **59** (2000), 265–78.

12. K. A. With and T. O. Crist. Critical thresholds in species' responses to landscape structure. *Ecology*, **76** (1995), 2446–59. K. A. With and A. W. King. Dispersal success on fractal landscapes: a consequence of lacunarity thresholds. *Landscape Ecology*, **14** (1999), 73–82. A. W. King and K. A. With. Dispersal success on spatially structured landscapes: when do spatial pattern and dispersal behaviour really matter? *Ecological Modelling*, **147** (2002), 23–39.

13. L. Fahrig. Relative effects of habitat loss and fragmentation on population extinction. *Journal of Wildlife Management*, **61** (1997), 603–10.

14. L. Fahrig. How much habitat is enough? *Biological Conservation*, **100** (2001), 65–74. K. A. With and A. W. King. Analysis of landscape sources and sinks: the effect of spatial pattern on avian demography. *Biological Conservation*, **100** (2001), 75–88.

15. G. P. Malanson. Dispersal across continuous and binary representations of landscapes. *Ecological Modelling*, **169** (2003), 17–24.

16. D. B. Lindenmayer, S. McIntyre and J. Fischer. Birds in eucalypt and pine forests: landscape alteration and its implications for research models of faunal habitat use. *Biological Conservation*, **11** (2003), 45–53.

17. D. E. Debinski and R. D. Holt. A survey and overview of habitat fragmentation experiments. *Conservation Biology*, **14** (2000), 342–55.

18. J. A. Bissonette and I. Storch. Fragmentation: is the message clear? *Conservation Ecology*, **6(2)**, (2002) 14. Available as www.consecol.org/vol6/iss2/art14; see also the review in K. McGarigal and S. A. Cushman. Comparative evaluation of experimental approaches to the study of habitat fragmentation. *Ecological Applications*, **12** (2002), 335–45.

19. J. Bogaert. Lack of agreement on fragmentation metrics blurs correspondence between fragmentation experiments and predicted effects. *Conservation Ecology*, **7(1)**, response 6 (2003). Available as www.consecol.org/vol7/iss1/resp6.

20. J. Bissonette and I. Storch. Understanding fragmentation: getting closer to 42. *Conservation Ecology*, **7(2)**, (2003), response 5. Available as www.consecol.org/vol7/iss2/resp5.

21. R. E. Plotnick and R. H. Gardner. A general model for simulating the effects of landscape heterogeneity and disturbance on community patterns. *Ecological Modelling*, **147** (2002), 171–97.

22. See, for example, J. Bascompte and R. V. Sole. Effects of habitat destruction in a predator-prey metapopulation model. *Journal of Theoretical Biology*, **195** (1998), 383–93. D. Alonso and R. V. Sole. The Div game simulator: a stochastic cellular automata model of rainforest dynamics. *Ecological Modelling*, **133** (2000), 131–41. P. Dube *et al.* Quantifying gap dynamics at the patch mosaic level using a spatially-explicit model of a northern hardwood forest ecosystem. *Ecological Modelling*, **142** (2001), 39–60.

23. M. P. Hassell, H. N. Comins and R. M. May. Species coexistence and self-organizing spatial dynamics. *Nature*, **370** (1994), 290–2.

24. J. R. Krummel *et al.* Landscape patterns in a disturbed environment. *Oikos*, **48** (1987), 321–4.

25. G. D. Peterson. Contagious disturbance, ecological memory, and the emergence of landscape pattern. *Ecosystems*, **5** (2002), 329–38.

26. D. Rafaelli. How extinction patterns affect ecosystems. *Science*, **306** (2004), 1141–2. E. S. Zavaleta and K. B. Hulvey. Realistic species losses disproportionately reduce grassland resistance to biological invaders. *Science*, **306** (2004), 1175–7. M. Solan *et al.* Extinction and ecosystem function in the marine benthos. *Science*, **306** (2004), 1177–80.

27. E. Lieberman, C. Hauert and M. A. Nowak. Evolutionary dynamics on graphs. *Nature*, **433** (2005), 312–16.

28. T. F. H. Allen and T. W. Hoekstra. *Toward a Unified Ecology.* (New York: Columbia University Press, 1992).

29. R. L. Specht and A. Specht. *Australian Plant Communities: Dynamics of Structure, Growth and Biodiversity.* (Oxford: Oxford University Press, 1999).

30. J. S. Pate and T. L. Bell. Application of the ecosystem mimic concept to species-rich Banksia woodlands of Western Australia. *Agroforestry Systems*, **45** (1999), 303–41.

31. G. J. Burch *et al.* Comparative hydrological behaviour of forested and cleared catchments in south-eastern Australia. *Journal of Hydrology*, **90** (1987), 19–42.

32. S. A. Townsend and M. M. Douglas. The effects of three fire regimes on stream water quality, water yield and export coefficients in a tropical savannah (northern Australia). *Journal of Hydrology*, **229** (2000), 118–37.

33. D. A. Saunders, R. J. Hobbs and C. R. Margules. Biological consequences of ecosystem fragmentation: a review. *Conservation Biology*, **5** (1991), 18–32.

34. D. Freudenberger. *Bush for the birds: biodiversity enhancement guidelines for the Saltshaker Project, Boorowa, NSW.* Report for Greening Australia. (Canberra: CSIRO Sustainable Ecosystems, 2001). D. B. Lindenmayer *et al.* A prospective longitudinal study of landscape matrix effects on fauna in woodland remnants: experimental design and baseline data. *Biological Conservation*, **101** (2001), 157–69.

35. F. S. Chapin III *et al.* Ecosystem consequences of changing biodiversity. *Bioscience*, **48** (1998), 45–52. F. S. Chapin III *et al.* Consequences of changing biodiversity. *Nature*, **405** (2000), 234–42. P. G. Risser. Biodiversity and ecosystem function. *Conservation Biology*, **9** (1995), 742–6. D. Tilman. The ecological consequences of changes in biodiversity: a search for general principles. *Ecology*, **80** (1999), 1455–74. D. Tilman. Causes, consequences and ethics of biodiversity. *Nature*, **405** (2000), 208–11. D. Tilman *et al.* Forecasting agriculturally driven global environmental change. *Science*, **292** (2001), 281–4. D. Tilman *et al.* The influence of functional diversity and composition on ecosystem properties. *Science*, **277** (1997), 1300–2. D. Tilman, C. L. Lehman and K. T. Thomson. Plant diversity and ecosystem productivity: theoretical considerations. *Proceedings of the National Academy of Sciences, USA*, **94** (1997), 1857–61. D. Tilman *et al.* Diversity and productivity in a long-term grassland experiment. *Science*, **294** (2001), 843–5. D. Tilman, D. Wedin and J. Knops. Productivity and sustainability influenced by biodiversity in grassland ecosystems. *Nature*, **379** (1996), 718–20.

36. A. Hector *et al.* Plant diversity and productivity experiments in European grasslands. *Science*, **286** (1999), 1123–7.

37. S. Diaz and M. Cabido. Vive la difference: plant functional diversity matters to ecosystem processes. *Trends in Ecology and Evolution*, **16** (2001), 646–55. F. Schlapfer and B. Schmidt. Ecosystem effects of biodiversity: a classification of hypotheses and exploration of empirical results. *Ecological Applications*, **9** (1999), 893–912.

38. M. W. Schwartz *et al.* Linking biodiversity to ecosystem function: implications for conservation ecology. *Oecologia*, **122** (2000), 297–305.

39. J. Bengtsson. Which species? What kind of diversity? Which ecosystem function? Some problems in studies of relations between biodiversity and ecosystem function. *Applied Soil Ecology*, **10** (1998), 191–199. F. D. Hulot *et al.* Functional diversity governs ecosystem response to nutrient enrichment. *Nature*, **405** (2000), 340–4. M. Loreau *et al.* Biodiversity and ecosystem functioning: current knowledge and future challenges. *Science*, **294** (2001), 804–8.

40. M. C. Emmerson *et al.* Consistent patterns and the idiosyncratic effects of biodiversity on marine ecosystems. *Nature*, **411** (2001), 73–7. D. A. Wardle *et al.* Can comparative approaches based on plant ecophysiological traits predict the nature of biotic interactions and individual plant species effects in ecosystems? *Journal of Ecology*, **86** (1998), 405–20.

41. D. A. Wardle *et al.* The influence of island area on ecosystem properties. *Science*, **277** (1997), 1296–9.

42. For example, see P. M. Attiwill *et al.* Nutrient cycling in forests of South-Eastern Australia. In *Nutrition of Eucalypts*, ed. P. M. Attiwill and M. A. Adams (Collingwood, Vic.: CSIRO Publishing, 1996), pp. 191–227.

43. W. Durka *et al.* Effects of forest decline on uptake and leaching of deposited nitrate determined from ^{15}N and ^{18}O measurements. *Nature*, **372** (1994), 765–7.

44. J. S. Pate and T. L. Bell. Application of the ecosystem mimic concept to species-rich Banksia woodlands of Western Australia. *Agroforestry Systems*, **45** (1999), 303–41.

45. V. Dunbabin, Z. Rengel and A. J. Diggle. Simulating form and function of root systems: efficiency of nitrate uptake is dependent on root system architecture and the spatial and temporal variability of nitrate supply. *Functional Ecology*, **18** (2004), 204–11. V. Dunbabin, A. Diggle and Z. Rengel. Is there an optimal root architecture for nitrate capture in leaching environments? *Plant, Cell and Environment*, **26** (2003), 835–44.

46. J. Walker *et al. Evaluating the success of tree planting for degradation control.* Final report, National Landcare Program. (Canberra, ACT: CSIRO Land and Water, 1998).

47. This topic was reviewed by C. R. Margules and R. L. Pressey. Systematic conservation planning. *Nature*, **405** (2000), 243–53.

48. J. R. Ive and K. D. Cocks. Incorporating multiparty preferences into land use planning. *Environment and Planning, B*, **16** (1989), 99–109. D. P. Faith *et al.* Integrating conservation and forestry production: exploring trade-offs between biodiversity and production in regional land-use assessment. *Forest Ecology and Management*, **85** (1996), 251–60. L. Recatala *et al.* Land use planning in the Mediterranean Valencian Region: using LUPIS to generate issue relevant plans. *Journal of Environmental Management*, **59** (2000), 169–84.

49. DEFRA. *Environmental Stewardship: Look after your Land and be Rewarded.* Promotional booklet. (London: Department of Environment Food and Rural Affairs Rural Development Service, 2005). DEFRA. *Environmental Stewardship: Entry Level Stewardship Handbook.* (London: DEFRA Rural Development Service, 2005). DEFRA. *Environmental Stewardship: Higher Level Stewardship Handbook.* (London: DEFRA Rural Development Service, 2005). DEFRA. *Environmental Stewardship: Higher Level Stewardship; Farm Environment Plan, Guidance Handbook.* (London: DEFRA Rural Development Service, 2005).

50. DEFRA *Environmental Stewardship: Higher Level Stewardship; Farm Environment Plan, Guidance Handbook.* (London: DEFRA Rural Development Service, 2005).

51. J. Whitfield. How green was my subsidy? *Nature*, **439** (2006), 908–9.

52. D. Kleijn and W. J. Sutherland. How effective are European agri-environment schemes in conserving and promoting biodiversity? Journal of Applied Ecology, **40** (2003), 947–69. D. Kleijn *et al*. Mixed biodiversity benefits of agri-environment schemes in five European countries. *Ecology Letters*, **9** (2006), 243–54.

53. S. G. Potts *et al*. Commentary on Kleijn et al. (2006). *Ecology Letters*, **9** (2006), 254–6.

54. Kleijn and Sutherland (2003), p. 964. (See Note 52.)

14 Function in fragmented landscapes

Restoration of agricultural landscapes, urban landscapes and infrastructure.

Much less work has been done on the effects of land use change and habitat fragmentation on processes in landscapes than on the spatial patterns of species. We do know that fragmentation compromises function and this allows water, salt and nutrients to be mobilised across partly cleared catchments. As might be expected, ecosystem function is better preserved in larger fragments.[1] Simple models[2] show that the landscape becomes dysfunctional and leaky after fragmentation, and the models reproduce the broad patterns observed in Australian catchments.[3] It is becoming clear that what fragmentation and land use change does is to alter the original pattern of biophysical features and species in the landscape (which has contingent biological origins); in doing so, it reduces water and nutrient use efficiency.[4] It appears that much of the small-scale pattern in landscapes is produced by self-organisation and SGC through local interactions, which result in an approach to something like maximum water and nutrient use efficiencies on the part of the whole. Agricultural development after clearing may increase the overall production of crops but at the cost of reduced overall water use efficiency. This is strongly reminiscent of the result discussed earlier that at about 50% reduction in coverage the relationships between pattern and process change from being dominated by reaction–diffusion relations (strong coupling) to one where the ability to find and colonise suitable habitat patches becomes the limiting factor (weaker coupling).

If we are to understand in detail how the various pieces of a land use mosaic fit together and how the overall landscape performs, then we need to study the interrelationships between the functions of the various components. Unfortunately there has been almost no detailed experimental or observational work that examines the effect of changing mosaic patterns on function and the movement of water and materials across landscapes.[5] Some work has been attempted on the relationships of habitat heterogeneity to the biodiversity and functioning of agricultural landscapes. For example, it is clear that some of the more dramatic changes in the populations of farmland birds in the UK over the past few decades have been the result of the large-scale changes in farming practices and in habitat heterogeneity at a range of scales.[6] It is possible to conceive of experiments that would replace various kinds of landscape heterogeneity at a range of scales to restore both biodiversity and function to modified landscapes. These would, however, require long-term and large-scale support.

In the work on landscape function the emphasis has largely been on the statistical properties of catchments in relation to things like hydrology and nutrient exports, reporting bulk catchment parameters rather than working at the more detailed level. The result is a body of work that allows generalisations to be made about the effects of land use change on hydrology and nutrient exports but does not give much guide as to how the present mosaic of land use might be modified to provide greater biodiversity or water and nutrient use efficiencies. Certainly, clearing of native ecosystems leads to more flashy stream and river flows and leakage of nutrients from catchments. Replacement of forests by agriculture is known to produce these results.[7] Examples of work on nutrient exports, land use change and population density were discussed in a previous chapter. Urban development, with its higher proportion of impermeable surfaces in catchments and numerous sources of nutrients and other pollutants, has a very strong influence on water quality and nutrient exports so that even quite small urban areas in catchment can dominate the movement of nutrients and pollutants.[8]

Agricultural landscapes

Agricultural landscapes and their crops and herds are designed to maximise production and profit. Production decisions are made on the basis of risk management and investment returns; the organisms we farm are selected for maximum growth rates and maximum seed or crop production. Because in the past there has largely been a single factor production focus, other factors tend to be downplayed and off-site impacts largely discounted. In short, we have focused on one or two forms of capital growth (financial and infrastructure capitals) at the expense of the natural capital. We are very dependent on a restricted suite of high-yield species and varieties; now that Western agricultural techniques have been spread across the globe, many of the crops grown are not appropriate for the biome that is being farmed. (Many originally temperate species and varieties are farmed in (sub)tropical and arid landscapes where they require high inputs of pesticides, water and fertilisers.) Water and energy use efficiencies are lower than in natural ecosystems; agricultural systems are leaky in terms of both water and nutrients because the overall leaf area index is frequently suboptimal and the soil is left bare for weeks or months on end. Water use efficiency of irrigated and rain-fed crops is low compared with that of the natural vegetation (which, over long time periods, approaches $MaxE_T$ states). Wallace compiled data that showed that agricultural crops only evaporated 10%–30% of the water applied, the rest being lost through drainage and runoff.[9] Some rain-fed crops in semi-arid and arid regions are as little as 5% efficient. Given the evident need for poverty reduction and food production in many tropical and subtropical countries there is much to be done in increasing agricultural water use efficiency, particularly the efficiency of use of the so-called 'green' water flows in catchments.[10]

As we have seen, the impact of off-site pollution and third party impacts from agriculture and urban development are widespread. Large areas of North America, the United Kingdom and Europe are suffering from what might be regarded as landscape and waterscape failure: pollution of groundwaters, rivers, lakes and coastal waters by the runoff of phosphorus and nitrogen compounds arising from long-term over application of fertilisers and animal wastes, as well as disposal of sewage and other waste waters.[11] This is compounded by the atmospheric trans-boundary transport of nitrogen and sulphur oxides arising from fossil fuels used in industry and electricity generation. Nutrient runoff is increased because many agricultural soils now contain more than three times the amount of phosphorus required for optimal plant growth; most of this phosphorus surplus is contained in the top centimetre or so. Land use change from woodland to pastoral grasslands increases surface sheet-flows during heavy rain and moves nutrients from paddocks into streams and rivers. The consequences of this nutrient runoff are groundwaters that exceed the guidelines for human consumption, and the eutrophication of surface and coastal waters, leading to harmful algal blooms. In some cases, for example phosphorus in Northern Ireland[12] and nitrogen in the Gulf States of North America,[13] it appears that the landscape is uncontrollably leaking nutrients from soil stores, something that is likely to continue for the foreseeable future. The antidote to this widespread leakage of nutrients is to try to reduce nutrient applications to the land and to balance crop demands with the rate of application. This approach is now enshrined in management guidelines (Best Management Practices, BMPs) and in farm plans that attempt to match nutrient supply and demand and balance the overall nutrient budgets.[14] BMPs are used as a management tool in many countries around the world.

Agricultural landscapes are also patchy, but the patch dynamics are not just a function of geomorphology, soils and climate; the natural scales also recursively interact with social, cultural, financial and transportation networks and flows. We have therefore imposed other scales of space/time patchiness and other processes over the top of the natural landscape. What we have frequently done is to forget that underlying the attempt to produce homogeneity at the paddock scale there remains a natural geomorphological and ecological scale of variability. This within-paddock variability in soil texture, moisture, nutrients and organic material was formed by geological, micro-topographic and geomorphological variability laid down by the interactions of the original ecosystems. Soil sampling reveals that there is considerable variability at scales of a few tens of metres or less,[15] which I argued earlier was a result of SGC: the emergence of soil micro- and macro-structure that arises from the interaction of geomorphology and small scale reaction–diffusion processes. This variability now manifests itself in the form of within-paddock variability in crop growth, yield and quality. Furthermore, it was quickly discovered that fertiliser application could be made more efficient and effective by targeting those areas of each field that would best respond to the applications.

This superimposition of a set of scales of organisation on top of the natural ecological and environmental scales of self-organised pattern and process is not constant in time. All forms of capital are not homogeneous in space and time. Being emergent properties of complex adaptive systems, these forms of capital have characteristic, even fractal, patterns of variability. By changing farming practices we have altered the interactions and the characteristic scales of human, social, financial and infrastructure capitals and the ways in which these have interacted with 'the rest of nature'. The foot-and-mouth disease outbreak in England was a classic example. Some surprising 'tipping points' have been found. Policy decisions, for example the EU Common Agriculture Policy (CAP) with its incentives and subsidies for a variety of outcomes, change the extensification and intensification of agriculture and so lead to altered interactions with natural capitals in many and various ways. Ernoult, Bureau and Poudevigne have studied the changing spatial patterns of agricultural activity and environmental variables over time in areas affected by the EU CAP by looking at the changing fractal dimensions of agricultural activity over time.[16] They showed that before intensification of agriculture there was a strong correlation between agricultural activity and landscape (natural capital) patterns, i.e. agricultural activities were spatially heterogeneous and were largely determined by the pattern of fundamental habitat variables such as aspect, slope, hydrology and soil types. After intensification (resulting from the introduction of the CAP) these correlations weakened as agricultural activities became more homogeneous and were largely determined by financial and economic forces. So globalisation is driving patterns of social and economic change that override the natural scales of heterogeneity that underlie the production processes. Little wonder that we see complex and surprising changes in biodiversity and ecosystem services.

Restoration of function and biodiversity in agricultural landscapes

If we are to restore biodiversity and function in agricultural landscapes we need to know more about the detailed interactions across scales between the various forms of capital and the connectivity between them. Pathways and connectivity are the keys to understanding process, rather than just the statistical patterns. Some of the most ambitious efforts to restore landscape function are being made in arid and semi-arid landscapes where considerable dryland salinisation is occurring as a result of reduced functional biodiversity and low water use efficiency ($MaxE_T$ is not achieved). Clearing has increased groundwater recharge under crops; biodiversity loss in the Australian wheat and sheep zone is rife.[17] At present the financially attractive farming and cropping options are 'leaky' and promote landscape salinisation, whereas native bush is much less leaky because of its high biodiversity and functional diversity. Somehow we need to try to achieve greater water use efficiency and improved biodiversity outcomes while also improving social and economic conditions for the rural communities. In all probability this will only be achieved through the design of new landscape and waterscape mosaics where sustainability is not achieved on every hectare, but overall an ensemble approach to a more sustainable 'win–win' solution (reduced recharge and increased profitability) is achieved.[18]

In the Murray–Darling Basin the landscape and waterscape renewal projects are grouped at small catchment and farm enterprise scale under the aegis of the 'Heartlands' project, an effort to simultaneously maximise many forms of capital and to produce sustainable landscapes, societies and enterprises. The 'Heartlands' project is an attempt to bring together a range of tools to ensure that water use efficiency, biodiversity and profitability are maintained so that rural and regional communities are financially viable and secure. Being 'in the red' financially is not a good precursor to 'being green' in terms of landscape and farm management. We simply do not have many options to offer farmers in degraded landscapes; we can describe the symptoms, but given our dependence on a restricted suite of crop varieties there are few proven remedies. We are short of process understandings at the relevant scales (paddocks and land use mosaics) and there is a strong influence of the uniqueness of 'place' (the unique outcome of contingent pattern and process developed through small-scale SGC) in each catchment, so it is hard to determine precisely what to do in any given situation. 'Heartlands' is about trying to build sustainable landscapes and waterscapes by using whatever tools are presently to hand, building new frameworks and models at relevant scales. It involves a large number of partnerships between various players: research and knowledge providers, LANDCARE groups, catchment management boards, and State and Commonwealth Government Agencies. A real attempt is being made to closely involve farmers and landholders in the generation of knowledge and the development of remedial measures. In this respect it is a model of a new kind of science, committed to delivering outcomes at relevant ecological, social and economic scales in the face of very complex scientific challenges. 'Heartlands' brings together teams of crop scientists, surface- and groundwater hydrologists, ecologists and those interested in the conservation of biodiversity to attempt to provide decision support tools for farmers and regional communities wishing to achieve a more sustainable landscape. Doing this through partnerships is also a significant social challenge, one that the world of science is ill fitted to deliver.

Mosaic farming techniques are being explored to try to achieve better 'triple bottom line' outcomes by using a variety of modelling approaches (all of which are recognised to be partial and limited in various ways). Physiological crop models are used to predict crop growth and water use; these are coupled in various ways to surface and groundwater hydrological models to predict recharge and stream flows with various spatial scenarios of agroforestry plantations, crop rotations and native 'bush' plots for the preservation and restoration of biodiversity.[19] Given what we now know about the fractal nature of catchments and the close connections between soil properties, small-scale flow paths, mosaics of land use and water quality, we simply do not know enough about the small-scale connectivity between land and water and how that is affected by clearing and agricultural activities. There is good evidence that there are many site-specific interactions between landscapes and surface and groundwaters, with source and sink areas connected by pathways determined by small-scale soil properties.[20]

Our models are partial and incomplete in this regard so, as yet, other than general statements about linking patches of natural vegetation by corridors, replanting groundwater recharge zones, constructing riparian buffer strips and avoiding gross erosion events during heavy rainfall, it is difficult to make specific recommendations to farmers about precisely what to do where on their farms to improve ecological and water quality outcomes. Groundwater recharge is highly episodic – in one study, 10% of rainfall events contributed over 85% of the total recharge[21] – so the impact of changed land use on groundwater recharge depends on the interaction of rainfall–recharge events with the spatial and temporal pattern of water use by crops and other vegetation. The altered spatial mosaic of land use must therefore also be complemented by crop rotations (management of resource availability over time) using deeply rooted plants such as Lucerne to fully utilise the soil water stores and to reduce deep recharge. Revegetation strategies can take more than a decade to begin to influence and improve water use efficiency because of the time it takes for trees and other perennial plants to establish and grow, and therefore there are time lags both in the reduction of recharge and the groundwater response. Simple empirical models of plant water use and groundwater flow rates show that small sloping catchments may show reduced salt exports in 10–20 years, but larger regional groundwater systems will take 100–200 years to come to a new equilibrium with the revegetated land surface.[22]

Groundwater systems are, on the whole, much less well understood than surface water systems; although there are large underground stores of water, overextraction is common so that revegetation strategies have to be seen in the light of irrigation and other strategies of conjunctive (combined surface and groundwater) use. Many groundwater systems contain water that is very old and therefore they represent a non-renewable resource for irrigation and other uses.[23] Any strategy that seeks to improve water use efficiency and make farming more sustainable will therefore have to take into account all the sources and sinks for surface and groundwaters (extraction, irrigation, 'blue' and 'green' water fluxes, groundwater recharge and discharge) and will take many years.

The crop science and forestry models are used in conjunction with design rules based on the best knowledge from landscape ecology for the preservation and restoration of biodiversity[24] (LUPIS was introduced in the previous chapter) to try to achieve an integrated optimal outcome for each demonstration site. The models and insights are then used as an input to a dialogue with the local communities to consider and influence land management decisions.[25] The science component of 'Heartlands' works in close collaboration with LANDCARE groups and catchment management groups to ensure uptake and adoption of the latest ideas. Taken all together, 'Heartlands' represents one of the most sophisticated examples to date of what might be called integrated land use planning to achieve multiple sustainable outcomes.[26] In recent years the Australian states have been experimenting with various kinds of market-based instrument (such as biodiversity auctions or tenders) for natural resource management in which landholders can bid for priority revegetation targets.[27] Because these targets are best met by market-based instruments in the context of economically viable farming operations, these studies have been supported by large-scale economic analyses of the viability of dryland and irrigated agriculture in the Murray–Darling Basin[28].

Attempts to try to see what the interactions are between land use, hydrology, biodiversity and production (economic outcomes) are in their infancy, but attempts are being made to push down this path around the world. For example, simple hydrological models are being combined with economic models and models for ecological surrogates (such as bird populations) to explore some of these interactions.[29] Similar work in the USA is trying to assess what might be done to build multiple capitals in farming catchments – a so-called 'multifunctional agriculture' – through improving social and economic capital in the farming community while simultaneously improving biodiversity, water quality and fish health, increasing carbon sequestration and decreasing greenhouse gas emissions.[30] Significantly, some of the indicated land use mosaics are both more productive and profitable than present practices as well as being better for other values such as biodiversity and water quality. Similarly, there is evidence that improved forestry practices may produce a number of ecological goods and services and thereby help alleviate rural poverty.[31] There are therefore some 'win–win' solutions to these difficult problems and it is possible to identify alternative 'Pareto' surfaces elsewhere in parameter space.

The question might be asked: what kind of intervention is going to be required to make a significant change in groundwater recharge and salinity? As discussed previously, the evidence points to the need for targeted, large-scale revegetation of catchments. Investigations have certainly revealed that there is a close link between vegetation cover and stream flows. Empirical studies such as paired catchment studies[32] and data from many catchments around the world[33] clearly indicate that forested catchments have higher evapotranspiration than cleared (grassland) catchments and those catchments with mixed land uses fall between the two; so 'green' water fluxes are a strong function of land use and vegetation type. As might be expected, forested catchments have higher water use efficiency than agricultural catchments, so that deforestation and clear felling increases stream flows and groundwater recharge, and reafforestation reduces recharge and stream flows.[34] Flow regimes in forested and cleared catchments differ by anything from 20%–30% to 100%; as might be expected, it is frequently the summer low-flow periods fed by groundwater flows that are more affected by the trees than high-flow periods in winter. So land use and climate interact to change the seasonality of 'blue' water flows in rivers and streams. In the natural state the flows of 'green' water in catchments are part of, and are controlled by, the SGC of interactions between organisms. The patterns and processes are subtly balanced with the biodiversity and climate. Once the SGC is broken then water use efficiency drops markedly.

Land clearing and pastoral and cropping activities in the Murray–Darling Basin have increased groundwater recharge in overgrazed paddocks and under crops such as wheat because of reduced water use efficiency.[35] The interaction between 'green' and 'blue' water flows is complicated by the time scales of plant growth, disturbance across a mosaic of land use types (e.g. by fire) and the groundwater response times so that, with fractal flow paths in catchments and the uneven distribution of rainfall over time, the shifting mosaic of agricultural and other land uses has an impact on the hydrology and water quality of streams at a wide range of scales from days to centuries. It means that the situation is spatially and temporally very complex and quite often it is difficult to either detect changes in the short term or detect the effects of individual management actions. This is precisely why it is possible to have public (and highly politicised) debates about evidence for change – or the perceived lack thereof – and the desirability of the continuation of 'business-as-usual' strategies. The groundwater response times of changed land use in some of these catchments are of the order of 15–20 years in sloping terrain, so revegetation may produce quite rapid improvements in water quality in the streams. Targeted revegetation in recharge zones (and therefore changing the land use mosaic) may be an effective strategy for reducing salinisation of these catchments but, worryingly, at least some results indicate that massive revegetation is going to be required (40%–50% of catchment area) before any significant impact is going to be made on salt mobilisation and stream salinity levels.[36] In these debates the evidence (such as it is) gets swamped by beliefs, culture and values.

Urban landscapes

Urban landscapes are also complex systems with emergent properties arising from interactions of governance, social and political factors with the built environment, infrastructure, energy, water and transport networks and the natural environment. Indeed, there is a continuum of pattern and process from the natural to the built environment with ecosystems, agricultural landscapes and the built environment varying across a wide range of space and time scales. Urban areas are dominated by the built environment: houses, apartments, office blocks, factories and roads. Cities have low energy and nutrient use efficiencies and require huge energy and materials subsidies to survive. It has been calculated, for example, that the city of London has an ecological footprint (the area of land required to produce all the required services) about 120 times the area of the metropolis. Although this is about equal to the area of the British Isles it does, of course, include global sources and sinks for produce and manufactured goods and services.

Over the years cities have grown up dependent on centralised services: energy, water supply and waste disposal, transport corridors, telecommunications and information flows. City engineers tend to be very conservative people: the technologies and engineering solutions presently in use in our cities have changed little in the past century or more, and many have Roman origins (for example, the use of aqueducts to bring water into the city from sources or storages outside). City sewer systems have changed little since the nineteenth century. As noted earlier, the driver has often been to break the faecal to oral link with minimal treatment by providing remote and unpolluted sources of water, and to transport wastes and waste water away from the city by using streams, rivers and coastal waters. Change is slow because we have a large number of cultural, social, infrastructural and financial 'sunk costs'. A number of factors are now driving change in what has become the business of urban water supply. Population growth in urban centres is causing demand to rise while competition for water between urban and agricultural uses in peri-urban and regional areas is causing concern over the security of future urban supplies. Thus there is a need for both supply and demand management. Supply and demand scenarios in Australia, for example, indicate that in future there will be an overall shortfall of about 30 Gl per annum due to demand outstripping the sustainable catchment yield by 2030.[37] Climate change is complicating the picture also. In Western Australia, for example, rainfall has declined sharply since the mid-1970s, so that runoff into the city's reservoirs has declined to about one third of what it was only 40 years ago (this aspect of sudden shifts in climate regimes will be discussed more fully in Chapter 16). If sustainable catchment yields fall by 10% as a result of climate change across Australia, the 30 Gl figure quoted above could rise by a factor of ten even if demand management policies are implemented. So the huge urban footprints, and the demands for resource supply and waste disposal, are placing severe stresses on the surrounding landscapes and waterscapes. This realisation alone is causing demands for urgent reviews of engineering practices in the urban water sector.[38]

Surprisingly perhaps, urban areas, with their large proportions of impervious surfaces (roofs, driveways, streets, parking lots, etc.) in their catchments, are actually net exporters of water. Studies of the overall water balance of cities consistently show that when stormwater flows and runoff from the urban area itself are included in the equation, more water is exported than is imported.[39] In a study of an urban catchment in a suburb of Canberra, the capital of Australia, Mitchell and others found that rainfall falling on the catchment was three times larger than the amount of water imported, and that evaporation was the largest loss term. She could find no longer-term storage or loss of water in the catchment over a period of 17 years (no overall catchment wetting or drying). On average the drinking water import equalled the storm water loss and was approximately two thirds of the overall loss of storm water and waste water. This result appears to be representative of a number of other urban water balance studies. So there is actually surplus water in urban areas, but the normal practice is to try to shed this storm water into drains, streams and coastal waters as fast as possible to minimise flooding. Because of the largely impervious nature of urban catchments storm run off is very 'flashy' in nature, with volumes rising and falling rapidly as rainfall events pass over the city. Thus urban areas not only change the overall water balance, they also change the spectrum of stream flows by changing the frequency and magnitude of flood events.[40] Because they tend to shed water rapidly after rain, urban areas contribute to the speed of propagation of flood events downstream. In terms of downstream water quantity and quality therefore cities change both the overall time averaged amount of water and nutrients exported (through storm water outflows and waste water discharges) as well as the frequency and magnitude of events. Simple modelling shows that downstream aquatic ecosystems are highly sensitive to such changes and can produce very non-linear responses to even small changes in the input spectrum of water and nutrients.[41] When these hydrological features are combined with the extraction of water from peri-urban rivers and streams to provide for secure storage and supply, then urban areas are responsible for some complex changes in regional hydrology that have major impacts on aquatic ecosystems.

Given the projected shortfall in the balance of supply and demand for urban water, there is a need to think seriously about both supply and demand management. Advances in technologies – including IT systems, membrane filtration, desalination, grey-water re use and recycling technologies – are making it ever more possible to consider cost-effective alternatives to the more traditional engineering solutions. Many new technologies are coming on stream. Indeed, there is a need to try to think through some of the challenges of managing urban water systems more sustainably as complex adaptive systems, which is what they are. As Beck has recently written, the challenge is as follows:

> Given the plethora of candidate unit process technologies, compose
> from these parts the whole of an entire infrastructure whose impact
> will be to restore – to the maximum extent possible (to some quasi-
> pristine, pre-city status) – the global cycles of materials circulating
> around the city and the spectrum of disturbances to which its
> surrounding aquatic environment is subject. Furthermore, achieve this
> composition subject to the constraint of using to the full the sunk
> societal investment in today's paradigms of sewerage and wastewater
> treatment systems, as we know it in the developed countries.[42]

In his paper, Beck was talking about the advent of high-performance integrated control systems and the ways in which they might be used to give better environmental performance and a smaller urban footprint (i.e. how integrated control systems might be used to more closely mimic the natural spectrum of upstream and downstream events). Beck places some emphasis on the word integrated and the fact that regional strategies are required to fully integrate the space and time variability in the various capitals that need to be maximised to obtain a more sustainable outcome. Successful demand management not only requires the application of new technologies; it also requires their successful adoption by society. So demand management is about values and beliefs as much as it is about technological advances, and these are truly CAS.

There are some innovative ideas around which could be used to address the supply question. Some are very simple. For example, above-ground rainwater tanks – even in semi-arid countries like Australia – can provide major benefits. Given the excess of rainfall over imported drinking water in most cities, a dwelling with a roof area of about $150\,m^2$ could capture and supply the water requirements of the household in most years. In Australia's arid climate it could supply all of the requirements even in drought years if water were recycled for toilet flushing and garden watering. So installing a 10 000 litre tank for each house captures rainfall, reduces storm flows and backs off the mains water supply. This practice stands up to stringent financial analysis and provides greater economic benefit to the community than the usual water supply and storm water management options.[43] Rainwater tanks are rarely installed in urban centres, although they are ubiquitous in rural areas beyond the reach of mains water supplies. There are concerns about the microbiological quality of tank water, and consequently in urban areas there are all kinds of regulations to stop connection of rainwater tanks in ways in which the tank water might (even by remote chance) back up into and contaminate the mains water supply. In fact it seems that the microbiological quality of tank water is good (a fact well known to rural people) and, particularly if tank water is used to provide the hot water service to the household, the risks of contamination are very low indeed.

(The thermal shock of running the tank water through the water heater kills most pathogens.) Nevertheless, regulations to prevent the installation of rainwater tanks to the household mains supply still prevent this practice in many urban areas. The installation of rainwater tanks in urban areas has surprisingly non-linear results when considered as part of an overall urban water strategy. Household-scale actions – house design and the choice of appliances – strongly determine the system dynamics. The precise impact on demand management depends on the temporal distribution of rainfall and the buffering capacity of the tank system, which together determine how often the mains water supply is drawn upon when the tank level is low. In addition, there are strong demographic factors in Western cities, where teenagers tend to take long showers. So the precise impact of the tank systems on supply and demand management depends on urban engineering decisions, climate and seasonality in rainfall, and the age structure, behaviour and population density of the people in the various suburbs that make up the city.[44] Overall, the upstream and downstream effects of installing rainwater tanks in urban areas are strikingly non-linear.

So Beck's challenge is complicated by the non-linear response of the coupled 'systems of systems' that makes up an urban water supply and waste disposal system. The challenge is further complicated by the convergence of technologies that is going on between IT, water supply and power systems. More and more there is convergence between distributed IT, water and power systems as utilities seek efficiencies and improvements in performance. Local and regional water and power systems are replacing the older, massive base-load power stations and monolithic utilities. Local sewer mining plants recover water for recycling onto parks, gardens and sports ovals, small-scale gas turbines provide peak load electric power generation for hospitals and other large buildings, and water is used for cooling and air-conditioning. As we shall discuss in Chapter 18 there is a rapid trend towards the use of market mechanisms for the management of water and power systems. With electrical power grids, for example, national electricity markets bid for supply contracts at intervals as short as 15 minutes so that price mechanisms are used to capture short-term advantage and generating plants can be turned on and off as market demands fluctuate. Connectivity is increasing as national and even transnational grids are interconnected – and there is no reason to assume that water will not eventually go the same way as power grids.

Mosaics of stocks and flows

Natural landscapes consist of mosaics of vegetation patches, each of which, through trial and error over time, approaches a robust MaxEnt 'neutral space'. These form HOT solutions to the expected spectrum of perturbations. Fractal flow paths transport energy (as carbon compounds) and materials between patches. Given the power law distributions of rainfall and flows, most transport of energy and materials happens as a result of infrequent major events. Disturbance, fragmentation and agricultural and urban development reduce biodiversity and the overall water and nutrient use efficiencies of the landscape. Flow rates between patches increase and the spectrum of perturbations changes character so that more frequent, smaller flow events are effective in moving materials within the landscape. HOT solutions break down. Restoration of landscape biodiversity and function seeks to replace as many patches as possible with high efficiencies and to mimic natural flow paths and regimes. This requires the monitoring of stocks of capitals 'within' patches and the perturbations and movements of materials 'between' patches. The preservation of resilience and robust HOT 'neutral spaces' requires paying attention to the distribution of pattern and process.

NOTES

1. D.A. Saunders, R.J. Hobbs and C.R. Margules. Biological consequences of ecosystem fragmentation: a review. *Conservation Biology*, **5** (1991), 18–32.

2. J.A. Ludwig *et al.* A leakiness index for assessing landscape function using remote sensing. *Landscape Ecology*, **17** (2002), 157–71.

3. G.P. Harris. The biogeochemistry of nitrogen and phosphorus in Australian catchments, rivers and estuaries: effects of land use and flow regulation and comparisons with global patterns. *Marine and Freshwater Research*, **52** (2001), 139–49.

4. J.A. Ludwig, D.J. Tongway and S.G. Marsden. Stripes, strands or stipples: modelling the influence of three landscape banding patterns on resource capture and productivity in semi-arid woodlands, Australia. *Catena*, **37** (1999), 257–73.

5. About the only work is that of B.K. Ferguson. Landscape hydrology: a component of landscape ecology. *Journal of Environmental Systems*, **21** (1992), 193–205.

6. T.G. Benton, J.A. Vickery and J.D. Wilson. Farmland biodiversity: is habitat heterogeneity the key? *Trends in Ecology and Evolution*, **18** (2003), 182–8.

7. G.P. Harris. Biogeochemistry of nitrogen and phosphorus in Australian catchments, rivers and estuaries: effects of land use and flow regulation and comparisons with global patterns. *Marine and Freshwater Research*, **52** (2001), 139–49. L.B. Johnson *et al.* Landscape influences on water chemistry in Midwestern stream ecosystems. *Freshwater Biology*, **37** (1997), 193–208.

8. L. Silva and D.D. Williams. Buffer zones versus whole catchment approaches to studying land use impact on river water quality. *Water Research*, **35** (2001), 3462–72.

9. J.S. Wallace. Increasing agricultural water use efficiency to meet future food production. *Agriculture, Ecosystems and Environment*, **82** (2000), 105–19.

10. J.S. Wallace and P.J. Gregory. Water resources and their use in food production systems. *Aquatic Science*, **64** (2002), 363–75.

11. S.V. Smith *et al.* Humans, hydrology, and the distribution of inorganic nutrient loading to the ocean. *BioScience*, **53** (2003), 235–45. Smith *et al.* show a strong effect of human population density on nutrient exports from catchments.

12. See, for example, R.H. Foy and A.E. Bailey-Watts. Observations on the spatial and temporal variation in the phosphorus status of lakes in the British Isles. *Soil Use and Management*, **14** (1998), 131–8. S.I. Heaney *et al.* Impacts of agriculture on aquatic systems: lessons learnt and new unknowns in Northern Ireland. *Marine and Freshwater Research*, **52** (2001), 151–63.

R. H. Foy, S. D. Lennox and C. E. Gibson. Changing perspectives on the importance of urban phosphorus inputs as the cause of nutrient enrichment in Lough Neagh. *Science of the Total Environment*, **310** (2003), 87–90.

13. R. B. Alexander, R. A. Smith and G. E. Schwarz. Effect of stream channel size on the delivery of nitrogen to the Gulf of Mexico. *Nature*, **403** (2000), 758–61. G. F. McIsaac *et al.* Nitrate flux in the Mississippi River. *Nature*, **414** (2001), 166–7.

14. See, for example, J. van Bruchem, H. Scheiere and H. van Keulen. Dairy farming in the Netherlands in transition to a more efficient nutrient use. *Livestock Production Science*, **61** (1999), 145–53.

15. See, for example, the variograms presented in A. B. McBratney and M. J. Pringle. Estimating average and proportional variograms of soil properties and their potential use in precision agriculture. *Precision Agriculture*, **1** (1999), 125–52.

16. A. Ernoult, F. Bureau and I. Poudevigne. Patterns of organisation in changing landscapes: implications for the management of biodiversity. *Landscape Ecology*, **18** (2003), 239–51.

17. See the maps of biodiversity and catchment condition for the Australian continent at www.nlwra.gov.au or the Australian Natural Resources Atlas and Data Library homepage at www.audit.ea.gov.au/ANRA.

18. L. Brennan *et al*. *Mosaic farming feasibility; a report of the Heartlands initiative*. Document HL11–04, June 2004. www.clw.csiro.au/heartlands (Canberra, ACT.: CSIRO Land and Water, 2004).

19. Z. Paydar and J. C. Gallant. Applying a spatial modelling framework to assess land use effects on catchment hydrology. In *Proceedings of the International Congress on Modelling and Simulation, Townsville, Australia, July 2003*, ed. D. A. Post, Volume 2, pp. 491–6. For a similar international perspective see M. V. Santelmann *et al*. Assessing alternative futures for agriculture in Iowa, USA. *Landscape Ecology*, **19** (2004), 357–74.

20. J. L. Weld *et al*. Identifying critical sources of phosphorus export from agricultural watersheds. *Nutrient Cycling in Agroecosystems*, **59** (2001), 29–38. M. Newson, A. Baker and S. Mounsey. The potential role of freshwater luminescence measurements in exploring runoff pathways in upland catchments. *Hydrological Processes*, **15** (2001), 989–1002. H. F. Kishel and P. J. Gerla. Characteristics of preferential flow and groundwater discharge to Shingobee Lake, Minnesota USA. *Hydrological Processes*, **16** (2002), 1921–34.

21. L. Zhang *et al*. Estimating episodic recharge under different crop/pasture rotations in the Mallee region. Part 2. Recharge control by agronomic practices. *Agricultural Water Management*, **42** (1999), 237–49.

22. W. R. Dawes *et al*. Biophysical modeling of catchment-scale surface water and groundwater response to land-use change. *Mathematics and Computers in Simulation*, **64** (2004), 3–12.

23. W. M. Alley *et al*. Flow and storage in groundwater systems. *Science*, **296** (2002), 1985–90.

24. J. R. Ive and A. O. Nicholls. *Ecological design principles*, Heartlands report HL4–01, May 2001. www.clw.csiro.au/heartlands (Canberra, ACT.: CSIRO Land and Water, 2002).

25. K. D. Cocks and J. R. Ive. Mediation support for forest land allocation – the SIRO-MED system. *Environmental Management*, **20** (1996), 41–52.

26. H. Cresswell *et al*. *Heartlands planning for sustainable land use and catchment health. A report of the Heartlands initiative*. Publication HL9–04. www.clw.csiro.au/heartlands (Canberra, ACT.: CSIRO Land and Water, 2004).

27. See, for example, J. Ward *et al*. (2005) *Market-based instrument approaches to implementing priority revegetation in the South Australian Murray-Darling Basin*. (Adelaide: CSIRO Land and Water Client Report, December 2005).

28. B. Bryan and S. Marvanek. (2004) *Quantifying and valuing land use change for integrated catchment management evaluation in the Murray-Darling Basin, 1996/97 – 2000/01.* Stage 2 report to the Murray–Darling Basin Commission. (Adelaide: CSIRO land and Water Client Report, November 2004).

29. N. Fohrer, D. Moller and N. Steiner. An interdisciplinary modeling approach to evaluate the effects of land use change. *Physics and Chemistry of the Earth*, **27** (2002), 655–62.

30. M.V. Santelmann *et al.* Assessing alternative futures for agriculture in Iowa, USA. *Landscape Ecology*, **19** (2004), 357–74. G. Boody *et al.* Multifunctional agriculture in the United States. *BioScience*, **55** (2005), 27–38.

31. D. Lamb, P.D. Erskine and J.A. Parrotta. Restoration of degraded tropical forest landscapes. *Science*, **310** (2005), 1628–32.

32. A. Best *et al. A critical review of paired catchment studies with reference to seasonal flows and climatic variability.* (Canberra, ACT.: CSIRO Land and Water technical Report 25/05; Melbourne: CRC for Catchment Hydrology technical Report 03/4; and Canberra, ACT.: Murray–Darling Basin Commission publication 11/03, 2003). Available from the respective websites.

33. L. Zhang, W.R. Dawes and G.R. Walker. *Predicting the effect of vegetation changes on catchment average water balance.* (Melbourne: CRC for Catchment Hydrology technical report 99/12, 1999).

34. B. Klocking and U. Haberlandt. Impact of land use changes on water dynamics – a case study in temperate meso- and macroscale river basins. *Physics and Chemistry of the Earth*, **27** (2002), 619–29.

35. G. Walker, M. Gilfedder and J. Williams. *Effectiveness of Current Farming Systems in the Control of Dry Land Salinity.* (Canberra, ACT.: CSIRO Land and Water, 1999).

36. N. Herron *et al.* Modelling the impacts of strategic tree plantings on salt loads and flows in the Macquarie River catchment, NSW, Australia. *Journal of Environmental Management*, **68** (2003), 37–50.

37. Data from unpublished projections by the Water Services Association of Australia, Melbourne, 2004.

38. See, for example, P. Troy. The management of water in Australian cities. *Dissent*, (Summer 2001/2002), 28–32.

39. V.G. Mitchell, T.A. McMahon and R.G. Mein. Components of the total water balance of an urban catchment. *Environmental Management*, **32** (2003), 735–46.

40. See, for example, M.B. Beck. Vulnerability of water quality in intensively developing urban watersheds. *Environmental Modelling and Software*, **20** (2005), 381–400.

41. I. Webster and G.P. Harris. Anthropogenic impacts on the ecosystems of coastal lagoons: modelling fundamental biogeochemical processes and management implications. *Marine and Freshwater Research*, **55** (2004), 67–78.

42. M.B. Beck. *Environmental Modelling and Software*, **20** (2005), p. 385.

43. P.J. Coombes and G. Kuczera. A sensitivity analysis of an investment model used to determine the economic benefits of rainwater tanks. *Proceedings of the 28th International Hydrology and Water Resources Symposium, Wollongong, NSW*, 10–14 November 2003. (Canberra, ACT.: The Institution of Engineers, Australia, 2003).

44. J.P. Kaye *et al.* A distinct urban biogeochemistry? *Trends in Ecology and Evolution*, **21** (2006), 192–9.

15 Environmental flows

The development of decision support systems in the ill-defined and uncertain world of landscapes, rivers and modified flow regimes.

As we move towards regional landscape and waterscape management, and as we attempt to find new land use mosaics and systems operation protocols to more closely mimic the world of 'the rest of nature', there is an increasing focus on what are called 'environmental flows': the water requirements of the aquatic ecosystems of our rivers and estuaries. The 'environmental flows problem' is a particularly revealing example of all the problems we have discussed so far: complexity of interactions within catchments, uncertainty, the lack of discriminating indicators and problems with linking indicators to management recommendations. Some of the more innovative solutions are also indicative of trends in natural resource management.

Agricultural and urban developments cause alterations to the natural flow regimes of rivers and estuaries through diversions, dams and water extraction as well as changed runoff characteristics. As we have seen, this is now a massive, worldwide problem. The flows in most of the world's major rivers are regulated to some degree. In addition, water quality is reduced through leakage and wash-off of nutrients from soils, crops and urban areas. Water quality is also reduced because of waste disposal and waste water discharges of various kinds. In Western countries considerable progress has been made in reducing nutrients and pollutants in what are called point source discharges (sewage overflows, waste water discharges and industrial waste streams) through improved treatment technologies and regulation. Water reuse has been adopted more slowly than pollutant removal so the hydrological modification of rivers and estuaries remains, even though the discharges are overall cleaner than they were. Nutrient removal from waste water discharges is now widespread in developed nations, so the nutrient impacts are now largely coming from diffuse landscape sources.[1] All in all, aquatic ecosystems downstream of agricultural and urban areas are degraded. The realisation that aquatic ecosystems are legitimate water users in their own right has focused a lot of attention in recent years on the recovery of these systems by restoration of more natural river flow regimes via discharge and storm water flows and improvements in land management practices.[2]

Largely because of a perception that chemical water quality data were 'noisy' and could not therefore be reliably interpreted, there has been widespread use of invertebrates, fish and other organisms to monitor river quality.[3] Most Western nations have programmes in place to monitor river health through the use of censuses of benthic (bottom-living) invertebrates. It is widely believed that these organisms are good integrators and indicators of river condition. The interpretation of the data in the context of environmental flows is not altogether easy, however (and it should be remembered that the original use of these techniques was to monitor point sources of toxic pollutants rather than either diffuse nutrient and sediment inputs or changes in flow). Even though the benthic invertebrate data are collected by using stringently controlled protocols, it is clear that there is much small-scale – riffle and reach scale – determination of the results of each of the samples. The statistical technique requires classification of the health of the river in question by the comparison of the samples collected with data from reference sites chosen to represent similar, but pristine, reaches.[4] Such reaches are becoming harder and harder to find, an impossibility indeed in many nations where the entire landscape and waterscape has now been modified by human activity. We should remember that freshwater biodiversity is being lost more rapidly than in any other habitat around the world.

We do know that the populations of benthic invertebrates in rivers are determined by a number of factors. Bunn and Arthington[5] put forward the following four basic principles:

1. flow is a major determinant of physical habitat in streams which in turn is a major determinant of community structure
2. life history strategies of aquatic organisms have evolved in direct response to the natural flow regimes
3. maintenance of natural patterns of longitudinal and lateral connectivity is essential for the viability of riverine species
4. invasion by exotic and introduced species is favoured by the alteration of flow regimes.

Of course this focuses largely on the physical flow requirements of the organisms in rivers. Throughout the environmental flows literature there is a tendency to conflate flows with river health and to use the tools designed to monitor river health to monitor flow regimes. We have already seen that there are as many off-river, landscape-scale impacts on the physical structure and sediment characteristics of rivers and streams as there are flow determinants. Unfortunately it appears that measures of river health are only weakly influenced by changes in flow, but strongly influenced by land use changes and point source toxicant discharges. Only at equilibrium, when all the increased sediment supply resulting from land use change has been flushed from the river, would point 1 apply: and as we have seen in Australian floodplain rivers equilibration times are much longer than 200 years. This is not an equilibrium world. It is therefore very hard to find definitive published accounts of the response of benthic invertebrate populations to changing flow regimes.

The critical logic steps in the science of environmental flows assume that there is a direct relations between flow and physical habitat (higher flows flush out fine sediments and lead to rougher and cleaner sediment types), and that habitat type is a strong determinant of the biodiversity of aquatic organisms. Analyses of numerous data sets from flow experiments and observations around the world do not show strong relations between changing flow regimes and aquatic biodiversity. Reviews and empirical analyses of data do seem to indicate that habitat is a strong determinant of biodiversity[6] but that flow is not a strong predictor of benthic biodiversity.[7] Proportional changes in hydrological variables such as mean annual flows are not strongly linked to ecological outcomes. This can only mean that factors other than flow are strong determinants of sediment type and habitat quality in rivers – and this must include catchment land use mosaics and the proportion of forested, agricultural and urban lands in the drainage area.

The things we do to ensure security of supply of 'blue' water for agricultural and urban supply (building dams, regulating and changing seasonality of flows, trapping floods and reducing floodplain inundation) have all had massive impacts on the natural aquatic biota. Changing flow regimes do appear to alter both the biodiversity of riparian ecosystems and the ways in which nutrients are cycled.[8] So the best we can do in many situations is to use the flow – physical habitat – biota linkage to try to preserve and restore aquatic communities in rivers while recognising that landscape and land use restoration is also critical for river restoration. As long as we can bring the nutrient and pollutant levels under control through careful attention to land use restoration and waste discharges then this is a beginning point in many river systems. Unfortunately, as discussed earlier, many river systems are heavily physically modified through land use change, and erosion is a major problem. River flows are now commonly characterised by much flashier flows than normal so that river geomorphology has been heavily modified in many regions. After land clearing and urban development, channels and banks are eroded and widened, and sand slugs lie in the river beds. Much fine sediment has been deposited in the beds of rivers and streams that were once dominated by cobbles and gravels. Not only has this had a big impact on the aquatic ecology (salmonid fish, for example, which depend on clean gravels and good water quality for successful spawning and recruitment, are under threat in many places) but widespread catchment modification and population growth means that it is therefore almost impossible to put the clock back.

Riverine waterscapes are as complex as the landscapes that they sit in, and there are many linkages between the habitat mosaics in the waterscapes and those in the surrounding landscapes.[9] The shifting pattern of habitats in rivers and their catchments have long been exploited by organisms but we have a rather poor understanding of the ways in which the two are linked, and the ways in which we have changed the patterns, processes and linkages, particularly at smaller scales. The close linkages between landscape and waterscape extend beyond water chemistry to the impact of soil development and terrestrial plant successions on aquatic biota over periods of hundreds of years.[10] Whereas some of the biotic determinants are external, some are also internal. For example, beavers, through their dam-building activities, are the ultimate ecological engineers, influencing both their own survival and the ecology of many other species. Niche construction by organisms – where organisms significantly influence their environments and those of others – is widespread and is a powerful feedback mechanism, which adds an extra level of complexity to the relationship between organisms and their environments.[11] Rivers and their catchments are not equilibrium systems: the biodiversity of both is maintained by the shifting dynamical patterns of habitats and communities over time scales from individual flood events out to postglacial scales and beyond. By imposing new frequencies and magnitudes of disturbance on top of what was already a shifting mosaic of interactions underwater (just as we have done on land) we have produced unexpected outcomes. As discussed before in the context of landscape ecology, we have a better knowledge of pattern than of process and we have tended to ignore the process linkages between the various temporal and spatial scales in rivers when we alter flow regimes.[12] Analyses of the altered pattern of species distributions may tell us that a river reach is degraded, but it rarely tells us what to do to repair or restore the damage.[13]

Catchments do show power-law-like relationships of flood flow events: few large events and many small ones. River geomorphology is usually determined more by the extreme flow events than by averaged flows and if we view the spatial and temporal scales of interaction at work in the river as a nested hierarchy then the effects of individual flood events will, in time, work their way throughout the system.[14] One product of river regulation and the provision of security of supply of 'blue' water for irrigation seems to be the homogenisation of spatial and temporal variability in rivers – effectively what we do is to flatten the power law graph down (reduce the slope) so that there are fewer large flood events and more smaller flow events – with a consequent impact on physical habitat and biodiversity. Downstream of urban areas, however, the situation is different, with higher storm flow frequencies in rivers arising from impervious areas in the catchment. We do not, it seems, fully understand what these opposite effects might have on aquatic biota coupled, as they are, with other changes in water quality due to land use changes. By concentrating on monthly (or less frequent) data collection we have missed an opportunity to study the linkages between land use, flow, in-stream habitat and biodiversity in more detail.

Decision support tools

Partly because of the complexities and fundamental uncertainties (and partly because of the contingent history and conceptual limitations of ideas in various countries) existing environmental flow assessment tools are many and varied. None approaches the required complexity. Tharme has written a very useful review of the methods used in 44 countries in six world regions.[15] The most commonly applied methodology appears to be what might be called the 'Tennant' method, after its originator in the USA.[16] In this method minimum flow standards are set after the collection of data on the linkages between field conditions, habitat and hydraulic and biological data. At least 25 countries use this method now, either in its full form or as a set of arbitrarily derived percentages of annual average flows, although it seems to be most widely used in Europe and North America. Habitat simulation methods are the second most widely used technique and exploit the linkage from flow–habitat–biota identified earlier as a critical set of steps. The cornerstones of the In-stream Flow Incremental Methodologies (known as IFIM) are physical and riverine habitat simulation programmes. They are the dominant methods in use in North America, although, as might be expected, Tharme noted the 'methodology's lack of ecological predictive capability'.[17] The third set of methodologies in use are what might be called holistic methodologies, involving a mix of hydrology-based methods, simulation techniques, expert judgements and workshops with stakeholders and communities. These are mostly in use in Australia and South Africa, and in Tharme's view represent the recent development of a more sophisticated methodology which takes a 'bottom-up' ecosystem-based, whole-of-basin view together with a 'top-down' interactive process. The South African DRIFT method (Downstream Response to Imposed Flow Transformation), for example, has four modules: a biophysical module, which examines the response of the river to flow changes, a socio-economic module, which describes the links between river users and their needs (including health issues), a module that creates a number of future scenarios, and an economic module, which examines compensation and mitigation costs.[18] Tharme notes in her review that assessment tools for environmental flows are not used world wide and that there are many gaps both in our knowledge and in the use of the available techniques. Given the need for techniques to advance sustainability and to balance the various capitals in catchments, this is an area that requires urgent attention.

Science meets politics

In response to the pressures on water and its productive uses in many countries, the environmental flow assessment techniques that have been developed have been built into various forms of Integrated Water Resources Management (IWRM). IWRM includes a variety of community consultation, participation and dialogue processes for conflict resolution and policy development, so that IWRM is a combination of science, expert opinion and consultation processes.[19] In the face of considerable uncertainty and in the absence of good data and information, we must rely on expert judgement and community consultation. Environmental flows are one place where a paucity of good science meets Realpolitik; the use of environmental flows assessment techniques around the world is most advanced in countries that have well-developed water policies and community involvement in decision making. Together we must face the uncertainty as best we can. The rise of 'water wars', disputes over water rights and the competing demands for a variety of productive and other uses have been made more pointed by the realisation that aquatic ecosystems are legitimate water users also, and that natural capital should have rights and values. Even if we could suddenly raise the quality of the information to hand, and unequivocally demonstrate the impact of flow management on natural values, we would still require consultative mechanisms to make decisions about the allocation of scarce resources to various uses. There are ethical aspects to this which go way beyond the instrumental and utilitarian values associated with modern science[20] and raise important issues about how competing values might be assessed and compromises achieved.[21]

What is happening all over the world, therefore, is the emergence of precisely the kind of 'postmodern' science that we have already discussed. New partnerships and collaborative relationships are required between science and the community.[22] Science and the community are coming together in places where holistic assessment techniques are being used to debate a series of differing values and trade-offs in an environment of uncertainty and partial knowledge. Overall, a new and more holistic global vision for water is slowly emerging.[23]

Because of drought, high water demand from irrigation and urban development and the evident environmental damage resulting from overallocation of surface ('blue') water supplies, this is nowhere more true than in the Murray–Darling Basin in Australia. Over the period from 2001 to 2004 the continent experienced a 1 in 100 year drought and reservoir storage levels fell to unprecedentedly low levels. The condition of the Murray River has been summarised in a number of reports.[24] Large areas of the River Red Gums that line the rivers as they flow through the desert have died because of a combination of increasing salinity, low water levels and a very long period since the last time the floodplain was inundated. Some 350 000 mature trees over an area of about 250 000 ha of flood plain are dying: an entire cohort of old trees has been lost. In addition large areas of Black Box woodland on the terraces beside the river, which would have been flooded less frequently, are also dead. The river is degraded along much of its length by excessive water extraction, flow regulation, overgrazing on the flood plain and habitat destruction resulting in salinisation. We have evidently crossed a threshold that would have been better avoided. The public outcry has focused a number of minds on the environmental flow requirements of the river, and a number of iconic floodplain sites have been earmarked for restoration and recovery. The processes of determining the environmental flow requirements of the Murray River have begun; and stakes are high because the Murray is one of the Australian rivers of poetry, song and legend. The Murray is part of the national heritage.

The Murray River is totally regulated, so the process must be to restore the longitudinal and lateral connectivity of the river and its floodplain and to share the scarce water between many strongly competing uses and values. To attempt to do this the Australian governments (Commonwealth and State) have relied heavily on holistic environmental flows assessment techniques and also on expert panels for advice about river condition and flow requirements.

The Snowy River has long been degraded by large-scale water diversions for the Snowy Mountains hydro-electric scheme. It has recently been the subject of a public outcry and water is now being returned to the river. As part of the process of deciding what the minimum environmental flow requirements are, a composite river condition index was created, which involved using the minimum value of a habitat condition and a biotic condition index. Habitat condition was measured by hydraulic and physical habitats, water quality, barriers to fish passage and the condition of riparian vegetation. Biotic condition was measured by vegetation (microphyte) condition, aquatic invertebrates and fish community indices.[25] As might be expected, the best correlations were between the invertebrate community indices and the indices for hydraulic and physical habitat, and the only significant correlates to the fish indices were those concerned with barriers to fish migration. Nevertheless the composite index was a better measure than the individual components and such composite indices are being more widely adopted throughout the Basin. Perhaps most importantly the composite index was a very useful way of presenting and summarising information and was a useful input to the expert panel process. As a unified and synthesized source of information it was a way of addressing some of the shortcomings of the expert panel approaches by making them less speculative and more repeatable, better structured and transparent.[26]

Holistic assessments

To try to return the Murray River to its former glory an independent expert reference panel on environmental flows was created, which used as its knowledge base the Murray Flows Assessment Tool (MFAT). The expert reference panel produced an initial confidential report, which provided scope for the choice of public scenarios for water to be returned to the river. Possible increases in the environmental flows in the river were assessed as scenarios around specified increases in river flows up to a maximum of 1500 Gl per annum. MFAT is not a predictive model; it is a decision support tool. As such it contains a combination of empirical data, past experience and expert opinion based on previous flow events and river condition. So MFAT links a hydrological model of the river capable of showing both flows and floodplain inundation in various river reaches to a transparent process of finding river condition indices for each flow scenario and river reach. MFAT links flows and floodplain hydrology to various ecological and other assets in the river: geomorphology, fish, birds, vegetation and algal blooms. Composite indices were used for each river reach. In each case preference curves for each outcome were constructed from expert judgement and by empirical data supported by consensus knowledge from the literature. MFAT allows these judgements to be made transparently and repeatably and was subject to extensive peer review and independent assessment of its performance. MFAT also brings all the supporting evidence together in one location and allows assessments of uncertainty to be explicitly stated. So MFAT represents one of the most extensive and politically charged examples of the use of environmental flow assessments based on all available knowledge, in an environment where uncertainty is acknowledged and treated transparently. It has been the basis of an extensive public debate over the future of the river and has led to Commonwealth Government commitments to purchase an initial 500 Gl of water for the river from the irrigation water market.

One of the greatest shortcomings of MFAT in my view is that it does not adequately represent the response of the river and its ecosystems to flood pulses and flow variability of the kind that used to exist before the river was regulated, beginning a century ago. It does not take into account the more complex view of the 'systems of systems' approach espoused here with the associated hysteresis effects and 'points of no return', nor does it use the information contained in multivariate measures. Although uncertainty can be incorporated, estimates were not widely used. These floodplain rivers are not equilibrium systems; they are on long-term trajectories, which are largely determined by very infrequent extreme flood events. The linkages between pattern and process across scales (including the properties of various kinds of SGC) lead to a level of complexity that is not currently widely appreciated or understood. Time since the last big flood is a frequently neglected aspect of 'deep time' in these systems. Like many other ecosystems these are not equilibrium systems – trajectories of change and multiple states abound. We do not do risk assessments or make expert judgements about the interactions between ecological factors, species or pressures on the system. The past or the present are probably not an effective guide to the future – particularly if flood frequencies have been changed by engineering or climate change (or both) – and we lack adequate process and mechanistic information to be able to make those linkages.

The river has been totally regulated and modified for a long time – including the introduction of exotic species – and we are now seeing the consequences in the demise of the native fish, in poor water quality and in the dead and dying trees. Planning for floodplain restoration, where the trees may live for 250 years or more, actually requires planning and action over decades, something we are not good at doing anywhere in the world.[27] We have discounted the effects of long-term change and deep time; and it is not just the flow regime in the river that has been changed. For example, many of the fallen trees that used to lie in the river (called 'snags' in Australia) have been removed; and they were covered in biofilms and provided a habitat for fish and other organisms. Snags are an important part of the river ecology[28] and are another excellent example of the very small impacting on the larger system properties. In addition, few people appreciate that although the river and its floodplain look degraded now, there are many more trees in the river corridor now than there were a hundred years ago. In the years after colonisation deforestation for construction, fences and fuel for the river boats was rife. This tree removal in the past, coupled with high grazing rates from stock, rabbits and feral goats in the present, appears to have had large-scale, long-term impacts through increased recharge and salinisation of the terraces alongside the river. So although there may be more trees than there were, the landscape is nevertheless badly degraded.

So we have changed many things in the Murray River. It will not be possible to restore many of the original flow and flood regimes because of all the engineering that has been done and because of all the other assets, values and capitals that now require access to the floodplains of rivers in the Basin. These other capitals require greatly altered seasonal flow regimes in order to ensure production and profit. Security for the natural ecosystems can now only be bought at the risk to other values, and the overlapping scales of pattern and process from the 'system of systems' will ensure a different outcome than before. In practical terms, how do we return a flood to the river now that it has been specifically engineered to prevent overbank flows? If we have only 500–1500 Gl of water for the river (and even 1500 Gl is only a little more than 10% of the total diversions from the river) how do we use this water wisely to obtain the best ecological, social and economic outcome in such a situation? Is it possible to save the few nominated iconic floodplain sites along the river by returning the flood flows to just those sites with the right magnitudes and return frequencies when the river has been engineered for totally different purposes? Remember that these CAS show power law distributions of many properties, including flood flow distributions. How do we restore such variability to the river and its catchment when we buy and sell the surface water in the basin, and manage the river through market mechanisms in which the water allocations are based on annual averaged flows? These are very difficult questions to which we have, at present, no adequate answer. Nevertheless MFAT has been valuable in that it has begun the process of the construction of a holistic assessment for the river. The potential benefits of various environmental flow scenarios can now be debated by society at large and the values obtained – ecological, social and economic – can be debated and traded off. This process will need to be supported by totally different kinds of science and institutional arrangements.

Landscape and waterscape management: the way forward

So what is the way forward in such complex matters? There are already, in the shadows, hints and examples of the kinds of approaches that we will need to take. For a start we have to acknowledge that we will probably never have the kind of detailed and precise knowledge of these systems that positivist science would like. Even if we could conceive of a huge data gathering project, pressure of events and political realities suggest that decisions would to be taken in short order anyway, long before some of the answers were in. So we will always be managing and setting policy in a data-poor environment. Some, in fact, have called for 'data-less' management, in recognition of the fact that we will never have the kinds of information we need.[29] Johannes, writing about a scale of problem similar to the Murray–Darling – the impossibility of ever collecting enough data to adequately manage tropical coastal fisheries by means of traditional fisheries management methods – calculated that even by using 'short-cut' assessment techniques it would take more than 1700 person-years to assess the artisanal fisheries of over 7000 Indonesian coastal fishing villages. He concluded that even simple precautionary management was not possible if it relied on quantitative information from all sites. We need, he wrote, to go further.

> We need the much greater simplifications of what might be called data-less management – that is, management carried out in the absence of the data required for the parameterisation and verification of models that predict effects of various management actions with useful statistical confidence limits.[30]

Data-less management does not mean managing without any kind of information; it draws on the best scientific knowledge to hand, on knowledge from other similar systems and on other forms of local, indigenous and anecdotal information. There are other forms of knowledge than science, other ways of knowing, and these need to be brought into play.

In truth most environmental management problems are exercises in data-poor environments, where we know we know some things, where we know there are some things we do not know and where we know there will always be unknown unknowns.[31] Wherever possible we do need prior warning of thresholds and strong hysteresis effects. It should also be remembered that the increasingly complex and networked world in which we live also leads to non-linear creativity and many path dependencies, and hence an additional degree of social and institutional 'unknowability'.[32] Johannes therefore argued that data-poor management is an imperative in this world and he rejected claims that it was not science. Perfect it may not be, but perfection is an unachievable goal; and data-poor management is certainly better than no management at all. Furthermore, if we are to try to maximise all forms of capital to obtain a more sustainable outcome, data-poor management will have to be carried out in an adaptive framework with full community and institutional consultation. So the challenge in a nutshell is to try to manage and maximise all forms of capital in a data-poor environment where surprises will occur and various forms of knowledge, beliefs and values must be recognised and traded off. All this must be done in a changing world, encompassing complex and interacting trajectories and cycles of economic, social and environmental change. The people that seem to accept this terrible reality most readily are those working with the problems of third world development and some of the best examples of tackling practical problems of sustainability with novel tools come from that literature. Ecologists working in the Western world would do well to pay more heed to those struggling to manage the day-to-day problems of population pressures, sanitation and landscape management in the third world.

There are a small number of initial experiments being carried out along these lines. One uses multi-agent simulation (MAS) techniques. In their review of the development of MAS, Bousquet and Le Page[33] quote Holling's definitions of three kinds of concept that have defined causality in ecological systems. The first was equilibrium (the balance of nature), the second was the existence of multiple stable states (nature resilient) and the third point of view was change and interaction in complex systems (nature evolving).[34] The third view is the one adopted here, in which 'the observations focus on the connectivity of the ecosystem's elements, their interactions and their organisation across scales'.[35] So a focus on the elements (agents) and their interactions, and the ways in which the context and connectivity change over time, is a different way of looking at the properties and development of systems. Thus MAS avoid some of the key problems with dynamical models discussed earlier, although it must be recognised that such models are still imperfect and in the early stages of development. Nevertheless MAS have been effectively used in ecological simulations in many contexts.[36] A parallel set of MAS have been developed in the social sciences and in computational economics to examine the properties and development of interacting social agents (and here 'agents' may be individuals, villages or other social groups).[37] The most interesting developments in this area have been in the fusion of ecological and social MAS in a spatial context for assistance with the management of common-pool resources. Bousquet and others have built a strong French group that has used CORMAS (Common-pool Resources and Multi-Agent Systems) to stimulate deliberative processes around resource management problems.[38] There is now a large literature on this subject.[39] What is interesting about CORMAS is that it is used as a stimulant for deliberative processes, i.e. rather like Management Strategy Evaluation in the fishing industry, the model is used in an adaptive sense to attempt to capture shifting beliefs and values as well as the dynamics of the resource management interactions. This kind of model has been used to simulate and analyse the interactions between players in the management of irrigation systems in Senegal.[40] CORMAS operates in an explicitly spatial framework, so it has strong parallels also with cellular automaton (CA) models in the interactions between adjacent grid squares. This kind of approach has been used to model and analyse the spatial interactions between the dynamics of land and water use around the fringes of Sao Paulo in Brazil.[41] The design and use of MAS models in a consultative and community-based context is part of an overall capacity building process and a process of 'opening the black box' to all players. The construction of the model is part of an overall learning process; by the scientists about community values and beliefs, and by the community about linkages and natural resource constraints and dynamics.[42] Lynam has used similar techniques in Mozambique and Zimbabwe to evolve a methodology for the analysis and management of 'locally complex systems in a globally complex world'.[43] In the Zambezi valley the agro-ecosystems are non-equilibrium evolving and adaptive systems. Lynam calls for 'theories of evolving and adaptive agents and institutions, and theories of hierarchically structured and adaptive ecosystems' to cope with the reality of the systems he is working with. Lynam also identifies a number of daunting problems:

- the problem of integration across scales using discrete data collected at one or a few scales
- integration of the many forms of knowledge available – and the predilection of scientists to believe their numerical models even when this knowledge is actually worse than the others
- the integration of various sources of uncertainty
- our limited ability to understand variability across scales and the uncertainties introduced by our analytical methods
- translating science and its model into languages and concepts that can be understood by a people most of whom have never seen a computer

These are fundamental problem for all natural resource managers – they are not peculiar to the Zambezi valley! Further development of the use of spatially discrete simulation by using simple schemata can be found in use in other countries. Lynam has collaborated with the developers of CORMAS to find ways of coupling MAS with Bayesian nets and belief models to bring prior knowledge and various forms of experience to bear on development problems in Africa.[44] This is about 'adapting science to adaptive managers' and finding ways to bring together what we know, the uncertainties in our knowledge and lacing them in an adaptive framework of participatory engagement with the people on the land. Given the uncertainties in our knowledge of natural resource systems, any attempt at integrated landscape or water resource management (IWRM), that seeks to achieve outcomes on the ground and in the water is going to require deliberative and participatory processes that use limited and uncertain knowledge.[45] At present Bayesian belief nets, MAS and other forms of simple models are the best we have. These models can be used as part of discourse-based and deliberative processes to try to find fair outcomes to the problems of valuation of multiple forms of capital and to try to find ways of balancing the multiplicity of pressures on natural resources and biodiversity in land and waterscapes. At present it seems that we are stuck with deliberative processes as the only means of trying to find ways to balance conflicting and incommensurate values and beliefs about the natural world.[46] New data and insights will improve the quality of the debate and might go some way to reducing the uncertainties, but they will never be eliminated, even with the most sophisticated expert systems informing the decision making process. In a world in which things change continuously at a range of scales and often in surprising ways, and a world in which our knowledge is partial, then the only practical response is one of discussion, experiment and learning.[47] Above all we must find ways to be more adaptive and flexible in our responses to the natural world.

NOTES

1. S. R. Carpenter *et al.* Non point pollution of surface waters with phosphorus and nitrogen. *Ecological Applications*, **8** (1998), 559–68.
2. R. J. Naiman *et al.* Legitimizing fluvial ecosystems as users of water: an overview. *Environmental Management*, **30** (2002), 455–67.
3. See, for example, R. H. Norris *et al.* Uses of biota to assess water quality: an international conference. *Australian Journal of Ecology*, **20** (1995), 1–227. Also the issue of *Freshwater Biology* on 'River Health': *Freshwater Biology*, **41** (2) (March 1999) and the papers therein.
4. See, for example, M. J. Smith *et al.* AusRivAS: using macroinvertebrates to assess ecological condition of rivers in Western Australia. *Freshwater Biology*, **41** (1999), 269–82. That paper also contains references to work in other countries, particularly the original work by J. F. Wright and others, who developed the RIVPACS models in UK in the 1980s.
5. S. E. Bunn and A. H. Arthington. Basic principles and ecological consequences of altered flow regimes for aquatic biodiversity. *Environmental Management*, **30** (2002), 492–507.
6. See, for example, W. J., Young *et al.* Improving expert panel assessment through the use of a composite river condition index – the case of the rivers affected by the Snowy Mountains hydro-electric scheme, Australia. *River Research and Applications*, **20** (2004), 733–50.
7. N. Lloyd *et al. Does flow modification cause geomorphological and ecological response in rivers? A literature review from an Australian perspective.* Technical report 1/2004, (Canberra, ACT.: Cooperative Research Centre for Freshwater Ecology, University of Canberra, 2004).
8. C. Nilsson and M. Svedmark. Basic principles and ecological consequences of changing water regimes: riparian plant communities. *Environmental Management*, **30** (2002), 468–80. S. E. Bunn and A. H. Arthington. Basic principles and ecological consequences of altered flow regimes for aquatic biodiversity. *Environmental Management*, **30** (2002), 492–507. G. Pinay, J. C. Clement and R. J. Naiman. Basic principles and ecological consequences of changing water regimes on nitrogen cycling in fluvial systems. *Environmental Management*, **30** (2002), 481–91.
9. C. T. Robinson, K. Tockner and J. V. Ward. The fauna of dynamic riverine landscapes. *Freshwater Biology*, **47** (2002), 661–77.

10. A. M. Milner *et al.* Colonisation and development of stream communities across a 200 year gradient in Glacier Bay National Park, Alaska. *Canadian Journal of Fisheries and Aquatic Science*, **57** (2000), 1–16.

11. D. Jones. Personal effects. *Nature*, **438** (2005), 14–16.

12. M. C. Thoms and M. Parsons. Identifying spatial and temporal patterns in the hydrological character of the Condamine-Balonne River, Australia, using multi-variate statistics. *River Research and Applications*, **19** (2003), 443–57.

13. G. P. Harris. Pattern, process and prediction in aquatic ecology. A limnological view of some general ecological problems. *Freshwater Biology*, **32** (1994), 143–60.

14. M. C. Thoms and F. Sheldon. An ecosystem approach for determining environmental water allocations in Australian dryland river systems: the role of geomorphology. *Geomorphology*, **47** (2002), 153–68.

15. R. E. Tharme. A global perspective on environmental flow assessment: emerging trends in the development and application of environmental flow methodologies for rivers. *River Research and Applications*, **19** (2003), 397–441.

16. D. L. Tennant. In stream flow regimens for fish, wildlife, recreation and related environmental resources. *Fisheries*, **1** (1976), 6–10.

17. R. E. Tharme. *River Research and Applications*, **19** (2003), p. 407.

18. J. King, C. Brown and H. Sabet. A scenario-based holistic approach to environmental flow assessments for rivers. *River Research and Applications*, **19** (2003), 619–39.

19. *Integrated Water Resource Management (IWRM): a way to sustainability.* InfoResources, Focus no. 1/03, Swiss Agency for Development and Cooperation. Available from www.inforesources.ch. An excellent manual on the whole process of choosing the right assessment methods, defining water requirements, modifying infrastructure, covering the costs and obtaining political and community backing can be found in M. Dyson, G. Bergkamp and J. Scanlon (eds). *Flow. The Essentials of Environmental Flows.* (Gland, Switzerland and Cambridge, UK: IUCN, 2003). Available from the IUCN website at www.iucn.org.

20. M. Acreman. Ethical aspects of water and ecosystems. *Water Policy*, **3** (2001), 257–65.

21. J. Bennett. Environmental values and water policy. *Australian Geographical Studies*, **41** (2003), 237–50.

22. N. L. Poff *et al.* River flows and water wars: emerging science for environmental decision making. *Frontiers in Ecology and the Environment*, **1** (2003), 298–306. (www.frontiersinecology.org)

23. W. J. Cosgrove and F. R. Rijsberman. Creating a vision for water, life and the environment. *Water Policy*, **1** (1998), 115–22.

24. M. Thoms *et al. Report of the River Murray Scientific Panel on Environmental Flows.* (Canberra, ACT.: Murray–Darling Basin Commission, 2000), www.mdbc.gov.au. R. H. Norris *et al. Snapshot of the Murray–Darling Basin River Condition.* (Canberra, ACT.: Murray–Darling Basin Commission, September 2001). (www.thelivingmurray.mdbc.gov.au)

25. W. J. Young *et al.* Improving expert panel assessments through the use of a composite river condition index – the case of the rivers affected by the Snowy Mountains Hydro-electric scheme, Australia. *River Research and Applications*, **20** (2004), 733–50.

26. P. Cottingham, M. C. Thoms and G. P. Quinn. Scientific panels and their use in environmental flow assessment in Australia. *Australian Journal of Water Resources*, **5** (2002), 103–11.

27. F. M. R. Hughes and S. B. Rood. Allocation of river flows for restoration of floodplain forest ecosystems: a review of approaches and their applicability in Europe. *Environmental Management*, **32** (2003), 12–33.

28. W. J. Young (ed.) *Rivers as Ecological Systems: the Murray–Darling Basin.* (Canberra, ACT.: Murray–Darling Basin Commission, 2001).

29. R. E. Johannes. The case for data-less marine management: examples from tropical near shore fin fisheries. *Trends in Ecology and Evolution*, **13** (1998), 243–6.

30. Ibid., p. 243.

31. This famous catch-phrase is taken from a quotation by the US Secretary of Defence, Donald Rumsfeld. It is now widely quoted. In addition to many websites, one source is H. Seely (ed.) *Pieces of Intelligence: the Existential Poetry of Donald. H Rumsfeld.* (New York: Free Press, Simon and Schuster, 2003). Seely attributes the full quotation to Rumsfeld talking at a Department of Defence news briefing on 2 Feb 2002.

32. R. W. Rycroft and D. E. Kash. *The Complexity Challenge: Technological Innovation for the 21st Century.* (London: Pinter, 1999).

33. F. Bousquet and C. Le Page. Multi-agent simulations and ecosystem management: a review. *Ecological Modelling*, **176** (2004), 313–32.

34. C. S. Holling. Simplifying the complex: the paradigms of ecological function and structure. *European Journal of Operational Research*, **30** (1987), 139–46.

35. Bousquet and Le Page, *Ecological Modelling*, **176** (2004), p. 315. (See Note 33.)

36. Reviewed in Bousquet and Le Page, *Ecological Modelling*, **176** (2004). (See Note 33.)

37. See, for example, N. Gilbert and J. Doran (eds). *Simulating Societies.* (London: UCL Press, 1994).

38. F. Bousquet *et al*. Cormas: common-pool resources and multi-agent systems. *Lecture Notes in Artificial Intelligence*, **1416** (1998), 826–37.

39. See www.cormas.cirad.fr/en/bibliog/article.htm.

40. O. Barreteau *et al*. Suitability of multi-agent simulations to study irrigated system viability: application to case studies in the Senegal River valley. *Agricultural Systems*, **80** (2004), 255–75.

41. R. Ducrot *et al*. Articulating land and water dynamics with urbanisation: an attempt to model natural resources management at the urban edge. *Computers, Environment and Urban Systems*, **28** (2004), 85–106.

42. O. Barreteau *et al*. Agent-based facilitation of water allocation: case study in the Drome River valley. *Group Decision and Negotiation*, **12** (2003), 441–61.

43. T. Lynam. Adaptive analysis of locally complex systems in a globally complex world. *Conservation Ecology*, **3 (2)**, 13 (1999); online at www.consecol.org/vol3/iss2/art13.

44. T. Lynam *et al*. Adapting science to adaptive managers: spidergrams, belief models, and multi-agent systems modelling. *Conservation Ecology*, **5 (2)** (2002) 24; online at www.consecol.org/vol5/iss2/art24. T. Lynam, R. Cunliffe and I. Mapaure. Assessing the importance of woodland landscape locations for both local communities and conservation in Gorongoza and Muanza Districts, Sofala Province, Mozambique. *Ecology and Society*, **9 (4)** (2004) 1; online at www.ecologyandsociety.org/vol9/iss/4art1.

45. J. Cain, C. Batchelor and D. Waughray. Belief networks: a framework for the participatory development of natural resource management strategies. *Environment, Development and Sustainability*, **1** (1999), 123–33.

46. M. A. Wilson and R. B. Howarth. Discourse-based valuation of ecosystem services: establishing fair outcomes through group deliberation. *Ecological Economics*, **41** (2002), 431–43.

47. C. S. Holling. From complex regions to complex worlds. *Ecology and Society*, **9 (1)** (2004) 11; online at www.ecologyandsociety.org/vol9/iss1/art11.

16 Evidence for global change

Global observing systems: evidence for change in the 'wide now' and in 'deep time'.

The nexus of information and computing technologies, new ways of observing both the biosphere and the anthroposphere, and the broadening of the community of interest around global environmental issues, has led to major developments in knowledge and policy around the world. Each new science has its one image – and in this area it is the NASA Apollo mission image of the Earth rising above the Moon. All at once the Earth was seen as a bounded, discrete and lonely blue ball in the black void of space. All of a sudden the finite nature of our home was made clear. Developments in communications and computing technologies, together with data from the space programmes of the major Western and other nations, have led to a revolution in the way we can image, measure and model global phenomena. If space programmes were originally spurred on by the arms race of the Cold War then what we are witnessing is a real 'peace dividend' from those investments in new technologies. Beginning with the early LANDSAT missions and developing through the NASA Earth Observing System and remote sensing programmes from Japan, Europe, India and other countries we have, since the 1970s, witnessed the rapid development of many sophisticated earth observing systems to measure and monitor atmospheric, oceanic and terrestrial patterns and processes. We have spacecraft in low Earth orbit, geostationary meteorological satellites and an ever-increasing array of atmospheric, oceanic and terrestrial sensors, from deep in the ocean to high in the atmosphere. This has led to huge conceptual and practical advances. Supercomputers routinely assimilate data from spacecraft and a huge array of other sensors to produce daily global weather maps and predictions. Sensors in space routinely monitor ocean currents, sea surface temperatures, cloud patterns, ozone holes, deforestation and land use change, and the global distribution of photosynthetic vegetation, to name but a few of the parameters of interest. Sensors in space are complemented by a growing range of smart and autonomous sensors on the ground and underwater, some even attached to animals like albatrosses, penguins and elephant seals in remote places like the Southern Ocean.[1] Tracking the movements of birds, fish[2] and mammals by satellite trackers is becoming routine, as is the measurement of a variety of environmental parameters such as sea temperature.[3] We have learned a lot about migration paths and the ocean environment from tagged animals in recent years. So we are even recruiting the planet's biodiversity to assist us with our environmental monitoring.

The space programmes of the major Western and other nations grew up alongside global science programmes like the International Geosphere–Biosphere Programme (IGBP), the World Climate Research Programme (WCRP), the global biodiversity programme (DIVERSITAS) and the International Human Dimensions Programme (IHDP) coordinated through the International Council of Scientific Unions (ICSU).[4] These programmes are now being brought together under the aegis of the Earth Systems Science Partnership. In conjunction with United Nations agencies such as the UN Environment Programme (UNEP) and operational agencies such as the World Meteorological Organization (WMO), ICSU assists with the coordination of three major Global Observing Systems: the Global Climate Observing System (GCOS), the Global Ocean Observing System (GOOS) and the Global Terrestrial Observing System (GTOS). These programmes will now work with the new Global Earth Observing System of Systems (GEOSS) to be housed within the WMO.[5] (The global science community is very fond of acronyms.) So a large-scale global science and coordination infrastructure has also been established in the past few decades to make all this happen; the way in which all that has been put together is worth a book in itself. The revolution in data has been accompanied by a conceptual revolution because, along with the technological challenge of collecting, storing and accessing all this data, we have faced the challenge of turning data into information and knowledge; and that means creating mental and numerical models. When the first global research products were being produced we suddenly had to begin thinking about Earth system science; and as if the physical, chemical and biological world was not complex enough, we also had to start thinking through the complex feedbacks between the biosphere and the anthroposphere, the human world. So there has been a well-coordinated knowledge revolution in the past three decades.

In the full context outlined above (i.e. combination of Earth observation, data and information systems, modelling and prediction) Earth system science was born in the late 1980s during the design of the NASA Earth Observing System. The Earth system sciences committee deliberations were chaired by Francis Bretherton and led to some key scoping documents[6] and to a detailed flow diagram – the first conceptual model for the fluid and biological Earth – which became known as the Bretherton diagram. The diagram was an attempt to bring together the major flows of energy and materials within the Earth system and to begin to build conceptual and mechanistic models of the interactions. It was, if you like, an attempt to formulate a prediction engine for the Earth system: an attempt to underpin the remotely sensed observations of the Earth with a process understanding of the key relationships and parameters.

There are important scientific programmes that are beginning to take us down the path to understanding the complexity of the global CAS. One, of great relevance here, is what is called 'sustainability science'.[7] Sustainability science seems to have arisen largely as an outgrowth from one of the major scientific initiatives of the past few decades: the IGBP.[8] This intiative has been in existence for more than 20 years and is concerned with the understanding of global ecology and biogeochemistry – the linkage of biology and ecology to the global cycles of nutrients and other key elements. With its accompanying programme, the IHDP, it attempts to explain much of the observed global dynamics. Sustainability science originates in what I might call 'hard science': the attempts to understand global processes through data gathering, hypothesis building and numerical modelling of the Earth's systems. It constitutes the coming together of terrestrial, atmospheric and oceanic science. This birth of Earth system science has been called a new Copernican revolution[9] because, instead of telescopes telling us of our true place in the universe, it instead turns the technology back towards Earth and tells us of our true place on this planet. So over the past three decades there has been a very great effort made to obtain data on what might be called the 'wide now': the global scope of biospheric and anthropospheric processes and impacts. We now have unprecedented information about natural global processes and the global impacts of human activities. We can monitor everything from the disappearance of Arctic ice cover to the patterns of planktonic biomass in the oceans, from the distribution of Sahelian dust to the disappearance of tropical forest cover.

Gathering information about change over time: monitoring deep time

Whereas there have been major steps forward in gathering knowledge about the 'wide now' we have made less progress in monitoring change over time. There some very good long-term (30–40 year) records of atmospheric gas composition, but there are relatively few sets of direct long-term observations of aspects of the biosphere.[10] This has a lot to do with institutional, personal and financial matters. Few institutions and individuals have been able to maintain interest, resources and stamina to continue data gathering for more than a few years at one site. A lot of programmes run for 3–5 years and then stop because students graduate and funding agencies lose interest. Even those that have managed to maintain long-term monitoring programmes have been subject to all kinds of pressures and vagaries in funding. Some long-term data sets have been achieved as much by luck as by good judgement and many have been continued clandestinely until further funding could be found. In the world of catchments and aquatic ecology the outstanding examples of long-term data sets are the Hubbard Brook studies of catchment biogeochemistry and acid rain by Gene Likens and his many collaborators in the USA, the long-term data sets from the English lakes begun by John Lund and continued over the years by many people from the Freshwater Biological Association, the Continuous Plankton Recorder data from the North Atlantic begun by Sir Alistair Hardy,[11] and the many long-term fishery records. Whereas the fishery records may span hundreds of years,[12] the data sets requiring chemical or biological analyses of samples have run for no more than 50 years and all went through various crises, but they survived political, social and technological change.

All the long-term ecological data sets show patterns of change spanning decades, driven either by climate variability or by anthropogenic change. The data show strong evidence of phase transitions – abrupt changes between regimes dominated by different groups of species – and evidence of hysteresis effects.[13] Once commercial fish populations are greatly reduced in numbers by fishing pressure, marine ecosystems may recover to a state quite different from that before the fishing began. These ecosystems do not come back the way they were. As we have seen, ecosystems are known to be non-linear amplifiers of climate variability[14] and may show abrupt periods of catastrophic change.[15] We have forgotten what the oceans were like before whaling and overfishing, what rivers and lakes were like before land clearing and eutrophication, and what biodiversity once existed. We forget that human societies have collapsed in the past a number of times.[16] This is not to say that all the trends are downwards: we have also forgotten that there are many places in the word where forest and tree cover was much lower one hundred years ago than it is now (e.g. parts of the Hudson Valley in New York, and the Murray–Darling Basin in Australia). There are also many places where water quality has improved dramatically as a result of pollution controls and improved technology (e.g. the Ribble Valley in northern England). Environmental quality during the Industrial Revolution was appalling in many places.

All the long-term records we have tell of fluctuations in the biosphere over time in climate, hydrology, populations and biodiversity. Some of the variability we see in long-term records is extrinsic, being due to changes in the Earth's orbital parameters. Some variability is due to extreme events such as volcanic eruptions, storm, flood and drought and the coupling of atmosphere, land and ocean in the Earth's heat engine and water cycles. Some variability is intrinsic, being due to internal ecosystem dynamics and SGC. Some is anthropogenic and can be traced to past 'collapses' and development activities. Many changes were driven by technological change and economic cycles – the Kondratiev cycles – in which new technologies were developed and resources exploited more efficiently and in new ways. Some, such as fire frequencies, are a complex interaction between exogenous, endogenous and anthropogenic factors.[17]

Much of the time series data that we have is seriously aliased: it was collected far too infrequently to fully sample the natural dynamics. Too many long-term data sets were collected monthly or even less frequently, thus totally undersampling the high-frequency dynamics we now realise are so very important in catchments and aquatic systems. Some climate reconstructions were overconservative in estimating the true variability of the global system. In many cases extreme events were not sampled. But once again technology is coming to the rescue. More and more sampling and data collection systems are becoming computer-controlled and available online, so that higher-frequency data can be collected automatically and continuously and stored digitally for later processing. So with institutional constraints, poor memories, lack of critical data, often rudimentary conceptual and prediction engines, and conflicting sets of values and beliefs there is little wonder that some aspects of change on this planet are a matter of debate. There are vigorous debates about what constitutes evidence of change and what we should do about it even if we accept the evidence.

The palaeo-record

It is impossible to do justice to all the work that has been done on the study of past climates and environments in a short section here. The reconstruction of past climates and environments – from hundreds of millions of years ago, to the so-called Milankovitch cycles of about 120 000 years driven by changes in the Earth's orbit, to the more recent postglacial era (<15 000 years) – has been achieved from a variety of proxy records buried in everything from tree rings to rocks and sediment cores from the oceans and lakes. It is possible to use stable isotope ratios, the fossil record, tree ring widths, pollen grains and other the remains of organisms such as diatoms and Foraminifera to reconstruct past climates and ecologies with great accuracy. Some cores preserve what are called varved sediments, in which (just as for tree rings) it is possible to discern annual events even as long ago as 100 000 years. Because the work is usually done on wood samples and on rock and sediment cores, it can be done much more easily within the usual funding and institutional arrangements for science than can long-term monitoring.

The overwhelming impression gained from all this work is that this planet is a very dynamic entity – more dynamic than we usually admit. Climate change driven by fluctuations in the orbital path of the Earth at time scales of over 100 000 years has driven massive environmental changes. Ice ages have come and gone and these, together with the movement of the continents by continent drift, have led to long-term evolutionary and biogeographic change. There have been large-scale extinctions in the past, including five 'great' extinctions,[18] and a mysterious series of fluctuations in global biodiversity with a periodicity of about 62 million years.[19] Although there are gaps and sampling biases in the fossil record, the evidence for the long-term cyclical behaviour of global biodiversity seems clear. As the palaeo-record becomes more complete it is becoming clear that abrupt change in climate and biodiversity is quite common. Stasis is unusual. The best-documented period is that before and after the last ice age. During these periods rapid climate swings occurred, sometimes lasting decades or a few centuries. In the period leading up to the last glacial period in North

Atlantic and Europe about 120 000 years ago there was a pulse of aridity lasting 438 years, which seemed to be associated with abrupt changes in the distribution of warm ocean waters originating in the Gulf Stream.[20] Short-term climate fluctuations can have decidedly non-linear effects on the biosphere.

Climate change: converts and doubters

Perhaps nowhere at present is the debate so heated as the debate over the evidence (or lack thereof) for anthropogenically induced climate change. As I noted in the Introduction, there are those who believe that the evidence is already very clear, and that the human race should take urgent action to correct the emission of radiatively active greenhouse gases into the atmosphere before it is too late. Most of the science community falls into this group, although there are some (regarded as mavericks) who are not convinced. There are also those (usually on the right of politics and aligned with big energy and business interests) who dismiss this as the usual 'litany' of green scaremongering, and who insist that 'business as usual' is just fine: indeed, more economic activity, greater resource use, greater greenhouse emissions and greater wealth generation is going to improve the world for everyone. Yes, we can see global warming in the past fifty or more years, and a range of biological responses. Tim Flannery has provided an excellent review of the evidence for warming and of the underlying science.[21] But is this evidence of change due to anthropogenic change or is it part of a natural cyclical pattern? In recent years the debate has centred on the Kyoto Accord: an attempt to put in place a global carbon emissions trading system to encourage control of future levels of atmospheric carbon dioxide and other greenhouse gases. Those who are not convinced by the evidence for anthropogenically induced global warming will, of course, have nothing to do with carbon trading, which is seen as a tax on energy and industrial production. Once again, this is really a debate about evidence for change, the significance thereof, and a very deep debate about intra- and intergenerational equity.

So what is the evidence? First, it is generally agreed that the evidence for rising atmospheric concentrations of carbon dioxide is incontrovertible. The records of increasing atmospheric carbon dioxide beginning with Keeling's data from Hawaii[22] are long-term and of high precision. Indeed, the evidence from air bubbles trapped in ice cores, when combined with the recent atmospheric measurements, does show that the present concentrations of carbon dioxide in the atmosphere are at levels not seen in the past 420 000 years.[23] Along with other radiatively active gases such as methane and chlorofluorocarbons, the atmospheric composition has changed considerably in the past two centuries since the industrial revolution. (Some would argue that the changes in atmospheric composition began earlier, with the dawn of the agricultural age, although the evidence for this is less clear.)[24] Nevertheless, the evidence here is good and widely accepted. In terms of atmospheric carbon dioxide concentrations, we are now in uncharted waters.

What is not widely accepted is what this means. Many argue on the basis of complex computer modelling of the coupled ocean, land and atmosphere system that it is possible not only to account for the temperature fluctuations of the past century or more – and attribute them to a mixture of natural events such as volcanic eruptions and to human activity – but also to develop scenarios for future climates and temperature rises based on the long lifetimes of the key gases in the atmosphere. This would be the 'consensus view' of groups like the International Panel on Climate Change, the predominant college of global change scientists. Reconstructions of the global temperature over the past 1000 years show the classic 'hockey stick' pattern of constancy (or a very slow decline) in temperature up to about AD 1800 – the handle – followed by a sharp kick up in the past 200 years – the blade. The IPCC uses a combination of observations and global coupled atmosphere, land and ocean models to reconstruct the temperature record of the past 1000 years and to make predictions for the next century. They can do this because of the long lifetime of greenhouse gases in the atmosphere, and they construct various future scenarios based on possible management and policy options. Yes, the models suffer from many of the problems discussed previously; nevertheless they are the best we can do with a global system that fluctuates on scales from minutes to centuries and metres to hundreds of kilometres. Nevertheless, it must be remembered that physicochemical models conform to the laws of conservation of mass and momentum and therefore perform better than ecological models that contain evolved and adaptive agents; furthermore, the models are now supported by some good empirical verifications, which increase our confidence in their predictions.[25]

The IPCC has concluded that there is now good evidence for anthropogenically induced climate change and that action at the global scale to reduce emissions of carbon dioxide is necessary, indeed urgent and overdue. Others argue that the jury is still out; even that all this is a kind of scientific sleight of hand designed to scare people and ensure that funding for science is continued. There are even arguments over whether historical climate reconstructions are valid and whether we need a new 'hockey stick'. These people point to the natural variability in the Earth system over geological time, and insist that it is not possible to sort out the signal from the noise – even that there is no signal, it is all just noise. In defence of their arguments they point to all the assumptions and uncertainties in the data and in coupled global models and insist that the warming predictions are flawed because of this.[26] Nevertheless, there are now some impressive empirical confirmations of the model predictions.

Although the global climate models do give us predictions about future trends, one thing that they will not be able to do is to predict sudden state shifts, hysteresis effects and 'tipping points' in the global climate system. We simply do not yet understand all the feedbacks and linkages between the atmosphere, the oceans, the cryosphere and the biosphere to be able to model these effects. There is every reason to assume that just as ecosystems show these kinds of jumps and irreversible changes then so too will the global climate system. Smooth changes over time are less likely than step functions and 'tipping points'. Attempts have been made of late to try to identify some of the key potential threats.[27] Among others, these include: cessation of north Atlantic deep water formation and abrupt changes in the Gulf Stream, instability of the Greenland and west Antarctic ice sheets, transformation of the Indian monsoon system, and changes in the frequency and magnitude of El Niño – Southern Oscillation (ENSO) effects, bistability or collapse of the Amazonian forests, and bistability of the Saharan (Sahelian) vegetation. Any one of these switches in state, or a combination of the above, can potentially shift the global climate system in abrupt and potentially irreversible ways. (By irreversible here I mean over time scales of import to the human population. Many of these are reversible in evolutionary and geological time scales – certainly not quickly enough to avoid major impact on the human population.) Thus climate science is beginning to tackle some of the more surprising properties of the Earth system. There is growing evidence that change over time will not be gradual.

What do the empirical data say? While we argue, what is going on out there on the planet? What we are seeing is certainly consistent with the model predictions and scenarios. Warming is happening. In the past 30 years or so there have been major hydrological changes in many parts of the world. Ice cover in Arctic lakes has been reduced, and the ice-free period is lengthening.[28] Tropical cyclones and hurricanes have also become stronger in the past 30 years.[29] Temperatures are rising in many places – temperature rises in the deep ocean are a particularly important indicator of change – and there are associated changes in many biological, phenological and ecological processes. We can now draw upon long-term data sets of plankton abundance from the oceans and from lakes,[30] long-term fisheries records,[31] and other meteorological and hydrological records. Recent meta-analyses of many more informal sets of observational data (such as arrival times of migrating birds and emergence dates for butterflies) spanning the past century all tell stories of change over time that are consistent with recent global warming.[32] In the past 50 years or so, species in the Northern Hemisphere have shifted their ranges towards the poles by 6.1 km per decade and spring events have become earlier by about 3–5 days per decade. Recent syntheses of large data sets now provide 'compelling' evidence of the effect of 'fingerprint' climate change on ecological processes.[33]

In addition to long-term trends, biological parameters also respond to shorter term fluctuations in ocean dynamics and climate associated with the Southern Ocean and with the El Niño – Southern Oscillation,[34] the North

Atlantic Oscillation,[35] fluctuations in the Gulf Stream[36] and the Pacific Decadal Oscillation.[37] So there is good evidence of rapid phenological, biological and ecological responses to both longer-term climate trends and decadal-scale variability. Most of the studies are driven by the wish to find evidence for anthropogenic change in ecological and biological as well as climatological and atmospheric signals. There clearly has been warming in the past 50 years, but this still begs the question as to whether what we are seeing is part of a long-term climatological trend driven by anthropogenic changes or a natural cyclical pattern of global warming – just one of a series of cyclical changes over time. Recent observations of events in the Arctic and Antarctic would argue that the trends we are seeing at the present time are not just part of a shorter-term cyclical warming. The melting of the Siberian permafrost and the collapse of ice shelves in the Antarctic would seem to be unprecedented in the past 10 000–12 000 years – since the last ice age.[38] Flannery argues that there is good evidence for a major shift in the oceanic thermal regime in the mid-1970s[39] and, even more worryingly, there is once again evidence for a slowing of the North Atlantic oceanic heat 'conveyor belt' and evidence for significant change in the Gulf Stream.[40] Equally, recent warming in the California Current seems to be unusual in at least the past 1400 years.[41] There is palaeoclimatic evidence that shows that if present polar warming trends continue we may see the melting of the Greenland ice cap and rapid sea-level rise by 2100, a situation not seen for the past 130 000 years.[42] So the rapid events of the past few decades do now seem to be set in a much longer-term and more important context. Lovelock carries the argument further and paints a gloomy scenario of positive feedback and runaway warming.[43] Whatever the future holds, I see a change in the debate: more and more people are convinced that climate change is real and that the time has come to seriously address the issue.

Hydrological changes

Hydrological changes are one of the major effects of climate change and variability. It is clear that there already have been major changes in hydrological variables as a result of even modest warming in the past century. In particular ice extent, glacier retreat and reductions in snowpack have been observed in many regions.[44] With more than one sixth of the world's population relying on glaciers and snowpack (rather than dams) for their water storage and supply, the widespread melting that is both occurring now, and predicted to occur with high confidence, has serious implications for future water availability.[45] The areas most affected are likely to be Central and North Asia, the Andes in South America and the northern USA and Canada in North America; areas where snowmelt provides a significant fraction of the water supply and dams are not adequate to buffer any potential climate-induced change. There is now strong evidence of rapid melting of glaciers and ice sheets, together with increased runoff from high-latitude regions.[46] As a result, significant sea-level rise is very likely in periods as short as a century.

Because of the seriousness of the global water situation, various studies of global hydrology have been made to estimate the effects of a warming world on water resources. The most complete modelling studies are those of the IPCC under the Special Report on Emissions Scenarios (SRES).[47] Nevertheless, the combined climate and population change scenarios for hydrological changes up to around 2050 are complex. There are differences between the predictions of the various climate models. Overall, it appears that while regions already water-stressed (around the Mediterranean, through the Middle East, into the Asian subcontinent and through to parts of China) will remain so, in other regions in the later parts of the predicted period population growth and water demand will become more important than the changes in supply due to climate change.[48] Land cover change has strong feedbacks onto climate change, so that adding agricultural expansion into the SRES scenarios produces significantly different climates in some regions.[49] Thus socioeconomic and developmental issues dominate in the next fifty years and the future path of the biosphere will depend on the policies and practices that determine urbanisation and agriculturally driven global environmental change.[50] Modelling indicates that many ecosystem services are at risk in Europe under climate change, owing to population growth and hydrological changes. Changes may be positive (increases in forest area or opportunities for bio-energy production) or negative (declining soil fertility and water availability, increased risk of forest fires) depending on the region.[51] Sustainability is going to depend on the balancing of capitals, on regional and catchment-scale development paths and on population trends, as well as on climate.

On land, rainfall and runoff are already declining markedly in places and increasing in others. A very complete tree ring record from Northern Pakistan indicates that the twentieth century was the wettest observed in the past 1000 years.[52] There is evidence of major anthropogenic change in the global hydrological cycle.[53] With the increase in evaporation driven by higher temperatures, drought is becoming more prevalent in some regions. In Australia rainfall distributions are heavily influenced by El Niño – Southern Oscillation events; the ENSO-induced droughts bring severe reductions in runoff and changes to the water levels and residence times in major storages.[54] One of the best examples of long-term change is in Western Australia, where since the mid-1970s the rainfall has declined by about 30% and the runoff into Perth's dams has declined by more than 50%. This decrease appears to be due to a sudden and marked increase in temperature in the Indian Ocean and a change in the latitude of the subtropical high pressure ridge over southern Australia: it has moved further south, so pushing the predominant westerlies further south also. So within the cyclical pattern of climate variability there is a long-term change. This is precisely what the consensus of the global climate models would predict – indeed, although the impact of the change is most prevalent in Western Australia, as predicted the effect is visible all across southern Australia, even to eastern Tasmania. The worrying and surprising thing about the Western Australia situation is that the change was not, as the models predicted, gradual. There was a downward step function in rainfall in 1976.

In the past two to three years Australia has been gripped by a 1 in 100 year drought and all major cities are on water restrictions. Runoff into Perth dams in 2001 was the lowest since 1914, the previous lowest year on record. Water levels in dams in the Murray–Darling Basin have been at unprecedentedly low levels and irrigation allocations have been zero in some cases. What has made the 2002–4 droughts so severe is that, compared with the last nearly equivalent drought in 1982, the temperature in the Basin has risen by over one degree, increasing the evaporation rate and worsening the drought. In practical terms, what all this means is that water planners have had to continuously revise their sustainable water yield baselines downwards and timeframes for water infrastructure investments, which were 25 years or more,[55] are now of the order of 5 years or less; and there was very little warning of the changes. In these circumstances the past is no guide to the future.

Supply management has taken on a new meaning. All options from desalination plants to canals to bring water down from rivers in tropical Western Australia have been considered. Demand management is also taking on a new urgency, and reuse and recycling schemes are also being developed rapidly. Now, yes, long-term climate modelling does indicate that 50 year periods of rainfall decline, as we are presently seeing in Western Australia, have occurred before. These would, however, have occurred with lower populations and temperatures and less land clearing and vegetation change; resilience is now lower even if rainfall returns to its previous level. Data from stalagmites in Western Australian caves indicate that the rainfall patterns of the past 30 years are unprecedented in the past 200 years, evidence that suggests that we are in totally new territory. We appear to be in a new climate regime together with much higher demands and reduced supplies in critical regions.

The factor most likely to be important for land and waterscape management is not so much the changes in the annual rainfall over the next fifty years – about which the present generation of models are in broad agreement – but the ways in which that annual amount is delivered and how that might change. If the frequency and magnitude of extreme events is also likely to change then this is going to have major implications for landscape and waterscape function as well as security of supply and demand management. As we have already seen, it is extreme events that move things around in landscapes and which control many ecological processes in both freshwaters and estuaries. So, as I discussed in the previous chapter with the example of the River Red Gums, changes to the distribution of floods and droughts can have major ecological implications. Rainfall is known to be log-normally[56] or power law distributed; some have argued that this is evidence of self-organised atmospheric properties. In his seminal paper on MaxEnt solutions for SOC systems, Dewar used atmospheric evidence gathered by Paltridge and others since the 1970s to bolster his case. It appears that the 'mean-annual configuration of horizontal energy fluxes in the Earth's atmosphere and oceans corresponds closely to a state of maximum global entropy production'.[57] Certainly the distribution of droughts in semi-arid regions seems to follow power law scaling, and there is evidence of more than one scaling regime in rainfall records.[58] Climate change will influence atmospheric circulation patterns, which, as a possible SOC process, is going to interact with the SGC of the landscape in some very complex ways which we do not yet understand.

Attempts have been made to create 'real' rainfall distributions from the outputs of the coupled atmosphere–ocean global circulation models by 'downscaling' from the rather coarse scale of the model grid cells to actual rain gauge data.[59] In this way it is possible to go from the broad-scale patterns of atmospheric circulations – both as presently observed and the ways in which they might change over the coming years – to drought and flood frequencies and rainfall intensities. Rainfall and water supply scenarios for Africa indicate that climate change will have the most serious effects in a mid-range rainfall band (500–1000 mm p.a.).[60] In this range surface drainage may decrease by as much as 50%. Many major African rivers originate in zones with this precipitation range; the climate scenarios indicate that flow variability will increase along with the frequency of periods of drought. Most of Southern Africa and a band from Senegal to Sudan appears to be particularly at risk. Like Western Australia, the Cape Town region is already experiencing serious drought.[61] Model climate scenarios for parts of Australia indicate declines in total rainfall in coming years – consistent with the observed changes in the past 30 years – but predict that the rainfall will arrive in fewer, more extreme events. This has significant implications for landscapes and waterscapes because of the non-equilibrium relationships between plant phenology, water use efficiency, hydrology and the responses of the aquatic flora and fauna. Because of the close link between vegetation and soil moisture we might reasonably expect that changes in rainfall event frequencies and magnitudes will affect groundwater recharge and the movement of materials in fragmented landscapes. Extreme events are when all the important things happen in landscapes and waterscapes: the geomorphology is restructured, materials and organisms are moved and events are set in train that can have consequences for centuries thereafter. Changes in overbank flow events, the timing of floods and the frequency of drought periods (and hence longer water residence times in storages) are already having impacts on, for example, the ecology of aquatic communities and the frequency of occurrence of toxic cyanobacterial blooms in weirs and storages.[62]

Changes to the frequency and magnitude of rainfall events will also have major implications for the performance and safety of engineered structures (weirs, dams and culverts), for flood frequencies in urban areas and for many other aspects of risk management in urban and rural areas. Preliminary estimates of the effects of climate change in parts of Australia indicate that despite an overall drying trend there may none the less be an approximate halving in the return time of extreme events and a 30% increase in the frequency of 1 in 40 year events.[63] This has important implications for the design, construction, operation and cost of infrastructure. Safety design and risk management strategies depend critically on the expected frequency and magnitude of extreme rainfall and flooding events. The cost of infrastructure is a very non-linear function of the design criteria when flood intensities and return times are altered. Costs may increase significantly for only a small increase in flood intensity and frequency, so it is important to make the climate change predictions correct, for a number of reasons.

Ecosystems distributed across landscapes and waterscapes are, to a degree, designed through trial and error and approach robust 'neutral spaces': HOT designs that are tolerant of expected perturbations but highly sensitive to unexpected events. Climate change, through changing both the means and the variances of climate, threatens landscapes and waterscapes in unexpected ways. The distributions of both 'green' and 'blue' water will change over time and interact strongly with the homoplastic structures and functions of ecosystems. We are becoming more and more susceptible to climate change, whether natural or of anthropogenic origins. As populations rise and we place more and more pressure on resources such as water, then we have fewer and fewer options for sustainable solutions. Resilience declines, risks increase and the past is indeed no guide to the future.[64] At the global scale, water resources are going to be one of the key pressure points for a sustainable future. Tragically, the regions of the globe that are predicted to be most under threat of climate change are those that are already short of water. If the future really does bring us surprises, 'tipping points', positive feedbacks and hysteresis effects then even books like those of Flannery (which has been called the 'Silent Spring' of climate change) are, if anything, going to be seen in hindsight as optimistic. Planning for as much resilience as we can manage is the only prudent option. The next fifty years really are going to be critical.

NOTES

1. M. D. Murray *et al.* How Wandering Albatrosses use weather systems to fly long distances. 1. An analytical method and its application to flights in the Tasman Sea. *Emu*, **102** (2002), 377–85. M. D. Murray *et al.* How Wandering Albatrosses use weather systems to fly long

distances. 2. The use of eastward-moving cold fronts from Antarctic Lows to travel west-wards across the Indian Ocean. *Emu*, **103** (2003), 59–65. M. D. Murray *et al.* How Wandering Albatrosses use weather systems to fly long distances. 3. The contributions of Antarctic Lows to eastward, southward and northward flight. *Emu*, **103** (2003), 111–20.

2. B. A. Block *et al.* Electronic tagging and population structure of Atlantic bluefin tuna. *Nature*, **434** (2005), 1121–7.

3. C. J. A. Bradshaw *et al.* The optimal spatial scale for the analysis of elephant seal foraging as determined by geo-location in relation to sea surface temperatures. *ICES Journal of Marine Science*, **59** (2002), 770–81.

4. For more information on ICSU, see www.icsu.org.

5. See the Editorial and news items in the journal *Nature*, **433** (2005), pp. 785 and 798.

6. *Earth system science; preview and overview. Documents prepared by the Earth system sciences committee.* (Washington, DC: NASA Advisory Council, May 1986). *Earth system science; a closer view. Report of the Earth system sciences committee.* (Washington, DC: NASA Advisory Council, January 1988).

7. See www.sustainabilityscience.org.

8. See www.igbp.kva.se.

9. H. J. Schellnhuber. Earth system analysis and the second Copernican revolution. *Nature*, **402** (1999) (supplement), C19–C23.

10. By long-term here, I mean data sets spanning 30–50 years. This, of course, is not long-term from the point of view of the biosphere or postglacial events, but ecology is a relatively new science and systematic observations only really began in the postwar period.

11. G. C. Hays, A. J. Richardson and C. Robinson. Climate change and marine plankton. *Trends in Ecology and Evolution*, **20** (2005), 337–44.

12. See, for example, D. H. Cushing. *Climate and Fisheries*. (London: Academic Press, 1982).

13. J. Duffy-Anderson *et al.* Phase transitions in marine fish recruitment processes. *Ecological Complexity*, **2** (2005), 205–18.

14. C.-H. Hsieh *et al.* Distinguishing random environmental fluctuations from ecological catastrophes for the North Pacific Ocean. *Nature*, **435** (2005), 336–40.

15. M. Scheffer *et al.* Catastrophic shifts in ecosystems. *Nature*, **413** (2001), 591–6.

16. Jared Diamond. *Collapse*. (London: Allen Lane, The Penguin Press, 2004).

17. J. L. Pierce, G. A. Meyer and A. J. T. Jull. Fire-induced erosion and millennial-scale climate change in northern Ponderosa pine forests. *Nature*, **432** (2004), 87–90.

18. D. Raup and J. Sepkoski. Mass extinctions in the marine fossil record. *Science*, **215** (1982), 1501–3.

19. J. W. Kirchner and A. Weil. Fossils make waves. *Nature*, **434** (2005), 147–8. R. A. Rodhe and R. A. Muller. Cycles in fossil diversity. *Nature*, **434** (2005), 208–10.

20. F. Sirocko *et al.* A late Eemian aridity pulse in central Europe during the last glacial inception. *Nature*, **436** (2005), 833–6.

21. T. Flannery. *The Weather Makers*. (Melbourne: Text Publishing, 2005).

22. C. Keeling *et al.* Interannual extremes in the rate of rise of atmospheric carbon dioxide since 1980. *Nature*, **375** (1995), 666–70.

23. J. R. Petit *et al.* Climate and atmospheric history of the past 420 000 years from the Vostok ice core. *Nature*, **399** (1999), 429–36.

24. See the report of the work by Ruddiman in *Science*, **303** (2004), 306.

25. M. N. Evans. The woods fill up with snow. *Nature*, **440** (2006), 1120–1.

26. See, for example, F. Pearce. Grudge match. *New Scientist*, 18 March 2006, **189** (2543), 40–3.

27. See the copy of Schellnhuber's map of global 'tipping points' reproduced in *Nature*. M. Kemp. Inventing an icon. *Nature*, **437** (2005), 1238.

28. C. R. Duguay *et al.* Recent trends in Canadian lake ice cover. *Hydrological Processes*, **20** (2006), 781–801.

29. K. Emanuel. Increasing destructiveness of tropical cyclones over the last 30 years. *Nature*, **436** (2005), 686–8. P. J. Webster *et al.* Changes in tropical cyclone number, duration and intensity in a warming environment. *Science*, **309** (2005), 1844–6.

30. M. Winder and D. E. Schindler. Climatic effects on the phenology of lake processes. *Global Change Biology*, **10** (2004), 1844–56.

31. See, for example, S. J. Hawkins, A. J. Southward and M. J. Genner. Detection of environmental change in a marine ecosystem – evidence from the Western English Channel. *Science of the Total Environment*, **310** (2003), 245–56.

32. G.-R. Walther *et al.* Ecological responses to recent climate change. *Nature*, **416** (2002), 389–95. C. Parmesan and G. Yohe. A globally coherent fingerprint of climate change impacts across natural systems. *Nature*, **421** (2003), 37–42. T. L. Root *et al.* Fingerprints of global warming on wild animals and plants. *Nature*, **421** (2003), 57–60.

33. G.-R. Walther *et al.* Consensus on climate change. *Trends in Ecology and Evolution*, **20** (2005), 648–9.

34. G. P. Harris *et al.* Interannual variability in climate and fisheries in Tasmania. *Nature*, **333** (1988), 754–7.

35. N. C. Stenseth *et al.* Ecological effects of climate variations. *Science*, **297** (2002), 1292–6. G. Beaugrand and P. C. Reid. Long-term changes in phytoplankton, zooplankton and salmon related to climate. *Global Change Biology*, **9** (2003), 801–17. V. Grosbios and P. M. Thompson. North Atlantic climate variation influences survival in adult Fulmars. *Oikos*, **109** (2005), 273–90.

36. D. G. George and A. H. Taylor. UK lake plankton and the Gulf Stream. *Nature*, **378** (1995), 139.

37. M. Winder and D. E. Schindler. Climatic effects on the phenology of lake processes. *Global Change Biology*, **10** (2004), 1844–56.

38. E. Domack *et al.* Stability of the Larsen-B ice shelf on the Antarctic Peninsula during the Holocene period. *Nature*, **436** (2005), 681–5.

39. Flannery, *The Weather Makers*. (See Note 21.)

40. D. Quadfasel. The Atlantic heat conveyor slows. *Nature*, **438** (2005), 565–6. H. L. Bryden, H. R. Longworth and S. A. Cunningham. Slowing of the Atlantic meridional overturning circulation at 25°N. *Nature*, **438** (2005), 655–7.

41. D. B. Field *et al.* Planktonic foraminifera of the California Current reflect 20th-century warming. *Science*, **311** (2006), 63–6.

42. J. T. Overpeck *et al.* Palaeoclimatic evidence for future ice-sheet instability and rapid sea-level rise. *Science*, **311** (2006), 1747–50.

43. J. Lovelock. *The Revenge of Gaia*. (London: Penguin, Allen Lane, 2006).

44. See, for example, the article on the reductions of snowpack depths in the Rockies by R. F. Service. As the west goes dry. *Science*, **303** (2004), 1124–7. There are similar reports of glacier retreat in the Alps and other mountain areas around the world, including the tropics and the Southern hemisphere: see J. Oerlemans. Extracting a climate signal from 169 glacier records. Published online 03 March 2005; doi 10.1126/science.1107046

www.sciencexpress.org; also A. J. Cook *et al.* Retreating glacier fronts on the Antarctic peninsula over the past half-century, *Science*, **308** (2005), 541–4.

45. T. P. Barnett, J. C. Adam and D. P. Lettenmaier. Potential impacts of a warming climate on water availability in snow-dominated regions. *Nature*, **438** (2005), 303–9.

46. T. F. Stocker and C. C. Raible. Water cycle shifts gear. *Nature*, **434** (2005), 830–3. J. Dowdeswell. The Greenland ice sheet and global sea-level rise. *Science*, **311** (2006), 963–4. E. Rignot and P. Kanagaratnam. Changes in the velocity structure of the Greenland ice sheet. *Science*, **311** (2006), 986–90. See also the Editorial (p. 1673), the News story (p. 1698), Perspectives (p. 1719, 1720) and associated articles (p. 1747, 1751, 1756) in *Science*, **311**: 5768, 24 March 2006.

47. N. W. Arnell. Climate change and global water resources: SRES emissions and socio-economic scenarios. *Global Environmental Change*, **14** (2004), 31–52.

48. C. J. Vorosmarty *et al.* Global water resources: vulnerability from climate change and population growth. *Science*, **289** (2000), 284–8.

49. J. J. Feddema *et al.* The importance of land-cover change in simulating future climates. *Science*, **310** (2005), 1674–8.

50. D. Tilman *et al.* Forecasting agriculturally driven global environmental change. *Science*, **292** (2001), 281–4.

51. D. Schröter *et al.* Ecosystem service supply and vulnerability to global change in Europe. *Science*, **310** (2005), 1333–7.

52. K. S. Treydte *et al.* The twentieth century was the wettest period in Northern Pakistan over the last millennium. *Nature*, **440** (2006), 1181–2.

53. M. N. Evans. The woods fill up with snow. *Nature*, **440** (2006), 1120–1.

54. G. P. Harris and G. Baxter. Interannual variability in phytoplankton biomass and species composition in a subtropical reservoir. *Freshwater Biology*, **35** (1996), 545–60.

55. Hydrologists commonly use 100 year baselines for planning water infrastructure if sufficient data are available; a practice no longer possible in many regions.

56. B. Kedem, and L. S. Chiu. On the lognormality of rain rate. *Proceedings of the National Academy of Sciences*, USA, **84** (1987), 901–5.

57. R. Dewar. Information theory explanation of the fluctuation theorem, maximum entropy production and self-organised criticality in non-equilibrium stationary states. *Journal of Physics*, A**36** (2003), 631–41 – quoted from p. 632.

58. R. F. S. Andrade, H. J. Schellnhuber and M. Claussen. Analysis of rainfall records – possible relation to self-organised criticality. *Physica*, A**254** (1998), 557–68.

59. S. P. Charles *et al.* Statistical downscaling of daily precipitation from observed and modelled atmospheric fields. *Hydrological Processes*, **18** (2004), 1373–94.

60. M. de Wit and J. Stankiewicz. Changes in surface water supply across Africa with predicted climate change. www.sciencexpress.org/ 2 March 2006/10.1126/science.1119929 (2006).

61. M. Rouault and Y. Richard. Intensity and spatial extent of droughts in Southern Africa. *Geophysical Research Letters*, **32** (2005), L15702, doi: 10.1029/2005GL022436.

62. Harris and Baxter, *Freshwater Biology*, **35** (1996). (See Note 54.)

63. Bryson Bates, personal communication.

64. W. N. Adger *et al.* Socio-ecological resilience to coastal disasters. *Science*, **309** (2005), 1036–9.

17 Values and beliefs

What we know, whether we believe it and whether we act on the information we have is conditioned by culture, values and belief.

In global science and remote sensing programmes there is a need for technological, institutional and intellectual resources to store, conceptualise, process and visualise the data coming in. There is a real data assimilation problem, which has to deal with errors and uncertainties as well as parameterisation and scaling issues. What are required are sources of data about the present status of resources and trends over time, conceptual models and prediction engines to assimilate the data and turn it into information, and institutions and systems to enable action to be taken where required. With the explosion of data and information systems in the past two or three decades, it is the institutional and governance systems that we are lacking the most. Data systems provide information, institutional and governance systems allow management action to be taken, but it is values and beliefs that ultimately determine whether anything is done.

In global meteorological observation and weather forecasting we now have some very sophisticated systems to receive the satellite observations as well as predictive models to assimilate the data as they are received. Models of the global atmospheric circulation are continuously updated by streams of detailed information about the present state of the atmosphere. Huge investments have been made in solving some of the problems of data fusion and assimilation across scales and between image and point source data. This improves forecasting skill and, as we can all see in our daily newspapers, four- to five-day forecasts are now routine and accurate. This is one case where the necessary science, technology, infrastructure and institutional arrangements are in place to effectively assimilate the data and turn them into useful products and outcomes. Other examples of action taken on the basis of monitoring information may be cited. These include the observation of rising CFC concentrations in the atmosphere and the realisation of a connection to the so-called 'ozone hole' in the stratosphere. The observations and process understandings were effectively turned into desirable outcomes through the Montreal protocol and the banning of CFCs in refrigeration and other industrial processes. Other examples are the reduction in emissions of sulphur and nitrogen oxides in North America and Europe, which were shown to cause 'acid rain' and an increase in the acidity of soils and surface waters with consequent damage to forests and fish populations, and the control of nutrient discharges to lakes, which caused nutrient enrichment (eutrophication) and widespread toxic algal blooms. Finally, I may cite the example of the International Whaling Commission, where clear evidence of declining whale numbers led to an international ban on whaling and the declaration of large marine reserves to protect whale species.

So there are clear examples where data on meteorology, global atmospheric chemistry, water quality and anthropogenic impacts on the populations of 'charismatic megafauna' have led to changing practices and regulation leading to desirable outcomes. Success seems to be achieved where the data are clear and the science is explicit, the models are not complex and easily communicated to both the public and managers, the alternatives are simple and effective, the political and economic pain is not too great and a strong lobby for action exists. In addition, there is a link between strong institutional and governance mechanisms and effective action. If society decides on a change in management practice, it is important to be able to make the decision 'stick'.

In most cases, however, the chain of events is much more problematical. Strong evidence of declining fish stocks in the world ocean has not led to the necessary cuts in total allowable catches and quotas. The whaling ban is now being questioned. In the area of water and catchments the picture is mixed at best, with rivers in many large basins around the world undergoing environmental decline through the construction of dams, flow extraction, degradation of water quality and loss of fisheries and biodiversity. In all of these cases the data are open to argument and interpretation, the evidence is not universally accepted, there are many players with differing cultures, values and agendas, the governance mechanism is problematical, the political and economic pain is great and there are many competing lobby groups. This is, in fact, the normal situation. So data and information are only a part of the story; whether or not the new knowledge is turned into action and policy depends on individuals, values and beliefs, cultural and institutional factors, and social and economic considerations. All the technology in the world will not achieve an outcome if these factors are not addressed.

In my view, this observation lies at the core of the debate over global warming. In the case of rising concentrations of carbon dioxide in the atmosphere the observational data are clear but the implementation of the Kyoto protocol has not been achieved or even widely agreed. This is a common observation from all attempts at knowledge management: technology is but a small part of the problem. By far the greatest part of achieving more sustainable outcomes is about ethics, trust, communication and collaboration between people and cultures. Roger Pielke has written about the nexus of prediction and policy making in the context of the atmospheric sciences and has made many of these points.[1] He has garnered three lessons learned from a career in science and technology policy research:

- effective use of predictions is only one component of the decision making process;
- prediction for science and prediction for policy are not the same thing;
- scientific prediction products may be complex and may be misused.

Pielke and Conant conclude that in the context of climate change science and its effect on policy

> policy-making focussed on prediction has run up against numerous political and technical obstacles, meanwhile alternatives to prediction – such as no-regrets adaptation and mitigation policies . . . have become increasingly visible. The prediction process can be said to work if the goals of climate policy – to reduce the impacts of future climate changes on environment and society – are addressed, independent of whether century-scale climate forecasts prove to be accurate.[2]

Scientists have to be careful about policy advocacy – and a focus on one or a few solutions – rather than on policy research, which might actually expand the range of options available. Policy decisions will be taken come what may, and will be taken in response to a flood of inputs from lobby groups, including scientists.

Communication between communities and groups is deeply contextual. We tell ourselves, and each other, stories that come from our sense of place, our values and culture. As Bateson realised, introducing new information into a community produces just the kinds of surprising and unexpected outcomes that are characteristic of complex adaptive systems. Stories, attitudes and values shift in response to the new information; some new information is accepted and some not. As David Snowden has written, information that we share is context-sensitive and cannot be conscripted. Information is only ever volunteered in context.

> We always know more than we can tell, and we will always tell more than we can write down. We only know what we know, when we need to know it.[3]

Knowledge is deeply contextual; it is triggered by circumstance. To find out what someone knows and to share information, we have to create a meaningful context for their knowing by asking a meaningful question or creating a suitable context. This goes back to theories of reflexive and recursive interactions in human communities and to the ideas of 'sense giving and sense receiving' of Polanyi. (This is exactly the old adage about writing things down . . . 'how do I know what I think until I see what I say?')

Communities and groups in society have very different views on what they know, how they know it, what more they need to know and whether they even want to know more. This is one of the basic problems with the communication of science and new information: it takes a long time and a lot of social interaction to achieve a consensus on the basic problem, the conceptual model of what some of the key interactions are, and agreement on a suitable course of action. This, together with the debatable status of evidence, models and prediction engines and the uncertain and partial nature of the data, means that to achieve progress requires a lot of social and cultural exchange and interaction. If scientists have one major failing in all this, it is the conviction that reason and rationality will prevail and that people will be convinced by resort to argument based on the known 'facts'. This is neither a reasonable nor a rational world, and there is precious little agreement on the 'facts' of the matter, much debate and little mutual learning!

This is a debate about values, beliefs and uncertainties. The science community needs to be more accepting of other points of view and be prepared to argue the case for logic and reason in a world which, by and large, does not accept those premises. I worry about statements that begin along the lines of 'if the scientific community is to recover its standing in the world'.[4] If the science community has a privileged position in the world it is because of the rigorous way in which it treats uncertainty and the transparency and testability of its assumptions. Science does sometimes have a problem with compromise. Do not get me wrong here; I have argued strongly for biophysical constraints on the human condition and I do not accept ontological relativism. The precautionary principle states that placing radiatively active gases in the atmosphere at levels unseen for the past 650 000 years is foolish, even if there are uncertainties in the feedback mechanisms and the expected outcomes. After all, this is not a controlled experiment – there is no other comparable planet to act as a control. I do accept epistemological relativism: people do have other values and beliefs – and views about the treatments and weights to be placed on the uncertainties – which clash with those of the science community. The science community should be careful about asserting moral or logical authority when there are large uncertainties. Science is not value-free and whether scientists like it or not they are totally engaged in a debate about the global future, which is debate about power, money, various other forms of capital and their values and fungibility, and intra- and intergenerational equity. There are many points of view and this is high-stakes global Realpolitik, played hard and fast. So this is an argument about shades of grey, not black and white – with the highest of stakes. We should welcome the key role of science in the debate, and avoid *ad hominem* arguments.

The development of new data and information systems, the realisation of the partial nature of our knowledge and the trend towards subsidiarity and empowering local communities has led to a broadened and deepened engagement between science and the community in the area of natural resource management. In areas such as catchment management and the management of fish stocks there have been numerous experiments with co-management and mutual learning, where instead of management agencies handing down decisions from the mountain top on stone tablets there has been a serious attempt to involve the local communities so that they have understanding of the issues and ownership of the outcomes. This trend has been accompanied both by the much greater availability of information through the Internet and the Web and by a rise in regional and local scepticism about science and the role of centralised agencies. Accountability and transparency are now required, and many of the management agencies (who themselves may have been downsized, delayered and deskilled by the moves towards small governments) have realised that the only way forward is to work with and through the local and regional communities who must actually manage the resource. Community ownership and empowerment is the best and most sustainable solution to the management of resources. Enlisting support is better than regulation. Regulation often does not work: indeed, people will usually find a way around strict regulatory frameworks. For example, it is much better to teach people about the disposal of liquid domestic and industrial waste, how to do it and what is required and why (and provide disposal stations to accept the waste) so that they are encouraged to do the right thing and understand the consequences of not doing so. Strict regulation and controls on dumping industrial wastes in urban sewerage systems usually results in the waste appearing in rural ditches in the middle of the night! Many coastal Australian cities now have painted signs on the roadside kerbs next to street drains, which say 'this drains to the bay'. Because many local residents are also keen fisherfolk, this reminder has sufficed to greatly reduce the impact of illicit waste disposal on coastal water quality and fish populations.

Integrated assessments and community engagement

The debate around climate change, the uncertainties in the modelling and the issue of the role of science in policy formulation is not quite as black and white as some commentators might insist. In addition to what might be called the 'hard science' of the global modellers there is an active debate going on around the construction and use of integrated assessments of the impact of climate change on the human dimension, as well as the recursive interactions that will be involved. As we learn about the effects of changing atmospheric chemistry, and policy is formulated in response, then the course of global affairs will change, as will the impact on global atmospheric chemistry. This is inevitably going to be a recursive debate as society slowly adapts to the knowledge and risk assessments. So the debate over the Kyoto protocol is just the first round in an ongoing series of interactions and should therefore be seen, not as an end in itself, but as an initial useful option.

Integrated environmental assessment (IEA) can be seen as a new method for combining science and policy development. An early definition was given as follows:

> the two defining characteristics (of IEA) are (a) that it seeks to provide information of use to some significant decision maker rather than merely advancing understanding for its own sake, and (b) that it brings together a broader set of areas, methods, styles of study, or degrees of confidence, than would typically characterise a study of the same issue within the bounds of a single research discipline.[5]

IEA is therefore a classic example of Ravetz's 'postnormal' science in that it brings together multiple viewpoints, values and data sets and attempts to synthesise them. IEA is a way forward that scales up the multi-disciplinary (even trans-disciplinary) challenges of global scales and engages with multiple stakeholders and communities.[6] This challenge of combining stakeholder values, disciplines, and differing models and data collected at a range of scales remains fundamental not only to this approach but also to the solution of the sustainability question.[7] There is a need to find ways to form bridges between values, communities and research agendas to solve this problem.[8] Ravetz has pointed out the present 'immaturity' of the approach, compared with other disciplines;[9] nevertheless these attempts at integrated assessments are unprecedented in the history of science and policy development.[10]

There are a number of integrated assessment models of climate change that have been used over the years and which examine the cost-effectiveness and the cost–impact and cost–benefit relationships of various abatement and other economic options.[11] The problem with all these models is that there are severe uncertainties, many of the basic assumptions are value-laden,[12] and there is no consensus as to the best methodology.[13] Just as with catchment models, some of the modelling uncertainties are such that it may not be possible to actually identify 'optimal' policy and management strategies because of the non-uniqueness of 'behavioural' models of the coupled environmental, social and economic system.[14] Structural uncertainty may be as great as parameter uncertainty; predictions of future events may be subjective, probabilistic and uncertain.[15] Because of this a range of approaches are being tried across a number of policy issues. Suggestions include reducing the complexity of the models to capture most of the system dynamics with greater confidence[16] (much like Data-Based Models); or defining a 'tolerable windows' approach where rather than precise predictions and solutions a set of 'knockout criteria' or 'guardrails' are set up and efforts are made to define solutions that stay within them.[17] In addition to climate change, other areas of active IEA development include the control of air pollution and of acid rain and critical nutrient loads to lakes.[18] In all cases as predictions are required further and further into the future there is a tendency to shift from deterministic models, to probabilistic order of magnitude assessments, and finally to sets of simpler 'knockout' boundaries and guardrail criteria.

A growing consensus is leaning towards a combination of science and participatory and deliberative processes, taking into account multiple perspectives and a diversity of actors.[19] The participatory process involves a broader community involvement in defining and evaluating the product of decision making (often involving the use and assessment of science and as input to what is often called 'evidence-based' decision making or policy) as well as greater involvement in the process of decision making itself. Citizens play many roles in these debates; the overall process has all the characteristics of a complex system.[20] As we have already seen in the case of foot and mouth disease in the UK, surprises can occur when complex systems reach 'tipping points', and if the incorporation of science into decision making is not transparent or effective and the process is not sufficiently participatory then negative outcomes, as with BSE in the UK, can readily occur. Global and systems-level challenges require quite new response mechanisms.

Two further trends are discernible. One is the development of regional or 'place-based' integrated risk assessments. Because of the huge challenge of integrating many factors and communities and the potential for hysteretic or synergistic effects in these assessments, there has been a move towards planning and vulnerability assessment at the regional or river basin scale.[21] The goal is not exact prediction but the identification and prioritisation of risks and future trends.[22] Second, in common with other approaches to complex adaptive system responses, multi-agent modelling is again being used as a method to evaluate possible futures. Learning is a key component of the human response to potentially catastrophic future scenarios. Janssen and de Vries write

> Our research demonstrates that a more thorough understanding of the role of ignorance and the features of social dynamics, as displayed nowadays in the international negotiations to reach a climate treaty, could add realism to and reduce the uncertainty in the plethora of published emission scenarios.[23]

Possible futures: mainstreaming the complex

The problem we have at the moment is that we have two camps: the 'business as usual' camp, which sees no threat in the climate scenarios, and on the other hand those who worry about biodiversity loss, land use change, melting ice, warming trends and changes in rainfall distributions. The 'business as usual' camp tends to focus on resource use, economic growth and wealth generation, and the use of market mechanisms for the efficient allocation of resources. If we take a multiple capitals and values approach then there is a real need to try to mainstream all the complexities of managing and balancing multiple capitals spread out across landscapes in real time. As we have already noted, there is a trend towards developing tools and techniques for the inclusion of market 'externalities': trans-boundary air pollution impacts, off-site and downstream impacts of water use. As we shall see in the next chapter, a number of methods are being developed to widen the scope of markets, although there are limitations in the use of price mechanisms for resource allocation in natural systems that show non-linearities and multiple stable states. If the forecasts of climate change are correct, then it will not be long before there is an urgent need to develop tools to achieve a 'consilience' of complex interests and capitals. If we are to achieve a 'stronger' form of sustainability then there is a need to mainstream the complex: to convince all parties, all camps, that the only way forward is to be able to manage the complex adaptive interactions between people, resources, economics and the natural world, all at once. If we take a resilient view of these interactions, rather than an equilibrium view, then we need to be cognisant of the precariousness of our present position. How far are we from a major change in the global system, a surprising change in state that may involve hysteresis? This view places a new emphasis on complex forms of integrated risk assessments. How, for example, do we begin to identify the points of rapid and non-linear change that may be close by, or how do we identify the new Pareto optima, the new, more efficient and sustainable options, which may be some way away from our present position? There are, at present, no simple answers to these questions. We do not have tools to examine the shape of non-linear 'stability landscapes' other than the kinds of multiple-state ecosystem models we have already discussed. The Resilience Alliance is working in this area and progress is being made – but we have a long way to go. Given the risks of global and climate change then there is a need to develop tools to assess and improve resilience: the ability to gracefully recover from shocks. Recent extreme storm events in the USA – Hurricanes Katrina and Rita in 2005 – and the tsunami in SE Asia have demonstrated that as populations, resource and energy use and urbanisation have increased then the resilience has declined. In the new, riskier world of land use and climate change it will be necessary for all enterprises to develop new skills in integrated risk analysis. Hurricanes and tsunamis threaten all kinds of social and economic infrastructure, and they show how precarious our present state is.[24]

NOTES

1. R. A. Pielke and R. T. Conant. Best practices in prediction for decision-making: lessons from the atmospheric and earth sciences. *Ecology*, **84** (2003), 1351–8.

2. Ibid., p. 1353.

3. D. Snowden. Complex acts of knowing: paradox and descriptive self awareness. *Journal of Knowledge Management* (special edition), Spring 2002.

4. M. Allen. A novel view of global warming (a review of Crichton's 'State of fear'). *Nature*, **433** (2005), 198.

5. E. A. Parson. *Searching for Integrated Assessment: a Preliminary Investigation of Methods and Projects in the Integrated Assessment of Global Climate Change.* (Cambridge, MA: John F. Kennedy School of Government, Harvard, 1994). Quoted from P. D. Bailey. IEA: a new methodology for environmental policy. *Environmental Impact Assessment Review*, **17** (1997), 221–6 (quote from p. 221).

6. G. P. Harris. Integrated assessment and modelling: an essential way of doing science. *Environmental Modelling and Software*, **17** (2002), 201–7.

7. P. Parker *et al.* The potential for integrated assessment and modelling to solve environmental problems: vision, capacity and direction. In *Understanding and Solving Environmental Problems in the 21st Century*, ed. R. Costanza and S. E. Jorgensen. (Amsterdam: Elsevier, 2002), pp. 19–39.

8. S. Cohen *et al.* Climate change and sustainable development: towards a dialogue. *Global Environmental Change – Human and Policy Dimensions*, **8** (1998), 341–71.

9. J. R. Ravetz. Developing principles of good practice in integrated environmental assessment. *International Journal of Environment and Pollution*, **11** (1999), 243–65.

10. P. Matarasso. Integrated assessment: rhetoric of models and perceptions of world futures. *International Journal of Environment and Pollution*, **11** (1999), 447–61.

11. For a review, see H. Dowlatabadi. Integrated assessment models of climate change: an incomplete review. *Energy Policy*, **23** (1995), 289–96.

12. J. P. van der Sluijs. A way out of the credibility crisis of models used in integrated environmental assessment. *Futures*, **34** (2002), 133–46.

13. E. A. Parson. Integrated assessment and environmental policy making; in pursuit of usefulness. *Energy Policy*, **23** (1995), 463–75.

14. A. T. Cocks *et al.* The limitations of integrated assessment modelling in developing air pollution control policies. *Environmental Pollution*, **102** (1998), 635–9.

15. E. A. Casman, M. G. Morgan and H. Dowlatabadi. Mixed levels of uncertainty in complex policy models. *Risk Analysis*, **19** (1999), 33–42.

16. R. Sinha *et al.* Reduced-form modelling of surface water and soil chemistry for the tracking and analysis framework. *Water, Air and Soil Pollution*, **105** (1998), 617–42.

17. G. Petschel-Held *et al.* The tolerable windows approach: theoretical and methodological foundations. *Climatic Change*, **41** (1999), 303–31.

18. D. S. Jeffries *et al.* The effect of SO_2 emission controls on critical load exceedances for lakes in southern Canada. *Water Science and Technology*, **39** (1999), 165–71. J. P. van der Sluijs. A way out of the credibility crisis of models used in integrated environmental assessment. *Futures*, **34** (2002), 133–46.

19. B. Kasemir *et al.* Integrated assessment of sustainable development: multiple perspectives in interaction. *International Journal of Environment and Pollution*, **11** (1999), 407–25.

20. J. R. Ravetz. Citizen participation for integrated assessment: new pathways in complex systems. *International Journal of Environment and Pollution*, **11** (1999), 331–50.

21. B. Yarnal. (1998) Integrated regional assessment and climate change impact in river basins. *Climate Research*, **11**, 65–74.

22. W. E. Easterling. Why regional studies are needed in the development of full-scale integrated assessment modelling of global change processes. *Global Environmental Change – Human and Policy Dimensions*, **7** (1997), 337–56. D. A. Boughton, E. R. Smith and R. V. O'Neill. Regional vulnerability: a conceptual framework. *Ecosystem Health*, **5** (1999), 312–22. J. Ravetz. Integrated assessment for sustainability appraisal in cities and regions. *Environmental Impact Assessment Review*, **20** (2000), 31–64.

23. M. Janssen and B. de Vries. The battle of perspectives – a multi-agent model with adaptive responses to climate change. *Ecological Economics*, **26** (1998), 43–65.

24. W. N. Adger *et al.* Socio-ecological resilience to coastal disasters. *Science*, **309** (2005), 1036–9.

18 Managing environmental, social and economic systems

The complex problem of managing the coupled 'system of systems': how it is also hedged about by values and assumptions about the way the world works. Some heterodox views of a more inclusive set of tools.

Many can perceive that this world of ours is becoming more and more complicated and fragile as a result of a host of linkages between technological, environmental, political, social and economic forces. The hurricanes that hit the southern USA in 2005 clearly indicated that many of our socioeconomic systems do not collapse gracefully. The problems of global sustainability and natural resource management are indeed 'wicked' problems where we are trying to deal with meso-scale interactive landscapes, emergent properties of the micro-scale agent behaviour and macro-scale constraints. Achieving solutions to many of these challenges will require us to think not just about single prescriptions but about the complexity of 'systems of systems', their properties and responses, and how the action and interaction of local components across and between scales can emerge as global outcomes. If we seek a more sustainable future then we are desperately in need of more, and better, tools for integrated assessments and prediction – or if not prediction, then at least monitoring and adaptive management. Environmental impact assessments need to be placed in an adaptive management framework: a framework characterised by less methodological, institutional and organisational rigidity.[1] We are very used to valuing things in monetary terms, but as global environmental problems press in upon us there is a real need to bring other factors and forms of capital into the equation. All this has to be done in a world where there is much more risk and surprise in store than we usually admit.

What lies in the shadows?

We have to find a way to balance values – economic, sociocultural and ecological values – and their complex and recursive interactions. These are early days and present efforts are partial and incomplete but, nevertheless, the past twenty or thirty years of the twentieth century might just be seen with the hindsight of history as a major conceptual turning point. These new ideas and concepts are still in the shadows as far as mainstream society is concerned but if the human population is to tackle the evident problems of global change, overexploitation of global resources (especially water) and loss of biodiversity, and to begin to restore the damage, then it will be necessary to begin to think seriously about the complexity of interaction in global systems and how to deal with it effectively. As the human population rises towards some upper limit – perhaps in the next fifty years or so – and our role as the dominant species on the planet becomes ever more evident, it is essential that we confront the interactions that underlie the necessity for sustainable and interconnected societies, economies and environments. Most of our present theoretical and policy tools lack the necessary sophistication to do this effectively.

For the first time in human history we appear to have reached the point where production is being limited by the stock of natural capital rather than human or financial capital. For the first time we are running out of resources – agricultural land, water and biodiversity – our stocks of natural capital. Natural capital is as essential for human wealth and productivity as any other kind of capital, be it financial, infrastructural, social or human. Natural capital provides many apparently free ecosystem services (everything from clean air and clean water to crop pollination)[2] which have been valued at many trillions of dollars[3] – much more than the global Gross Domestic Product. Senator Gaylord Nelson is quoted as saying 'the economy is a wholly owned subsidiary of the environment'[4] so new, more inclusive market structures will be one way to ensure that the balance is maintained. To be sustainable the planet now requires a balance between all kinds of capital – including financial capital – because to be sustainable now requires money. Various indices of sustainable economic welfare have been developed to try to assess the present state of nations from more than just financial measures – more ethical measures if you like – and to achieve some kind of balance between capitals.[5] Almost all of these indices indicate a reduction in ethical wealth in Western nations since the 1970s, despite rapid growth in GDP. Analysis of all forms of stocks and flows indicates reductions in natural and other capitals while financial capital has increased. Nevertheless, many Australian farmers have told me 'I'd love to be green but I am in the red'. In other words, we cannot do without money: local, regional and global ecological restoration is going to require wealth to achieve it. Poverty is a crucial global barrier to environmental restoration.

As we have seen, the real challenges for restoration of the planetary ecology lie in the complex meso-scale zone between paddocks and global dynamics, where people, biodiversity, pattern and process meet at regional scales. Although some argue that 'small is beautiful', it really isn't always going to be possible to be sustainable on every hectare, so the construction of land use mosaics and a consequent understanding of spatial complexity will be critical. Stocks and flows will need to be balanced across scales through the construction of mosaics of stocks connected by fractal flow paths. Deficiencies in some areas will be made up by subsidies from others, as already happens. It is the actions of individual people acting in a regional context that, in the end, are going to make the difference.

A more inclusive (and complex) set of tools

What is going on is a revision of what the sociologists call 'problematization' or 'methodologizing': how problems are defined and tackled and by whom. Traditionally, problems would have been defined by scientists and academics with a particular disciplinary or methodological view of the problem. As the old saying goes 'when you have a hammer in your hand every problem is a nail'. Now there is a demand for integration, systems thinking and transdisciplinary science, which requires cross- and interdisciplinary discussion, fusion, agreement and innovation. This is hard and takes time. Some scientists with a strongly reductionist and narrow disciplinary focus will never manage it. Over time problems are becoming larger, more complex and inclusive of many disciplines and hence 'ways of knowing'. New sources of information are being brought to the table.

The kind of 'knowing' that is brought to the table is very context-sensitive. The way in which we think about resources, name them, and manage them is no exception. This is all tied up with the language we use. Because we live in a predominantly modernist world, we tend to favour a system of semiotics and language that lends itself to codification, quantification and predictability or accountability.[6] Semiotics, world-making and logical typing go hand in hand.[7] The modern era, with its fascination with markets and other financial vehicles, is a good example because 'numerical objectification and utility constitute the ontological prerequisites for the creation of marketable objects'.[8] Thus the way in which we name and explain features of the world around us are highly context-sensitive and culturally determined. Markets for goods and services have been known for centuries, but markets for goods like water and carbon and for ecosystem services like those provided by the biosphere are quite new. In trying to bring the natural world into the world of markets and finance we suffer from problems of the use of a numerical epistemology.

Water institutions (legal, administrative and policy) are undergoing unprecedented change worldwide.[9] In the past 20 years or so, particularly since the rise of globalisation with its emphasis on efficiency, productivity and international competitiveness, there has been a simultaneous drive in many countries towards subsidiarity and the introduction of market reforms in natural resource management (NRM). This has not been a universal trend, however; there are distinct regional differences. In countries that came under the sway of the Chicago School and which have felt the full force of the Thatcher–Reagan economic reforms (e.g. the USA, the UK, Australia) and those that have been strongly influenced by similar World Bank policies (e.g. Chile) there has been a rapid move towards corporatisation or privatisation of public assets and infrastructure (especially water management assets) and the full application of market mechanisms. For example, the UK has privatised its regional water companies and Australia trades most of its surface waters. On the other hand, in countries that have retained social democratic governments (such as Scandinavia and most of Western Europe) there has been a greater emphasis on state intervention and subsidies. In an extensive review of water pricing policies around the world, Johansson *et al.*[10] have examined the state of pricing policies for irrigation in many countries. Water reform has been implemented in many countries with the prime aim of improving efficiency and effectiveness; nevertheless, they conclude that market mechanisms alone do not necessarily achieve the most efficient results, that some mechanisms are easier to implement than others, and that governments still have an important role to play in providing stable policy and institutional frameworks within which markets can operate.

Perhaps the biggest problems with present markets lie in their inability to include what have been called externalities and public goods; both may be items that are difficult to define and quantify. Markets require defined rights and clear title to enable trades to take place. The definition of rights and other legal entitlements by its very nature defines what is internal and external to the market. There is therefore a kind of circularity here. For a market to exist there must be externalities; and the drive towards profit and efficiency will inevitably entail cost-shifting to entities external to the market arena.[11] To be able to trade in ethical wealth would require the trade in goods and services to include things such as off-site impacts and third-party effects, and other (ecological) goods and services. Such more inclusive markets are now beginning to be developed so that the broader definition of wealth may be factored into the 'triple bottom line' of social, environmental and economic goods and services. Markets require defined rights for buyer and seller but ethical wealth must also include other rights and responsibilities in addition to the water. The definition of a broader basket of rights in areas such as natural resources and biodiversity is not easy, and in many cases is experimental at present. None the less markets can inform decision makers in powerful ways and will doubtless expand and grow. Around the edges of orthodox macro- and micro-economic theory and practice we are seeing the development of a number of what might be called heterodox economic persuasions. This has been particularly true in the areas of economics concerned with environmental and water management. Although most of these developments and conversations have been confined to the pages of academic journals there have none the less been some important influences on environmental and natural resource management policies.

In the realm of complex adaptive systems and economics (for there are significant analogies in terms of the behaviour of individual agents in the market)[12] the field of evolutionary economics has developed to address the issues of growth, innovation and the development of economies. Rycroft and Kash have discussed the role of self-organised learning and path dependence in innovation and the development of new products and markets through 'network learning in practice'. They argue that increasing complexity in network interactions is a major challenge for firms operating in global markets.[13] Some authors[14] have argued for the relevance of the kinds of Darwinian, algorithmic approaches that Dennett[15] would espouse; indeed, the role of evolution in the marketplace has been discussed by evolutionists as well as economists.[16] Markets are a kind of CAS, with each agent taking independent investment decisions based on partial information in a global marketplace. As with ecological theory it is necessary to keep a vial of Dennett's Universal Acid to hand to ensure that we do not fall into unnecessary constructivist paradigms.[17] 'Cranes' will do just fine; we do not need teleological 'sky hooks'. This view of the generation of complexity from algorithmic processes is echoed by Foster and others who, as with biological systems, see the role of self-organisation as crucial in economics as elsewhere in life.[18] Indeed, the modelling of information transfers and knowledge exchange has been borrowed from physics[19] and applied to the modelling of self-organisation in financial market systems.[20] Evolutionary economics allows for long-term population growth, technological change, cyclical behaviour (as is observed in the so-called Kondratiev cycles, for example) and innovation in market dynamics so that it does not assume static solutions and the strict adherence to equilibrium conditions. Biological theories must be used with care in social contexts (and vice versa) but nevertheless there are some new and interesting cross-fertilisations occurring between the social and biological sciences, which may serve to impart more realism into economic models and ideas. Foster and Ball, for example, have recently used the full complex systems analogy and argument, including the structure of scale-free ('small-world') networks, to develop a critique of orthodox economics and to argue against simplistic analyses of 'the firm' in isolation from its network, of neoclassical linear, equilibrium theory, and of optimisation.[21] Thus while ecological and economic modelling (indeed, ecology and economics) share some intellectual foundations, they also share similar criticisms of their techniques of analysis, modelling and prediction.

Are NRM markets workable?

This concept of small-scale actions and choices leading to large-scale emergent properties of NRM and economies is of great importance to the ways in which we might manage water through trading mechanisms. The establishment of rights and markets makes all the usual kinds of equilibrium economic assumptions about utility and the 'invisible hand' of the market. A view of economics as SGC systems focuses more on the complexities of the definitions of various kinds of roles, rights and responsibilities held and played both by water itself (as a private, public and environmental good) and by the market players (as irrigators, farmers, urban dwellers and members of the broader society). Furthermore, the markets that have been established for water tend to focus on annual allocations and annual average flows. Markets can only work if the entities to be traded are in many ways predictable and definable. The kinds of catastrophic and hysteretic changes that characterise ecosystems make it very difficult for market solutions to cope.[22] From the point of view of the environment as a SGC system, annual averages mean nothing; much more important are the distributions of flood and drought in space and time and the ways in which the infrastructure established to deliver security to the water users modifies the frequency distributions on which the ecosystems of the rivers depend. This would be merely an academic argument but for the fact that at a recent Council of Australian Governments (COAG) meeting the Australian governments committed A$500M to buy water in the open market to replace environmental flows in the Murray River. This represents a major wealth transfer from the farming community to the river. So we are now faced with the issue of how best to use the water. What does 'smart' water look like, and how do we best restore ecological function and biodiversity in a fully regulated river system in which the infrastructure is specifically designed to contain and attenuate precisely the kinds of floods that the floodplain of the river requires?

It is for this reason that fundamental criticisms of market mechanisms are not just an academic exercise. Such criticisms cut to the core of the present fascination with market solutions (particularly for water management) and whether these will ever provide efficient and effective long-term solutions to resource allocation and lead to good environmental outcomes. There are certainly those voices that would deny that this is possible. Market solutions are favoured by those who espouse instrumentalist and utilitarian positions – and see the natural world as instrumental to human needs – whereas a more objectivist view sees intrinsic value in the natural world. Economists see water markets as a means of increasing efficiency and effectiveness, and there is a real problem with assessing the many and varied use and values of water. Therefore water markets, with their focus on quantification and objectification and their attendant externalities, are seen by many as only a partial solution. There is a really important debate here.

The market-based solutions so favoured by economic rationalists are largely based on the Coase Theorem. Coase's Theorem seems to say in plain English that clearly defined property rights can assure that the 'polluter pays' and that the market will ensure that businesses have an incentive to adopt techniques to reduce pollution. This requires little government intervention and is therefore more efficient than the alternative, which is to tax companies for polluting – the so-called Pigouvian tax system. So what Coase's Theorem attempts to do is to improve efficiency and 'internalise the externalities' by defining and assigning rights to tradeable goods and services through quotas, licences and legal rights. Although this is an excellent idea and certainly can influence behaviour in certain circumstances, the problems lie in the fundamental assumptions of defined property rights, low bargaining costs, perfect competition and the absence of wealth and income effects. All these are difficult to define in practice. It is frequently difficult to define property rights to environmental goods and services, which are often mobile, complex entities that vary in space and time.[23] To Coase it made no difference who obtained the initial property rights: assuming low transaction costs, the results were the same. Of course, it does matter who has the property rights – they are a gift of wealth and power. Without compensation, markets tend towards power law distributions of wealth: few rich and many poor. What the application of the Coase Theorem reflects is the historical separation of idealised economic theory from the world of the environment and society, and the difficulty in applying idealised theories to real world entities. Nevertheless, this theorem is the fundamental basis of the 'robust design' of the new Australian water reform package.[24]

In my view the most fundamental criticism of this theorem and of much economic theory lies in what might be called the 'Multiple Prisoners' Dilemma' problem and the emergent effects of many small decisions taken by market players with partial information. This problem is typical of many common pool resource management problems such as water, fisheries and forestry. In any real-world market situation, where the flows of information are inevitably going to be imperfect, the usual assumptions that pertain to the achievement of optimality and maximal utility – 'constant returns to scale, infinite divisibility, free entry, dispersed ownership of each grade of factor, shared knowledge, complete markets' – are going to be ideal situations.[25] Where there are two or more players with imperfect information, the Multiple Prisoners' Dilemma applies; any multiple-player situation has surprisingly complex and unexpected outcomes.[26] This is particularly true if there are multiple rounds of play – and there is a memory of what happened before and who did what to whom last time around – and if there are marked inequalities and asymmetries between players.[27] Market players change their preferences in response to the decisions of others. If information flows are imperfect there are always incentives to cheat. Micro-motives lead inevitably to macro-behaviour.[28]

The canonical economic theory assumes that participants in the market are entirely rational and self-regarding (and have perfect information). 'Economic man or woman' is supposed act in this way. Clearly this is not always so because of issues of memory, trust, betrayal, the actions of third parties and other indirect, multiple-player effects. The dynamics of social and economic networks are complex and do not always lead to perfect 'economic' behaviour; over time both non-cooperative and altruistic patterns of behaviour may develop. The behaviour of third parties is critical. Nowak and Sigmund have concluded that 'the evolution of cooperation by indirect reciprocity leads to reputation building, morality judgement and complex social interactions with ever-increasing cognitive demands'.[29] Recent work focuses on the extent to which the actions of others – which may frequently exhibit preferences that are of bounded rationality or are other-regarding – may be influenced by a small number of 'economic' players in the market so that although there are many imperfect actors the overall market dynamics are as theoretically required. Depending on the circumstances, it is possible for a small number of 'economic' players to influence the overall market behaviour; equally, the converse is true. Work in this area aims to develop 'better predictions of actual aggregate behaviour than does traditional economic theory'.[30]

Bernholz has shown that the only way to produce any kind of sensible outcome to make a number of unrealistic assumptions in the models; even then it is still necessary to assume perfect information flows between parties.[31] So the Coase Theorem is only ever going to be an idealised cartoon of the real-world market situation. Reality is a market with poorly defined rights, imperfect information flows and multiple players who act on local information and change their decisions in response to the actions of others. No wonder that markets produce complex behaviours and do not always produce the expected outcomes. McKay and Bjornlund have analysed the outcomes of some of the recent Australian water market mechanisms and have concluded that the rational pursuit of personal gain through the application of market mechanisms does not always produce the best social and environmental outcomes.[32] Water is a special kind of good, with many kinds of values, some of which are amenable to market valuations, and some of which are not.[33] There are things that markets can and cannot do – they have a role to play – but so do other policies and institutional arrangements to define the scope of market activity and to produce public good and other desirable outcomes. Allocative efficiency in economic policy is just one part of a broader strategy to produce sustainable outcomes for society and its environment. Sustainability requires the management of wealth and many other forms of capital. Therefore the debate should not be whether we are for, or against, the use of market instruments; rather, it should be about how to set such mechanisms in a broader framework to obtain, as it were, 'the best of both worlds'. We must be careful to achieve a balance between the needs of the markets (and the ways in which through logical typing, objectification and quantification they structure uses and values) and the needs of other values, uses and benefits, which may not be so easily defined or traded.[34]

In an attempt to design a robust system for tradeable water entitlements, Young and McColl[35] have tried to find ways of setting water markets in the context of other regulatory and institutional frameworks to ensure the best outcome – efficient markets within a framework in which externalities and social considerations are managed effectively. Young and McColl have tried to design a system that delivers maximum benefits 'across heterogeneous landscapes, through time as circumstances change' and when several objectives and problems are being managed simultaneously (as is usually the case.) Using the Tinbergen Principle, they argue that in any robust system there is a need for as many instruments of control as there are dimensions to the problem (and instruments of control include other mechanisms than just markets.) Arguing from Mundell's Principle of market classification, they also insist that any market instruments must be focused on the objectives on which they have most effect. Finally, using the Coase Theorem, they argue for a trading system with low transaction costs. Putting all this together with three fundamental goals – distributive equity, economic efficiency and the appropriate management of externalities – Young and McColl came up with the following table of possible instruments in a robust scheme for water management.

Policy objective	Distributive equity	Economic efficiency	Externalities
Scale: individual	Entitlement	Access allocations	Use licences
Scale: total system	Water allocation plans	Trading protocols	Integrated catchment plans

Thus Young and McColl see the need to have access allocation mechanisms and trading protocols embedded in a system of water allocation plans, integrated catchment management plans and other licences to ensure that an equitable and sustainable system is achieved. In a changing and complex world this type of overall scheme can set targets based on a steadily improving knowledge of the complex and emergent entities that must be managed. Most Australian 'matters for target' are condition indicators (e.g. nature and extent of native vegetation, river health indicators, etc.)[36] rather than measures of stocks and flows (although targets for salinity and nutrient exports from catchments are used). Targets can, however, be set on the basis of knowledge of biophysical constraints: regional stocks and flows assessments of various capitals, which provide for non-market outcomes and the protection of cultural and other values. The use of biophysical indicators to balance and constrain regional capital stocks and flows requires 'smart' targets to be set for complex and changing entities and, if necessary, the development of specific institutions and governance frameworks to manage these entities as needs arise. Tinbergen's Principle would call for new management structures to be established to manage specific externalities as needs arose. Market mechanisms could be used if appropriate. As conditions change a robust scheme like this can evolve and change over time to suit changed conditions. Effectively what Young and McColl have designed is a robust system of structures designed to be flexible and resilient enough to accommodate changing knowledge and climate. The efficiency principle would merely try to minimise the number of instruments as far as possible to achieve effective control. Young and

McColl have made an excellent start, but given the kinds of complexities that we now understand apply to the management of landscapes and waterscapes with human interventions at a variety of scales, there is plenty of scope for innovation and intellectual input in this area.

Environmental economics attempts to treat environmental assets like commodities and to achieve the most socially efficient use of resources. In this regard it is still a utilitarian and instrumentalist discipline. Ecological economics, on the other hand, 'extends the boundaries of analysis of environmental problems to include both economics and ecology'.[37] In an attempt to include a broader suite of goods and services, ecological economists have begun the tackle the issues of the valuation of ecosystem services and other kinds of externalities not usually factored into the marketplace.[38] Ecological economics attempts to bring to the table other forms of capital – other stocks and flows – in addition to the financial.[39] In particular it focuses on natural capital and the value of ecosystem goods and services.[40] Yes, there are problems with the definition of natural capital and there has been some debate around the concept because of the basic incommensurability of monetary and other values.[41] Others bewail the state of ecological knowledge and theory and lament its inability to produce coherent accounts of the human–environment interface.[42] The problem lies in trying to use techniques such as avoided costs, contingent valuation, hedonic pricing, travel cost methods or other methods to try to turn the properties of complex non-linear ecosystems into monetary values (some have even attempted to use property valuation techniques[43]). The assumptions and limitations of the various techniques are frequently not well matched to the complex and non-linear properties of the natural world. These properties require techniques for valuation under uncertainty.[44] Chee writes

> for most of us, the cognitive burden imposed by attempting to grapple with ecosystem dynamics influenced by stochasticity, inter-connectivity, nonlinear interactions and spatial and temporal lags in ecosystem responses is overwhelming.[45]

Right now ecologists, conservation biologists and economists are talking different languages – for example 'much of economics of biodiversity remains to be written'[46] – and there are those who argue strongly that orthodox economics not only works against sustainability but is also essentially 'ungreenable' in its present form because of problems with biophysical scarcity, discounting, the hegemony of global markets, substitutability, monetary limitlessness and the structural problems of complex systems.[47] Nevertheless, we simply have to try to find ways of bring various values together so as to more closely match the activities of the anthroposphere to those of the biosphere because whether we like it or not the interpenetration of the two is becoming ever more complex and difficult to manage. The stocks and flows of other capitals can be used to set the biophysical, social and cultural context within which market activities can proceed.

Attempts are being made to bring economics and ecology together, most particularly by the Beijer Institute in Stockholm. Working from the Beijer Institute, Dasgupta and Mäler have tried to 'uncover ways in which the price system is capable of functioning as a resource allocation mechanism'.[48] Price systems can be efficient allocation mechanisms for resources if the transformation possibilities between goods and services are of a particular mathematical type – a convex set – and economists 'rely on the convexity assumption, always hoping that it is not an embarrassing simplification'.[49] We know that ecosystems have properties that do not comply with this assumption, so a search is being undertaken for ways of combining the complex properties of natural systems with those of the ideal world of economics. There certainly are situations in which price mechanisms cannot be used to construct efficient allocation mechanisms; these include situations in which there are positive feedback processes.[50] They are equally problematical in situations where there are multiple stable states, hysteresis effects or other strong non-linearities. It is precisely for this reason that the ecosystems in which we know that state flips, multiple stable states and hysteresis effects occur (e.g. shallow lakes, estuaries, fire and grazing regimes in rangelands and savannahs) are constantly being used as case studies for these new kinds of economic analyses. Dasgupta and Mäler also point out in their paper that it is precisely these positive feedbacks, multiple stable states and thresholds that render the 'environmental Kuznets curve' an invalid concept. The 'environmental Kuznets curve' is a form of economic reasoning that says that it is possible to destroy or pollute the environment when a country or region is poor. Trade and development improve the environment through increased income, because richer people can afford to fix up the environment later. Substitutability between manufactured and natural capital is not possible if hysteresis and thresholds render change irreversible. This is an important consideration in discussion of 'strong' and 'weak' sustainability.

Signals, incentives and regulations

The conclusion from all this is that markets and price mechanisms can be used in certain situations if the properties of the system in question (or even the range of properties in question) lend themselves to such an approach. We do know that all-encompassing equilibrium assumptions (single stable states and reversibility in space and time) are not universally valid, so the management framework must include other policy instruments, including taxes, regulations, incentives and other forms of what have been called 'social contrivances'.

Ian Wills has moved beyond the usual equilibrium orthodox view of economics to view markets as an imperfect means of seeking non-market signals and incentives.[51] He discusses at length the problems of coordination of the economy and the environment and the reasons, and remedies, for such lack of coordination. He also realises that even the best of present structures and practices provides but poor information and incentives to properly cost and include various kinds of externalities. Markets provide signals and incentives based on changes in marginal values and utility. Biophysical constraints and resource use targets provide signals based on absolute scarcity and values. In discussing the properties of coupled social, economic and environmental systems, Wills concludes that lack of information and uncertainties are inescapable. Errors will inevitably be made, so a strategy of monitoring and nimble adaptation is the best possible within boundaries set by fundamental constraints.

There are two kinds of sustainability – or two extremes of a spectrum of possibilities. The 'strong' sustainability constraint, as it is called, requires the human race to maintain and not deplete the planet's stocks of natural capital: biodiversity, ecosystem services and renewable and non-renewable resources.[52] This leaves future generations with the same resources and possibilities as we enjoyed. All the previous discussion shows that this 'strong' constraint is not being adhered to in the world in which we find ourselves. Equally, there are real problems with the use of the usual kinds of treatments for externalities in any discussion of intergenerational equity. For example, use of the Coase model of resource trading is impossible because there is no information flow to future generations, who cannot participate in the market.[53] Nevertheless there is debate about what is the best strategy for intergenerational equity. Following pioneering work by Solow and Hartwick the debate centres on the degree of substitutability between natural and manufactured capital.[54] Solow and Hartwick assumed substitutability between the two forms of capital and suggested that intergenerational equity was preserved if the total stock of all forms of capital was preserved, and that rents from the exhaustion of resources were invested for the benefit of future generations. Many therefore espouse a 'weak' form of sustainability in which natural capital may be degraded as long as we match our activities to those of the natural world and substitutes are created.[55] So sustainability is both about the ways in which we treat the future through discount rates and the like, and about interconversions of the various forms of capital. Sustainability is hard to achieve if non-linearity, multiple stable states and hysteresis are known to occur. Time lags and action at a distance are also complicating factors. It just may not be wise to exhaust some forms of natural capital. The exercise of identifying what has been called 'critical' natural capital had been worked through in the UK in the context of water resources and supply, with the conclusion that with present management the natural capital was not being maintained.[56] Further analyses have been used to determine the size and nature of the sustainability gap between the present and the 'strongly' sustainable state.[57]

Footprints and 'stocks and flows'

There is now a large literature on these more inclusive forms of economics. Two major trends have emerged: one attempts to measure the ecological 'footprint' of cities, regions and nations[58] and the other uses 'stocks and flows' models in a form of accounting for the consumption of goods and services.[59] As with the accounting of critical natural capital, the overall pattern of ecological footprints is also unsustainable.[60] Using data from 1997, Wackernagel and his collaborators worked through the detailed example of Italy's footprint and then used the methodology to analyse the global footprint country by country. The methodology accounts for the through put of energy and resources in each nation and translates these into the biologically productive areas required to produce these flows. These areas were then compared to the available area and productivity of each nation. The result was a ratio in hectares per capita, which was negative if the required footprint was larger than the available area. Most nations were negative, ranging from −6.8 for Singapore and −3.8 for Japan (i.e. the required resource footprints for Singapore and Japan are 6.8 and 3.8 times the productivity of their respective land areas). The USA had a ratio of −3.6 and most Western European nations were in the −2.0 to −3.0 range. Few nations were positive; ranging from 14.3 for Iceland, 12.8 for New Zealand, to Australia 5.0, Brazil 3.6 and Canada 1.9. The overall global ratio was found to be about −0.7, indicating that the global consumption of resources exceeds the area that can sustainably produce them.[61] If the footprints are calculated on a per capita basis the results look very different, particularly for countries like Australia and Canada, which have large land areas and relatively small populations. On a per capita basis the footprints range from 10 hectares per capita for the USA, 8 for Australia, 5–6 for Western Europe and Japan, less than 2 for China and 1 for India. These footprints, and the ways in which they are calculated, are now a source of some debate in the world because of pressures to restrain water use and carbon and other emissions. Should all countries abide by per capita energy and materials use targets? Or should countries like Canada and Australia be able to have higher per capita usage offset by their large land areas? These are difficult ethical choices.

The use of stocks and flows models at regional and local scales is an attempt to place the local or regional economy in the context of its use (and/or distortion) of the flows of materials and energy. Cities, for example, draw resources from large areas around them and usually have very large water catchment areas made possible by dams, diversions and interbasin transfers of water. Similarly, the disposal of storm water and waste water streams from large cities may severely affect large surrounding regions. Jansson and co-workers[62] calculated the freshwater flows appropriated by the cities and nations surrounding the Baltic Sea and showed that the water and resource footprint was 8.5–9.5 times the area of the Baltic Sea and its drainage basin. There have also been attempts to place regional or ecosystem-specific stocks and flows models in an economic context – to fuse, if you like, the flows of financial and natural capital and resources.[63] These models are explicitly static, linear and equilibrium constructs, which attempt to link the anthroposphere to the biosphere. They are a first step down a long road. Despite the acknowledgement that this is but a first step these models have been the sources of some controversy. Economists in particular are unhappy with the attempts to model the biophysical constraints surrounding the market economy.[64] They seem to feel that market substitution will take care of the resource limitations implied; none the less, as an ecologist, I do not see how market forces and price mechanisms can substitute for the fundamentals of life, particularly water, biodiversity and other non-market values. I agree with Ayres that boundless technological optimism is misguided.[65] A new consilience is required here.

Given the shortcomings of market economics (when used as the sole means to manage natural capital) I do not see how we can escape using stocks and flows frameworks to provide just, equitable and fair biophysical signals and incentives to all. Markets can exclude the poor, whereas biophysical constraints apply to all, regardless of status or income. There are some excellent examples of changed behaviour and innovation resulting from water restrictions in Australian cities. Water restrictions frequently result in much larger cuts in per capita water use than the planners anticipate.

New institutions from old

While we are having problems getting global collaboration on issues like carbon emissions and climate change – the global atmosphere is a classic 'tragedy of the commons'[66] – there are none the less many examples of successful management of the commons at local and regional scales.[67] Although human tinkering has produced numerous models of landscape change, it has also produced a variety of institutional and governance arrangements, some of which achieve long-term, intergenerational sustainability. These are precisely the kinds of 'social contrivances' mentioned earlier: self-organised, community-based, collective self-governance systems for the management of the commons at regional scales. These governance arrangements employ sanctions to encourage collaboration rather than defections and so combat the problems of the Prisoner's Dilemma. They depend on building and maintaining trust within communities and usually employ ways of knowing other than science. The comparative analysis of these institutional arrangements by the school of 'new institutionalism' has shown that the structure of the resource system and the attributes and behaviours of the appropriators are critical success factors.[68] Ostrom has concluded that successful and sustainable management of the commons requires the following conditions to hold at local and regional scales:

- Recognition of rights to organise, together with collective choice arrangements,
- Clearly defined resource boundaries so that the rules can be devised and managed by the resource users,
- Congruence between management rules and local conditions so that compliance with the rules is easy to monitor,
- Effective monitoring of the resource by monitors accountable to the users,
- Graduated and effective sanctions for non-compliance,
- Low-cost adjudication and conflict resolution mechanisms,
- An organised set of nested governance arrangements (to cope with issues of scale) and
- There must be established procedures for revising the rules.[69]

There are many examples of sustainable self-organised, collective resource management institutions around the world: some in the Swiss Alps, for example, have lasted many hundreds of years. Equally, there are many unsuccessful examples of complex situations in water management, for example, where lack of clear definitions, system uncertainties, lack of effective monitoring and inappropriate governance arrangements have led to resource depletion and conflict. Nevertheless, it is clear that there are many opportunities for the development of appropriate regional, self-organised, collective institutions. This is consistent with the trend towards subsidiarity as long as the higher-level governance arrangements are properly nested and truly allow this. Devolved, collective institutions require good information about resource flows and their variability in space and time together with effective adaptive management arrangements to cope with uncertainty. This is another example of regional constraints – a unique sense of local 'place' – producing local solutions. The factors that lead to the successful establishment of effective self-organised institutions are still a matter of debate and research, but we should learn from 'what works' and apply what we can, particularly in situations where market failure is probable. Globalisation, and the increasing interpenetration of the anthroposphere and the biosphere at a range of scales, presents a particular challenge to the management of common pool resources at local scales in ways that promote community equity and sustainability. Dolšak *et al.* write that

> multiple studies tell the same old stories. Central governments initiate the dismantling of local, well-functioning and self governing systems, leading to governance failures at the coarser scale. The introduction of private property and market economy leads to the deterioration of common-pool resources and communities.

The interests of users across scales are frequently in conflict. Allocation of rights to resources is a political process; access can be limited by the structure of macro-level institutions and by the human and social capital available to actors at the various levels. Increasing complexity is driving a capacity challenge as well as making the set of adaptation strategies larger and more interconnected. Furthermore, incremental and linear responses do not cope well with changing complex, emergent and non-linear contexts.[70]

NOTES

1. B.F. Noble. Strengthening EIA through adaptive management: a systems perspective. *Environmental Impact Assessment Review*, **20** (2000), 97–111.
2. For an excellent recent review of the classification, description and methods of valuation of ecosystem services, see R.S. de Groot, M.A. Wilson and R.M.J. Boumans. A typology for the classification, description and valuation of ecosystem functions, goods and services. *Ecological Economics*, **41** (2002), 393–408. G.C. Daily *et al.* Ecosystem services: benefits supplied to human societies by natural ecosystems. *Issues in Ecology*, **2** (Spring 1997), 2–16. C. Kremen. Managing ecosystem services: what do we need to know about their ecology? *Ecology Letters*, **8** (2005), 468–79.
3. R. Costanza *et al.* The value of the world's ecosystem services and natural capital. *Nature*, **387** (1997), 253–60.
4. Gaylord Nelson. The bankruptcy files. *Wilderness*, (Summer, 1994).
5. See R. Costanza, J. Farley and P. Templet. Quality of life and the distribution of wealth and resources. In *Understanding and Solving Environmental Problems in the 21st Century*, ed. R. Costanza, and S.E. Jorgensen, pp. 221–58. (Amsterdam: Elsevier Science, 2002).
6. J. Kallinikos. Predictable worlds: on writing, accountability and other things. *Scandinavian Journal of Management*, **12** (1996), 7–24.
7. N. Goodman. *Ways of World Making.* (Indianapolis: Hackett, 1978). Gregory Bateson. *Mind and Nature: a Necessary Unity.* (Glasgow: Fontana/Collins, 1980).
8. J. Kallinikos. Cognitive foundations of economic institutions: markets, organisations and networks revisited. *Scandinavian Journal of Management*, **11** (1995), 119–37.
9. For a review and a discussion of some key case studies, see R.M. Saleth and A. Dinar. Institutional changes in global water sector: trends, patterns and implications. *Water Policy*, **2** (2000), 175–99.
10. R.C. Johansson *et al.* Pricing irrigation water: a review of theory and practice. *Water Policy*, **4** (2002), 173–99.
11. A. Vatn and D.W. Bromley. Externalities – a market model failure. *Environmental and Resource Economics*, **9** (1997), 135–51.
12. P. Ball. *Critical Mass; How One Thing Leads to Another.* (London: Arrow Books, 2005).
13. R.W. Rycroft and D.E. Kash. *The Complexity Challenge: Technological Innovation for the 21st Century.* (London: Pinter, 1999).
14. G.M. Hodgson. Darwinism in economics: from analogy to ontology. *Journal of Evolutionary Economics*, **12** (2002), 259–81.
15. D.C. Dennett. *Darwin's Dangerous Idea: Evolution and the Meanings of Life.* (London: Allen Lane, 1995).
16. N. Eldredge. Evolution in the marketplace. *Structural Change and Economic Dynamics*, **8** (1997), 385–98.

17. For a discussion of constructivist epistemology in complexity and economics, see J.-L. Le Moigne. On theorizing the complexity of economic systems. *Journal of Socio–Economics*, **24** (1995), 477–99.

18. J. Foster. The analytical foundations of evolutionary economics: from biological analogy to economic self-organization. *Structural Change and Economic Dynamics*, **8** (1997), 427–51. J. Foster. Competitive selection, self-organization and Joseph A. Schumpeter. *Journal of Evolutionary Economics*, **10** (2000), 311–28. U. Witt. Self-organization and economics – what is new? *Structural Change and Economic Dynamics*, **8** (1997), 489–507. G. Buenstorf. Self-organisation and sustainability: energetics of evolution and implications for ecological economics. *Ecological Economics*, **33** (2000), 119–34.

19. M. Ruth. Evolutionary economics at the crossroads of biology and physics. *Journal of Social and Evolutionary Systems*, **19** (1996), 125–44.

20. A. Ponzi and Y. Aizawa. Criticality and punctuated equilibrium in a spin system model of a financial market. *Chaos, Solitons and Fractals*, **11** (2000), 1739–46.

21. J. Foster. From simplistic to complex systems in economics. Proceedings of the 'Economics for the Future' Conference, Cambridge, UK, Sept 2003. Ball. *Critical Mass*. (See Note 12.)

22. This focus on ecosystem dynamics, basins of attraction and non-linear dynamics in socio-economic systems is characteristic of the work of the Resilience Alliance. See, for example, B. H. Walker *et al.* Resilience, adaptability and transformability in socio-ecological systems. *Ecology and Society*, **9(2)** (2004), 5. http://www.ecologyandsociety.org/vol9/iss2/art5.

23. M. Borgerhoff Mulder and P. Coppolillo. *Conservation: Linking Ecology, Economics and Culture.* (Princeton, University Press, 2005).

24. M. D. Young and J. C. McColl. Robust reform: the case for a new water entitlement system for Australia. *Australian Economic Review*, **36** (2003), 225–34. M. D. Young and J. C. McColl. Robust design: designing tradable permit and allocation systems for the long term. Proceedings of the Policy Research Experts Symposium on *Economic Instruments for Water Demand Management in an Integrated Water Resources Framework*, June 14–15, (2003), Ottawa, Canada.

25. P. Samuelson. Some uneasiness with the Coase Theorem. *Japan and the World Economy*, **7** (1995), 1–7, quoted from p. 1.

26. See the extended discussion of this and other complex effects arising from the interaction of local agents in Ball, *Critical Mass*. (See Note 12.)

27. P. Taylor. *Unruly Complexity: Ecology, Interpretation, Engagement.* (Chicago, IL: Chicago University Press, 2005).

28. T. Schelling. *Micromotives and Macrobehavior.* (New York: Norton, 1978).

29. M. Nowak and K. Sigmund. Evolution of indirect reciprocity. *Nature*, **437** (2005), 1292–8.

30. C. F. Camerer and E. Fehr. When does 'economic man' dominate social behaviour? *Science*, **311** (2006), 47–52.

31. P. Bernholz. Property rights, contracts, cyclical social preferences and the Coase Theorem: a synthesis. *European Journal of Political Economy*, **13** (1997), 419–42.

32. J. Mckay and H. Bjornlund. Recent Australian market mechanisms as a component of an environmental policy that can make choices between sustainability and social justice. *Social Justice Research*, **14** (2002), 387–403.

33. H. H. G. Savenije. Why water is not an ordinary economic good, or why the girl is special. *Physics and Chemistry of the Earth*, **27** (2002), 741–4.

34. S. Beder. Charging the earth: the promotion of price-based measures for pollution control. *Ecological Economics*, **16** (1996), 51–63.

35. M. D. Young and J. McColl. *Defining tradable water entitlements and allocations: a robust system.* Paper presented to the Policy Research Experts Symposium on *Economic Instruments for Water*

Demand Management in an Integrated Water Resources Framework, June 14–15, 2004, Ottawa, Canada.

36. See the lists of 'matters for target' at www.nlwra.gov.au or www.nrm.gov.au.

37. I. Wills. *Economics and the Environment: a Signaling and Incentives Approach*. (Melbourne: Allen and Unwin, 1997).

38. H. Mooney, A. Cropper and W. Reid. Confronting the human dilemma. *Nature*, **434** (2005), 561–2.

39. For a discussion of the concepts of valuation and of differing sets of 'values' in economics and ecology, see S. C. Farber, R. Costanza and M. A. Wilson. Economic and ecological concepts for valuing ecosystem services. *Ecological Economics*, **41** (2002), 375–92.

40. R. Costanza *et al*. The value of ecosystem services: putting the issues in perspective. *Ecological Economics*, **25** (1998), 67–72.

41. W. E. Rees and M. Wackernagel. Monetary analysis: turning a blind eye on sustainability. *Ecological Economics*, **29** (1999), 47–52.

42. M. J. Harte. Ecology, sustainability, and environment as capital. *Ecological Economics*, **15** (1995), 157–64.

43. I. A. Curtis. Valuing ecosystems goods and services: a new approach using a surrogate market and the combination of a multiple criteria analysis and a Delphi panel to assign weights to the attributes. *Ecological Economics*, **50** (2004), 163–94.

44. S. C. Farber, R. Costanza and M. Wilson. Economic and ecological concepts for valuing ecosystem services. *Ecological Economics*, **41** (2002), 375–92.

45. Y. E. Chee. An ecological perspective on the valuation of ecosystem services. *Biological Conservation*, **120** (2004), 549–65 (quote from p. 560).

46. G. Heal. Editorial. Economics of biodiversity: an introduction. *Resource and Energy Economics*, **26** (2004), 105–14.

47. M. Wackernagel and W. E. Rees. Perceptual and structural barriers to investing in natural capital: economics from an ecological footprint perspective. *Ecological Economics*, **20** (1997), 3–24. A. Fenech *et al*. Natural capital in ecology and economics: an overview. *Environmental Monitoring and Assessment*, **86** (2003), 3–17.

48. P. Dasgupta and K.-G. Mäler. The economics of non-convex ecosystems: introduction. *Environmental and Resource Economics*, **26** (2003), 499–525.

49. Ibid., p. 499.

50. D. Starrett. Fundamental non-convexities in the theory of externalities. *Journal of Economic Theory*, **4** (1972), 180–99.

51. Wills, *Economics and the Environment*. (See Note 37.)

52. H. Daly and J. Cobb. *For the Common Good*. (Boston, MA: Beacon Press, 1989). D. Pearce, A. Markandya and E. Barbier. *Blueprint for a Green Economy*. (London: Earthscan, 1989). H. Daly. *Steady State Economics*, 2nd edn. (Washington, DC: Island Press, 1991).

53. J. Pasqual and G. Souto. Sustainability in natural resource management. *Ecological Economics*, **46** (2003), 47–59.

54. R. M. Solow. Intergenerational equity and exhaustible resources. *Review of Economic Studies*, Symposium, 1974, 29–45. J. M. Hartwick. Intergeneration equity and the investing of rents from exhaustible resources. *American Economic Review*, **67** (1977), 972–4.

55. See C. Folke *et al*. *Investing in Natural Capital: the Ecological Economics Approach to Sustainability*. (Washington, DC: Island Press, 1994). F. Hinterberger, F. Luks and F. Schmidt-Bleek. Material flows vs. 'natural capital'. What makes an economy stable? *Ecological Economics*, **23** (1997), 1–14.

56. P. Ekins. Identifying critical natural capital. *Ecological Economics*, **44** (2003), 159–63. P. Ekins. Identifying critical natural capital; conclusions about critical natural capital. *Ecological Economics*, **44** (2003), 277–92. P. Ekins and S. Simon. An illustrative application of the CRITINC framework to the UK. *Ecological Economics*, **44** (2003), 255–75.

57. P. Ekins *et al.* A framework for the practical application of the concepts of critical natural capital and strong sustainability. *Ecological Economics*, **44** (2003), 165–85.

58. M. Wackernagel and W. Rees. *Our Ecological Footprint: Reducing Human Impact on the Earth.* (Philadelphia, PA: New Society Publishers, 1996).

59. L. Gordon, M. Dunlop and B. Foran. Land cover change and water vapour flows: learning from Australia. *Philosophical Transactions of the Royal Society of London*, B**358** (2003), 1973–84.

60. M. Wackernagel *et al.* National natural capital accounting with the ecological footprint concept. *Ecological Economics*, **29** (1999), 375–90.

61. For the application of this analysis to North America, see M. Senbel, T. McDaniels and H. Dowlatabadi. The ecological footprint: a non-monetary metric of human consumption applied to North America. *Global Environmental Change*, **13** (2003), 83–100.

62. A. A. Jansson *et al.* Linking freshwater flows and ecosystem services appropriated by people: the case of the Baltic Sea drainage basin. *Ecosystems*, **2** (1999), 351–66.

63. D. Jin, P. Hoagland and T. M. Dalton. Linking economic and ecological models for a marine ecosystem. *Ecological Economics*, **46** (2003), 367–85.

64. See the discussion in J. M. Gowdy and A. F. Carbonell. Towards consilience between biology and economics: the contribution of Ecological Economics. *Ecological Economics*, **29** (1999), 337–48.

65. R. U. Ayres. Cowboys, cornucopians and long-run sustainability. *Ecological Economics*, **8** (1993), 189–207.

66. Peter Barnes has suggested a solution in the form of a publicly owned Sky Trust, which would pay dividends to all who, after all, collectively own the atmosphere as a commons. It would set biophysical limits on carbon emissions and operate a cap and trade system of permits. See P. Barnes. *Who Owns the Sky?* (Washington, DC: Island Press, 2001).

67. P. Schuster. The commons' tragicomedy. *Complexity*, **10** (2006), 10–12.

68. E. Ostrom. *Governing the Commons: the Evolution of Institutions for Collective Action.* (Cambridge: Cambridge University Press, 1990).

69. N. Dolšak and E. Ostrom. The challenges of the commons. In *The Commons in the New Millennium*, ed. N. Dolšak and E. Ostrom, pp. 3–34. (Cambridge, MA: MIT Press, 2003).

70. N. Dolšak *et al.* Adaptation to challenges. In *The Commons in the New Millennium*, ed. N. Dolšak and E. Ostrom, pp. 337–59. (Cambridge, MA: MIT Press, 2003).

19   Linking multiple capitals in a changing world

Finding ways to understand and manage the interactions of the many forms of capital that together lead to sustainability.

The linkage of economic and ecological concepts and models requires us to be more realistic. Ecological systems are not linear, equilibrium systems; somehow we must find a way to link economic activity to the dynamics and resilience of natural systems. Deutsch and her collaborators wrote

> We envision that the development of indicators of ecosystem performance to capture critical natural capital in the context of resilience will become an increasingly important area for both research and policy in the coming years.[1]

Of course, there is a changing view that economies and societies are also non-equilibrium CAS and have similarly dynamic properties – so the challenge is to find ways to link the environmental–socioeconomic systems-of-systems. Science will play a role in this linkage as a generator of new knowledge, but it must do so in a much more engaged and interactive form and with the recognition of complexity. Whatever form sustainability science takes, a form of 'postnormal' science will be involved.[2] Orthodox economics assumes at least short-term equilibrium and the applicability of concepts of marginal utility and essentially instrumental values. Economic models assume 'well-behaved' linear dynamics around equilibria. We are going to need a heterodox economics and a set of governance arrangements that does not use outdated physics-based assumptions.[3]

Valuation of ecosystem services in the world of CAS and resilience should perhaps be more about avoidance of catastrophic change than trying to place a value on averaged properties of systems. New ideas are starting to flow through in this area; already concepts of valuation are changing towards more realistic ideas around thresholds and 'tipping points'.[4] In a discussion of complex systems and valuation, Limburg and others wrote

> As we conceive of them, none of the existing valuation methods, economic or ecological, adequately allows for all the dimensions that distinguish the marginal from the non-marginal: no single valuation scheme will work well over all circumstances. We must develop indicators of which set of system conditions we find ourselves in, or moving toward.

We have already discussed the problems of prediction and complexity, and of partial and incomplete data. The resilient and adaptive capacities of CAS and socioeconomic systems are more related to the existence and preservation of mechanisms[5] – materials and energy flows and the mechanisms that sustain them are to be valued more than states.

Whereas Limburg, O'Neill and others have used catastrophe theory and the models of bifurcations to demonstrate that valuation techniques are presently lacking,[6] Scheffer and others have used similar models to show that social change may similarly follow surprising and highly non-linear future courses.[7] Janssen and Carpenter have looked at the response of a lake to a variety of management philosophies, value sets and cultures, by means of multi-agent modelling techniques.[8] The hysteretic response of lakes to phosphorus inputs has been discussed previously; when this interacts with a variety of beliefs about ways to manage lakes, some surprises are in store. An approach that attempts to minimise phosphorus loads leads to a 'time bomb' with long-term accumulation of phosphorus in the sediments. Command and control management approaches cause the lake to cycle through all possible states. Only an adaptive learning approach (in which agents learn from and adapt to unexpected changes in the state of the lake) can produce a resilient response on the part of the lake. This is not the 'optimum' state from the lake's point of view, but it is resilient to stochastic perturbations and to other forms of uncertainty. So 'weak' sustainability in a learning environment is probably the best we can achieve for now, but is this going to be sufficient in the long run? Will it avoid collapse?

Ecological modernisation

The 'weak' form of sustainability – in which human activities and the economy must be more closely matched to the flows of materials and energy in the natural world – has become popular in the context of reuse, recycling and clean production. It has been argued that 'it is not the availability of resources which limits global economic growth but the ecological consequences of man-induced material streams'.[9] It has thus been further argued that the sustainable economy is a dematerialised economy – one in which the life-cycle material intensity per unit of service is minimised. This has led to the concept of reductions in resource use, which lead to concomitant increases in profitability. Some of these ideas seem to have originated in Europe as part of the development of what has been called ecological modernisation: the incorporation of ecological systems thinking into social, political and economic discourse.[10] Ecological modernisation favours the reduction of the environmental impact of advanced industrial societies through dematerialisation and the development of knowledge- and service-based industries. It also advances the causes of innovation, pollution and risk reduction, environmental protection and the alignment of national policy goals around these themes. Ecological modernisation certainly sees important changes in the risk profile of advanced societies, with the major risks changing from proximate risks of disease, starvation and poverty to less easily perceived risks associated with technologies of various kinds.[11] Ecological modernisation is seen as a way for societies to move towards reductions in industrial and environmental risk – but some see a centralised social democracy as necessary for this new path to be followed effectively.[12] Critics of ecological modernisation see two future challenges in the implementation of ecological modernisation. First, ecological modernisation is only 'weakly' sustainable and the process of globalisation is accompanied by attempts to displace and externalise many environmental and social costs.[13] Globalisation and the rise of multi-national companies are also frequently incompatible with the requisite attention to unique local and regional features of place. Second, it appears that some aspects of ecological modernisation have been captured by economists who see it as a corollary to conventional efficiency measures. It may well be that a more radical policy approach is going to be required – one more consistent with a 'stronger' version of sustainable development.[14]

The use of a simple, equilibrium model of nature as a model for the way in which we should manage our affairs is also a primarily European development, which reached its fullest development in the form of industrial ecology.[15] Industrial ecology has similarities to the 'weak' form of sustainability in that it attempts to improve efficiencies of resource use and to match the inputs and outputs of energy and materials with the capacity of the environment. Industrial ecology is thus seen as an arm of sustainable development[16] although it has been criticised as being business-as-usual with a green tinge. These concepts have been used in the redesign of industrial parks and other innovative industries. It has been shown that it is certainly possible to reach 'Factor 4' reductions in the intensity of material flows in industry and to maintain or improve profitability so that 'dematerialisation' of the production process is achievable.[17] There are many good examples of what has been called Natural Capitalism in existence; the Rocky Mountain Institute in Colorado is a major exponent of these approaches.[18] There are still those, however, who criticise industrial ecology and maintain that these ideas remain in the intellectual sphere rather than being incorporated into the mainstream of economic and social policy.[19] There are certainly the same problems with the implementation of these ideas as there are with the construction and use of stocks and flows models – complexity, emergent surprises, uncertainty[20] – and these may account for the lack of mainstream acceptance by government and industry. Others criticise ecological modernisation precisely because is it only a 'weak' form of sustainability. These authors place greater emphasis on the other values that environments and societies hold, values that are not effectively included in market economics.[21] Market economics and instrumental reason are necessary but not sufficient.

In countries that have introduced market reforms there has been a parallel devolution of power to local and regional groups of various kinds and hence growing subsidiarity. Market mechanisms allow for competition between local and regional groups for resources, including transfers of water within and between catchments. A water transfer is also a wealth transfer. Thus the increased complexity of a world of water markets is accompanied by an increased focus on the capacity of local and regional groups to manage and compete in a world of much increased complexity. In recent decades, as governments have moved to reduce their expenditure and rates of taxation in the names of efficiency and smaller government, we have witnessed the demise of farm extension schemes and the large centralised NRM agencies that not only managed resources but also provided information to others to do so. Just as NRM policies have changed and become much more complex, we have also witnessed reductions in education programmes and support, and the de-skilling of state agencies.

The response to market reforms

In countries that have gone through the water reform process there have been rapid institutional and social changes. Instead of large-scale monopolistic state agencies, funded by the taxpayer, which supplied water and treated wastes and acted in the public interest to ensure public health and support economic development (and were, in a way, both poacher and gamekeeper), the privatisation of water boards made it necessary to restructure responsibilities for governance and regulation so that pricing and regulatory tribunals were established. The roles of environmental protection agencies were also changed in order to separate the roles and responsibilities for environmental management. The state no longer bore all the sovereign risk. (This means, essentially, that we are not often dealing with what Young and McColl would call 'robust' governance schemes.) As water boards became corporatised or privatised their governing boards became aware of liability and risk management issues and promptly took action to spread or share risk with others. New intermediaries arose (contractors, lessees and lessors, insurers, international mergers and holding companies) so that there is now a lack of clarity around who is responsible when things go wrong, such as lack of supply security, pollution incidents, public health issues, etc. This has been an area characterised by much ingenuity and innovation in terms of financial vehicles, governance arrangements and risk management scattered across government institutions, water companies and small-to-medium enterprises. Furthermore, these many new intermediaries frequently have conflicting views, values and interests.[22] Medd and Marvin[23] see this as a classic case of the emergence of complexity both within and between systems.

Water is once again an excellent example of the changes under way in this area. Roe and van Eeten have described the challenges and innovations surrounding the management of water in large-scale complex systems such as the Everglades, the Columbia River Basin and the San Francisco Bay delta area in the USA. In each case a management regime is emerging 'which brings together engineers, ecologists, line operators, regulators and modellers'.[24] The complexities and risks of balancing (among other things) power generation, environmental flows and ecological restoration required the development of multi-disciplinary teams to bring the full range of required skills to bear and to begin to trade off conflicting objectives and views. Because of the complexities and uncertainties, and the totally new management problems that were being generated in the absence of established decision support frameworks, the teams resorted to gaming techniques to explore the full range of opportunities and solutions. This situation is merely going to worsen as time goes by and as more and more of our urban and industrial infrastructure becomes more and more interdependent. With the development of small-scale water recycling plants, micro-turbines for power generation, co-generation plants and other forms of distributed infrastructure there is a growing interdependency between water, electricity, gas and oil as sources of water and energy.[25] Equally, the ability to trade electricity spot prices on hot days (when air conditioning is in great demand) – and when some of that electricity is generated by hydro-electric power plants – means that there is a very close connection between market forces and factors such as environmental flows in rivers downstream of dams. This growing interpenetration of complex infrastructure, market forces and the environment increases the complexity of the management challenges. What is going on here is the development of collaborative natural- and social-science-based management, which attempts to find solutions for landscape-scale problems.[26]

Integrated catchment and water management

Some of this self-same trend is seen in the huge increase in the number of Integrated Catchment Management (ICM) plans and Integrated Water Resource Management Plans (IWRM). As we have seen these can, and should, be seen as the frameworks that sit around trading activities. We are reframing the water and NRM debate to build more ecological realism: building in catchment- and watershed-scale management plans in the context of social and economic forces and incorporating consultative processes to take a more inclusive view of the many values of water. This trend has deep historical roots.[27] It requires a radical rethink of the institutional framework in which we manage water, particularly in a world in which water markets are so common. National responses to this challenge vary depending on the particular political and social and economic policy context in each case.[28] In this respect Australia is an unusual example in that it has the Murray–Darling Basin Commission

(MDBC), an intergovernmental body set up specifically to manage the water resources of the Basin across State and Territory borders. The first water agreement to share water between the Australian States was signed in 1914, so the MDBC has a long history.[29] The MDBC uses a highly consultative process of ICM and has presided over a long-term process of water reform in the Basin. The events in the Murray–Darling Basin have been complex and politically charged, and the process of debate and reform continues. In a way it is a classic case of the tensions and trade-offs required to put ICM or IWRM in place: attempting to balance the various values placed on water with social, economic and political factors in a democratic system. International experience with ICM plans is mixed, with some claiming that we are actually (again) confusing means with ends. Wallace[30] would prefer that rather than focus on the process we focus on realistic targets, highlighting barriers to achievement and working to overcome them. I think others would agree with him.[31] The path to greater sustainability and the rational use and management of water resources is a work in progress; much has been learned, but we have a long way to go.

Integrated approaches to catchment and resource management (ICM and IRM) are widely used around the world as a means of bringing together information, resource users and managers, community interests and policy groups to achieve more sustainable and unified outcomes, and to attempt to manage market externalities. Bellamy and Johnson[32] listed the motives for IRM as follows:

- Degradation of land, water and vegetation resources in rural areas
- Government commitments to a range of national strategies and treaties requiring on-ground action by local communities
- Fragmentation of decision making across numerous public agencies and industry bodies
- Trends towards the devolution of stewardship of natural resources
- Certification of the ecological integrity of rural commodities as an increasing market force
- Increasing need for multiple use management and the diverse values placed on natural resources
- Increasing community expectations for involvement and higher standards of accountability and transparency

Tackling these 'wicked' problems is a major challenge for trained resource managers and ecologists, and an even bigger challenge for laypersons in the community. The IRM process is still largely experimental and does not always succeed; none the less the aim is to create and improve community ownership of management strategies, improve awareness of key processes, foster the development of new institutional arrangements and establish an ongoing participatory process. In many cases the conditions for successful collective co-management of common pool resources outlined above are not met.[33] Consequently, sustainable resource management is not achieved.

In some jurisdictions ICM is a legislative requirement and the regional catchment boards or committees established under the ICM process have statutory powers. Some are able to set legislative targets for stocks and flows. In other cases ICM is merely a stated policy goal. Fragmentation has long been an issue – in terms of a multiplicity of single-issue approaches to resource use, in terms of disciplinary conflict and in terms of institutional mandates. In many cases institutional arrangements and boundaries between special interest groups make integrated solutions difficult to achieve.[34] Whatever the particular status of the local groups, the intent is clear: to produce agreed and integrated resource management plans that have strong local and regulatory support. The goal is a bold and courageous one and the overall picture is mixed. In some cases the means (the process) becomes an end in itself and little is achieved other than endless meetings.[35] Many landholders do not merely want empowerment through access to information; rather, they want expert advice and assistance with the implementation of sustainable and viable solutions.

The water reform process in Australia has seen the establishment of both privatised water companies (for the supply of both urban water and irrigation water supplies) and various kinds of regional or catchment-based management authorities (CMAs). The differing mandates and governance purposes of these entities can be a source of conflict. Privatised water companies are beholden to their shareholders and are required to maximise shareholder value. Urban and agricultural enterprises, which depend on water for profit, are focused on how much water there is and how to obtain more, either through more dams and infrastructure or through increased recycling. CMAs, on the other hand, are focused more on other values and capitals, particularly public good assets and natural capital. This can lead to conflicting goals and purposes.

In the Australian context the water reform process has been overseen by the Council of Australian Governments (COAG): the council of the Commonwealth Prime Minister and the State Premiers. Financial incentives provided by the Commonwealth drove the States to comply with more open and economically efficient policies around NRM. To be able to trade an asset on the market requires both title and secure access, so the development of water markets has been accompanied by a series of reforms to the land and water tenure and water allocation acts. Title to land and water has been separated and, in an environment where drought and flood ensure great variation in entitlements from year to year, the allocation process has been changed to a guaranteed proportion of the available runoff. Thus the advent of effective trading regimes requires a number of policy and legal changes. As with the UK water reforms, there have been knock-on effects. Security and securitisation is an issue. There is some nervousness on the part of mortgage lenders if the productive base of farms in arid areas (their water allocations) can be traded away separately from the land. In this case there is an issue of the remaining value of the land asset. Similarly, there is considerable nervousness on the part of many water users because of the possibility of large-scale water trading within and between catchments. Water is wealth for the community, so entire communities could be seriously disadvantaged if large fractions of their water were traded away. This is precisely why Commonwealth intervention has again been required to encourage the Australian States to engage in a national water market. In addition, the A$500M environmental flows allocation for the Murray River has proved to be difficult to find. Communities are reluctant to trade away their rights to water.

Localism and regionalism: management at the meso-scale

What is emerging from the shadows is a concept of adaptive environmental management that uses markets and other regulatory instruments at regional scales and which engages a learning community. The challenge is to assemble and manage natural resources, together with agriculture and urban settlements, in a sustainable manner. Bringing socioeconomic considerations into play in a 'triple bottom line' calculation adds extra dimensions of complexity through the interaction of factors such as transport links, energy and water distribution networks, infrastructure and enterprises of various kinds, and the reach of capital. These are the definitive 'wicked problems' of Dovers because of uncertainty and ignorance, overlapping scales, and novel management and policy options. The final level of complexity involves the rediscovery of Bateson's work in the context of individuals, families and communities as reflexive learning entities, particularly in the light of the technological advances in mobile and personal communications. Vera John-Steiner[36] has written of creative collaboration where individuals and communities together create their futures. Overall, then, what is emerging is a highly complex recursive and evolving epistemology involving science, individuals and communities with an overall goal of adaptive management and sustainability. We must pay heed to the social construction of mind and the possibilities that this presents.[37]

What is relevant here is the concept of local communities as the basis of what might be called eco-localism.[38] Employing local support and commitment to build a community economy with a sense of place is an idea that has been around for many years[39] and has gone by a number of names. The basic idea has been to espouse the advantages of local self-sufficiency or at least local dematerialisation and reuse and recycling. This puts a radically modern spin on the self organised, collective management institutions that (with the right institutional arrangements) produce sustainable resource management. This is an argument about scale, place and social capital, which is certainly applicable in developing countries. Eco-localism asserts the importance of local sustainability as opposed to the large-scale globalised enterprises, which become separated from local concerns and focus more on profit, global finance and market share. It has been possible to use the concepts of natural capital, footprint analysis and regional stocks and flows assessment to assess the sustainability of alternative regional development paths through models that compare these analyses to changes in quality of life.[40] Certainly, the trend, even in developed Western countries, is towards regionalisation and devolution; with the rise of the information age and the speed of communications and transport, smaller enterprises can be established almost anywhere. Many authors are beginning to foresee the rise of local and regional clusters and new, more distributed and decentralised economies, which have the potential to be more sustainable environmentally, socially and economically.[41] The tendency towards subsidiarity and regional economic development is driving similar trends,[42] although we are still in the realm of 'weak' sustainability.

There is no doubt that what we are seeing is a major change in paradigms. Economics and ecology are struggling to come to terms with valuation problems; individuals, communities and institutions are being required to be more adaptive in a world of complexity, change and uncertainty. In a commentary to celebrate the tenth anniversary of the journal *Ecological Economics*, Gowdy and Carbonell describe the big changes that have occurred in the past decade in the way economists look at the natural world and ecologists look at the economy; a change brought about by the evident interaction of the anthroposphere and the biosphere.[43] We are the first species to show strong global interaction at this scale, so we are very much making this up as we go along. There are no precedents to guide us. They assert that science has 'entered that age of the breakdown of disciplinary boundaries' and argue that although this is easier for some natural sciences because it does not involve a rethink of most basic assumptions, the consilience of biology and economics is proving much more difficult. They place a lot of the blame on economists, who have failed to come to grips with the realities of complex systems and strong recursive non-linearity in the world. Much environmental degradation can be seen as a form of 'tragedy of the commons' brought about by the Prisoner's Dilemma problem[44] and this has institutional implications for knowledge management, information flows and a much more deliberative and adaptive strategy. This point has been further taken up by Wilson and Howarth,[45] who espouse a deliberative strategy for the valuation of ecosystem and other forms of capital. If monetary equivalents are not to be obtained then it will require a debate about social equity to solve some of these most difficult problems. They see discourse-based methods with groups of people as an adjunct to the other methods discussed above. Finally, to link back to themes introduced previously, the development of ecological economics has brought about a real 'postnormal' science, fully engaged with society and evolving new transdisciplinary techniques to solve some of the most difficult issues of the day.[46]

Multiple-attribute decision making

> Implementation of an ecosystem approach to NRM requires evaluation of a broad array of ecological services in a multidimensional, community-based watershed approach that empowers people to make informed management decisions.

So wrote Tony Prato in an introduction to a paper on multiple-attribute decision-making approaches to NRM.[47] Multiple-attribute decision analysis is but one example of a large body of work on multi-criterion analysis or MCA. MCA is a way of trading off various kinds of incommensurate values as part of a non-market valuation process. It avoids the problems with contingent valuation, cost–benefit analyses and the other valuation techniques discussed earlier because it does not require the assignment of monetary values to ecological goods and services (which is a matter of ethical debate) and it allows preferences and cultural biases to be specifically included and weighted in the consultation process. Basically, MCA is a way of ranking a series of options based on various criteria and weights. The criteria may be of various kinds; monetary, ecological, and social or cultural. Various kinds of algebraic MCA models then allow these criteria and weights to be combined to produce a set of ranked options. The process is open, involving dialogue and debate around the criteria and weights. MCA techniques have been used to derive management plans for landscapes, rivers and farming systems of various kinds.[48] This requires a conceptual model of the problem at hand, so that the attributes to be weighted are relevant to the options chosen. If this is not the case then management actions based on the attributes will not achieve the desired ends.

Notwithstanding the problems with cost–benefit and other more financial analyses, attempts are being made to come up with realistic recommendations for landscape renewal by using these techniques. In the case of the dryland salinity discussed earlier in the context of the Murray–Darling Basin in Australia, Hajkowicz and Young used benefit–cost analyses to examine a variety of revegetation and landscape renewal options.[49] What they showed was that over large areas revegetation was not economically feasible because it would be necessary to revegetate as much as 50% of the landscape to control the dryland salinity problem and to save only 3% of the land. They concluded that it was necessary to target remediation plans so as to save carefully chosen productive, ecological and infrastructure assets in these catchments. In some cases cost–benefit analysis of various landscape remediation scenarios are combined with environmental benefits indices based on MCA-like techniques. The resulting landscape investment models can also be used to carefully target investment in remediation projects. I discussed the problems of nutrient movement, erosion and sediment generation in catchments in earlier chapters, and specifically discussed the case study of the Murray–Darling Basin at some length. We know a lot about the sources and sinks of salt, nutrients and sediments in the Basin. This has now been the focus of an analysis to target remediation efforts based on an evaluation of a range of attributes including salinity, water yield, nitrogen and phosphorus runoff, stream sediment concentrations, soil erosion and carbon sequestration. These attributes have been used to define an optimum investment pattern within the confines of a programme budget.[50] The strategic landscape investment model showed that highly targeted investment in just 4% of the area studied in New South Wales was capable of producing significant benefits. Again, this analysis was based around a good deal of prior knowledge about pattern and process in the study area. Nevertheless it does show that economic and MCA techniques can be used to effectively target remediation activities.

Complexity and restoration

Pretty well this entire planet is now managed in one way or another; there are few independent pristine areas. From the equator to the poles, everywhere is affected to some degree by climate change and the global transport of various pollutants. Ultimately, restoration should be our goal: from an ethical stance, mere management and conservation is not sufficient. This is going to be a very hard task. Restoration and management require not only understanding of many fundamental processes in landscapes,[51] but also an ability to observe, understand and predict the outcomes of purposeful interventions in catchments and landscapes of various kinds. I have argued that there are some fundamental constraints on what we can know about ecological systems and that we must accept that we will always have to act on the basis of imperfect knowledge. A deeper understanding of the properties of CAS is going to be essential. The key paradigm shift has been to begin to understand how to link the local to the global: how the actions and interactions of individual agents (be they organisms or individual people) can scale up to system properties.[52] Complex systems show the emergence of often quite surprising properties. The traditional approach of science has been reductionist: to take complex entities apart and to seek simple models. CAS require a quite different approach, which attempts to understand the statistical ensemble properties of the whole system, together with all the extreme events, surprise, emergence and hysteresis that we so often see. Merely complicated answers to truly complex problems do not suffice.

The lessons for sustainability are clear and go beyond science. Human influences on the planet are largely controlled by individual choices and decisions made by people, usually acting on local knowledge. Farmers, for example, take individual decisions about paddock and farm management based on the local climate, soil types and their estimates of risk and financial success. The decision making process is complex and recursive, being based on local knowledge, on regional patterns of social, economic and ecological processes, and on higher-level emergent patterns arising from ethics, value systems and global commodity prices. All human societies have a well-defined sense of place[53] and a long-term memory of landscape and culture.[54] Giddens argues that in a world of radicalised modernism our sense of place is disembedded and fragmented because social activity is 'lifted out' of its local context and set instead in large-scale expert systems of production, transport and marketing.[55] It is easy to see how clashes can arise between different groups (e.g. farmers and conservationists) where ethics and values can differ markedly, arising as they do from different contexts and contingent histories and memories. There is a clash of 'sense giving' and 'sense receiving' even when listening to the same words.[56] Trust breaks down. Couple this with a degree of indeterminacy and risk management and the stage is set for problems.

With ideas of chaos, CAS and the rejection of pure and instrumental reason floating around in society for the past thirty years or more it is hardly surprising that the Western world has moved on beyond the modern era's reliance on concepts of reason, progress and truth. Ecological theory is based on arguments from design, and on concepts of balance and equilibrium. Thus the world of radicalised modernity as laid out by Giddens is, as he asserts, a truly radical departure from past epistemologies: a radically new synthesis is emerging. Instead of treating the world as simple, linear and seeking universals, the world is now seen as non-linear, complex and recursive. Our knowledge is partial and contingent. The modern world has seen dramatic reorganisation of the human perceptions of space and time.

Nevertheless, despite the extreme views of some 'postmodernists', who espouse total epistemological relativity, there are relationships and physical laws with great predictive power and generality. These underpin and make possible the biological world of CAS. We have good foundations to stand on and we must use what we know, even if, for now, it is partial and incomplete. In the contextual and recursive world of ecology, sociology and economics we should not expect the same degree of universality and predictive power as we see in physics; but 'physics envy' has long been a problem in biology and other related disciplines. What is emerging is a more ethical, contingent set of explanations based more on the data and on experience than on reason and physical theories.[57] As John Ralston Saul has pointed out, a truly ethical view recognises the complexity and contingency of this world – it truly is a form of systems thinking. An ethical world view is an appropriate view to hold in a world of CAS, recognising as it does context, relationship and recursive interaction. To quote Saul, ethics is 'a sense of the other and of inclusive responsibility': an adaptive epistemology based on doubt and on justice, equity and fairness. An ethical approach is also accepting of doubt and ignorance as a useful characteristic of our reality.

For the ICM process to be successful it requires clear goals and targets for on-ground outcomes, and congruence between the aims and objectives of the various players. Achieving sustainable goals at regional scales increases the level of difficulty; first, there are many players and many aims and objectives to reconcile and second, what must result from any regional resource management plan is a mosaic of land uses and environmental values. This is the challenge of designing and restoring a complex adaptive system with environmental, social and economic processes and scales overlapping in subtle and interactive ways. All this requires an adaptive management and consultation process that is able to monitor progress, learn from mistakes and move forward accordingly. We begin to see why it is so hard to do this in practice.

Norton[58] has advocated the development of a more universal Earth ethic, which attempts to bridge the gap between the two extremes of instrumental and intrinsic values, and moves beyond objectification and the rise of a globalised 'placeless' set of (largely economic) values. Norton argues that it is essential that we move beyond the arguments between adherents of the two philosophies, that we cease trying to sort types of capital and that we value the uniqueness of place. He places value in discussions and debates over possible trajectories and processes that increase resilience and suggests an 'adaptive management model as a way of understanding human-nature interactions from the viewpoint of a community adapting to a larger, changing eco-physical system'.[59] Strong sustainability and intergenerational equity are ensured through a sense of responsibility ('a sense of the other and of shared responsibility') and through monitoring of progress, deliberative processes and the inclusion of other values.

A new world order is emerging from the shadows. It is a world with a different set of values from the instrumentalist, corporatist world of globalisation, economic efficiency, profit and shareholder value. It is a more ethical world – a world of systems thinking – that recognises and indeed exploits bounded complexity and variability instead of trying to control or eliminate it. A 'triple bottom line' world requires profitability, variability, diversity and compassion. It will be a world in which CAS are understood and in some cases guided towards more sustainable futures.

NOTES

1. L. Deutsch, C. Folke and K. Skanberg. The critical natural capital of ecosystem performance as insurance for human well-being. *Ecological Economics*, **44** (2003), 205–17.
2. A. Muller. A flower in full blossom? Ecological economics at the crossroads between normal and post-normal science. *Ecological Economics*, **45** (2003), 19–27.
3. See the review of M. Borgerhoff Mulder and P. Coppolillo. *Conservation: Linking Ecology, Economics and Culture.* (Princeton, NJ: Princeton University Press, 2005) by R. L. Nadeau. Why

can't we graft a green thumb on the invisible hand. *Trends in Ecology and Evolution*, **20** (2005), 588–9.

4. K. E. Limburg *et al.* Complex systems and valuation. *Ecological Economics*, **41** (2002), 409–20.

5. S. R. Carpenter *et al.* From metaphor to measurement: resilience of what to what? *Ecosystems*, **4** (2001), 765–81.

6. A. A. Batabyal, J. R. Kahn and R. V. O'Neill. On the scarcity value of ecosystem services. *Journal of Environmental Economics and Management*, **46** (2003), 334–52.

7. M. Scheffer, F. Westley and W. Brock. Slow responses of societies to new problems: causes and costs. *Ecosystems*, **6** (2003), 493–502.

8. M. A. Janssen and S. R. Carpenter. Managing the resilience of lakes: a multi-agent modelling approach. *Conservation Ecology*, **3 (2)** (1999), 15. www.consecol.org/vol3/iss2/art15.

9. F. Schmidt-Bleek. Toward universal ecology disturbance measures: basis and outline of a universal measure. *Regulatory Toxicology and Pharmacology*, **18** (1993), 456–62.

10. For a useful review of the history and development of the ideas behind ecological modernization, see the foreword to a special journal issue: J. Murphy. Ecological modernization. *Geoforum*, **31** (2000), 1–8.

11. See U. Beck. *Risk Society: Towards a New Modernity*. (London: Sage, 1992).

12. M. J. Cohen. Risk society and ecological modernization. *Futures*, **29** (1997), 105–19.

13. D. Pepper. Sustainable development and ecological modernization: a radical homocentric perspective. *Sustainable Development*, **6** (1998), 1–7.

14. M. S. Andersen and I. Massa. Ecological modernization – origins, dilemmas and future directions. *Journal of Environmental Policy and Planning*, **2** (2000), 337–45.

15. R. Isenmann. Industrial ecology: shedding more light on its perspective of understanding nature as a model. *Sustainable Development*, **11** (2003), 143–58.

16. J. Huber. Towards industrial ecology: sustainable development as a concept of ecological modernization. *Journal of Environmental Policy and Planning*, **2** (2000), 269–85.

17. F. Hinterberger, F. Luks and F. Schmidt-Bleek. Material flows vs. 'Natural capital'. What makes an economy sustainable? *Ecological Economics*, **23** (1997), 1–14.

18. See, for example, L. H. Lovins, A. B. Lovins and P. Hawken. *Natural Capitalism: Creating the Next Industrial Revolution*. (New York: Little, Brown, 1999). L. H. Lovins and A. B. Lovins. Natural Capitalism: path to sustainability? *Corporate Environmental Strategy*, **8** (2001), 99–108.

19. J. Ehrenfeld. Industrial ecology: a new field or only a metaphor? *Journal of Cleaner Production*, **12** (2004), 825–31.

20. F. den Hond. Industrial ecology: a review. *Regional Environmental Change*, **1** (2000), 60–9. R. U. Ayres. On the life cycle metaphor: where ecology and economics diverge. *Ecological Economics*, **48** (2004), 425–38.

21. J. Hukkinen. Eco-efficiency as abandonment of nature. *Ecological Economics*, **38** (2001), 311–15. C. Hamilton. Dualism and sustainability. *Ecological Economics*, **42** (2002), 89–99.

22. C. Johnson and J. Handmer. Water supply in England and Wales: whose responsibility is it when things go wrong? *Water Policy*, **4** (2002), 345–66. W. Medd and T. Moss. Knowledge and policy frameworks for promoting sustainable water management through intermediation. EU RTD project *New intermediary services and the transformation of urban water supply and wastewater disposal systems in Europe – intermediaries*. Final report; deliverable 7.3 Contract # EVK1-CT-2002-00115. (2005). See www.irs-net.de/intermediaries.

23. W. Medd and S. Marvin. Complexity and spatiality: regions, networks and fluids in sustainable water management. In *Managing the Complex: Philosophy, Theory and Applications*, ed. K. A.

Richardson. Vol. 1 in Managing the Complex. (New York: The Information Age Publishing, 2004), pp. 491–502.

24. E. Roe and M. van Eeten. Some recent innovations in improving ecosystem functions and service reliability. *Global Environmental Change*, **13** (2003), 155–8.

25. M. Heller. Interdependencies in civil infrastructure systems. *The Bridge* **31** (4) (Winter 2001). (Washington, DC.: National Academy of Engineering, 2001).

26. S. A. Mullner, W. A. Hubert and T. A. Wesche. Evolving paradigms for landscape scale renewable resource management in the United States. *Environmental Science and Policy*, **4** (2001), 39–49. E. Roe and M. van Eeten. Reconciling ecosystem rehabilitation and service reliability mandates in large technical systems: findings and implications of three major US ecosystem management initiatives for managing human-dominated aquatic-terrestrial systems. *Ecosystems*, **5** (2002), 509–28.

27. J. D. Priscoli. Water and civilization: using history to reframe water policy debates and to build new ecological realism. *Water Policy*, **1** (1998), 623–36.

28. R. M. Saleth and A. Dinar. Institutional changes in global water sector: trends, patterns and implications. *Water Policy*, **2** (2000), 175–99.

29. D. J. Blackmore. Murray-Darling Basin Commission: a case study in integrated catchment management. *Water Science and Technology*, **32** (No. 5–6) (1995), 15–25.

30. K. J. Wallace. Confusing means with ends: a manager's reflections on experience in agricultural landscapes of Western Australia. *Ecological Management and Restoration*, **4** (2003), 23–8.

31. F. C. van Zyl. Integrated Catchment management: is it wishful thinking or can it succeed? *Water Science and Technology*, **32** (No. 5–6) (1995), 27–35.

32. J. A. Bellamy and A. K. L. Johnson. Integrated resource management: moving from rhetoric to practice in Australian agriculture. *Environmental Management*, **25** (2000), 265–80.

33. E. Ostrom. *Governing the Commons: the Evolution of Institutions for Collective Action.* (Cambridge: Cambridge University Press, 1990).

34. A. K. L. Johnson, D. Shrubsole and M. Merrin. Integrated catchment management in northern Australia. *Land Use Policy*, **13** (1996), 303–16.

35. K. J. Wallace. Confusing means with ends: a manager's reflections on experience in agricultural landscapes of Western Australia. *Ecological Management and Restoration*, **4** (2003), 23–8.

36. V. John-Steiner. Creative collaboration. (Oxford: Oxford University Press, 2000).

37. J. Bobryk. The social construction of mind and the future of cognitive science. *Foundations of Science*, **7** (2002), 481–95.

38. For an excellent review of this topic, see F. Curtis. Eco-localism and sustainability. *Ecological Economics*, **46** (2003), 83–102.

39. Curtis provides an excellent historical review. Some of the key references are: P. Ekins. *The Living Economy: a New Economics in the Making.* (London: Routledge, 1986). R. Douthwaite. *Short Circuit: Strengthening Local Economies for Security in an Unstable World.* (Totnes, England: Green Books, 1996). H. Daly and J. Cobb. *For the Common Good: Redirecting the Economy toward Community, the Environment and a Sustainable Future.* (Boston, MA: Beacon Press, 1994). D. Korten. *The Post-Corporate World: Life after Capitalism.* (San Francisco, CA: Berret-Koehler Publishers, 1999).

40. C. Collados and T. P. Duane. Natural capital and the quality of life: a model for evaluating the sustainability of alternative regional development paths. *Ecological Economics*, **30** (1999), 441–60.

41. G. R. Walter. Economics, ecology-based communities, and sustainability. *Ecological Economics*, **42** (2002), 81–7. H. P. Wallner. Towards sustainable development of industry: networking, complexity and eco-clusters. *Journal of Cleaner Production*, **7** (1999), 49–58.

42. D. Gibbs. Urban sustainability and economic development in the United Kingdom: exploring the contradictions. *Cities*, **14** (1997), 203–8. D. Gibbs. Ecological modernization, regional economic development and regional development agencies. *Geoforum*, **31** (2000), 9–19. I. Deas and K. G. Ward. From the 'new localism' to the 'new regionalism'? The implications of regional development agencies for city-region relations. *Political Geography*, **19** (2000), 273–92.

43. J. M. Gowdy and A. F. Carbonell. Towards consilience between biology and economics: the contribution of Ecological Economics. *Ecological Economics*, **29** (1999), 337–48.

44. G. L. Cannibal and G. M. Winnard. Managing the tragedy: an inter-disciplinary model for managing the environment as interacting chaotic hierarchy. *Futures*, **33** (2001), 147–60.

45. M. A. Wilson and R. B. Howarth. Discourse-based valuation of ecosystem services: establishing fair outcomes through group deliberation. *Ecological Economics*, **41** (2002), 431–43.

46. A. Muller. A flower in full blossom? Ecological economics at the crossroads between normal and post-normal science. *Ecological Economics*, **45** (2003), 19–27.

47. T. Prato. Multiple attribute decision analysis for ecosystem management. *Ecological Economics*, **30** (1999), 207–22.

48. T. Prato. Multiple attribute evaluation of landscape management. *Journal of Environmental Management*, **60** (2000), 325–37. G. Strassert and T. Prato. Selecting farming systems using a new multiple criteria decision model: the balancing and ranking method. *Ecological Economics*, **40** (2002), 268–77. T. Prato. Multiple-attribute evaluation of ecosystem management for the Missouri River system. *Ecological Economics*, **45** (2003), 297–309.

49. S. Hajkowicz and M. D. Young. An economic analysis of revegetation for dryland salinity control on the Lower Eyre peninsula in South Australia. *Land Degradation and Development*, **13** (2002), 417–28.

50. S. Hajkowicz *et al.* The strategic landscape investment model: a tool for mapping optimal environmental expenditure. *Environmental Modelling and Software*, **20** (2005), 1251–62.

51. R. V. O'Neill. Recovery in complex ecosystems. *Journal of Aquatic Ecosystem Stress and Recovery*, **6** (1999), 181–7.

52. J. H. Holland. *Emergence: from Chaos to Order*. (Reading, MA: Addison-Wesley, 1998).

53. G. Seddon. *Sense of Place: a Response to Environment, the Swan Coastal Plain*. (Nedlands, WA.: University of Western Australia Press, 1972). George Seddon. *Landprints: Reflections on Place and Landscape*. (Cambridge: Cambridge University Press, 1997).

54. S. Schama. *Landscape and Memory*. (London: HarperCollins, 1995).

55. A. Giddens. *The Consequences of Modernity*. (Stanford, CA: Stanford University Press, 1990). David Harvey. *The Condition of Postmodernity*. (Oxford: Blackwell, 1989).

56. M. Polanyi. *Knowing and Being*. (London: Routledge and Kegan Paul, 1969).

57. E. Fox Keller. *Making Sense of Life: Explaining Biological Development with Models, Metaphors and Machines*. (Cambridge, MA: Harvard University Press, 2002). J. R. Saul. *On Equilibrium*. (Toronto: Penguin Books, 2001).

58. B. G. Norton. Biodiversity and environmental values: in search of a universal earth ethic. *Biodiversity and Conservation*, **9** (2000), 1029–44.

59. Ibid., p. 1043.

20 Community, capacity, collaboration and innovation

The ability to understand and manage complex problems, the role of individual and community capacity: innovation, integration and synthesis, future communities.

An ethical, system-based approach that acknowledges many ways of knowing is a very new way to operate for many people. It is essential to examine and be open to the position of the *other*: other beliefs, cultures, values and ways of knowing. This is the only truly ethical position to take. It is so much easier to argue from a narrower position of simplistic belief and conviction, which provides a false sense of certainty and security.[1] This is particularly true if instrumental reason[2] is employed (and it often is). The acknowledgement of the need for an ethical system framework places a strong emphasis on listening, on relationships[3] and on learning and adapting[4] at the levels of individuals, communities and institutions. Working as part of a complex adaptive system requires individuals and institutions to be facilitators rather than the more usually observed *modus operandi* of command and control. Indeed, and exactly as Handy foretold,[5] this is an age of unreason, of choice and flexibility, of the importance of little things and the effects of small decisions writ large. Nevertheless this is also the age of inclusion and ethics, so even small decisions must be couched in the landscape of context, consultation, networks and relationships.[6] Given the uneven and distributed nature of both biodiversity in the biosphere and cultures and values in the anthroposphere, this argues for the importance of subsidiarity and maximising local and regional autonomy. Consultative and facilitatory behaviour implies a willingness to surrender sovereignty and place your fate in the hands of others. This will not happen without a good deal of trust, something that takes time to develop because trust is only built up through continuous reinforcement by behaviour that is ethical. So there is a paradox here: in a world that is changing very rapidly, relationships and trust are only built up relatively slowly. Building trust and relationships therefore requires some priority and effort in a world where some act in haste out of conviction.

Operating in this new world challenges the capacity of individuals and groups. All our lives are journeys of growth and development; we continuously experience new things and learn from them as we grow.[7] Because of the close linkages between work and the rest of our lives, the personal journey is what Andrew Olivier would call the working journey;[8] in addition, the individuals are inevitably part of groups and therefore their growth is to be seen in the context of institutions and communities. This is very much the approach that Bateson first proposed and applied in the context of family counselling.[9] Again, there is a form of double democratisation in operation here because the process of growth and learning must go on both at the level of the individual and also the institution or community – even the nation – and the two inevitably inter-act. Porter[10] was among the first to write about 'clusters': groups of industries and communities that became globally significant and competitive through the development of unique regional strategies. The same idea can be applied to regional clusters dedicated to a more sustainable future. Fukuyama[11] has shown how trust and networks at the community level – social capital – are essential for healthy and thriving communities.[12] So if we are to tackle some of the really wicked problems, particularly those at the regional scale, then we will need to build capacity and social capital at the individual and community levels, taking regional factors and accidents of geography, history and climate into account. It is important to reiterate that wealth is an important driver of sustainability – poverty makes poor choices – so any move forward has to combine wealth gen-eration as well as the other forms of capital.

People and institutions grow at different speeds and can easily fall out of step. If the growth rates of personal and community capacity differ then what inevitably happens is that people leave and go elsewhere to find challenge and reward. Key employees and participants in the magic circle leave to find new challenges to suit their capacity at the time. Thus the 'brain drain' is not just an international issue; it is an issue between and within all kinds of communities and institutions. This is a major issue in many third world countries. It is also an important issue for rural and regional communities in developed Western countries. Loss of capacity to urban centres is a significant problem; de-skilled communities lack innovative and productive capacity. They also lack the ability to respond to changing times. There is therefore an urgent need to rethink the relationships between the urban and the rural, particularly when most of the 'green' NGOs have their main constituencies in urban populations and their objectivist conservation values do not reflect the more utilitarian rural values.

The growth in personal capacity over time was studied extensively by Elliott Jaques. He and his co-workers devised a model for understanding work in terms of problem complexity and the time span of discretion (before it is possible to judge outcomes) and also to map the capacity of individuals to deal with these different levels of ambiguity and uncertainty as it develops over time.[13] Platt argues that this personal growth is an essential human characteristic, an invol-untary search for meaning and personal identity.[14] As defined by the scheme developed by Jaques and others, work levels I–III are operational work, making things, producing things, project managing, directing business units; levels IV–V are concerned with weaving the strands together and shaping the future of organisations though strategy and vision. Levels VI and VII are concerned with the most complex tasks and those with the longest time frames, having an impact between 10 years and 50 years or more into the future. They are about shaping societal values. These are the tasks of national and international corporate citizenship, of revealing and previewing a variety of possible futures, and of building relationships that create and sustain a shared future for multiple stakeholders and diverse value systems.[15] It is vital for communities either to possess these higher level capacities or to have access to them.[16]

The capacity of individuals grows with time at different and predictable rates. Capacity here is about an ability to cope with uncertainty and complexity, and an ability to 'think systems' and juggle future options. We can all do this to some degree but some are much better at it than others. This is not about making value judgements around whether higher capacity is better; people are different and mature at different rates. Society needs all sorts in order to function effectively. Capacity, it is generally believed, cannot be taught; either people grow and mature so that they can handle uncertainty and cope with complexity or they do not. There is, however, the possibility that capacity can be learned with age.[17] Certainly there are changes in cognitive function as people age, and these are not always for the worse. From my own experience, what increases capacity is not book learning but a complex adaptive systems view and an ability to be a context-sensitive observer of events. So it is possible that capacity is about being able to recognise and remember contexts, and what the appropriate action was in a given context. This is a skill that can, at least, be encouraged, if not taught. Certainly, mentoring of individuals and communities can increase sensitivity to context and complexity in many situations. In a way capacity is rather like manners: both can be taught (or at least encouraged) and both require sensitivity to the 'other' in context. Capacity, though, is not a prescribed set of behaviours, but a flexible and adaptive set of responses to constantly evolving contexts.

Now it is possible to criticise all this and assert that all that Jaques and his co-workers have come up with is yet another modernist totalising scheme to place people in pigeonholes and to judge and order the lives of individuals. To some extent I agree. Far better, it might be argued, in a world of complexity and highly radicalised modernity, to give individuals the skills to cope for themselves so that they can find their own ways through the maze of relationships and tasks that life throws at us. This is the kind of approach that Bateson, I am sure, would have favoured – to see the individual in context and to provide each person with the skills to recognise, name, understand and explain to others what is going on in and around his or her life. In this way it is possible to build a self-healing community – a self-organising community if you like – created by empowering the agents. Communities of all kinds must treasure, reward and retain their high-capacity people: loss of capacity over time leads to dysfunctional communities and loss of all forms of capital. Florida has written about the competitive advantages of creative communities and classes in society, and has shown that there is no substitute for talent, tolerance and technology.[18] Rycroft and Kash have discussed the role of non-linear creativity and network learning in innovation, together with the importance of integration and synthetic decision making.[19] Institutions and communities face a challenge in terms of leadership, capacity and collaboration if we are to solve some of the most pressing problems around sustainability. There was a time when it was possible to manage through focusing largely on internal management and community issues (work levels I through II or III in the Jaques framework). Now we live in a more complex world, which demands outcomes and more ethical solutions the challenges lie at higher work levels IV, V and VI (perhaps even VII, the sphere of global citizenship): we have to look further ahead and around, and manage upwards and outwards just as much as we do downwards and inwards. As the global context becomes more complex, so leadership becomes more critical in terms of being able to translate and integrate that context and interpret it for others.

What most NRM and research agencies – even at regional levels – do not yet understand is that they are now required to operate in a world of changing level VI and VII networks and institutions.[20] Globalisation of enterprises and markets ensures that it is no longer possible to manage successfully at level II or III. As time has gone by over the past 30 years the complexity of the management tasks for all institutions has greatly increased. Water management agencies have changed from being merely dam builders and water deliverers, to agencies that must now manage multiple capitals – including financial, environmental and social outcomes – in a globalised environment. Privatised water companies now have global reach. They own and manage distributed and interconnected infrastructure incorporating IT systems, energy generation and water supply and recycling plants, even media and network content. Risk profiles have changed and become much more complex. All institutions require level IV 'weavers' and interpreters to succeed in this environment. Lack of this level of work in organisations exposes institutions to greatly increased risks. Rycroft and Kash show how the lack of such a level of network complexity acts as a barrier to innovation in this globalised world.[21]

Innovation: generating new ideas

As Andrew Olivier[22] points out, this brave new world of complexity, values and 'wicked problems' is a particularly difficult cultural challenge for many professions, not just for science. To be successful at finding out new things and solving problems is something that requires constant practice, long training, intense focus and dedication. Many scientists like to work in relative isolation from the world of relationships, politics and compromise. Scientists like to think science is value-free and totally objective. Of course, it is not, but nevertheless most successful science is done at work levels I–III by breaking complex problems up into bite-sized chunks and focusing on soluble problems one by one.[23] Successful careers in science are built around successful problem solving, and in deliberately picking the right problems at the right time. Successful careers in science are not usually built around lengthy and unproductive struggles with complexity, uncertainty and indeterminate problems. That means that there must be a bridge from the science at bench level to the vision and management of science institutions at the turning of the new millennium as society and governments require more and more of the funding for science to come from external sources. The commoditisation of science and many other professions, and the demands from society to look out more and focus on outcomes relevant to social and economic needs, has been a real driver for change on the culture and behaviour of many professions. Trust in networks becomes a major issue here as society becomes more and more sceptical and demanding, driven as it is by both cultural and technological changes making access to information much more widespread. There is a now an active debate about both the means and the ends of many contentious research programmes and technologies. The frequent reliance by the professions on instrumental reason does not sit well with many parts of society. Ethics demands that we focus on outcomes rather than on the shorter-term means to frequently ill-defined ends. There is a real communication challenge to be able to build trust between those working at different levels of work and complexity, and between institutions and the community.

Science, innovation and the search for sustainability have become part of a larger enterprise where we seek non-zero sum games and increasing returns spread throughout a network of relationships. This requires improved coordination between entities and individual and organisational learning throughout the network.[24] Right now there is still too much focus on short-term, tactical innovation. Throughout the commoditisation of science – with its short-term focus on rates of return and shareholder value – there is a need to focus on the longer term. At the enterprise and community level, although there must be a focus on wealth creation and profitability, there must also be a focus on building new options and sustainable enterprises for the future: the 'third horizon' of Baghai, Coley and White.[25] Too much focus on today's problems and on tomorrow's returns ensures that we do not end up with a suitably adaptive strategy to meet future challenges, and that the mould of today's imperatives is never broken. This is what all communities require, those far-sighted and iconoclastic individuals who can see farther than most[26] and who can break out of the tyranny of the present. Even so, these individuals must obtain wider ownership of their visions, and this requires work to ensure local adoption and acceptance, capturing the benefits of the vision in the short term and paving the way for future growth and development of all. Robert Wright has written about the importance of the growth of non-zero sum games: games in which all are winners rather than the more usual pattern of winners and losers.[27] The development of non-zero solutions to the coming bottleneck is going to be critical.

So, are we organising ourselves to meet the challenge? Around the world there is growing interest in collaboration models, linkage programmes, etc., associated with a move towards greater collaboration in science, business and government and the establishment of various kinds of collaborative fora, networks and institutions. Level IV entities are being constructed in response to need. Many of these initiatives are designed to connect teams of researchers with users and those able to deliver outcomes for private and public benefit. For example, in Australia there are Co-operative Research Centres (CRCs), there are Network Centres of Excellence in Canada, and the Vth and VIth Frameworks require extensive collaboration between individuals, research institutes and countries in the European Union.[28] We are also seeing the development of a number of major collaborative research and management programmes; some pertinent examples are the Chesapeake Bay programme and the Comprehensive Everglades Restoration Plan programme in the USA, the RELU programme in the UK, and projects such as the Moreton Bay Waterways and Catchment Partnership in Australia.[29]

Throughout the Western world we are seeing a number of common economic trends, all centred on increased economic efficiency and effectiveness: privatisation, private–public partnerships, and the 'third way' are being combined with innovative models of regional outsourcing and service delivery. Public–private partnerships (PPPs) are all the rage in many areas, such as the water industry, health and education. Too much emphasis on competitive market structures can hinder innovation. Creative collaboration within and between networks seems to lead to better outcomes – and to the competitiveness of nations.[30] Many of the bigger multi-disciplinary research and management programmes are therefore now characterised by complex partnerships between government agencies and jurisdictions, universities, and private companies. These level IV or V partnerships commonly take 3–5 years to establish successfully as the various actors align their aspirations and values. The fluidity and greater complexity of relationships is becoming a serious management challenge. They are leading to an increased complexity and workload both for the network participants themselves and for staff in other parts of institutions involved. Going down this road is a challenge for all.

There is, therefore, a focus on new models of excellence – models that directly link discovery to outcome in a network culture. Higher-level leadership calls for the communication of hope for the future and the development of new sets of values. A new model for science excellence is also emerging: not just excellence in science but also excellence in delivery, adoption, innovation and economic/environmental impact *and in working with and through others to achieve these ends*. This trend requires new and more complex modes of operation, changes in old (often monolithic) institutions and new modes of thought and behaviour.

All of these external trends and institutional responses raise issues of how institutions identify and work with effective collaborators in a changed marketplace. It should be remembered that organisations are themselves complex adaptive systems with very complex cultures and institutional dynamics.[31] Basically, this is about the whole business of establishing relationships and working in teams, and the issues of congruence between behaviours, structures and desired outcomes. The necessary governance and accountability structures must also be developed to encourage the required behaviour and support the individuals at the front line. Hierarchical rather than facilitatory organisations find it difficult to cope with individuals who wander across institutional silos, creating new relationships and transdisciplinary solutions to complex problems. It usually ends in tears unless the organisation changes.[32] We simply have to recognise that it is very difficult to 'manage' (in any traditional sense) non-linear creativity and innovation in synthetic, transforming networks.[33] But we must find a way.

Integration and synthesis: achieving outcomes

Problem identification and solution increasingly requires synthetic analysis and decision making. Integration and synthesis within and between disciplines are major issues. This is the problem of changing from single research groups (which may be in discovery mode and in a strongly competitive environment with contestable funding) to larger teams and outcomes with true integration of outputs and delivery against a larger goal or outcome but with explicit milestones (sometimes set by non-scientists) along the way. I have already mentioned programmes like the Rural Economy and Land Use (RELU) programme in the UK, set up as a response to the foot and mouth disease outbreak. If this is to be successful then integration between agricultural and food science, ecology, hydrology, regulatory policy, sociology and market economics is going to be essential. Simply grouping activities together into a co-ordinated programme of disciplinary research does not achieve the required level of integration for the new and more complex environment. Integration is, in essence, quite a difficult social process, which requires building effective communication and trust between groups to facilitate a shared understanding of problems, values, vocabularies and meanings. It takes time and effort to achieve success, and that means really working hard at communications and sharing of knowledge and prejudices. The challenge is to link disparate 'communities of practice' together into a single 'community of interest'. Reaching a common understanding of shared goals and objectives is difficult because of 'symmetries of ignorance' caused by their respective cultures and their use of different knowledge systems.[34] We constantly underestimate the difficulty of this task.

Science and other communities carry much implicit knowledge. Communication between institutions, communities and cultures is not easy. Each group sees reality in different ways and there is often a gap between the 'sense giving' of one group and the 'sense receiving' of another with the same statements. In building a 'community of interest' allowance must always be made for other interests, values, cultures and beliefs. Researchers have a habit of becoming too close to the science and not being sensitive to the needs and beliefs of others. Hubris and 'not seeing the wood for the trees' is a common behaviour pattern. A purchaser–provider model of science requires knowledgeable purchasers and ethical providers. We are slowly but surely moving beyond purchaser–provider models to true partnerships where all players are prepared to surrender some sovereignty and resources to a combined entity to achieve a common goal and shared benefits. This is not easy to achieve and there are many failures along the way, often because individuals and institutions place their interests above those of the group.

Although many argue that excellence in scientific discovery is a matter for lone 'boffins', in fact the process of creativity and discovery is a team effort. Scientists commonly use informal global networks[35] and meetings to share, develop and peer-review ideas. No human being is an island; social interaction is essential for the development and honing of new ideas. Creativity requires both social interaction and periods of introspection. The key aspects of creativity are periods of quiet withdrawal, time to 'daydream' and ponder new ideas and the time to make linkages across disciplines. Unfortunately in the commercialisation of science the focus on outcomes has merely added more and more jobs into the individual's job jar. The creative scientist is now required to think up new ideas, work them through, write papers and patent ideas, network extensively, market the ideas and ensure the delivery of outcomes to society. If this whole process is not managed carefully then creative individuals initially end up working outrageous hours. Either they suffer burn out, to the detriment of their health and personal relationships, or the creativity suffers – or both. One real issue has been that different institutions are different distances down the path of change to network cultures. Many are, as yet, not ready to make the bold step into a more uncertain and fluid world. This is particularly true of hierarchical and bureaucratic institutions that do not trust individuals to operate without strong checks and balances, and those institutions bound up with strong legal frameworks. Inertia is strong in such cases. Many of the most creative people now operate in this environment outside of institutional restrictions as lone 'brains for hire'.

Recent work on team sizes, network structures and the creation of creative enterprises in the arts and the sciences – including Broadway theatres – shows some common attributes.[36] Network performance is very much influenced by the number of 'old timers' (experienced people with team experience and many contacts) versus newcomers. Successful and high-performance teams had a judicious mix of innovative newcomers and highly networked 'old timers'. Teams consisting entirely of 'old timers' tended to be conservative and set in their ways, so a mix of newcomers provided spice and new ideas. Teams made up entirely of newcomers performed poorly, having poor networks and more isolated clusters. Teams with the right mix of skills underwent a 'phase transition' or 'tipping point' as the number of 'old timers' increased so that the networks coalesced and became more interconnected. As we have already seen, many collaboration networks are 'small world' or scale-free, and recruitment around hubs (which is what is going on here) produces a kind of 'rich-get-richer' effect.[37] High-performance teams require a judicious mix of experience and new talent. Although Broadway seemingly reached a steady state in its collaboration and network structure in the 1930s – and has stayed roughly constant ever since with about seven members per team – economics, ecology, social psychology and astronomy do not yet seem to have found the required optimal number. Teams in these areas are mostly in the range of two to four team members and still growing.

Network cultures built on trust encourage and facilitate parties to come and go as the goals change over time. The initial discussions must be about the nature of the challenge and what kind of team structure we need to solve it, rather than about narrow sectoral interests and revenue sharing. This is a reflection of a greater fluidity, of a more complex view of the balance of risk and return. Such programmes become living, evolving structures built around skilled individuals with adherence to common goals. It is really important to include a number of high-capacity 'old timers' with wide networks and lots of experience on any team. Goals for individual and entities must support and reinforce flexible and collaborative behaviour: simple revenue goals usually drive perverse behaviour. Partnerships that recognise higher risk and return, rather than trying to nail everything down in initial agreement, are the goal to be sought. A willingness to allow for risk and flexibility is desirable, so open, flexible arrangements rather than rigid centre agreements are the best way forward. The true test of success is for agencies and individuals to agree to pool resources and demonstrate a willingness to allow others to direct resources and manage teams for the common good. True partnerships are characterised by a willingness to surrender individual and jurisdictional sovereignty for common goals.

There will be a need to define the goals and the governance structures to encourage and support the individuals at the front line. There is much individual risk in these enterprises, particularly when dealing with cultures in conflict. Successful network cultures turn competitors into collaborators,[38] but it must be recognised that success in this arena is frequently beyond the power of individuals. Structures and relationships are fluid and changing:

one of the distinguishing characteristics of network culture is that walls which once seemed secure become permeable screens which create possibilities for the emergence and evolution of new organizational systems and structures.[39]

Failure must not be held against individuals if external factors conspire against success. Organisations will need to be flexible and adaptive and keep the external world under constant review. There is indeed a need to look outwards and upwards.

Finally, the ultimate challenge is a requirement to do this both nationally and internationally. Solutions to sustainability issues require integration across the entire innovation system – from academia to industry clusters – in an environment where regional strategies will differ markedly for reasons of culture, history, infrastructure, facilities, etc. Nevertheless in the new economy and emerging global network culture '*competitors must learn to collaborate*'.[40] If this collaborative strategy is pursued by communities, and fully developed, it will place them in a position of 'cognitive advantage', which is, in itself, a competitive advantage in a rapidly changing world. As networks of trust and relationships expand, new opportunities will arise. The response will be non-linear and very creative.

Future communities

As we have begun to appreciate the complexity of the global situation – the interdependence of humans and the biosphere, the uncertainty of our knowledge and the need to develop and preserve all forms of capital – we have begun to build a growing literature around the topic of what future communities might look like. First and foremost for a sustainable outcome there is a need for a new engagement between humans and nature. In the past conservation biology has tended to set nature apart from humans through the protection of the last great wild places on Earth. David Western has called for a new form of conservation philosophy, science and practice, which 'must be framed against the reality of human dominated ecosystems, rather than the separation of humanity and nature underlying the modern conservation movement'.[41] Humans must learn to collaborate with nature, not compete with it. This has been echoed in more recent papers and as I and others have noted this is a very significant change in emphasis which is, in itself, a major challenge to the conservation movement and many NGOs.[42] The sustainability of future communities seems to lie in the interaction of social, environmental and economic capitals with a focus at the local level because of the vagaries of climate, biogeography and resources.[43] Sustainability requires the interaction between all capitals, all people, all networks and all of nature – involving therefore the 'ordinary' or the 'rest of nature' as well as the special wild places – so that development and capacity building is not just an issue for the third world, it is an issue for us all. The problem of global sustainability requires a lift in capacity on the part of all communities and in particular a re-engagement between rural and urban communities. Social capital development is critical if this is to succeed. In fact, while forms of localism and community-based development are a key part of rural development programmes in the third world, there is an equal need for such programmes in the first and urban worlds as well. Even in the West, economic development in regions is dependent on cultural and social capital, strong networks and the capacity of local communities and entrepreneurs.[44]

The need for capacity building as part of development was recognised by Sen[45] among others. Access to human and social capital, networks, and information and communications technologies are a key part of community and social development in the postmodern world. With ICT infrastructure and skills it is possible for even remote rural and regional communities to combine the best of local knowledge with links to other urban and international capabilities.[46] Through ICT, communities of interest may be disparate and distributed. Effectively what can be built is a kind of 'small-world' network around a community of interest, with many local links and fewer long-range connections to various forms of distributed capitals. It is equally important for urban communities to link effectively with rural and regional communities around the world, sharing knowledge and financial resources. Bunge sees the world as a network of interconnected systems and argues that this is a world view quite different from past concepts.

> The systemic approach to social policy-design is quite different from libertarianism and totalitarianism: it attempts to involve the interested parties in the planning process, and designs social systems and processes likely to improve the individual well-being, revising the plans as often as required by the changing circumstances.[47]

This argues for an approach to sustainability characterised by a shifting mix of policies and institutions that encourage flexibility and choice. Taylor calls this an 'unruly complexity'.[48] We should not underestimate the difficulty of the challenge we face.

Social networks suffer from both communication and complexity constraints. Annen has shown how social capital development and the construction of inclusive networks can be thought of as a kind of multiple-player prisoner's dilemma.[49] To build social capital not only is it important for the network players to behave cooperatively, it is also essential for the other players to know about the trustworthiness of others. So social capital is more than simply membership of various organisations, clubs and networks; it is also dependent on information flows about trustworthiness, capacities and complexity as well as rewards and sanctions for good or bad behaviour. Networks are useful ways to think of some of the processes that underlie community development – and there are both the 'vertical' networks of commodity and market chains as well as the 'horizontal' chains of innovation and learning.[50] Some have used Actor Network Theory (ANT) to analyse the power relationships involving financial, technological and other entities in the commodity chains and communities.[51] Networks in regional areas can produce regional hot spots or clusters of innovation around key industries, often based around particular geographical, resource or community assets that can be exploited or built upon. Many of these clusters have 'small-world' characteristics with much local interaction, but also with long-range links to skills and resources in the wider world. These appear to be the kinds of networks to be encouraged.

NOTES

1. The critique of instrumental reason and situational ethics is well outlined by J.R. Saul in *Voltaire's Bastards* (London, Penguin Books, 1993), *The Unconscious Civilisation* (Toronto, Penguin Books, 1997) and *On Equilibrium*. (London, Penguin Books, 2001).

2. Instrumental reason may be defined as 'the eclipse of ends'. It reason is therefore a notion of reason that values efficiency above all, and therefore justifies means over ends.

3. M. Schluter and D. J. Lee. *The R-option*. (Cambridge: Relationships Foundation, 2003).

4. P. M. Senge. *The Fifth Discipline; the Art and Practice of the Learning Organisation*. (Milsons Point, NSW: Random House Australia 1992).

5. C. Handy. *The Age of Unreason*. (London: Arrow Books, 1990).

6. R. W. Rycroft and D. E. Kash. *The Complexity Challenge: Technological Innovation for the 21st Century*. (London: Pinter, 1999).

7. A. R. Platt. *The First Imperative*. (Market Harborough, UK: Matador, 2004).

8. See A. Olivier. *The Working Journey*. (Johannesburg: Andrew Olivier, 2003). Copies available from the web address www.theworkingjourney.com.

9. G. Bateson. *Steps to an Ecology of Mind*. (St Albans, Herts: Paladin, 1973).

10. Michael Porter has written extensively about the competitiveness of nations, and the global interaction between innovation strategies and regional 'clusters' which leads to wealth generation and reform. See M. E. Porter. *The Competitive Advantage of Nations*. (New York: The Free Press, 1990).

11. F. Fukuyama. *Trust: the Social Virtues and the Creation of Prosperity*. (New York: The Free Press 1995).

12. Much has been written about social capital; some would argue too much (see, for example, C. Kadushin. Too much investment in social capital? *Social Networks*, **26** (2004), 75–90). Nevertheless I find the concept useful as a broad catch-all for social networks, information flows and trust that can support capacity building and innovation at the local level. For a very thorough review of the concept of social capital and its important role in national policy – including a discussion of the numerous definitions – see the paper by the Australian Productivity Commission. *Social capital: reviewing the concept and its policy implications*, Commission Research Paper, 2003 – available from the APC website www.apc.gov.au.

13. E. Jaques. *A General Theory of Bureaucracy*. (London: Gregg Revivals, 1976). E. Jaques and K. Cason. *Human Capability; a Study of individual Potential and its Application*. (Arlington, VA:

Cason and Hall and Co., 1994). G. Stamp and C. Stamp. Well being at work; aligning purposes, people, strategies and structures. *International Journal of Career Management*, **5** (3) (1993).

14. Platt, *The First Imperative*. (See Note 7.)

15. This is well explained by Andrew Olivier in his book about the 'working journey' (see Note 8). Gwynne Dwyer sees the United Nations as a level VI/VII enterprise to build a multi-lateral world order, and asserts that this is a 100-year project, not yet complete. See G. Dwyer. *Future: Tense: the Coming World Order*. (Melbourne: Scribe, 2006).

16. B. Dive. *The Healthy Organisation*. (London: Kogan Page, 2002).

17. See, for example, E. Goldberg. *The Wisdom Paradox: How Your minds Can Grow stronger as Your Brain Grows Older*. (New York: The Free Press, 2005).

18. R. Florida. *The Rise of the Creative Class: and How it's Transforming Work, Leisure, Community and Everyday Life*. (New York: Basic Books, 2002).

19. R. W. Rycroft and D. E. Kash. *The Complexity Challenge: Technological Innovation for the 21st Century*. (London: Pinter, 1999).

20. Dwyer, *Future: Tense*: (Note 15) gives an excellent summary of the changing shape of the international world order and the risks of the next 50 years.

21. Rycroft and Kash, *The Complexity Challenge*. (See Note 19.)

22. Olivier, *The Working Journey* (see Note 8). Science is but a microcosm of a much larger problem for professions and private companies. The nature of the 'Requisite Organisation' has changed markedly in recent decades. See E. Jaques. *Requisite Organisation: the CEO's Guide to Constructive Structure and Leadership*. (Arlington, VA: Cason, Hall and Co., 1989). Dive, *The Healthy Organisation*. (See Note 16.)

23. See the discussion of the commoditization of science in R. Levins and R. Lewontin. *The Dialectical Biologist*. (Cambridge, MA: Harvard University Press, 1985), and in S. Crook, J. Pakulski and M. Waters. *Post Modernisation: Change in Advanced Society*. (London: Sage Publications 1992).

24. J. Urry. *Global Complexity*. (Cambridge: Polity, 2003). Rycroft and Kash, *The Complexity Challenge*. (See Note 19.)

25. M. Baghai, S. Coley and D. White. *The Alchemy of Growth: Building and Sustaining Growth in your Company*. (New York: Orion, 1999).

26. To misuse a quote from Isaac Newton, those who see farther than most do frequently do so by 'standing on the shoulders of giants' – again, relationships are important because you can only stand on the shoulders of friendly and trusted giants!

27. R. Wright. *Non-zero; History, Evolution and Human Cooperation*. (London: Abacus Books, 2001).

28. See www.nce.gc.ca/media/newsrel/2001/120301_e.htm and http://europa.eu.int/comm/research/fp6/index_en.html.

29. For details on these programmes and useful links see www.chesapeakebay.net, www.evergladesplan.org, www.relu.ac.uk, www.healthywaterways.org.

30. Rycroft and Kash, *The Complexity Challenge*. (See Note 19.)

31. K. J. Dooley. A complex adaptive systems model of organization change. *Non-linear Dynamics, Psychology and Life Sciences*, **1** (1997), 69–97.

32. Handy. *The Age of Unreason*. (See Note 5.)

33. Rycroft and Kash, *The Complexity Challenge*. (See Note 19.)

34. See *Communities of Interest: Learning through the Interaction of Multiple Knowledge Systems*. Proceedings of the 24th IRIS Conference (ed. S. Bjornestad *et al.*), August 2001, Ulvik, Department of Information Science, Bergen, Norway, pp. 1–14 (www.cs.colorado.edu/~gerhard/papers/iris24.pdf).

35. V. John-Steiner. *Notebooks of the Mind: Explorations of Thinking*, revised edn. (Oxford: Oxford University Press, 1997). V. John-Steiner. *Creative Collaboration*. (Oxford: Oxford University Press, 2000).

36. R. Guimera *et al*. Team assembly mechanisms determine collaboration network structure and team performance. *Science*, **308** (2005), 697–702.

37. A.-L. Barabasi. Network theory – the emergence of the creative enterprise. *Science*, **308** (2005), 639–41.

38. M. Taylor. *The Moment of Complexity: Emerging Network Culture*. (Chicago, IL: Chicago University Press, 2001).

39. Ibid., p. 260.

40. Ibid., p. 260.

41. D. Western. Human-modified ecosystems and future evolution. *Proceedings of the National Academy of Sciences, USA*, **98** (2001), 5458–65.

42. R. J. S. Beeton *et al*. Most of nature. *Science* (2007), submitted. J. Pretty and D. Smith. Social capital in biodiversity and management. *Conservation Biology*, **18** (2003), 631–8. K. S. Bawa, R. Seidler and P. H. Raven. Reconciling conservation paradigms. *Conservation Biology*, **18** (2004), 859–60. H. Doremus. Biodiversity and the challenge of saving the ordinary. *Idaho Law Review*, **38** (2002), 325–54. M. Chapin. A challenge to conservationists, p. 17–31 excerpted from *World Watch* magazine, November–December 2004.

43. M. Lehtonen. The environmental-social interface of sustainable development: capabilities, social capital, institutions. *Ecological Economics*, **49** (2004), 199–214.

44. I. J. Terluin. Differences in economic development in rural regions of advanced countries: an overview and critical analysis of theories. *Journal of Rural Studies*, **19** (2003), 327–44.

45. A. K. Sen. *Commodities and Capabilities*. (Oxford: Oxford University Press, 1987). A. K. Sen. *Development as Freedom*. (New York: Anchor Books, 1999).

46. A. Blackwell and R. Colmenar. Transforming policy through local wisdom. *Futures*, **31** (1999), 487–97. T. Stevenson. Communities of tomorrow. *Futures*, **34** (2002), 735–44.

47. M. Bunge. Systemism: the alternative to individualism and holism. *Journal of Socio-economics*, **29** (2000), 147–57.

48. P. Taylor. *Unruly Complexity: Ecology, Interpretation, Engagement*. (Chicago, University Press, 2005).

49. K. Annen. Social capital, inclusive networks, and economic performance. *Journal of Economic Behavior and Organization*, **50** (2003), 449–63.

50. J. Murdoch. Networks – a new paradigm of rural development. *Journal of Rural Studies*, **16** (2000), 407–19.

51. B. Latour. The powers of association. In *Power, Action, Belief: A new Sociology of Knowledge?* ed. J. Law (London, Routledge and Kegan Paul, 1986), pp. 264–80.

21 A new environmental paradigm

The challenge of rebuilding regions in an environment of decentralisation, pluralism and subsidiarity: the new 'wickedly' complex environmental paradigm.

So the challenge that is before us is to attempt to manage and restore multiple capitals and assets of different kinds (ecosystem structure, biodiversity, resources, the quantity and quality of water, human settlements) as well as their interactions across scales, and to do this at regional or watershed scales over time periods long enough to achieve something akin to intergenerational equity. Our starting place is from mostly highly modified landscapes and waterscapes and we must do this with limited resources and information. There have been many attempts to restore landscapes at local scales and many local successes but, overall, the indicators show that more needs to be done. Local successes do not eliminate large-scale decline – and vice versa. We must find ways of causing the whole to become more than the sum of the parts: there must be more integration and the exploitation of synergies and the benefits of SGC. It is clear that just scattering 'best management practices' across landscapes does not bring us to where we need to be; we need to find ways to exploit the non-linear interactions, synergies and emergent properties of the pandemonium of natural interactions (which we understand but poorly) to add value to what we may do ourselves.

What we are trying to do is to take the present (largely fragmented) landscape of natural, human, social and financial capital and make it more robust by restoring ecosystems and replacing assets of various kinds. Across the landscape we are already placing new assets (e.g. agroforestry plantations) in land use mosaics to suit multiple outcomes: urban subdivisions, improvement of biodiversity and water quality, salinity control, environmental flows, generation of new annuities and revenue streams from carbon trading. We are already using a variety of tools to provide signals and incentives; market-based instruments, auction schemes and incentive payments of various kinds have been instituted to achieve a variety of outcomes concerning biodiversity and ecosystem services. We are attempting to satisfy as many purposes as possible, with the hope of exploiting SGC and other non-linear interaction mechanisms. We are attempting to rebuild more robust and resilient land use mosaics incorporating more sustainable ecological and socioeconomic outcomes. The requirement is for the highest degree of intergenerational equity and the closest approach to robust states and MaxEnt solutions even though we know that we cannot be fully sustainable on every hectare. We require management and policy tools that exploit public and private investment on public and private lands to the maximum benefit, and effective instruments to ensure that adequate rents and compensation are paid, and we require market-based instruments and collective incentives to encourage the utmost community compliance and enthusiasm. We have precious few tools to do this; land use planning with GIS is only a beginning. It is possible to identify situations where a more balanced and system-oriented management regime is required. We know, for example, that widespread plantation forestry uses water and reduces stream flows for a period of 25–50 years after planting,[1] so the forestry industries should be required to purchase licences for their water use. Sometime in the future we may envisage plantations balancing carbon sequestration credits with water use licences.[2]

Balancing multiple capitals

Slowly but surely communities and governments are insisting on the balancing of multiple capitals in landscapes and waterscapes. Other values in addition to profit are being added to the list of desirable properties. Agriculture is being balanced by incentives for ecosystem services and biodiversity, fisheries management is being expanded to include ecosystem management and the preservation of marine biodiversity, land clearing is being controlled and the many and various impacts of climate change are being actively debated. Jurisdictions around the world are trying to use a raft of instruments and incentives both individually and in combination to achieve more sustainable outcomes. Market-based instruments, auctions, tax relief, rural adjustment schemes and interest rate subsidies are just some of the tools being used. What these schemes do is to place restrictions on what is 'private' on private land and constrain the freedom to use licences and quotas for water and access to fisheries and other common pool resources. This frequently causes anger, conflict and demands that compensation be paid. We have not yet learned all the lessons from the 'new institutionalism' school and frequently do not design the governance arrangements to be sustainable.[3] Nevertheless societies in many countries are demanding more balanced outcomes and are demanding a say in the ways in which public and private assets are managed on (and in) public and private lands and waters. Essentially what is happening is that interests are growing in public goods and moves are afoot to reinstate public rights over such goods on private land. This is a key development in the management of the 'whole of nature'.

There is a high degree of complexity here because of the impact of globalisation and market segmentation on the intensification and extensification of agriculture. In many Western countries a small number of supermarkets control significant fractions of the food market and they are driving greater efficiencies of scale, price reductions, improvements in quality and a consequent increase in intensification and a reduction in the number of farm enterprises. The overall terms of trade for agricultural products have been declining for fifty years. Farm subsidies also distort global markets so that apart from large, efficient, corporate farm enterprises the terms of trade for smaller enterprises are poor. As I have shown, most farm enterprises are financially marginal. So how do we ensure sustainability for rural societies? One way is to bring other capitals – especially natural capital – into the equation. To provide incentives for improved environmental management, some espouse stewardship payments, others market-based instruments (MBIs) of various kinds. In truth, however, neither approach comes close to solving the basic financial conundrum for farm enterprises. Although MBIs of various kinds do bring externalities into the wider market for ecological goods and services, it is unlikely that stewardship payments or MBIs will be large enough to provide financial security for farm enterprises. Is society prepared to put up enough funds for, say, biodiversity auctions to make a significant difference to profitability? I doubt it. If we use expenditure on national parks as an example, an inquiry in Queensland showed that expenditure on parks around Australia in 1997–8 ranged from A$0.73 per hectare per year in South Australia to A$24.80 per hectare per year in New South Wales.[4] In most states the expenditure was in the A$5–10 per hectare per year range. If this is representative of what Australians believe is required to manage the biodiversity of the continent on a per hectare basis, then it is not sufficient to make a difference to agriculture. What we are left with in Western countries is an increasing trend towards the corporatisation, consolidation and intensification of farming; and a problem of social and environmental sustainability on the rural landscape. De-ruralisation is a global problem.[5] In many Western countries the trend is being reversed by higher-income groups from urban centres buying up rural land in peri-urban rings 1–3 hours travelling time from the cities. This 'tree-change' phenomenon is widespread but all it does is to raise rural land prices beyond the reach of financially marginal rural communities. Hobby farmers do serve to balance capitals in rural areas by introducing environmentally friendly farming techniques, including reduced stocking rates and organic practices. Nevertheless these strategies can only be practised by those with off-farm incomes.

De-ruralisation and social decline in rural areas is widespread. The age structure of rural populations in Australia is being distorted by the flight of high-capacity young people and young families to urban centres. If we are to manage the 'whole of nature' we are going to have to find ways of ensuring equality of opportunity in rural areas and ways of funding sustainable environmental and agricultural management. In all probability that will also include a judicious mix of policy instruments to drive innovation in manufacturing and service industries in rural and regional areas, and encourage off-farm activities and income. At the same time, set-aside policies and policies that allow for, and manage, the process of reversion of farmland to natural vegetation will be required. Tragically, the present set of global policies and agricultural subsidies encourage land clearing and the destruction of native vegetation in the third world while driving de-ruralisation and the reversion of farming land in the West. We still have not found a successful policy mix to ensure sustainability across all forms of capital in all regions. I, with others, favour a policy mix that would more effectively balance and grow all forms of capital, and make investments that specifically tackle the problems of health, poverty and environmental management.[6] We have not yet seen the end of globalisation, despite strong arguments criticising neo-liberal economic policies.[7] In the face of population growth, AIDS, climate change and environmental degradation – including the possibility of surprises and hysteresis effects – a more sustainable future requires a robust and resilient set of policies.

We now know that fragmented efforts do not achieve anything other than fragmented benefits, and that policy instruments must be integrated and even correctly sequenced in time to achieve the necessary ends. Institutional arrangements are critical. In many parts of the world there are experiments in subsidiarity being carried out, in which local and regional communities are being empowered to make investments at those scales. In the Australian context the capacity to truly comprehend the nature of the tasks at hand is not uniform across governments, catchment management authorities and regional natural resource management committees. There are strong regional differences in social capital between communities. Some communities are well networked and open to innovation; others are positively resistant to change so that new ideas are actively suppressed.[8] Some are well advanced, and have the necessary tools to begin the tasks; others are at a much earlier stage of social, institutional and knowledge development and are just coming to grips with all the complexity of forming investment plans, setting targets and monitoring performance. All the 'C' words come into play – complexity, connectivity, context, contingency, climate change, community and capacity – as regional groups come to grips with the realisation that micro-process leads to macro-scale outcomes. The fact of cross-scale interactions in the formation of paradoxical catchment properties, fractal flow paths and the modification of soils and hydrological properties is not well understood. The challenges of innovation in a globalised economy are also not widely appreciated. System thinking is poor. There is little appreciation of non-linear interactions and the possibilities of emergence.

Partial information and the incentives and opportunities in the market system for individuals to shirk their responsibility to the community or group to which they belong leads to unanticipated and undesirable outcomes.[9] Equally, complexity can arise from mixed policy signals: restrictions on the 'private' together with a focus on free market solutions to NRM problems. Micro-incentives can produce macro-behaviour of surprising and unintended kinds, so social context and connectivity is just as important as ecological and biophysical connectivity. Interactions within the coupled social, economic and ecological systems are non-linear, there is much temporal and spatial variability in pattern and process across a wide range of scales, and emergence and surprise are rife. Many predictive and conceptual models are based on incomplete evidence; knowledge and evidence are partial and uncertain. Any attempt to treat the coupled 'system of systems' as a static entity leads to surprises and failure. There is therefore a personal and institutional strategic gap[10] between goals and reality.

One of the key considerations in the sustainability of landscapes, waterscapes, communities and the various forms of capital involved is a matter of scale. Globalisation sees the world at global scales; but the global is made up of many local communities, regions and places with differing cultures, values and beliefs. Ethical considerations demand that we do not treat the complex global 'system of systems' as a unitary whole but that we respect the differing cultures and values of the other. There are some difficult issues here around the ways in which we perceive and value economic, social and environmental goods and services. One of the problems we face in the management of natural resources, particularly when we attempt to empower local communities, is that the values and beliefs of central governments (often focused on globalisation and the competitiveness of nations) are not those of local and regional communities, who see such policy trends as threats to jobs and the local ways of life. Those attempting to build capacity in local groups can easily be caught between conflicting value sets and purposes. The governance arrangements are not properly nested. Local economies are often based on premises quite different from those of global ones; informal economies, even 'black' markets, may be the basis of local cultures and these may exist side-by-side with global commodity trading. Land use and revegetation decisions are indeed often determined by local cultural traditions of land tenure and beliefs about cultivation and pastoral practices.

There is a complete contrast between the orthodox story of neoclassical economics and what might be called 'sustainability economics'.[11] As Walter points out, the key performance indicators of classical economics are profit, personal wealth and the Gross Domestic Product (GDP) of nations 'and its major rituals are consumerism, wage labour, and capitalistic entrepreneurship'. Neo-classical economics assumes that 'greed is good' and that there are no unavoidable limits to production. There is a nascent movement towards including the 'externalities' in large-scale economic models, but these are bedevilled by valuation problems and a lack of absolute values. In Walter's view, a sustainability economics would have as its central story the adaptability of communities in the face of environmental limitations and change, 'including the value of learning by doing, the importance of monitoring and assessment, and the need for stewardship and capacity enhancement'.[12] There is work going on to develop alternative and more complete indicators of sustainable welfare that go beyond the more narrow financial indicators such as GDP growth, but these are scale-dependent.[13]

Once we go beyond neo-classical economics and begin to include other indices and forms of capital, then scale becomes important as we begin to define the region of interest and the stocks and flows involved.[14] Lawn has identified three key factors in determining whether a sustainable solution can be found. He identifies these as (a) ensuring that strong sustainability is achieved through matching the flows of energy and materials to the regenerative and assimilation capacity of the regional ecosystems, (b) ensuring distributive equity and (c) ensuring allocative efficiency. Markets can achieve some of these goals quite well – and this approach is now widely used in the case of water – but markets need to be hedged about by controls to ensure that individual behaviour does not distort overall performance through the multiple prisoners' dilemma. Furthermore, Lawn points out that markets cannot achieve all these goals because, although markets do provide information about the scarcity of one thing relative to another, relative prices are not the entire story. In the context of sustainability and biophysical constraints it is absolute prices (defined by other values) that are important because of the non-substitutability of many of the key forms of natural capital. Biophysical assessments set the regional market context in terms of assessing the fundamental biophysical constraints (e.g. the overall supply of water in a catchment) and also in determining the impact of past economic activity on key resources and natural capital.

There is a really important message for water markets contained in Lawn's analysis. The order in which these policy goals are addressed is critical. What we have tended to do in the past is to use water markets to solve the allocation problem first, and then make adjustments to ensure distributive equity and biophysical sustainability. But this clearly does not work well. Any glance at the situation in many irrigation areas around the world demonstrates this. Lawn argues convincingly that the policy goals of equity and sustainability should be solved first, and goes further to assert that this is the only way to solve Jevons' paradox. This paradox – the fact that increasing resource (water) use efficiency reduces production costs and thus leads to an increase in production, so placing more pressure on the environment – is widely observed. There are many cases in Australia where increased water use efficiency leads to increased production and profit and does not lead to a return of water to the environment (the intended outcome). This argument cuts to the core of the debate between resource economists about the use and limitations of market economics.

So a sustainable resource management policy at the local to regional scale is a complex thing to achieve. It requires a broad policy mix as well as considerable community capacity, and recognition of uncertainty, partial knowledge and complexity of interaction. Weisbuch has attempted to model these interactions in societies with models incorporating complex network interactions and spatial distributions of agents together with features of cognition and other social factors.[15] Although the results of these models are almost impossible to validate, they nevertheless demonstrate enormous complexity, abrupt state transitions and surprising properties very different from those produced by standard economic models based on concepts of equilibrium, perfect knowledge and total rationality. Some argue that just as the 'economy is a wholly owned subsidiary of the environment' it is also a wholly owned subsidiary of society and that society cannot ever be seen as static or at equilibrium.[16] I began in Chapter 1 by discussing the evidence for Kondratiev cycles in the global economy and the social and technological drivers that underpinned them. Perhaps the key thing to remember here is the concept of 'deep time'; what we need are measures and indicators of trajectories, path dependencies and change over time in very complex systems.[17] Where we presently are is dependent on contingent history; events are continuously unfolding and 'becoming' and the order in which we do things is just as important as what we do.[18] Local and regional community and context is important. Large universal frameworks fail to capture the richness of the true scales of pattern and process. Work by Holling and others in the Resilience Alliance has analysed the nature and extent of social change and has linked this to the problems of natural resource management. Inertia and sudden hysteretic shifts in public opinion appear to have causes similar to those of similar phenomena in ecosystems; feedbacks and information flows are just as non-linear and contingent as they are in nature.[19] Walker and his co-workers have used this kind of analysis to study changes in opinions and management practices in the Goulburn–Broken catchment in Australia, linking the hysteresis and non-linear, multiple states of ecosystem dynamics to other external social and economic drivers.[20] They lay out a schema for the analysis and adaptive management of resilience in social–ecological systems through a series of steps: (i) the analysis and description of the key processes, ecosystem dynamics and drivers, (ii) the exploration of possible external shocks, visions of the future and plausible policies, (iii) analysis of the resilience of the coupled 'system of systems' and (iv) a thorough stakeholder evaluation of possible policy and management options. What this approach does do is to give us hope: nothing is ever fixed and there is great opportunity for change and improvement in the ways in which we manage our affairs and those of the planet. We return again to complex local and regional solutions to difficult non-linear problems.

More recently, Walker and others from the Resilience Alliance have discussed the resilience, adaptability and transformability of social–ecological systems.[21] The view of ecological and socioeconomic systems as resilient rather than static focuses on the system properties, which promote 'the capacity of the system to absorb disturbance and reorganise while undergoing change so as to retain essentially the same function, structure, identity and feedbacks'.[22] This view sees socioecological systems occupying non-linear landscapes of state space with basins of attraction separated by ridges and hills of instability. The most important feature then becomes the 'precariousness' of the system: how close is it to a position of instability, how deep is the local basin of attraction (how resistant is it to change?) and what is the likelihood that the entire landscape of state space will change and throw the system into a deeper, but undesirable, basin of attraction? If the system is likely to be seriously perturbed by climate change or some extreme event (fire, flood or storm), will the system be catastrophically altered or will the system degrade 'gracefully' to ensure opportunity for rescue or recovery? There are many recent examples (hurricanes and tsunamis) to show that many present human-dominated socioecological systems do not degrade 'gracefully' in the face of natural disasters.[23]

So in addition to restoring landscapes and waterscapes by a mixture of public and private investments we must also pay attention to the 'precariousness' of the overall design. In the face of climate change and biodiversity loss, a non-linear emergent view of landscapes and waterscapes demands that we must build in as much robustness and resilience as possible. As far as possible we must try to return systems to the kinds of 'neutral' spaces that they came to occupy through trial and error over millennia. HOT designs are precarious in the face of unexpected perturbations, so as we move into combinations of climate regimes and land use patterns that have not been seen before we can expect surprises and large-scale hysteresis. What, then, is the likelihood that landscape and waterscape designs arrived at through a process of subsidiarity and co-design – involving the local community in the development of the necessary knowledge and in the decision-making process, and ensuring behavioural change through the use of market-based instruments and other incentives – will be more robust and less precarious than now? The present Western emphasis on globalisation, economic growth and shareholder value is clearly not moving in the right direction. Systems are becoming more precarious, not less. The growing adoption of markets and incentives for ecosystem services and other forms of natural capital is an attempt to 'balance the books' and restore some robustness but, at present, we are not fully capturing the synergies between local and larger-scale properties. Most local communities do not have the capacity to do this.

Decentralisation, pluralism, regionalism and subsidiarity

The drive towards subsidiarity, which is part and parcel of the 'third way' and has been widely adopted around the world, has major implications for the development of policy and management practice. There is a particularly good example of this in the recent Australian water management debate. After a period of particularly severe drought in the period 2000–02 various policies were proposed to provide effective water supply and management in Australia – some wise and some less so. In particular, as always happens during droughts in Australia, a number of old schemes were revived to turn around various north-ern rivers and redirect the water south to the people and irrigators in need. There is even a new scheme to build a canal to take water from tropical rivers in North-Western Australia down to Perth. In response to some of the more madcap schemes proposed in the media at the time, a group of 'concerned scientists' met in the Wentworth Hotel in Sydney in an attempt to inject some realism into the debate and to balance the debate around biophysical realities and the value of ecosystem services. (In effect, this was an attempt to balance the capitals in a debate that had become focused around profit and investment security.) This group rapidly became known as the Wentworth Group. The Wentworth Group's influential blueprint for a living continent and for a national water plan[24] invoked water market reforms and regionalism as a solution to the problem of increased water use efficiency. This is in the context of an already existing series of water reforms over the previous decade, spearheaded by the Murray–Darling Basin Commission and involving extensive use of 'cap and trade' mechanisms to ensure more efficient allocations and some improved water use efficiency in the Basin. The Wentworth Group's pronouncements were influential and led to a new National Water Initiative from the Commonwealth Government, to be delivered through regional catchment boards. Rather quickly the prescriptions of the Wentworth Group began to be criticised, in particular their preferred means of implementation of the new water plan: decentralised regionalism. This part of the plan was criticised for being simplistic and ignoring a lot of national and international experience with the complexities of this kind of delivery mechanism.[25] In particular the criticisms focused on the problems of defining regions and the difference between administrative regions, biophysical regions and democratic or social regions (and echoing Medd and Marvin's vision of human spaces as fluid, negotiated, hybrid spaces). Certainly, regional decentralisation does seem to produce more just and equitable solutions to the problems of natural resource management partly because they can be tailored to the local peculiarities and needs. Further criticisms centred on the complexities and difficulties of defining and dealing with the complex concepts and realities of 'community' in regional areas (in particular the complexities and inequalities of power, gender and wealth).[26] There are not only geographical communities of place but also imagined communities of nations or countercultures; these can be based on interests, imagination, intention or even resistance.[27] (This is perhaps one reason why there is, as yet, no agreement on a Basin-wide water market in the Murray–Darling Basin.) Communities are fluid and negotiated phenomena but are nevertheless important concepts and means of identity for most people in rural, regional and urban centres. Communities may be identified through discourses, geographies and practices, all of which are undergoing rapid change in these complex times.[28] This is particularly true in situations such as the UK foot and mouth outbreak where, as I discussed earlier, the 'system of systems' fought back in surprising ways.

Critics of the Wentworth Group also saw problems with their apparently simplistic view of the relationship between 'world class science' and the community.

There can be a chasm between the managerial language of modern science and the aspirations of communities with quite different values and beliefs. Science is but one source of knowledge that can be fed into a deliberative process to seek solutions to these 'wicked' problems. I agree with the Wentworth Group's critics who call for a process by which experts and citizens in communities 'co-produce' the knowledge that they require to solve the complex policy issues that they face. Communities can, on occasion, be very resistant to change (particularly that imposed from outside), so bringing in new knowledge as an agent of change can be a fraught and discouraging process.

What the new model of landscape and waterscape management calls for is a kind of recursive co-management in which institutions will be required to surrender sovereignty to local and regional groups. Institutions are required to be facilitatory rather than acting in command and control mode.[29] In terms of levels of work and capacity, subsidiarity works best when there is attention paid to the requisite tasks and levels of complexity, and when there is a deliberative process to ensure agreement on both means and ends.[30] This requires a lot of commitment and hard work by all parties, and no little risk, but the results justify the effort required. I find it interesting to note that in the UK we are seeing the establishment of a national resilience committee and the development of regional resilience teams (RRTs) and forums (RRFs) to handle 'disruptive challenges' of various kinds. The tasks of these groups are emergency planning, flood defence, civil contingencies and the protection of critical national infrastructure. This is a recognition that the world (even the world of water) is becoming 'riskier' and that formal roles for regional agencies and devolved administrations must be worked out before the event. There is still much work to be done to satisfy the various needs of central, regional and local governments and to determine how

> the multitude of activities relevant to resilience, involving institutional roles, policy instruments, interests, knowledge bases and technological capabilities, be coordinated and with what implications?[31]

This work is becoming ever more urgent as the interlinking of critical water, power and IT infrastructure in distributed systems makes management ever more complex and challenging.

Co-production of the requisite knowledge requires all parties to recognise that all knowledge is partial and incomplete, that evidence is debatable and that there are various ways of knowing determined by culture, semiotics and values. I still argue strongly for biophysical realities – after all, the overall supply of water in catchments is limited by rainfall and climate – but there are many ways of knowing and science does not necessarily have precedence over other forms of knowledge. Even if we agree that there is an 'enduring, underlying reality', asserting the 'epistemic sovereignty' of science limits the debate and constrains choices. A focus instead on 'epistemological pluralism' reinstates consideration of ways of knowing and their manifestation in institutions.[32] In an important paper Piers Blaikie has opened the debate about knowledge, community, power and evidence in a postmodern world where many see knowledge as entirely socially constructed.[33] I do not agree with those who advocate social constructionism[34] – I fall back, once again, on ontological realism and epistemological relativism – but I do agree that there is plenty of room to 'negotiate the facts' and that much can be gained from doing this.[35] Just as there is a need to debate the 'facts' of science and its application to the management of water and natural resources, there is an equal need to debate the 'facts' of economic and social theory that so dominate our lives – more so than the science in fact. A broader debate about theory, policy and power will lead to a more 'just sharing of power and influence' in a changing world.[36]

The new environmental paradigm

The increasingly pressing nature of more and more 'wicked' problems in environmental management, particularly water issues, is leading to a changing paradigm for environmental management. This new environmental paradigm involves recognition of the precariousness of the present state, decentralisation, systems thinking, and deliberative processes[37] and ethical considerations of justice, equity and fairness. It also implies adaptive institutional arrangements. It challenges the modernist technocratic view of the pre-eminence of science and goes well beyond the usual oppositional stance of 'green groups' and many NGOs.

A new environmental paradigm directly addresses the issues of knowledge, evidence and uncertainty and cuts to the core of the quandary around democracy and technology. As more and more of our problems and management issues become more complex and must rely on scientific and technological inputs, there is an urgent need to build trust, understanding and capacity at the community level.[38] Institutions must be reinvented to be more responsive, less hierarchical and more facilitatory in their approach to the many voices and many values and beliefs of disparate communities. And Steel and Weber state

> central to this effort are innovative, decentralised institutional arrangements which delegate significant authority to either private citizens, program managers within existing bureaucracy, or market based mechanisms.[39]

In the USA this approach has been called ecosystem management (EM) and brings together my arguments about community, the 'rest of nature', and decentralisation. Again to quote Steel and Weber in the context of EM in the USA many now contend that effective environmental programs require complex, collaborative partnerships among diverse government, civic and business actors at the state and local levels.[40]

This expands the scope of institutional arrangements in both space and time: from the local community to other levels of governance.

'Wickedly complex' problems have brought to light a number of shortcomings of the modernist, globalised approach; not the least the inability to deliver tailored regional solutions. The link between the new environmental paradigm, subsidiarity and 'third way' thinking is also clear because of the need for capacity and social capital at the local and regional level to be able to deal with such complex problems in a devolved manner. So the argument comes full circle at this point through the linking of the various forms of capital, complexity, uncertainty, capacity and subsidiarity into policy.[41] Above all what is required is the development of some vision and strategy at the local level. Democracy is more than universal suffrage and fair elections; democracy is also about freedom, local self-government (in the full meaning of the phrase) and the resolution of problems in an open society.[42]

Given the complexity of the world we are in – to misquote Margaret Thatcher – There Is No Alternative – TINA to this distributed and decentralised approach. (And of course Mrs Thatcher was famously denying the existence of anything called 'society' and pushing a market-based approach.) This argument has, perhaps, been most eloquently put by David Korten in his book *The Post-Corporate World*.[43] Drawing on his long experience in global development programs, Korten uses many of the same complex systems arguments that I have used here and reaches the same conclusions. He draws a number of lessons from what he calls 'life's ancient wisdom'.

- Life favours self-organisation: 'the freedom of the one depends on the responsible use of that freedom in relation to the needs of the many.' Individuals can make a difference and small actions can have major consequences.
- Life is frugal and sharing: local economies should be based on frugal use, equitable allocation and efficient reuse of water, energy and materials. This is a restatement of the strong sustainability argument.
- Life depends on inclusive, place-based communities, which are based around regional differences in climate, geography and resources.
- Life rewards cooperation: 'shared spaces create shared destinies and interests' and these are best served by collaboration.
- Life depends on boundaries: local communities should look to their borders so that they may maintain integrity and coherence in the face of global pressures. (This is not to say that 'small-world' networks should

not exploit long-range linkages; Korten merely argues that these should be managed locally.)

- Life banks on diversity, creative individuality and shared learning: this is an argument for capacity, creativity and the development of diversity and social capital.

This is precisely the same set of criteria for sustainable resource use as those developed by the 'new institutionalism' school.[44] Korten goes on to use these lessons from life to argue for a set of similar design criteria in the construction of sustainable communities in the face of global pressures. Although he does not suggest ways of achieving this outcome from where we are now, the trick is going to be to recognise the essential tension between the local and the global, and their path-dependent interdependence. What Urry calls 'glocalisation' has no coordinating centre – it is therefore 'complexity without telos' – with properties that depend on local decisions taken in the emergent context of the whole.[45]

What is emerging is a new, negotiated and fluid set of relationships between the local, the regional and the global with integrated stocks and flows of capitals. A new form of cross-scale ethics is emerging to deal with the difficult trade-offs and possibilities.

NOTES

1. A. Best *et al.* (2003) *A critical review of paired catchment studies with reference to seasonal flows and climatic variability*. (Canberra, ACT: CSIRO Land and Water technical Report 25/05; Melbourne: CRC for Catchment Hydrology technical Report 03/4; and Canberra, ACT: Murray–Darling Basin Commission publication 11/03). Available from the respective websites.

2. R. B. Jackson *et al.* Trading water for carbon with biological carbon sequestration. *Science*, **310** (2005), 1944–7.

3. E. Ostrom. *Governing the Commons: the Evolution of Institutions for Collective Action*. (Cambridge: Cambridge University Press, 1990).

4. Local Government Association of Queensland. Public inquiry into management of National Parks in Queensland. LGAQ, Brisbane.

5. T. M. Aide and H. R. Grau. Globalisation, migration and Latin American ecosystems. *Science*, **305** (2004), 1915–16.

6. J. Sachs. *The End of Poverty: How we can Make it Happen in our Lifetime*. (London: Penguin Books, 2005).

7. J. R. Saul. *The Collapse of Globalism and the Reinvention of the World*. (London: Penguin Books, 2005). S. Lewis. *Race Against Time*. CBC Massey Lecture Series. (Toronto: CBC Canada, 2006).

8. BTRE. *Focus on Regions*, No. 4: *Social Capital. Information paper No. 55*. (Canberra, ACT: Bureau of Transport and Regional Economics, Department of Transport and Regional Services, 2005). Available from www.btre.gov.au.

9. Ostrom, *Governing the Commons*. (See Note 3.) G. L. Cannibal and G. M. Winnard. Managing the tragedy: an interdisciplinary model for managing the environment as interacting chaotic hierarchy. *Futures*, **33** (2001), 147–60.

10. F. E. Harrison. The concept of the strategic gap. *Journal of General Management*, **15** (1989), 57.

11. G. R. Walter. Economics, ecology-based communities, and sustainability. *Ecological Economics*, **42** (2002), 81–7.

12. Ibid., p. 87.

13. P. A. Lawn. Scale, prices, and biophysical assessments. *Ecological Economics*, **38** (2001), 369–82. The discussion following leans heavily on Lawn's paper.

14. Ostrom, *Governing the Commons*. (See Note 3.)

15. G. Weisbuch. Environment and institutions: a complex dynamical systems approach. *Ecological Economics*, **34** (2000), 381–91.

16. M. Zafirovski. Reconsidering equilibrium: a socio-economic perspective. *Journal of Socio-economics*, **31** (2002), 559–79.

17. J. Urry. *Global Complexity*. (Cambridge: Polity, 2003).

18. J. Hukkinen. From groundless universalism to grounded generalism: improving ecological economic indicators of human-environmental interaction. *Ecological Economics*, **44** (2003), 11–27.

19. M. Scheffer, F. Westley and W. Brock. Slow responses of societies to new problems: causes and costs. *Ecosystems*, **6** (2003), 493–502.

20. B. H. Walker *et al.* Resilience management in social-ecological systems: a working hypothesis for a participatory approach. *Conservation Ecology*, **6 (1)** (2002), 14. Available online at www.consecol.org.vol6/iss1/art14.

21. B. H. Walker *et al.* Resilience, adaptability and transformability of social-ecological systems. *Ecology and Society*, **9 (2)** (2004), 5. www.ecologyandsociety.org/vol9/iss2/art5.

22. Ibid., p. 2.

23. W. N. Adger *et al.* Socio-ecological resilience to coastal disasters. *Science*, **309** (2005), 1036–9.

24. The Wentworth Group. *Blueprint for a Living Continent: a Way Forward from the Wentworth Group of Concerned Scientists*. (Sydney: World Wildlife Fund Australia, 2002). The Wentworth Group. *Blueprint for a National Water Plan*. (Sydney: World Wildlife Fund Australia, 2003).

25. M. B. Lane, G. T. McDonald and T. H. Morrison. Decentralization and environmental management in Australia: a comment on the prescriptions of the Wentworth Group. *Australian Geographical Studies*, **42** (2004), 1103–15.

26. The complexity of the concept of community, and the fallacies that can grow up around various simplistic views of the nature of especially rural communities, are well displayed in an editorial in the *Journal of Rural Studies* in 2004. See I. Hodge and S. Monk. The economic diversity of rural England: stylised fallacies and uncertain evidence. *Journal of Rural Studies*, **20** (2004), 263–72.

27. R. Liepins. New energies for an old idea: reworking approaches to 'community' in contemporary rural studies. *Journal of Rural Studies*, **16** (2000), 23–35.

28. R. Liepins. Exploring rurality through 'community': discourses, practices shaping Australian and New Zealand rural 'communities'. *Journal of Rural Studies*, **16** (2000), 325–41.

29. B. F. Noble. Institutional criteria for co-management. *Marine Policy*, **24** (2000), 69–77.

30. Ostrom, *Governing the Commons*. (See Note 3.)

31. W. Medd and S. Marvin. From the politics of urgency to the governance of preparedness: a research agenda on urban vulnerability. *Journal of Contingencies and Crisis Management*, **13** (2005), 44–9.

32. S. Healy. Epistemological pluralism and the 'politics of choice'. *Futures*, **35** (2003), 689–701.

33. P. M. Blaikie. Post-modernism and global environmental change. *Global Environmental Change*, **6** (1996), 81–5.

34. S. Jones. Social constructionism and the environment: through the quagmire. *Global Environmental Change*, **12** (2002), 247–51.

35. P. Taylor. *Unruly Complexity: Ecology, Interpretation, Engagement*. (Chicago, IL: Chicago University Press, 2005).

36. G. Aplin. Environmental rationalism and beyond: toward a more just sharing of power and influence. *Australian Geographer*, **31** (2000), 273–87.

37. B. S. Steel and E. Weber. Ecosystem management, decentralization, and public opinion. *Global Environmental Change*, **11** (2001), 119–31.

38. Ostrom, *Governing the Commons*. (See Note 3.)

39. Steel and Weber, *Global Environmental Change*, **11** (2001), p. 119. (See Note 37.)

40. Steel and Weber, *Global Environmental Change*, **11** (2001), p. 120.

41. L. White. Connection matters: exploring the implications of social capital and social networks for social policy. *Systems Research and Behavioral Science*, **19** (2002), 255–69.

42. M. A. Rudd. Live long and prosper: collective action, social capital and social vision. *Ecological Economics*, **34** (2000), 131–44.

43. D. Korten. *The Post-Corporate World: Life after Capitalism*. (San Francisco, CA: Berrett-Koehler Publishers, and West Hartford, CT: Kumarian Press, 1999; reprinted by Pluto Press, Annandale NSW Australia, 2000).

44. Ostrom, *Governing the Commons*. (See Note 3.)

45. Urry, *Global Complexity*. (See Note 17.)

22 Emergent problems and emerging solutions: developing an 'ecolophysics'?

So what can we make of the world we are in? Paying attention to pattern and process at small scales, complex valuations and reconciliations.

So the emerging solutions require a new world view. The first, and in my view the most important, change in world view has been the acceptance and understanding of a dynamic, non-linear, non-equilibrium view of complex systems; and the ways in which the actions of biological and social agents working with simple rules based on local information can produce emergent system-level properties. This 'unruly systemism'[1] – the action of agents in a recursive context – is a middle ground between the totally reductionist, individualist view and the structuralist view of system dynamics.[2] This view allows for high degrees of non-linearity, surprises and hysteresis effects: precisely what we observe in nature. It is also a way of understanding the behaviour of meso-scale entities, landscapes and waterscapes – but not necessarily being able to predict what is going to happen. This 'networked' view of nature seems to show up many consistent patterns associated with scale-free (or 'small world') networks, which occur in everything from networks of interacting enzymes in cellular metabolism to social networks across continents. I think Bateson would have been proud to see the ways in which some of his ideas have developed and taken root. Not only are individual people and families best seen in 'context' but these concepts have been a powerful ways of exploring and explaining much of what we see around us. In a complex and recursive world view, context is everything.

Perhaps equally important is the realisation that the properties of these networked complex systems lead naturally to self-organisation. There is very good evidence for the almost ubiquitous occurrence of self-organised patterns in nature and in the human sphere: everything from soil properties to stock markets. So interfering in nature without taking into account the self-organised properties of the biosphere and the anthroposphere can lead to surprises such as the collapse of species distributions, for example, when the distribution pattern comes from the interactions of the pandemonium in the 'tangled bank' and the habitat is fragmented into pieces smaller than the characteristic scale of the SGC. So the world of emergence, SGC and networks shows us how micro-scale interactions in everything from soils and sediments to human societies and communities – and frequently these are at scales that we have hitherto neglected – can lead to complex meso-scale behaviour of landscapes, waterscapes and human societies. We also require much better information upon which to base our monitoring, evaluation and reporting. This is where a total revolution in sensor webs, computing power and visualisation techniques will come to our aid. High-frequency monitoring networks, which deliver data from previously unthinkable spatial and temporal scales, are rapidly becoming a reality.[3] The reaction–diffusion interactions between populations and species and their environments at small scales are the source of much small-scale dynamics and patterning. A non-equilibrium view of the world suddenly turns 'noise' (a source of variance to be controlled and averaged) into 'signal' and evidence of true process emerges. The neglect of micro-scale interactions leads to some fundamental uncertainties and difficulties in interpreting evidence for change. Meso-scale systems – systems that have been called 'middle-number' systems because they contain a sufficient number of interacting components as to be almost impossible to comprehend[4] – show very deep recursive complexity, which can lead to unpredictable behaviour. All in all we are dealing with systems in which modelling and prediction have some fundamental shortcomings and uncertainties. Despite the meso-scale difficulties, the properties of the macro-scale entities – the so-called 'large number' systems – frequently show statistical properties that are comprehensible. In addition, SGC in non-linear reaction–diffusion systems clearly leads to larger-scale biophysical constraints – system properties very like the MaxEnt solutions of the strictly SOC thermodynamic systems that the physicists build.[5] So emergence and SGC take us from a non-linear, non-equilibrium view at small scale, through the difficulties of the world of meso-scale interactions – the world of reality for many of us two metre tall primates – through to statistical properties and thermodynamic constraints at the global scale. Just maybe the computing and sensor revolution will finally bring home to us some aspects of the true nature – the context – of the world in which we live.

It would be good to be able to have some early warning of system crashes and the approach to thresholds or critical points. We need measures of the precariousness of our present position. After all, if we think in terms of resilience, complex attractors and multiple stable states rather than global equilibria, what we require is an estimate of the shape of the overall 'stability landscape'. We must recognise that all these coupled 'systems of systems' inhabit changing 'stability landscapes' with basins of attraction interspersed with unstable mountain peaks and steep-sided cols. We must also recognise that these 'landscapes' change with time as climate and other large-scale constraints change over time. The robust HOT systems have arisen by trial and error and will show resilient responses to external perturbations. Furthermore we have discussed the distinct possibility that small-scale events (the micro-world of pattern and process) can have important emergent properties, causing surprise and even strong hysteresis. So are there any tools that might give us an early warning of imminent disaster – a measure of precariousness? The answer is very few, but there are some things in the shadows, and here we can exploit the approaching 'singularity', the convergence in technologies that we can use to monitor the natural world in real time and at high frequencies.

Ecolophysics

We can obtain a useful pointer from the world of finance and economics – and here we are exploiting the analogies between the dynamics of stock markets (driven by the actions of traders working on partial information) and the dynamics of natural systems. The application of physics to the high-frequency dynamics of markets (using data on market fluctuations at scales of minutes) has resulted in a discipline called financial physics or econophysics.[6] This is a new and controversial field, but one in which a lot of effort is being expended; after all, any tool that might warn of an impending market crash would be worth a fortune. (The financial world is depending more and more on very rapid expert systems to read information and make market trades before other people. In this way margins can be significantly improved although, presumably, the advantage will be less when everyone is doing this.) Nevertheless econophysics has developed some tools which, their developers claim, can identify a pattern of fluctuations in market prices prior to market crashes.[7] This work is mostly by Didier Sornette and his collaborators, who looked for particular signatures of market bubbles and crashes characterised by 'a power law acceleration of the market price, decorated by log-periodic oscillations'.[8] Anti-bubbles seem also to be preceded by log-periodic fluctuations in stock prices, but in this case by price declines and deceleration in the log-periodic fluctuations. These signals of an approach to crashes, which themselves are statistical outliers on power law or 'fat-tailed' distributions, are presumed to be characteristic of complex systems which show self-organisation, complex attractors, fractal properties and occasional 'land-slides' (to use the sand pile analogy discussed earlier).

This work is controversial; there is some difference between advocates of this heterodox, non-equilibrium form of economics and the more orthodox adherents of the traditional discipline.[9] Once again this is a dispute between those who see market equilibria and those who see a much richer set of dynamics arising from individual choice based on partial information in complex settings. Nevertheless, evidence is mounting that stock market crashes are preceded by identifiable signals. If this kind of analysis was possible with high-frequency ecological data, then might it be possible to get some early warning of impending abrupt changes in state – a kind of 'ecolophysics' perhaps?[10] This approach would require a complete change in attitude towards sampling and 'noise' in ecological data. First, it would require the collection of high-frequency (even minute scale) data from large numbers of sites. This would require a new approach to sampling, web-based and wireless communications systems, and large amounts of data storage. Nevertheless the technology now exists to do this. In catchments and water monitoring we are already seeing the beginnings of a 'high-frequency' wave of new data.[11] Conventional approaches fail to capture the full range of spatial and temporal variability in stream and river systems[12]. New high-frequency data will require a reassessment of past practices and interpretations. It has even been suggested that the difference in understanding will be enormous; as great as the difference between listening to a Beethoven symphony at the rate of one note every minute or so, and listening to the real thing.[13] Second, we must also look for changing spatial patterns in ecological systems. Spatial patterns (waves, spirals, chequer-board patterns) arise from internal reaction–diffusion dynamics and are characteristic of non-linear reaction–diffusion systems. These systems also exhibit 'extremal' behaviour such MaxEnt behaviour and power law statistics.[14] Cellular automaton versions of these models exhibit 'gliders' and other forms of patterns well known in CA and algorithmic models.[15] So there might be profit in measuring and monitoring the changing characteristic length scales of ecosystems.[16] Third, rather than controlling the 'noise' by averaging and eliminating it, it would require us to recognise that the 'noise' is, in fact, a valuable signal. We should look for signals amid the 'noise' in the time series and spatial patterns, by using the new technologies at our disposal. Certainly we are already seeing new fractal properties and obtaining insights into catchment and ecosystem function. Can we see signals of forthcoming 'flips' between multiple stable states and impending crashes as well? There are already some suggestive data.[17] I noted earlier that state flips in models of ecosystems showing strong multiple stable states and hysteresis were associated with chaotic bifurcation points. There appear to be signals of the approach to such points.[18] Whatever the future might hold, there is evidence for the importance of the small in determining the properties of the large.

Meso-scale mosaics and 'wicked' problems

Perhaps the most important application of such techniques will be to identify the critical source areas and connections between stocks and flows in landscapes and waterscapes so that it might finally be possible to make small-scale, local interventions and asset replacements add up to something more at the regional scale. What we desperately require is to find a way to ensure that small-scale, local interventions by river trusts, community groups and catchment management agencies interact non-linearly and synergistically so that what 'emerges' are more sustainable landscapes and waterscapes. At the moment there is little or no connection between localised actions, recovery plans or restoration activities. If we are to make ecological engineering possible then we will need to be able to exploit the emergent properties of localised actions. As we move towards more distributed power, water and other infrastructure on the landscape, as agriculture becomes more corporatised and intensive, and as urban development proceeds in higher-density, more energy-efficient forms then there will be opportunities to look closely and with new eyes at the interconnections between the anthroposphere and the biosphere. The kinds of capitals that we wish to link are themselves emergent properties of the underlying pandemonium. We must find ways to exploit the variability, connectivity and emergent properties of interconnected capitals, and we must find ways of doing this with highly water-, nutrient- and energy-efficient, low-entropy systems.

Management of the 'rest of nature' is the management of all of nature: multiple capitals and values across heterogeneous landscapes and waterscapes all at once. The focal scale – the meso-scale or regional landscape scale – is sandwiched between the higher-level macroscopic constraints of the biosphere and the micro-scale properties of 'hot spots', patches and small-scale pathways. As I have discussed, the higher-level properties are functions of biophysical constraints, MaxEnt-like properties of ecosystems, evolved homoplastic structures of various kinds, climate and contingent biogeography, disturbance and extreme events, and the multiple states and hysteresis of the system-level response. The higher-level constraints also include the large-scale ecological 'footprint' of the region, the stocks and flows of energy and materials into and out of the region that constrain choice and action. The stocks and flows assessments determine the extent to which the biophysical constraints are being circumvented by subsidies of energy, water and other materials and ways in which the precariousness of the present state is being altered by these subsidies. The micro-scale properties are a function of reaction–diffusion relationships between patches across scales, food chains and other kinds of interspecies interactions in the natural capital, and the physiology and stoichiometry of the dominant functional groups. Micro-scale properties of a region are also influenced by choices made in the management of other forms of capital: the small-scale interactions between human, social, transport, infrastructure and financial capital.

The micro- and the macro-worlds are connected by fractal flow paths and by the emergent properties of the lower-level pandemonium. These properties in turn constrain the lower-level interactions – they act as context and constraints on the patch dynamics. So meso-scale management of the 'rest of nature' requires knowledge of these higher-level constraints on actions and choice, the analysis of multiple states and hysteresis effects as they affect community and policy options, and the determination of the precariousness of the present state through monitoring and analysis of the high-frequency signals from the micro-world. The connections made across scales by water and energy infrastructure, transport mechanisms, diffusion and dispersion, ensure that this is not an equilibrium world.[19] Transdisciplinary and multi-scaled approaches are going to be necessary to understand these interactions between a variety of processes across scales.[20] There will be much indeterminacy and uncertainty, but we seek the 'win–win–win' solutions that provide multiple benefits.[21] I am sure that there will be new possibilities and surprises.

Water is the medium of exchange in land and waterscapes. It is the process of reaction and diffusion between 'hot spots' and patches – the exchanges of water, energy and materials across boundaries – which form the economy of nature. So boundaries and the exchanges across them are an essential feature of life. These small-scale exchanges become self-organised into macro-scale patterns and constraints, and form the basis of the complex meso-scale, 'middle number' systems in which we live. So 'green' water flows and small-scale pattern and process are critical to the provision of the ecosystem services on which all life depends. Water is an essential medium of connectivity; when we change water availability, either through climate change or by engineering works, we change the non-linear reaction–diffusion relationships of landscapes and waterscapes in subtle and unforeseen ways. The cross-scale interaction of the SGC patterns with trophic and other interactions form the basis of the hysteresis effects and state 'flips' that we seen in these coupled systems. There is strong evidence for SGC in landscapes and waterscapes but also that the scaling regimes are discontinuous and multi-fractal. The economy of life is evidently self-organised at a variety of levels and scales, as is shown by the existence of homoplastic and other complicit structures in ecosystems and across biomes. As these structures arise from interactions between species and agents in complex adaptive systems, we are limited by the time scales required to rebuild such entities. The things we value most, the ecosystem services, are emergent, and often secondary, properties of ecosystems, which arise from the micro-scale interactions of many species.[22] We value the properties arising from the underlying pandemonium. We have, in the past, largely neglected the fine-scale individual and micro-processes that lead to these structures. The final, observed, set of trajectories over time is constrained by evolutionary design, by stoichiometry and by the 'sunk costs' and 'kludges' of contingent history. The outcome depends on complex interactions between biodiversity, dispersal, geomorphology and climate together with external extreme events (fire, flood and drought), which perturb the trajectories. This is the essence of the uniqueness of 'place'. Equifinality is characteristic of these systems; there are many contingent routes to similar solutions.

The fundamental properties of landscapes and waterscapes have been revealed by the many (uncontrolled) experiments that we have already done on this planet at the meso-scale. We have cleared land and built cities and towns, fragmented landscapes and waterscapes, altered connectivity, radically changed nutrient inputs, reduced biodiversity and changed trophic structures through hunting and overfishing. We have constructed new functional mosaics and flow regimes to suit our needs for production and security. In doing so we have revealed many of the surprising, non-linear properties of these coupled systems – the systems have frequently 'bitten back'. Hysteresis effects, sudden 'flips' between states, irreversible step functions and changes in the frequency and magnitude of extreme events have been recorded in many systems. History shows us that it is not easy to manage integrated environmental, social and economic systems at these scales. Irreversible changes due to combinations of deforestation, soil loss, erosion and climate change have defeated human societies in the past.[23] There is much more uncertainty and surprise than we accept, even now, and we do not have a good record of adaptability and personal and institutional flexibility in response. This is a contingent and uncertain world of 'becoming' rather than 'being'.

Emerging solutions

In my view this calls for a revision of the 'modern', humanist tradition. The essential values are correct – secular humanism values the 'other' – but the ideas about reason, control and predictability require revision. These complex adaptive systems (particularly the systems with which we are familiar on a day-to-day basis – cities, landscapes, waterscapes, markets and human communities – which show complexity, uncertainty and unpredictability) are not susceptible to pure reason, will, or the traditional scientific method. There is more risk and uncertainty in daily life than most would like to admit. So more data will help, but will not provide all the answers. These meso-scale, 'middle number' systems appear to us to be capricious, unpredictable and contrary: there are surprises, unexpected consequences and things do go wrong. Things do indeed 'bite back'; the unexpected properties of complex systems add a whole new dimension to risk management.[24] This, perhaps, is one of the fundamental reasons why many human societies have failed in the past. Reason is not everything; context is important and many decisions are based on values, cultures and beliefs. Evidence of change may be hard to come by until it is too late; and simple remedies, or remedies based on incorrect assumptions, lead to neglect of important signals and/or failed remedial strategies. Evidence is usually debatable when viewed through inadequate epistemological telescopes; this is particularly true if the changes going on around us are relatively slow, so that each generation comes to believe that their circumstances are the 'way things are supposed to be'. We have very poor memories for 'deep time', and just about everything we do is focused on short-term fixes.

The evidence does, however, give cause for optimism. Although there is much small-scale pattern and process that generates emergent properties and the complexities of SGC, there is none the less good evidence that reintroduction of species can on occasion rebuild ecosystems – even tropical rainforests, which are regarded as the icons of biodiversity and complexity.[25] What has been done around the globe time and time again is the destruction of the larger species that provide structure and context for other species. Deforestation is still rife, riparian vegetation is lost from rivers, seagrass beds and coral reefs are being destroyed. We have replaced these highly patterned three-dimensional ecosystems with simplified and, for us, more productive systems, which effectively mine resources for our use. Micro-flora and fauna are replacing macro-flora and fauna. If soil and nutrient resources are not depleted by previous deforestation and erosion, and if the climate has not changed beyond the tolerance of the species, then forests can regrow over quite short time periods: decades to a century or two. If too much biodiversity is lost during the clearing process then all the original species will never return. Trophic cascades do matter. Nevertheless urgent attention to the functional mosaics and structure of the 'rest of nature' can retain significant biodiversity and function at landscape and waterscape scales. Restoration of all forms of capital at these complex meso-scales is an urgent priority. If we are to manage landscapes and waterscapes effectively then they will need to be populated by profitable and productive enterprises supported by viable social units and communities. This goes to the heart of the cultures, values and beliefs of global populations and to the relationships between urban and rural populations.

It is, of course, a lot easier to conserve the natural capital (in the form of reserves and parks) separately from the social, human and financial capital. Even though such a strategy does not ensure long-term sustainability, even for big parks, it is widely adopted. Adding in the people does add significantly to the overall complexity and difficulty because of the social, cultural and economic contexts and the cross-scale interaction, but there seems to be no other way in the long run. Splitting up systems into components removes any possibility of SGC and emergence and this, presumably, is why merely adding best management practices together in the landscape does not produce the desired effect. Somehow we have to encourage and build towards the SGC and constraints that natural systems exhibit.

It is hardly surprising therefore that the call for a Wilsonian 'consilience' has been heeded, but many go further and call for a more context sensitive consilience of the natural and social sciences with the humanities. This is very much a debate about what we know, how we know it and what we do about it. Costanza, for example, writes

> the consilience we are really searching for, I believe, is a more balanced and pluralistic kind of 'leaping together', one in which the natural and social sciences and the humanities all contribute equitably. A science that is truly transdisciplinary and multiscale, rather than either reductionistic or wholistic is, in fact, evolving, but I think it will be much more sophisticated and multifaceted in its view of the complex world in which we live, the nature of 'truth' and the potential for human 'progress' than the enlightenment thinkers of the 17th and 18th centuries could ever have imagined.[26]

Just as there is a 'panarchy' of natural systems[27] with interactions between systems across scales, there is also a social panarchy with connection between disciplines, beliefs, institutions and communities across scales. The situation is made more complex by the fact that human communities operate at different levels of work and have different capacities to cope with interactions, networks and complexity. Thus there are some highly complex workings out of the relationships between societies and the natural world as change occurs. What is regarded as 'true' changes over time as the natural, social and economic contexts change.

The lack of equilibrium, the paucity of good models and the fundamental uncertainty surrounding these recursive systems is very much exemplified by our track record in managing common pool resources. Our management of water, forestry and fisheries around the world has a similar track record: a record of poor management through overexploitation and overallocation, inability to value other ecosystem assets and a lack of sustainability. We can begin to see why. First, the nature of the resource itself is often assumed to be more homogeneous in space and time, and more predictable, than it really is. (This, for example, was one of the reasons for the demise of the great northern cod fishery.) We tend to use averages when fluctuations are its very nature. So, second, our actual knowledge of the magnitude of the resource is usually assumed to be a lot better than it really is. Third, we find it very difficult to trade off the other, usually incommensurate, ecosystem values and services. A largely utilitarian view of the world does not help, particularly when market instruments tend to drive a push for maximisation of efficiency, profit and shareholder value over other values.

Complex valuations

The problems of complex valuations are nowhere more difficult that in the construction of regional, system-level, water benefits accounts. If we are to manage water at the system level then there is a need to define, compare and trade off the various kinds of services and benefits that water provides: everything from aesthetic values to breeding water birds, greenhouse gas sources and sinks, to water quality and the value of irrigated crops. This brings together all the problems discussed in this book:

- the role of climate and variability in rainfall and runoff, and the existence of abrupt changes and changes in the frequency and magnitude of extreme events,
- the competing demands and values of 'green' versus 'blue' water in rural and urban settings and the effects of existing land use mosaics on the coupling between fluxes at a range of scales,

- the role of land use change in influencing the balance of 'green' and 'blue' water and the role of 'green' water in the provision of ecosystem services of various kinds,
- the ability not only to account for the effect of present land use change patterns but also to predict the effects of future management alternatives in the form of new mosaics of land use, water and energy use and infrastructure construction,
- the trade-offs between incommensurate measures and the value sets of various benefit types and domains; social, economic and environmental,
- the trade-offs between various forms of capital and the question of 'strong' sustainability and intergenerational equity,
- the use of deliberative, regulatory, markets and other instruments and governance mechanisms to provide a more sustainable use pattern, which values capitals other than profit and security of supply.

We have a major disjunction between the biophysical measures and predictive tools and the social and economic measures and tools at our disposal. Social values and psychometric classes do not equate with biophysical measures and monitoring outputs, particularly when all these are complex entities. Furthermore, there is a severe problem with synthesis and integration across scales and between individual projects and measures and a more integrated assessment of the totality of measures and capitals and what an alternative future might look like. How do we value and equate Rotary Clubs (social capital), financial investments and profit (financial capital) and the numbers of water birds or predators in ecosystems (natural capital)? Indeed, how do we value extreme events and variability, when these are detrimental to financial capital and essential to natural capital? In a world of change – and in a world in which natural capital is becoming ever more scarce and critical – a single-minded focus on security and economic efficiency does not provide for future gains in effectiveness or resilience in the face of change. We are still dependent on natural capital and ecosystem services, and always will be. This makes us dependent on complex entities, which produce variability and are driven by it. How best therefore to manage and value the interpenetration of the biosphere and the anthroposphere? How do we set targets for, value and trade emergent entities when we know that there are scaling regimes with sharp scale breaks between them? This is indeed 'immature' science, sociology and economics. When we have invested as much time in these questions as that invested in the creative maximisation of economic efficiencies, utilities and rents, then a more sustainable future may be assured.

Because of the key roles that both 'green' and 'blue' water play in providing connectivity and in maintaining ecosystem services, water plays a very complex role in maintaining the 'commons' for us all. Attempts to own, manage and alienate water flows for private benefit are therefore to be seen in a much broader context. So must the competing demands and purposes of private companies (focused on shareholder value) and the many new kinds of devolved public institution (river trusts, catchment management authorities and the like), which manage the public good aspects of the very same resource. The widespread – and growing – tendency to see water as something to be managed and traded as a private good must be balanced by the requirements for 'strong' sustainability and equity for all global inhabitants. This is not, at present, being managed effectively. Other values are vitally important for long-term sustainability. There are important issues about values, rights and equity here. There is yet another 'tragedy of the commons' that must be avoided.

Poor information, poor long-term memories, denial, incommensurate values and a philosophy of discounting evidence of deleterious change ('after all, we don't know for certain, do we . . . ?') frequently leads to the multiple prisoners' dilemmas and the 'the tragedy of the commons'. No wonder that we are seeing the slow rise of more robust management frameworks incorporating market trading systems where appropriate, but hedged about by other forms of institutional, legal and regulatory controls. Slowly but surely, adaptive co-management, utilising forms of knowledge other than pure science and other institutional frameworks, is being instituted around the world to manage common pool resources.[28] An optimist would say that, slowly but surely, the historical and modernist drive towards individual utility and self-interest (Adam Smith's 'invisible hand') is being replaced by altruistic common interest (Ruitebeek and Cartier's 'invisible wand'), which emerges in the co-management of natural resources in many communities if allowed to do so. To trade more effectively in environmental goods and services we need to graft a green thumb onto the 'invisible hand' of the market.[29] Management with little information (or even no information) is better than no management at all. The rush to institute market mechanisms for trading water and other natural resources in many western countries will eventually be (and is already being) tempered by other instruments that deal with issues of inequality as justice, equity and fairness become more and more the concerns of communities.

Managing complex entities

Mark Everard has reviewed the various river and catchment management schemes in place in the United Kingdom.[30] By and large these are implemented through a variety of foundations, trusts and other regional bodies funded from a variety of public and private funds. In all cases the intention is to maximise the various benefits of water and catchments (ecosystem services, freshwater fisheries (particularly salmonids), agriculture, flood mitigation, tourism and aesthetic values) in a landscape very much influenced by the foot and mouth disease outbreak in 2001. As discussed earlier, the foot and mouth disease outbreak drove home the point that tourism and recreation were by far the largest income source for rural communities, so that maintenance of the landscape values and recreational fisheries associated with 'Beautiful Britain' is paramount. Many of the river management plans are based around the need for improved farm practices and soil, manure and nutrient management. The overall impression gained from the review is that ecosystem functions and services are growing in importance in a policy environment that was, previously, more focused on economic and social outcomes. The new, more balanced, policy environment requires investment in multiple outcomes where disciplinary and geographical fragmentation and perverse subsidies did not encourage the kinds of integrated landscape-scale outcomes required. Indeed, the river trusts seem to have arisen to address precisely this policy need: a more integrated and community-based investment vehicle. Voluntary organisations have addressed the gaps in existing policies. Everard notes that the UK community is paying twice for damaged ecosystems: once through agricultural subsidies that encourage intensive farming practices and again, afterwards, through remediation programmes. New forms of EU stewardship payments and the programmes of the Water Framework Directive are beginning to address these needs but, nevertheless, there is a real need to find sustainable investment programmes that are capable of balancing a variety of capitals and values. Everard concludes that integrated water and catchment management requires placing ecosystem services at the core of sustainable development, thinking at larger scales, finding appropriate economic and regulatory signals and incentives, and providing new forms of leadership for both the voluntary and private sectors. Everything I have said in this book argues along similar lines.

Michael Young has spent many years working on the design of management systems for these common pool natural resources. As he points out, what is required is an efficient and robust system for managing sustainable investment and resource use, which achieves 'equity, environmental integrity and economic efficiency'.[31] In what I regard as a much neglected book, Young succinctly catalogues the shortcomings of market economics and notes that markets are not, on the whole, ecologically friendly. The continued search for economic efficiency leads to both intra- and intergenerational inequities, so that true sustainability requires mechanisms and instruments that ensure equity both within and between generations. Young makes the valid point that the true distinction between 'strong' and 'weak' sustainability is whether or not it is required that environmental quality is maintained within each generation, or whether some 'borrowing' between generations is allowed with compensation allowed for at later times. Correctly, in my view, Young argues for efficiency in economic policy as a means to achieving good environmental outcomes (the use of market mechanisms and the elimination of perverse trade and agricultural subsidies, for example), but sees the need for compensation and wealth redistribution mechanisms to tackle the problems of inequity in the short and long term. Sustainability requires equity and ethical solutions, in the here and now but especially over 'deep time'. If resource use is to be made sustainable, there is a very strong argument to be made for correct pricing of resources in the form of 'polluter pays' and 'consumer pays' policies. Arguing from economic theory, Young also calls for specific institutions and mechanisms to manage particular externalities, and this can be achieved either through regulation or through market mechanisms. Of course, none of this would be music to the ears of the 'business-as-usual' merchants and those who would deny that there is any kind of environmental problem in the world and who would argue that maximising profit and minimising cost is the best strategy. Nevertheless those working in third world development would surely agree. Aid workers have known for some time that sustainable wealth generation happens when people work together to manage local ecosystems effectively.[32] What I have found fascinating in the writing of this book is the fact that many of the most advanced tools and techniques for community dialogue and the balancing of cultures and values are to be found in use in the third world where the funding comes from philanthropic, aid and NGO funds. It is high time that these techniques were also used New York, London and Sydney, where they are as much in need of application.

Markets can be used to manage systems where the costs and feasibility of reversing a decision and restoring an equivalent set of environmental values or opportunities are low and where the significance of the decision is also low. With the correct allocation mechanisms and institutional and legal arrangements, markets can work well under these circumstances. As the possibilities of the irreversible loss of values and opportunities increases and the significance of decisions or actions increases (e.g. there is a real potential for lack of intra- or intergenerational equity) then market mechanisms need to be increasingly hedged about by tight institutional or regulatory rules. At the extreme, where reversibility is impossible and the significance of decision making or action is very high, then transparency, dialogue, deliberation and citizen-based decision making is essential.[33] In all cases real prices must be charged for resources and the winners must compensate the losers in Pareto optimal solutions, even across generations.

There are guides to action in the literature and there is an active debate in what might be called 'progressive politics' about the best ways to manage our affairs, and the affairs of the world, in changing times.[34] Biodiversity conservation responds directly to national and institutional governance.[35] There is an awareness of the urgency and complexity of the present predicament, particularly in the context of the third world. There have been ideas in the shadows for

years but there is a now a need to bring ecological and environmental considerations into the social and economic debate. These 'systems of systems' are now
one. Global politics needs an injection of just management of the commons.
Even though I did not set out to write a political text, any deep reading of the
ecological, social and economic literature, together with an epistemology which
views the world in ethical terms as a complex and recursive 'system of systems',
sees the shortcomings of a predominantly market- and efficiency-based global
economy. The motivations of those who would 'reclaim the commons' become
clear.[36] Although I do not necessarily see another world as inevitable, there are
certainly opportunities (and needs) for a new future as this Kondratiev cycle
turns to new directions. The ideas of recursive interaction in complex systems
are likely to be one of the determinants of how we proceed over the coming years.
Certainly they lie at the heart of many thoughts about government reforms and
the management of natural resources, especially water.

As I noted earlier, the water industry has been at the forefront of government
and governance reforms in Western and other countries. Cost-effectiveness, allocation efficiency and market reforms have been at the heart of water management systems over the past decade. They characterise what has been called the
New Public Management (NPM), which has been touted as a paradigm shift in
Western countries, but is probably not so.[37] NPM is a series of initiatives centred
on efficiency and effectiveness, service quality, decentralisation, subsidiarity,
smaller government, competition, outsourcing and the privatisation of service
delivery; it is simply an outgrowth of a modern, instrumentalist philosophy in
which objectification and quantification are favoured. (It goes hand in hand
with other 'scientific' management techniques like Total Quality Management
(TQM).) To varying degrees these types of initiative have been used in many countries where government services are now delivered through private companies
and other 'third way' providers. Control and the management of externalities
are supposed to be achieved through performance contracts and public service
charters. As I already noted, the application of NPM to water management has
led to a rapid proliferation of risk reduction strategies, new intermediaries and
new players in the market place as sovereign risk is shed from governments
to private corporations. Due diligence now requires corporations to assess all
forms of risk to their profitability and licence to operate, including environmental and other risks. The application of NPM to the management of science
breeds a culture of compliance and not innovation; it also discourages higher-
level (level IV and V) performance, which is critical to the success of transdisciplinary entities. It is far too easy to set performance goals and milestones at
too low a level. In a resource-limited world, this behaviour is frequently used
to ensure that such bold ventures are stillborn. The widespread application of
NPM to science agencies and government business enterprises is seeing a flight

of high-level talent away from such highly regulated and risk-averse institutions to more creative and flexible arrangements, such as individual consulting and research contracts. TQM and time sheets never fostered creativity. There are ever increasing opportunities for creative individuals to make effective contributions through more flexible vehicles.

The uncertainty and partial nature of environmental data represent a fundamental challenge to programmes run under the sway of NPM. I have already shown how in the area of environmental flows it is quite difficult to demonstrate that management actions result in improved ecological condition. It is also hard to set baselines and targets. In the world of NPM, and largely because of the complexity of the issues and systems being managed, if the contracts do not set adequate targets and goals then the service delivery falls short of expectations. A recent paper for DEMOS in London by Chapman[38] discusses the impact of complex adaptive systems on the NPM and the ways in which the system does indeed 'bite back' in unexpected ways. In the context of water, the huge *Cryptosporidium* outbreak in Sydney a few years back is an excellent example of the unexpected system failure, and the inability of performance contracts written without prior knowledge of the unexpected to cope at the moment of crisis. This is one of the reasons why less and less risk is accepted and institutions become more and more conservative in their approaches and attempt to shed risk to others. So Young's points still hold: management of complex resource systems such as water will always require a mixture of policy tools, some market-based for the simple and well-known situations, others with regulatory frameworks for more risky situations, and finally deliberative processes for community interaction and consensus building. One size does not fit all but there are some fundamentals. Full pricing is essential and compensation must be paid. People are concerned about fairness and make judgements on environmental decision making and management policies along these lines. Universal principles exist, and more contextual principles of distributive, procedural and interactional justice play important roles in the ways people think and act. Syme *et al.*[39] write

> on all three dimensions of justice, the equitable distribution of goods
> and burdens is important but not the sole principle, as other
> principles are also taken into account, such as efficiency,
> environmental rights, and rights to economic welfare.

In the management of water in particular the industry has to take public perceptions of justice, equity and fairness into account as it develops its service provision and risk management strategies. The future is an externality in itself; intergenerational equity and 'strong' sustainability require a more inclusive valuation system than is presently seen in NPM, together with institutions that can enforce the rights of future generations.[40]

There is a stark distinction between market-based frameworks for the management of common pool resources (much loved by the instrumentalists and lovers of New Public Management) and the model based around collective management or co-management. These two perspectives begin from quite different assumptions about the nature of people and society.[41] Advocates of NPM and market reforms see humans and society primarily as markets and market actors. Proponents of co-management see humans and society in cultural and social contexts that are not reducible to purely market terms. NPM sees government primarily in terms of efficiency and effectiveness, whereas proponents of co-management see a cultural and social role for government above that of pure efficiency. Market-based reforms assume that when there are no discrepancies between public and private interests then all will act in the public interest. This is clearly not so. A further distinction lies in the degree to which government institutions and agencies are prepared to surrender sovereignty to community interests and groups. Power sharing is an essential feature of what might be called 'radical-modernity', including true subsidiarity and cooperative management of resources.[42] Finally, there is the issue of uncertainty and risk management, and the degree to which market assumptions can operate in a complex and constrained world hedged about with multiple and incommensurate values.

All institutions – scientific institutions, corporations and government jurisdictions – must realise that a greater focus on ethics is slowly but surely being demanded by an ever more sceptical and educated populace. The Web really is an excellent source of information for community groups and NGOs. Thus practices and policies that have been the norm for decades are giving way to those with greater transparency and democratic involvement. We have moved from governments accepting the sovereign risk to an outsourced state of NPM where efficiency is all, risk management is paramount and the complexity of interactions brings new risks and opportunities. A new form of social capital is required to prosper in this newly interconnected world. Collaboration, partnerships and trust are the watchwords, and these require new skills and greater capacity to cope with complexity and relationships of a kind not seen before. Science, for example, has to change out of 'transmit' mode and more often into 'receive', and lift the level of work that it does. Society has problems it wants solved and sees science not as some kind of monastic religion but as a fully integrated source of particular skills and ways of knowing useful things. I believe that Giddens is correct in saying that an entirely new epistemology is emerging – one of complexity, uncertainty and surprise – and we now do recognize that we are living in a world of complex and interacting 'systems of systems'.

N O T E S

1. I have adapted this term from Peter Taylor, *Unruly Complexity: Ecology, Interpretation, Engagement* (Chicago, IL: Chicago University Press, 2005), because although we must take a systems view of the interaction of agents we must avoid falling back on some kind of totalising framework that does not allow of recursive interactions, surprise and hysteresis.

2. M. Bunge. Systemism: the alternative to individualism and holism. *Journal of Socio-Economics*, **29** (2000), 147–57.

3. D. Butler. Everything, everywhere. *Nature*, **440** (2006), 402–5.

4. G. P. Harris. *Phytoplankton Ecology*. (London: Chapman and Hall, 1986). T. F. H. Allen and T. W. Hoekstra. *Toward a Unified Ecology*. (New York: Columbia University Press, 1992).

5. A. R. Plastino, M. Casas and A. Plastino. A nonextensive maximum entropy approach to a family of nonlinear reaction-diffusion equations. *Physica*, A**280** (2000), 289–303.

6. J. Feigenbaum. Financial physics. *Reports on Progress in Physics*, **66** (2003), 1611–49. Similarly, the discipline of 'social physics' studies the emergent properties of societies: everything from the behaviour of crowds to traffic jams. See P. Ball. *Critical Mass: How One Thing Leads to Another*. (London: Arrow Books, 2004).

7. There are many papers on the topic written by Sornette and his collaborators. See, for example, A. Johansen and D. Sornette. Modeling the stock market prior to large crashes. *The European Physical Journal*, B**9** (1999), 167–74. D. Sornette and A. Johansen. Significance of log-periodic precursors to financial crashes. *Quantitative Finance*, **1** (2001), 452–71. W.-X. Zhou and D. Sornette. Evidence of a world-wide stock market log-periodic anti-bubble since mid-2000. *Physica*, A**330** (2003), 543–83.

8. A. Johansen and D. Sornette. The Nasdaq crash of April 2000: yet another example of log-periodicity in a speculative bubble ending in a crash. *The European Physical Journal*, B**17** (2000), 319–28.

9. P. Ball. Culture crash. *Nature*, **441** (2006), 686–8.

10. I am not the first to coin this term. In an analogy similar to econophysics and the context discussed here, the term appears to have been coined by Marcel Ausloos in Belgium.

11. D. Scholefield *et al.* Concerted diurnal patterns in riverine nutrient concentrations and physical conditions. *Science of the Total Environment*, **344** (2005), 201–10.

12. I. A. Malcolm, C. Soulsby and A. F. Youngson. High-frequency logging technologies reveal state-dependent hyporheic process dynamics: implications for hydroecological studies. *Hydrological Processes*, **20** (2006), 615–22.

13. J. W. Kirchner *et al.* The fine structure of water quality dynamics: the (high frequency) wave of the future. *Hydrological Processes*, **18** (2004), 1353–60.

14. M. Pascual and F. Guichard. Criticality and disturbance in spatial ecological systems. *Trends in Ecology and Evolution*, **20** (2005), 88–95.

15. A. Adamatsky, A. Wuensche and B. De Lacy Costello. Glider-based computing in reaction-diffusion hexagonal cellular automata. *Chaos, Solitons and Fractals*, **27** (2006), 287–95.

16. R. L. Habeeb *et al.* Determining natural scales of ecological systems. *Ecological Monographs*, **75** (2005), 467–87.

17. M. Rietkerk *et al.* Self-organized patchiness and catastrophic shifts in ecosystems. *Science*, **305** (2004), 1926–9.

18. W. A. Brock and S. R. Carpenter. Variance as a leading indicator of regime shift in ecosystem services. *Ecology and Society*, **11**(2) (2006), 9. www.ecologyandsociety.org/vol11/iss2/art 9/. S. R.

Carpenter and W. A. Brock. Rising variance: a leading indicator of ecological transition. *Ecology Letters*, **9** (2006), 308–15.

19. These ideas are spelled out in more detail in L. H. Gunderson and C. S. Holling. *Panarchy: Understanding Transformations in Human and Natural Systems.* (Washington, DC: Island Press, 2002).

20. P. M. Haygarth *et al.* The phosphorus transfer continuum: linking source to impact with an interdisciplinary and multi-scaled approach. *Science of the Total Environment*, **344** (2005), 5–14.

21. J. A. Foley *et al.* Global consequences of land use. *Science*, **309** (2005), 570–4.

22. C. Kremen. Managing ecosystem services: what do we need to know about their ecology? *Ecology Letters*, **8** (2005), 468–79.

23. J. Diamond. *Collapse.* (London: Allen Lane, The Penguin Press, 2004).

24. E. Tenner. Why Things Bite Back: Predicting the Problems of Progress. (London: Fourth Estate, 1996).

25. D. M. Wilkinson. The parable of Green Mountain: Ascension Island, ecosystem construction and ecological fitting. *Journal of Biogeography*, **31** (2004), 1–4.

26. R. Costanza. A vision of the future of science: reintegrating the study of humans and the rest of nature. *Futures*, **35** (2003), 651–71. (Quote from pp. 653–4.)

27. Gunderson and Holling, *Panarchy.* (See Note 19.)

28. J. Ruitenbeek and C. Cartier. *The Invisible Wand: Adaptive Co-management as an Emergent Strategy in Complex Bio-economic Systems.* Occasional Paper 34, Centre for International Forestry Research, Bogor, Indonesia (2001). www.cifor.cgiar.org.

29. See the review of M. Borgerhoff Mulder and P. Coppolillo. *Conservation: Linking Ecology, Economics and Culture.* (Princeton, NJ: Princeton University Press, 2005) by R. L. Nadeau. Why can't we graft a green thumb on the invisible hand. *Trends in Ecology and Evolution*, **20** (2005), 588–9.

30. M. Everard. Investing in sustainable catchments. *Science of the Total Environment*, **324** (2004), 1–24.

31. M. D. Young. *Sustainable Investment and Resource Use: Equity, Environmental Integrity and Economic Efficiency.* Man and the Biosphere Series, Vol. 9. (Carnforth, Lancs: UNESCO and Parthenon Publishing, 1992).

32. J. Giles. Ecology is the key to effective aid, UN told. *Nature*, **437** (2005), 180.

33. M. D. Young. Inter-generational equity, the precautionary principle and ecologically sustainable development. *Nature and Resources*, **31** (1995), 16–27. See also D. M. King. Can we justify sustainability? New challenges facing ecological economics. In *Investing in Natural Capital: the Ecological Economics Approach to Sustainability*, ed. A. M. Jansson *et al.* (Washington, DC: Island Press, 1994), pp. 323–42.

34. W. Hutton. *The World We're In.* (London: Abacus Books, 2002).

35. R. J. Smith *et al.* Governance and the loss of biodiversity. *Nature*, **426** (2003), 67–70.

36. N. Klein. Reclaiming the commons. *New Left Review*, **9** (2001), 81–9. I. Wallerstein. New revolts against the system. *New Left Review*, **18** (2002), 29–39.

37. L. E. Lynn, Jr. A critical analysis of the New Public Management. *International Public Management Journal*, **1** (1998), 107–23. D. G. Mathiasen. The New Public Management and its critics. *International Public Management Journal*, **2** (1999), 90–111.

38. J. Chapman. *System Failure: Why Governments Must Learn to Think Differently.* (London: DEMOS, 2002). Available from www.demos.co.uk/catalogue/systemfailure.

39. G. J. Syme *et al.* Ecological risks and community perceptions of fairness and justice: a cross-cultural model. *Risk Analysis*, **20** (2000), 905–16.

40. E. Padilla. Intergenerational equity and sustainability. *Ecological Economics*, **41** (2002), 69–83.

41. W. Dubbink and M. van Vliet. Market regulation versus co-management? *Marine Policy*, **20** (1996), 499–516.

42. E. Ostrom. *Governing the Commons: the Evolution of Institutions for Collective Action*. (Cambridge: Cambridge University Press, 1990). R. Plummer and J. FitzGibbon. Some observations of terminology in co-operative environmental management. *Journal of Environmental Management*, **70** (2004), 63–72.

23 Avoiding collapse

The 'fourth way' of recursive complexity and uncertainty: a richer debate about emergence, resilience and constraints, and about complexity, capacity and institutions.

In his recent book *Collapse*, Jared Diamond has looked at the fates of many previous human societies.[1] Many societies have failed in the past because of environmental problems, but some have survived for long periods by being cognisant of, and responding to, environmental constraints. Whatever we face as a result of our unprecedented interconnection with the natural world, complacency is not a good strategy under the present circumstances. Diamond catalogues the reasons for failure:

> Failure to anticipate the impending environmental collapse because of surprise, an incorrect sense of place or other unexpected ecological interactions,
>
> Failure to perceive imminent changes because of slow or imperceptible change, or a lack of evidence, or a disagreement about what constituted evidence (there is a lesson here about climate change),
>
> The application of apparently rational behaviour, often arising from the 'tragedy of the commons',
>
> Irrational behaviour, greed, poor decisions and denial,
>
> The application of unsuccessful solutions.

Many of these we have discussed here; the reasons for the past collapses of human societies are still with us. We are the first generation to realise the true nature and magnitude of regional and global constraints. The present nexus of increasing population, energy and resource demands, climate change and biodiversity loss, together with changing network architectures, increases the risks. Ecological surprise, hysteresis effects, uncertainty and debates about evidence are characteristic of the complex, non-linear world in which we live. The situation is further complicated by the existence of time lags and the perceptual problems of action at a distance. Lovelock takes a pessimistic view of our future prospects in his book *The Revenge of Gaia*.[2] He sees a world driven towards irreversible warming by positive feedbacks. Whatever the future holds we are rapidly learning about the nature of the world, and the constraints to our possible responses to it, and it is a race against time to see whether we can avoid past mistakes. Our rapidly increasing knowledge of environmental change is running hard up against cultural, institutional and personal constraints on our responses. Sustainability clearly requires an improved knowledge of the fundamental characteristics of the resources we are trying to manage, together with appropriate institutions to manage complex and emergent biophysical and social entities at local and global scales. We are not there yet. I remain an optimist but it will need quantum leaps in our thinking to pass through the bottleneck that Wilson foresees: not incremental thinking, but some real shifts in knowledge, culture and values.

The most important message from all the foregoing is that ethical system thinking is the key to the future. This is not a new idea. Indeed, it is an idea that was part of early religions. Respect for the system was what the ethical laws of the Jews were about centuries ago.[3] So the existential position of the human species is succinctly put in terms of the inevitable conflict between our curiosity, the human search for knowledge, novelty and self-identity, and the need to respect the 'system of systems' in which we must live. Once again Bateson got it right; in criticising the widespread adoption of expediency and the general ignorance about biological reality, he wrote

> Lack of systemic wisdom is always punished. We may say that the biological systems – the individual, the culture and the ecology – are partly living sustainers of their component cells or organisms. But the systems are none the less punishing of any species unwise enough to quarrel with its ecology.[4]

And the Millennium Ecosystem Assessment makes it clear that the global system is now taking the strain for globalised economies and material progress.[5]

We now know that despite the entreaties of the 'business as usual' merchants this is simply not possible, even in the absence of any environmental problems. Technological change has revolutionised the world in which we live, even if we wished to deny that human impact on the biosphere is widespread, pervasive and threatens not just our future but also the future of many other species. I think the evidence is compelling that technological advance and a focus on utilitarian ends and instrumental reasoning has brought us to the point where many measures of natural capital are in decline. Resilience has been compromised by loss of natural capital as well as the ever-increasing connectivity.[6] The next fifty years are probably going to be critical as we reach (and hopefully pass through) a crunch point in natural capital as well as the projected 'singularity' in computing, information and telecommunications technologies. But this is not a recipe for despair. This recognition of the state we are in is the first stage of doing something about it – after all, we do have the power to understand, name and explain the global condition and our place in it. With awareness and recognition comes a will to act. We have many examples of sustainable collective action to use as models; we can turn old institutional models into new, more appropriate systems of governance. Attention to inequalities and reconciliation of local and global interests is a high priority. As Diamond points out there is a race on in Western countries between the exponential increase on externalities and the exponential increase in knowledge and the will to act.

These issues go to the heart of how we might manage some of the great issues of the day:

> Climate change – using a mix of market-based and other incentives to reduce carbon emissions and achieve greater energy use efficiency (infrastructure and financial capital).
>
> Landscape and waterscape restoration in a regional context – using a mix of incentives to restore biodiversity and ecosystem services (natural capital). This will require finding efficient, profitable and constrained solutions to some complex issues.
>
> Building from local and regional restoration work to achieve global outcomes – taking account of connectivity and networks of influence.
>
> Finding new ways to monitor, evaluate and report progress towards a new set of 'smarter' targets, taking complexity and emergent properties into account.
>
> Solving some of the institutional issues around adaptive management and the interactions between the various communities of interest and jurisdictions.
>
> Finding new ways to discern and manage risk and resilience; finding techniques to assess the precariousness of the global situation.
>
> Building regional community capacity to ensure support and longevity for restoration programmes (social capital).
>
> Ensuring that individuals possess the necessary knowledge capital to be active and effective players in markets and society. Encouraging individuals to gain the necessary knowledge to take ethical decisions.
>
> Rethinking the distribution of research funding to ensure a greater supply of 'patient' dollars for blue skies inquiry (knowledge capital and creativity) as well as brokering and building transdisciplinary teams to solve these 'wickedly' complex problems (science as social action).

The micro- and the macro-

Many of these solutions lie in the realm of the signals and incentives provided to individuals to take ethical decisions. Much economic theory remains at odds with reality. We are, at present, largely unable to provide clear guidance for individuals taking decisions under conditions of complexity and partial information. The macroscopic properties of the biosphere emerge from the pandemonium of small-scale pattern and process. Critical source areas of various kinds (e.g. hydrological, nutrients, biodiversity) are linked across scales by reaction–diffusion processes – many of them non-linear – into a complex inter-weaving of pattern and process. Fluctuations of many properties in space and time are indicative of the underlying generating mechanisms and may be good indicators of change. If we use the wrong concepts and have not properly iden-tified the underlying mechanisms, little wonder that neither do small-scale actions to restore and manage landscapes and waterscapes usually add up to larger-scale outcomes, nor do large-scale prescriptions and policies work at the smaller, local scale. The signals and incentives we presently employ do not achieve sustainability or change for the good. Social capital is also a product of 'social physics' and individual choice. In this new, complex and riskier world the key role for governments is to recognise the constraints and set clearer goals, and to encourage investment in the presently neglected capitals: infrastructure, and collective social and knowledge capital. Governance arrangements must be nested in ways to suit biophysical reality.[7]

One of the most intriguing aspects of all this is the realisation that we are almost certainly trying to do this with insufficient evidence. The full realisation that small-scale interactions between individuals lie at the heart of the dynamics of both the anthroposphere and the biosphere forces us to accept that we only have partial and incomplete data upon which to base signals and incentives. Most of the environmental data that we have is woefully inadequate. As some-one is reported to have said 'we would never attempt to run the economy based on the kinds of data we have for the environment'. Debates rage over partial information, and firm stands are taken on major environmental issues on the basis of largely inadmissible evidence. Our predictive capability is less than we believe. More and more of our decision support tools are beginning to recog-nise this. Granted, huge investments and advances have been made in global observing systems; nevertheless we are still not addressing the complexities of systems that are fundamentally complex adaptive systems (CAS) and which fre-quently show surprise and hysteresis. Many of the things we would wish to value and protect are complex and emergent entities showing multi-fractal properties and much high-frequency – even paradoxical – variability. The human push for security attempts to reduce natural variability to a 'flat line' and in doing so eliminates fundamental properties of the ecology. Microscopic pattern and pro-cess both produces meso-scale complexity and is set in the context of larger-scale constraints. Thus markets and securitisation are in conflict with nature. A strong sense of place and the human scale of things, as well as a propensity to discount the future, work against us in planetary management. There are, therefore, two imminent crises: a crisis in the stocks and flows of energy and materials, biodiversity loss and the degradation of ecosystem services, coupled with a philosophical and epistemological crisis in terms of what we know about what is happening and what choices we make and institutions we establish to do something about it.

We are beginning to face the exponential rise in externalities that arise from our fascination with market economics, short-term profit and shareholder value, and we are beginning to factor other values into the financial markets we love so much. The institutions we presently have are not up to the task. We are beginning to realise that in the face of increasing global risks there is actually a close link between long-term profitability and resilience. (Interestingly, it is the large financial and insurance houses that have first realised the significance of climate change. Climate change is already one of the biggest factors contributing to insurance claims so it is directly impacting on their bottom lines. They are responding by changing risk profiles and premiums.) We are beginning to realise that conservation and restoration requires financial, human and social capital and that profitability requires the preservation of natural capital. Already our 'extended mind' of networked sensors in space and underwater gives us unprecedented reach and global coverage. These data contribute daily to the debate about global warming, extreme events and other kinds of anthropogenic impact. I foresee the day when complex signals from the CAS properties of various forms of capital will contribute to early warning signs of impending risks. Although the incorporation of this information into decision making is often painful and frequently fraught with political and cultural difficulties, eventually we must envisage its incorporation into new forms of multi-criterion analysis, market structures, targets and other incentives, which include new and improved representations of uncertainty and risk. So, increasingly, we turn to the interaction of people and biodiversity; to the interactions of social and natural capital in a complex and uncertain world. We cannot avoid the practical implications of the fact that our knowledge is 'heterogeneously constructed', bearing aspects of both reality and socially and culturally determined semiotics and metaphor.[8] Debates will continue. Science, rather than asserting priority, must engage in a series of messy debates about possibilities and options. Bateson was essentially correct: attempting to understand and change a 'heterogeneously constructed' system from the inside is very difficult. Boundaries and networks are negotiable and fluid.

Monitoring robustness and resilience

What breeds resilience are properties such as diversity, redundancy, modularity, connectedness, feedbacks and openness. These are all properties of landscape and waterscape mosaics across which are distributed various forms of capital. If we are to avoid collapse then all forms of capital need to be robust and resilient to change. Maintaining redundancy and diversity in landscapes and waterscapes comes at a cost, but this is a cost that must be balanced against the benefits of resilience in the face of changes in the spectrum of perturbations arising from land use and climate change at global scales. Resilience, after all, is the ability of a system to cope with change and stay intact.[9] Robust forms of capital also require an ability to be adaptable and even transformable if change is required. Whereas the present focus of monitoring, reporting and evaluation (and the so-called 'matters for target') is on measures of ecosystem condition and health, measures designed to monitor resilience would be different. These indicators would monitor the stocks and flows of capitals, the approaches to MaxEnt 'envelope' states, the spectrum of perturbations and the responses to it. This requires monitoring both means and variances across a range of scales, and watching for signals of the approach of thresholds and sudden changes in state. Resilience measures would also monitor systems and institutions that enhance adaptability and transformability.

Thus we must develop a new set of performance measures for 'all of nature' which encompass social, economic and environmental robustness and resilience. Natural systems have developed robust HOT states through trial and error over the millennia. We know that the responses of ecosystems in landscapes and waterscapes are conditioned by some deep evolutionary constraints: stoichiometry, molecular biology, physiology and trophic interactions linked by diffusion and dispersal through the environment. We are beginning to discern the major features of the catchment physiology and trophic cascades upon which the resilience of natural landscapes depends. The challenge we face is to design and develop suitable measures and responses for all capitals in short order. There are two key questions. The first is how to define the 'precariousness' of the present situation. We need to find ways to reach out into the non-linear space that lies beyond our present experience. How do we identify the 'tipping points' that lie beyond the scope of everyday experience (and models)? As global factors change (population, climate, biodiversity, etc.) we are moving into new dynamics and areas of risk. How do we identify where we are close to the edge of thresholds and therefore which issues to tackle first? This will require an analysis of the non-linearities and emergent properties of these coupled systems. We are finding more and more of these as we study natural systems more closely – both globally and regionally – adding a new dimension to integrated risk assessments. The second is the flipside of the first. If we can identify the 'tipping points' how do we then balance the various kinds of values and capitals that we have in ways which increase resilience? How do changes in these capitals arise from their interactions and push us closer to precarious states? What tradeoffs do we need to make and where do the new Pareto optima lie? This is a real problem in complex systems definition and dynamics, and the models we usually use do not reveal these properties.

What we require are new Pareto optima: new ways of maximising utility and minimising externalities. As Coombes and Kuczera have shown in the context of urban water systems,[10] because of the evident non-linearity of distributed water systems, and because of sunk costs, contingent technological developments and other constraints in policy and management practice, we are presently working to a very constrained Pareto frontier in terms of cost and water use efficiency. They write 'traditional solutions for water supply, sewage disposal and stormwater management are selected from an artificially limited set of separate technical solutions that form a constrained solution space'. So there is, in fact, a much broader constrained set of Pareto optima outside the present solution set. But given the constraints and the highly non-linear and emergent behaviour of these systems, how do we identify that wider solution space and find newer, better solutions? We know that our present solutions are suboptimal from a number of perspectives. How do we make the leap across the minefields of hysteresis and non-linearity to a better set?

What we do know is that what we presently regard as Best Management Practices (BMPs), if spread out across the land and waterscapes, simply do not take us to where we need to be – they are not sufficiently sustainable. The problem we have is that because of problems with actually determining the outcomes of management actions for all the reasons discussed above (in terms of our partial knowledge of improved ecosystem health, biodiversity, water quality, etc.) what tends to happen is that BMPs are set in terms of management actions rather than outcomes. Introduction of BMPs may result in long-delayed environmental outcomes as large soil nutrient pools are either built up or depleted; the results of BMPs may be hard to identify for decades.[11] Thus compliance with recommended management practices is taken as a good measure of progress when, in fact, the outcomes are often ill-defined at best.

So a monitoring, evaluation and reporting scheme for resilience would be very different from what we do now. It would include analysis and performance monitoring, which specifically looks for non-linearities 'in the shadows' (or in our peripheral vision) to reveal impending surprises and thresholds. It would also treat the variability we presently observe in new conceptual frameworks. In a way we are already being forced down this track. Many of the policy questions about water management that are presently being asked in the context of major national and international initiatives – such as the Water Framework Directive and the Australian National Water Initiative – are extremely difficult to answer. In many cases data analysis techniques and knowledge derived are insufficient. We need new tools to link complex performance and condition measures to management actions that improve environmental outcomes. When water allocation decisions end up in a court of law then minds will soon be focused on better measures.

Recognising constraints

In the face of all the difficulties associated with monitoring, evaluation and reporting there are those who argue that we should simply employ input and output controls rather than set performance targets based on 'fuzzy' outcomes or condition measures or use market mechanisms. This is the approach that is already in use in farm plans and nutrient budgets, emissions controls and caps on irrigation water extractions. This approach can be applied more broadly. It is possible, for example, to set input and output regulations region by region using footprint and 'stocks and flows' measures. Within the biophysical constraints set by regional biogeography, geology and climate, resource trading mechanisms and other self-organised collective institutional arrangements can be used to give market signals and incentives for innovation and efficiency gains. Prices for natural resources must be allowed to rise so as to reflect supply and demand – resource rents must be realistic. As resource prices rise then other substitutes will be developed where possible (e.g. renewable energy sources, bio-diesel, etc.), but there will be cases where there is no substitute and biophysical targets must be set and met. Market signals only reflect relative scarcity, so that biophysical controls must be used to reflect the absolute scarcity of key non-substitutable resources. To move towards 'stronger' sustainability we can regulate or cap water, energy and materials use and lower targets year by year. Technological solutions may solve some problems, but not all. 'Dematerialising' the economy is only a partial solution. Ratcheting down resource use to meet regional biophysical targets will reduce footprints over time and bring the stocks and flows of regions more into line with reality. We are, as ever, constrained by all kinds of path dependencies in our technologies and institutions and by the present lack of good predictive models and measures. The kinds of tools we are developing – more robust decision support tools used to stimulate debate and dialogue – are necessary when the stakes and the uncertainties are high. Regional and global constraints should not be seen as punitive. Water restrictions in urban areas have already demonstrated that there is a positive response to fair and equitable limits on resource use. In the face of ever-tightening resource availability we should expect to see all kinds of innovative solutions and non-linear forms of creativity arising from adaptive network strategies and transformations.

There is an inherent tension between a more partial and instrumentalist view of knowledge in a complex world and the existence of biophysical constraints. Throughout this book I have espoused a relativist epistemology while advocating a sturdy objective realism. An adaptive management regime will be required to recognise the existence of constraints and 'tipping points': boundaries to our choices and actions. We must seek greater resilience. This trend is consistent with the calls for a more open community dialogue about possible futures and is supported by the development of the Web and other tools for the measurement and dissemination of information. Cooperation is encouraged by disclosure and strongly influences the outcomes of multiple prisoners' dilemma games.[12] Cooperation and disclosure increases trust between community members. Norton believes that we should move towards 'strong' sustainability and hold open options for the future. He sees the maintenance of resilience as essential for intergenerational equity and wishes to 'distinguish economic policies that protect and expand opportunities from those that destroy and limit future options'. Norton would define 'strong' sustainability as 'an intergenerationally measurable index of opportunities embodied in resilient ecological systems that have maintained their integrity'.[13] Markets and individual behaviour are understood to be constrained by global and regional stocks and flows: by supra-economic biophysical constraints. Norton also sees that we need to find a way forward between the instrumental and intrinsic value systems and do away with the problems of quantification and naming of entities, seeking instead an alternative value system 'which recognises a continuum of ways humans value nature, values processes rather than only entities, is pluralistic and values bio-diversity in place'.[14] He sees merit in a community debate about possible future trajectories in the context of transparency and both intra- and intergenerational equity.

This changing system dynamic is a major challenge for governments, institu-tions, NGOs, communities and individuals. As Michael Young has concluded, it really is necessary to have institutions and instruments matched to the external-ities and other challenges that require management. In a changing and adap-tive world institutions and instruments also need to change with the changing circumstances. Already we can see that to avoid rural collapse it is necessary to find new coalitions around sustainable land- and waterscape management. Coalitions are needed dedicated to balancing the forms of capital to ensure (among other things) profitable and sustainable communities, higher-quality health outcomes, biodiversity conservation, high water quality and the preser-vation of cultural and heritage values.[15] This is very much a postoppositional, post-'green' and post-NGO agenda encompassing new forms of partnerships and collaborations with the capacity to cope with extremely complex and interactive scientific, social, medical, economic and cultural issues. We do not have much time.[16]

Balancing all forms of capital in such a complex world is indeed a place where the possibility of irreversible action and change is high, and the risks and decision-making stakes are high also. Market failure is rife. So this is why com-munity dialogue and other forms of collective deliberative processes are rapidly re-emerging. Old institutional models can still apply at local scales. At present there is no other way to attempt to balance the many and incommensurate values associated with the wise use of resources and the management of land-scapes and waterscapes *with people on and in them*. We simply do not have ways of making choices about values and resources that are not fungible and which morally and ethically cannot be valued solely in monetary terms – although we are trying hard to develop mechanisms to do this. The only way forward is to use market mechanisms and other incentives where we can, and to set targets and other goals in order to manage externalities and other values. New valuation sys-tems for water are being developed[17] which will allow us to think in new ways and define new goals for river management. These new valuation techniques allow us to think about upstream and downstream values in new ways, and to place values on the costs and benefits of storage and abstraction at various places in catchments.[18] Similarly, climate change and climate variability require that there are some quite sophisticated systems for defining environmental flows and minimum baseline conditions so that accepted rule-based mechanisms can be used to define environmental and other needs. We have some way to go in this area, particularly in a world of non-linearities and hysteresis.

> The first-best solution would be to define a set of minimum baseline conditions and then establish a mechanism that allows some-trade off among objectives as supply and demand conditions change by season and through time.[19]

Recursive complexity

So this is very much a 'radically modern' world: we have moved on beyond the strictures of structuralism, the debates about deconstruction and theory, and beyond the ideas of constructivism and various forms of relativism.[20] We are beyond 'left' and 'right', even beyond the 'third way'; this is, if you like, the 'fourth way'. We are now in an era of uncertainty and emergence coupled with synthetic thinking. We are trying to find ways of understanding, naming and explaining the features of the world around us by using new tools. The natural resource management policy questions are rapidly becoming more complex and frequently exceed the capacity of the science community to provide answers. In response the science is changing as fast as it can. We now seek explanations for both the properties of parts *and their recursive interactions in the context of the systems in which they are embedded.* Dennett abhors 'greedy reductionism' (remember the 'universal acid'? – it is cranes not skyhooks!)[21] and Wilson sees a place for this technique as means of entry into a complex world.

> Complexity is what interests scientists in the end, not simplicity . . . The love of complexity without reductionism makes art; the love of complexity with reductionism makes science.[22]

This recursive complexity also means that there is a need for a willingness (and capacity) to consider many points of view and many issues simultaneously. Single-issue solutions to complex problems rarely suffice. Synthetic thinking is required.

Capacity

Promoting a richer and more complex debate is a challenge for individuals and institutions alike. It requires high-capacity individuals to stimulate and participate in such debates, both in rural and in urban communities. It also requires institutions (which are often too risk-averse and centrally focused and therefore far too rigid and bureaucratic) to allow high-capacity individuals to do what they do best. The new complex network culture requires individuals who can see further than most, who can plan for diverse outcomes and allow for equifinality, and who can conceive of new partnerships and collaborations to achieve them. All communities require capacity; Richard Florida has shown that societies and communities that foster talent, tolerance and the requisite networking technologies are more creative and prosperous.[23] What is required is disruptive innovation and creativity: and disruptive is a key word! Disruptive, transgressive and creative behaviours are not often accommodated in the more traditional communities.[24]

There are precedents for nations successfully tackling complex and very hard questions, and succeeding in making social transformations. Perhaps the best example is that of South Africa, which made the transition from the apartheid era to that of the 'Rainbow Nation'. Led by Clem Sunter and others, South Africa began by looking at a series of possible environmental and political scenarios and then engaged in a national dialogue about the options and challenges.[25] The result is history. With the right political leadership and collective will it can be done. What is required is both the knowledge and a programme of 'knowledge as social action' to engage the community and facilitate change as well as a willingness to collectively face the future. Ilbury and Sunter have taken what they learned from the South African transformation and called it 'scenario planning in action'.[26] They describe a four-step process, which requires: first, an analysis of the fundamental rules of the game (which are becoming clear); second, an assessment of key uncertainties over which we have no control and the construction of plausible and relevant scenarios from those uncertainties; third, the setting out of options presented by those scenarios; and last, decisions can be made based on options presented by the scenarios. This is, if you like, a strategic planning process that allows for, and incorporates, uncertainty into the process. As the complexity of our recursive global engagement grows, more and more companies, regions and nations need to engage similar processes. Whatever happens, knowledge without social engagement, dialogue and collective action will never change anything.

Individuals can make a difference

If there is one message in all this it is that individuals can make a big difference. We can engage in social dialogues and improve our knowledge and capacity for ethical decision making. We can all get more involved in the policy debate. Those of us in resource-hungry Western-style economies can all live more sustainable lives, we can all adopt practices which reduce our ecological footprint and we can all, as Tim Flannery shows, adopt practices that will have only modest impacts on our lives but will have major impacts on energy consumption, the greenhouse effect and global warming.[27] It is not difficult to radically improve water and energy use efficiency at the individual level by installing quite simple conservation and reuse technologies. Cost-effective efficient and renewable energy technologies are now available, which can cut consumption in half. We *can* make a difference. This means that communities face a capacity challenge, to understand the issues better, the learn more about complexity and uncertainty and be more adaptive and less risk-averse. This means bringing all views, values and skills to the table in a more deliberative process. We must search for solutions that work with the natural world rather than against it. We must search for new, more sustainable institutions and collective governance arrangements. After all it is the search for a particular kind of certainty and security that has, to some degree, brought us to the present situation. There are alternatives that are no less rich – in many ways – some based on older self-organised models of trust and collective action.[28]

Creativity

Social capital is critical; more and more, and aided by the new technologies, social capital is reaching across institutions, communities and individuals, breaking down old barriers between corporations, institutions, disciplines and social groups. In the end I side with Handy: as far as possible reduce the power of the centre and fully empower the disciplinary and outlying units to make what accommodations with this new and complex world they find necessary.[29] We need coordination not control . . . and certainly do not discourage disruptive, non-linear creativity that arises from adaptive network strategies. Handy has also recently been arguing that creativity and a strong focus on efficiency, profitability and revenue growth do not sit well together. Creativity is something that takes time; and time is something that few have in this busy world of efficiency and shareholder value. Some of the most promising and creative opportunities now lie between the spheres of influence of various disciplines and cultures, so in addition to capacity building we need translators – walking Babel Fish if you like[30] – people who can communicate across boundaries, and in different languages, bringing groups together and sparking creativity and innovation. Traditional institutional arrangements are not keeping up with the pace of change or the complexity of the challenge.

It is no longer possible to think about maximising and managing all forms of capital in landscapes in isolation from broader-scale, even global, social and economic policy. Tilzey has, for example, in an analysis of the future of biodiversity conservation and agriculture in the UK,[31] concluded that if 'strong' sustainability is to be achieved then an integrated rural policy is required. In accordance with Young's analyses discussed above, Tilzey identifies the problems with the present neo-liberal ('market productivist') policies of many governments and the World Trade Organization in which costs are minimised, profits maximised and externalities largely unmanaged. Tilzey is critical of the attempts to 'green' high-input agriculture through programmes such as integrated farming systems (IFS) and integrated crop management (ICM). Although IFS and ICM address some of the problems with modern agriculture and attempt to achieve environmental benefits without major increases in cost, they are nevertheless seen as a form of 'weak' sustainability because they do not address the heavy use of external fuel and fertiliser subsidies or the use of pesticides. Intergenerational equity is not assured. The globalised trade in agricultural produce and the existence of huge and perverse subsidies are major factors leading to poverty and widespread environmental degradation. In short, what is required is a new vision for a more sustainable management regime, using biophysical constraints and regulations, using market mechanisms where possible, and managing externalities as Young has suggested. There is a major problem globally with the separation of conservation areas from people[32] and with the relationship between biodiversity conservation and poverty.[33] We have reached the point where the entire globe is the 'whole of nature'. Global biodiversity, climate and biogeochemistry are threatened. Agriculture is the largest global threat to biodiversity if it is measured by bird populations – the best-known taxonomic group.[34] It is hardly surprising that those with long experience of working with third world development, and vigorous spokespersons for those countries, are calling for new ways and a change away from neo-liberal practices, which do not balance all forms of capital effectively and which lead to poverty and biodiversity loss.[35] I am not one to suggest that we all go back and live in caves. There is a need for food and water for all, for development and for human dignity and freedom. The next fifty years are going to be a real challenge as populations rise and more and more land will be required for food production.[36]

In an empirical sense we need to learn more from 'what works'. In addition to learning more from what we have already done, largely by chance and by tinkering for generations, it would be a good thing, for example, to be able to try out a large-scale series of alternative experimental options at landscape scales – and see what works and what does not. Darwinian selection of ecosystem properties is possible[37] so that what we have been doing around the world is a huge distributed land and waterscape management experiment. We can learn much from has worked, and what has not, in the past. This includes social and economic institutions as well as landscape mosaics.[38] This is very much the socio economic and biophysical approach to what are often called genetic search algorithms in computing: allowing random perturbations and picking the ones that work. There are, of course, ethical considerations here so the options would need to be designed with care; none the less the idea has merit.

Recent work indicates that there may well be new land use practices that can support higher biodiversity without compromising agricultural production. Two approaches have been advocated: either wildlife-friendly farming (which boosts populations of wildlife on farmland but may compromise yields) or land sparing (which increases yields but only on a portion of the landscape). These are early days, and more empirical knowledge is required, but nevertheless there do seem to be land-sparing methodologies that lie in mosaic patterns that maintain yield and improve biodiversity on the remaining spaces.[39] We are seeking new water management strategies that use a mixture of natural and technological solutions distributed across the landscape. In essence, what we are trying to achieve is a kind of 'Factor 4' for agriculture in the form of a distributed mosaic of practices that as far as possible preserve the emergent properties of multiple capitals. We also seek new distributed rather than centralised institutional and governance arrangements. This is consistent with Tilzey's calls for integrated rural planning but, of course, would also need to have water management and other elements of a more sustainable farming system built in. There are recent attempts to integrate the many factors involved – from hydrology to governance – and describe a new future for landscapes and waterscapes, but as yet these are somewhat speculative and necessarily descriptive.[40]

The need for innovation

Perhaps one really important message for society that comes out of all this is the importance of investment in long-term 'blue skies' thinking at the present time. To find a way into this problem we should return to Bateson and his science that as yet has 'no satisfactory name'. In a paper about the origins of postnormal science Tognetti writes

> the growing recognition of irreducible uncertainty, as is particularly evident in complex global problems that cannot be controlled and that have in large part resulted from just such attempts to control natural systems, has led to a new social context in which, according to Ravetz, 'any science that assumes certainty and relegates the most urgent problems to "externalities" will be seen as increasingly irrelevant and bizarre'.[41]

The key characteristic of postnormal science is that a plurality of value systems and a multiplicity of perspectives inform the decision-making process. As long ago as the 1950s Bateson saw that 'one of the major fallacies of the scientific community is the premise that it is possible to have total control over an interactive system of which oneself is a part', a fallacy that he also viewed as one of the major sources of social and individual trouble. He saw false presumptions of an ability to 'control' and 'manage' ecosystems through quantitative measurement as a primary source of error in ecological science.[42] This leads directly to the need for the use of partial and incomplete models as part of a process of social dialogue and deliberation where the stakes are high and the uncertainties are large.

Postnormal science is inescapably radical.

> By emphasizing the uncertainties and value loading of policy-related science, it implicitly contradicted centuries of conventional wisdom for science, in which uncertainty was tamed, ignorance suppressed, and the supposedly value free character of science proclaimed as a great value. It subverts the 'boundary-work' of scientists in the policy domain, whereby they have established a monopoly of expertise on policy problems with a technical component.[43]

The environment of radical modernism in which we now live requires new forms of issue and risk management. The evident problems with the ways in which science has been used in the management of BSE, foot and mouth disease and GMOs and the debate around climate change are excellent examples of the need to work in new ways.[44] Secrecy, control and lack of transparency are changing to a more open acceptance of a variety of values and beliefs about the problems we confront. De Marchi and Ravetz worry that if present trends and practices continue, the lack of transparency may totally erode trust in institutions and governance and undermine any wish for innovation and the search for solutions to land and water management. The extensive use of social dialogue is essential if we are to move in the direction of 'stronger' sustainability;[45] as we develop ever greater and extended communities we shall have to embrace risk and uncertainty rather than trying to banish it.[46] This places a premium on the need to develop and cherish trust between all parties, something that is in the realm of postnormal politics as well as postnormal science.

Science (knowledge capital) as social action

We find ourselves embedded in 'Unruly Complexity' practising 'ecology as social action'.[47] What we require are a series of what Rycroft and Kash have called 'network transformations': conceptual leaps and innovative solutions to integrated, synthetic problems.[48] Science is traditionally a level II–III activity in terms of Jaques's levels of work analyses. Work proceeds piecemeal as problems are broken down into short-term soluble projects. The kind of postnormal science we are discussing here requires an altogether higher level of social and knowledge capacity – up to levels IV and V in Jaques's terms. At these levels, time scales of influence and design are much longer and the complexity of the tasks in hand – collaboration models, partnerships, deliberative processes, group learning, weaving and revealing of new adaptive solutions, coalitions and ways of knowing – is much higher and more complex. This could be said to be even more complex than Mode II science (which, according to Gibbons *et al.*, is 'science in the context of its application'[49]).

What we are discussing here is a Mode III postnormal science in which there is an ongoing redefinition of the problems and researchable questions through an adaptive and recursive dialogue between experiment and monitoring at catchment scales and engagement between science and the broader community. These are what Rycroft and Kash call highly innovative 'adaptive network strategies'. This is, if you like, 'scientific systemism' where research projects must be seen in the context of their recursive interaction with an ongoing evolution of values and beliefs. This means that scientists are involved in doing science, talking about it and listening to the views of others in a reflective, deliberative context. Many scientists and bureaucrats are not comfortable working in this realm and, even if they attempt it, they are often thwarted by institutional and political forces designed to reduce risk and constrain freedom of communication and action. There is too much short-term thinking and a focus on compliance rather than innovation.

'Stronger' sustainability

To approach a 'strong' sustainability constraint will require a massive research effort at landscape scales, looking for more sustainable methods and patterns of production and trying to maximise production as well as water and nutrient use efficiency through new crops, new irrigation and rotation techniques, and improved pest management. All this has to be done in an environment where improved water quality and biodiversity conservation is matched with a focus on human and social capital, heritage and cultural values, region by region around the world. One key question is the degree to which we can substitute natural for physical capital, and renewable for non-renewable energy supplies. If we are to move from 'weak' to 'strong' sustainability there will have to be a greater understanding of how it might be possible to combine natural and artificial capitals and functions in a new economic framework involving both the public and the private sectors.[50] In a world of distributed infrastructure and ecological patch dynamics, what is substitutable for what? What precisely is fungible and how? This task will require the judicious use of models of various kinds and varying degrees of complexity, matched by community and institutional involvement and collaboration. Much of the knowledge gained will only be achieved through empirical inquiry and adaptive experimentation: this is too complex a task for computer simulation alone. We have, after all, done a very large number of landscape and waterscape management experiments already through widespread land use change, river regulation and modification. Different countries use different policy mixes; different regions have differing contingent histories and biogeographies. This is a kind of science not yet implemented at regional and global scales: multi-disciplinary (even transdisciplinary), long-term, large-scale, integrative, adaptive and largely empirical.

To achieve 'strong' sustainability will require working within natural constraints: a close approximation to natural systems, which maximise water and nutrient use efficiency (the 'extremal' MaxEnt solutions discussed previously) and to systems that are flux matched at a range of scales so that, for example, vertical and horizontal fluxes of water and nutrients are matched much more closely to those of the regional ecosystems. This will require the establishment of targets and goals for the management of externalities that are more complex and 'smarter' than those presently used. I retain the forlorn hope that even in this much more complex world targets may be found that are no more complex to establish and manage than the present ones, and that perhaps a set of regulatory and market mechanisms may be found to manage them in concert, but they will not be simple annual averages as are used commonly now. For example, they will need to include variance terms as well as means and may include combinations of indicators with thresholds for action. In addition it will probably be necessary to institute management practices that explicitly introduce extreme events and perturbations (e.g. fires, floods and droughts) into these mosaic systems as well as the management (and trading?) of the interaction effects. This is a radically modern version of the 'new institutionalism', incorporating signals and incentives of a very complex kind into local collective management arrangements and perhaps merging them with local market-based instruments of various kinds. Even so there will always be the problem of the fact that we will be attempting to monitor and trade secondary entities, entities such as water quality, which are dependent on other non-traded entities and functions. If we wish to go down the track of multiple market solutions, then how all-encompassing does this have to be to be sustainable? I can only, for the time being, foresee 'guardrail' solutions to these problems that live within constraints and, hence, frame market activity.

It certainly will not be possible to be 'strongly' sustainable on every hectare, so there will be a need to find ways of managing both pattern and process in space and time and for compensation across deep time (human generations) so that assets and values are not lost. This is where we need information about stocks and flows across mosaic landscapes and waterscapes and about possible trade-offs, all set in an environment of justice, equity and fairness reached through deliberative processes.[51] The information requirements of doing this will be horrendous. To this extent there is probably much that can be done with an eye to mimicking natural systems with their characteristic fractal and power law patterns of behaviour; however, how we produce as much food as we do now (or more) in a more variable and patchy environment is a matter for urgent study. For example, how do we return more natural environmental flow patterns in rivers (with their characteristic statistical patterns of floods) when the agricultural production dependent on the irrigation water has to be more constant and secure? Smart water use is going to be quite different in future.

Perhaps the most pressing problem is that of the existence of many and various forms of incommensurate values. Regional by region it is essential that we find ways of combining and balancing a variety of capitals – financial, natural, human, social, infrastructural – and merging these with innovative technological, behavioural and cultural solutions to the problem of finding new Pareto frontiers. While recognising the irreplaceable nature of nature (at least in biodiversity terms) it is nevertheless possible to replace some of the natural ecosystem services with human technology (distributed water reuse and treatment plants, for example). We must find ways of achieving greater and more sustainable fungibility. Even after many years, more work still needs to be done to reconcile the incommensurate and antithetical values and assumptions of economics and the environment.[52]

It is time to move on. The urgency of the problems we face demands new solutions: nineteenth century economics arose from an eighteenth century political economy, twentieth century ecology arose from similar eighteenth and nineteenth century ideas. The challenge of the twenty-first century is to rethink many of these outdated ideas. We will need new land and water use patterns and mosaics, new market and regulatory structures that include the present 'externalities', new forms of science that deal with its 'externalities' also, new institutional and governance arrangements, new value sets that are more ethical and inclusive, and new cultures. If we are to survive the bottleneck of the next fifty years the search for innovative and more inclusive value combinations is urgent – and this means making what are presently incommensurate values commensurate with 'strong' sustainability. The present global arrangement of dominant neo-liberal policies is demonstrably not so, neither is the present enterprise of science: both suffer from 'externalities', and the recursive 'system of systems' which includes the environment and the human species is showing the strain. The tools are there in the shadows; the challenge is to find new combinations of policies and knowledge that move us rapidly forward.

This really is a case for 'stronger' sustainability: a more equitable arrangement of capitals and of stocks and flows throughout the interconnected biosphere and anthroposphere. Ethics and equity – redistribution and compensation – are the dominant issues. This is about justice, equity and fairness to all on the planet – intra- and intergenerational equity and the recognition of the rights of all denizens of the biosphere. Once we realise that avoiding collapse is in the interest of all, we may find the will to act.

NOTES

1. J. Diamond. *Collapse*. (London: Allen Lane, The Penguin Press, 2005).

2. J. Lovelock. *The Revenge of Gaia*. (London: Allen Lane, The Penguin Press, 2006).

3. A. R. Platt. *The First Imperative*. (Market Harborough, UK: Matador, 2004).

4. G. Bateson. Conscious purpose versus nature. In *To Free a Generation: the Dialectics of Liberation*, ed. D. G. Cooper. (New York, Collier Books, 1968), pp. 34–49.

5. See the Millennium Ecosystem Assessment Synthesis Report at www.maweb.org; also E. Stokstad. Taking the pulse of Earth's life support systems. *Science*, **308** (2005), 41–5.

6. W. N. Adger *et al.* Socio-ecological resilience to coastal disasters. *Science*, **309** (2005), 1036–9.

7. E. Ostrom. *Governing the Commons: the Evolution of Institutions for Collective Action*. (Cambridge: Cambridge University Press, 1990).

8. P. Taylor. *Unruly Complexity: Ecology, Interpretation, Engagement*. (Chicago, IL: Chicago University Press, 2005).

9. B. H. Walker *et al.* Resilience, adaptability and transformability of social-ecological systems. *Ecology and Society*, **9 (2)** (2004), 5. www.ecologyandsociety.org/vol9/iss2/art5.

10. P. J. Coombes and G. Kuczera. *Moving towards a systems understanding of integrated water cycle management*. (Brisbane, National Water Sensitive Urban Design Conference, 2002). G. Kuczera and P. J. Coombes. A systems perspective of the urban water cycle: new insights, new opportunities. *Water Sensitive Urban Development – A Vision for Sustainable Water Resources*, 26–28 April 2001. (Port Stephens, NSW: Stormwater Industry Association Regional Conference, 2001.)

11. The long time lags between changes in agricultural practice, management actions and ecological outcomes are well illustrated by the history of eutrophication in Lough Neagh in N Ireland. See, for example, R. H. Foy and S. D. Lennox. Evidence for a delayed response of riverine phosphorus exports from increasing agricultural catchment pressures in the Lough Neagh catchment. *Limnology and Oceanography*, **51** (1, part 2) (2006), 655–63. Similar problems are caused by the slow rate of groundwater movement. Reductions in nitrogen surpluses in the farms surrounding Lake Rotorua, NZ, will not be reflected in improved water quality for 30–70 years. See D. Gordon and U. Morgenstern. Groundwater delay time in the Lake Rotorua catchment. *Water Resources Update*, **6** (2004), 4. (Wellington, NZ: NIWA).

12. S. T. Schwartz and K. Zvinakis. Reputation without repeated interaction: a role for public disclosures. *Review of Accounting Studies*, **5** (2000), 351–75.

13. B. Norton. Resilience and options. *Ecological Economics*, **15** (1995), 133–6. (Quotes from p. 135.)

14. B. G. Norton. Biodiversity and environmental values: in search of a universal earth ethic. *Biodiversity and Conservation*, **9** (2000), 1029–44. (Quote from p. 1029.)

15. J. Sachs. *The End of Poverty: How we can Make it Happen in our Lifetime*. (London: Penguin Books, 2005). R. Siegfried. *Keeping the Rainbow: the Environmental Challenge for Africa and the World*. (Cape Town: Africa Geographic, 2002).

16. S. Lewis. *Race against Time*. CBC Massey Lecture Series. (Toronto: CBC Canada, 2006).

17. A. Y. Hoekstra, H. H. G. Savenije and A. K. Chapagain. An integrated approach towards assessing the value of water: a case study on the Zambesi basin. *Integrated Assessment*, **2** (2001), 199–208.

18. I. M. Seyam, A. Y. Hoekstra and H. H. G. Savenije. Calculation methods to assess the value of upstream water flows and storage as a function of downstream benefits. *Physics and Chemistry of the Earth*, **27** (2002), 977–82.

19. M. D. Young and J. C. McColl. Robust reform: the case for a new water entitlement system for Australia. *Australian Economic Review*, **36** (2003), 225–34.

20. M. Taylor. *The Moment of Complexity: Emerging Network Culture*. (Chicago, IL: Chicago University Press, 2001).

21. D. C. Dennett. *Darwin's Dangerous Idea*. (London: Allen Lane, The Penguin Press, 1995). (Quoted from pp. 81–2.)

22. E. O. Wilson. *Consilience: the Unity of Knowledge*. (New York: Knopf, 1998).

23. R. Florida. *The Rise of the Creative Class: and how it's Transforming Work, Leisure, Community and Everyday Life*. (New York: Basic Books, 2002).

24. R. W. Rycroft and D. E. Kash. *The Complexity Challenge: Technological Innovation for the 21st Century*. (London: Pinter, 1999).

25. B. Huntley, R. Siegfried and C. Sunter. *South African Environments into the 21st Century*. (Cape Town: Human & Rousseau Tafelberg, 1989).

26. C. Ilbury and C. Sunter. *The Mind of a Fox: Scenario Planning in Action*. (Cape Town: Human & Rousseau Tafelberg, 2001).

27. T. Flannery. *The Weather Makers*. (Melbourne: Text Publishing, 2005).

28. Ostrom, *Governing the Commons*. (See Note 7.)

29. Charles Handy. *The Age of Unreason*. (London: Arrow Books, 1990). Rycroft and Kash, *The Complexity Challenge*. (See Note 24.)

30. Taken from the translating Babel fish of the *Hitchhiker's Guide to the Galaxy* that broke down communication barriers and caused wars as a result! See D. Adams. *The Hitchhiker's Guide to the Galaxy*. www.bbc.co.uk/cult/hitchhikers/guide/babelfish.shtml.

31. M. Tilzey. Natural areas, the whole countryside approach and sustainable agriculture. *Land Use Policy*, **17** (2000), 279–94.

32. See D. Western. Human-modified ecosystems and future evolution. *Proceedings of the National Academy of Sciences, USA*, **98** (2001), 5458–65; also H. Doremus. Biodiversity and the challenge of saving the ordinary. *Idaho Law Review*, **38** (2002), 325–54. J. Pretty and D. Smith. Social capital in biodiversity conservation. *Conservation Biology*, **18** (2003), 631–8. K. S. Bawa, R. Seidler and P. H. Raven. Reconciling conservation paradigms. *Conservation Biology*, **18** (2004), 859–60. M. Chapin. A challenge to conservationists. *World-Watch*, Nov–Dec 2004, pp. 17–31.

33. W. M. Adams *et al.* Biodiversity conservation and the eradication of poverty. *Science*, **306** (2004), 1146–9. J. S. Brashares *et al.* Bush meat hunting, wildlife declines, and fish supply in West Africa. *Science*, **306** (2004), 1180–3.

34. R. E. Green *et al.* Farming and the fate of wild nature. *Science*, **307** (2005), 550–5. The other major threats are climate change and disturbance to global biogeochemical cycles.

35. D. C. Korten. *The Post-Corporate World: Life After Capitalism*. (San Francisco, CA: Berrett-Koehler Publishers, and West Hertford, CT: Kumarian Press, 1999).

36. D. Tilman *et al.* Forecasting agriculturally driven global environmental change. *Science*, **292** (2001), 281–4. D. Tilman *et al.* Agricultural sustainability and intensive production practices. *Nature*, **418** (2002), 671–7.

37. W. Swenson, D. S. Wilson and R. Elias. Artificial ecosystem selection. *Proceedings of the National Academy of Sciences, USA*, **97** (2000), 9110–14.

38. Ostrom, *Governing the Commons*. (See Note 7.)

39. R. E. Green *et al.* Farming and the fate of wild nature. *Science*, **307** (2005), 550–5.

40. S. Hajkowicz *et al.* Exploring future landscapes: a conceptual framework for planned change. (Canberra, ACT: Land and Water Australia, 2003). Available from www.lwa.gov.au.

41. S. S. Tognetti. Science in a double-bind: Gregory Bateson and the origins of post-normal science. *Futures*, **31** (1999), 689–703. The quotation from Ravetz is in Tognetti's text and

is cited as taken from J. Ravetz. Economics as an elite folk-science: the suppression of uncertainty. In *Keynes, Knowledge and Uncertainty*, ed. S.C. Dow and J. Hillard. (Aldershot: Edward Elgar, 1994).

42. S.S. Tognetti. Science in a double-bind: Gregory Bateson and the origins of post-normal science. *Futures*, **31** (1999), 689–703. (Quote from p. 691.)

43. J. Ravetz and S. Funtowicz. Post-Normal Science – an insight now maturing. *Futures*, **31** (1999), 641–6.

44. B. De Marchi and J.R. Ravetz. Risk management and governance: a post-normal science approach. *Futures*, **31** (1999), 743–57.

45. M. O'Connor. Dialogue and debate in a post-normal practice of science: a reflexion. *Futures*, **31** (1999), 671– 87.

46. S. Healy. Extended peer communities and the ascendance of post-normal politics. *Futures*, **31** (1999), 655–69.

47. P. Taylor, *Unruly Complexity*. (See Note 8.)

48. Rycroft and Kash, *The Complexity Challenge*. (See Note 24.)

49. M. Gibbons *et al.* *The New Production of Knowledge*. (London: Sage Books, 1994).

50. See the special section in the *Economist* magazine. How many planets? A survey of the global environment. July 6th 2002, 16pp., also G.C. Daily and B.H. Walker. Seeking the great transition. *Nature*, **403** (2000), 243–5. See also J. Sachs, *The End of Poverty*. (See Note 15.)

51. Ostrom, *Governing the Commons*. (See Note 7.)

52. J. Foster. Between economics and ecology: some historical and philosophical considerations for modelers of natural capital. *Environmental Monitoring and Assessment*, **86** (2003), 63–74.

Index